NEUROBEHAVIOURAL DISABILITY AND SOCIAL HANDICAP FOLLOWING TRAUMATIC BRAIN INJURY

Neurobe ,iioural disability (NBD) follows many forms of serious ' .un injury and is a major constraint on social independence. This book brings together a group of leading academics and practising clinicians to provide an overview of the nature of NBD, considering how it translates into social handicap, and what can be done to address associated problems, through social and behavioural rehabilitation, vocational training and family education.

This fully revised edition takes into account advances in the field, exploring the range of cognitive, emotional, and behavioural effects of brain damage most commonly associated with damage to the frontal and associated structures of the brain that govern social behaviour. This edition also features increased emphasis on psychological interventions, as well as new chapters on brain imaging, pharmacotherapy and assistive technology for disability.

Neurobehavioural Disability and Social Handicap Following Traumatic Brain Injury is essential reading for clinical psychologists, psychiatrists and neurologists working in brain injury rehabilitation. The book will also be of interest to relatives of those with brain injury seeking better knowledge to understand neurobehavioural disability, as well as the growing number of therapy care assistants, case managers, support workers, and social workers responsible for the day to day care of brain injured people in the community.

Tom M. McMillan is Professor of Clinical Neuropsychology at the University of Glasgow, UK.

Rodger Ll. Wood is Professor Emeritus of Clinical Neuropsychology, Swansea University, UK.

Brain, Behaviour and Cognition
Series editors: Glyn W. Humphreys and Chris Code

For a complete list of titles in this series, please visit www.routledge.com/Brain-Behaviour-and-Cognition/book-series/SE0542

NEUROBEHAVIOURAL DISABILITY AND SOCIAL HANDICAP FOLLOWING TRAUMATIC BRAIN INJURY

Second edition

*Edited by Tom M. McMillan and
Rodger Ll. Wood*

Routledge
Taylor & Francis Group

LONDON AND NEW YORK

Second edition published 2017
by Routledge
2 Park Square, Milton Park, Abingdon, Oxon OX14 4RN

and by Routledge
711 Third Avenue, New York, NY 10017

Routledge is an imprint of the Taylor & Francis Group, an informa business

First edition published in 2002 by Psychology Press

British Library Cataloguing in Publication Data
A catalogue record for this book is available from the British Library

Library of Congress Cataloging in Publication Data
Names: McMillan, Tom M., editor. | Wood, Rodger Ll.
(Rodger Llewellyn) editor.
Title: Neurobehavioural disability and social handicap following traumatic brain injury / edited by Tom M. McMillan and Rodger Ll. Wood.
Description: 2nd edition. | Milton Park, Abingdon, Oxon; New York, NY: Routledge, 2017. | Includes bibliographical references and index.
Identifiers: LCCN 2016033802 | ISBN 9781138923928 (hbk : alk. paper) | ISBN 9781138923935 (pbk : alk. paper) | ISBN 9781315684710 (ebk)
Subjects: LCSH: Brain damage—Patients—Rehabilitation. | Brain damage—Social aspects.
Classification: LCC RC387.5. N46 2017 | DDC 617.4/810443—dc23
LC record available at https://lccn.loc.gov/2016033802

ISBN: 978-1-138-92392-8 (hbk)
ISBN: 978-1-138-92393-5 (pbk)
ISBN: 978-1-315-68471-0 (ebk)

Typeset in Bembo
by Keystroke, Neville Lodge, Tettenhall, Wolverhampton

CONTENTS

PART IV
Service delivery and development   231

CONTRIBUTORS

Nick Alderman is Director of Clinical Services and Consultant Clinical Neuropsychologist, Brain Injury Services, Partnerships in Care. He is acknowledged as one of the UK's foremost experts in the management of challenging behaviour secondary to acquired brain injury and has over thirty years' experience working in and leading neurobehavioural rehabilitation services. Previously, he held senior posts in the Brain Injury Rehabilitation Trust and the National Brain Injury Centre (Kemsley Unit), St Andrew's Hospital, Northampton. He currently holds a number of academic appointments including Visiting Professor at the University of the West of England and Honorary Professor at Swansea University.

Fiona Ashworth is a Clinical Psychologist working in neuro-rehabilitation, with a special interest in the application of psychological therapies following acquired brain injury. Fiona trained at the University of Oxford, specialising in neuro-rehabilitation at the Oxford Centre for Enablement. She has over 10 years' experience working with people with acquired brain injury, since beginning her clinical career at the Oliver Zangwill Centre. Fiona currently holds a Senior Lecturing position at Anglia Ruskin University and continues to work at the Oliver Zangwill Centre. She contributes to research and wider literature with a focus on innovations in psychological approaches. Fiona has pioneered the use of Compassion Focused Therapy with people with acquired brain injury and this is one of her principal research areas. Fiona regularly presents her clinical work and research at international conferences and provides training and supervision within her specialisms.

Erin Bigler is a clinical neuropsychologist and Professor of Neuroscience and Psychology at Brigham Young University where he has directed the Brain Imaging and Behavior Laboratory for the past 26 years. He is board certified in clinical neuropsychology by the American Board of Professional Psychology. He is a past-president of the International Neuropsychological Society and the National Academy of Neuropsychology.

Breda Cullen obtained her BA (Hons) and MSc in psychology from Trinity College Dublin, following which she worked in research posts in Ireland, Australia and New Zealand, primarily in the area of dementia and old age psychiatry. She completed her clinical psychology training in Glasgow, specialising in neuropsychology and rehabilitation, then worked in acute neurosciences and rehabilitation services within NHS Greater Glasgow and Clyde. She is a member of the BPS Specialist Register of Clinical Neuropsychologists. Dr Cullen currently works full-time as a Research Fellow within Mental Health and Wellbeing. Research interests include executive function assessment, functional neuroimaging, psychological therapies and rehabilitation in neurological conditions, and epidemiology of cognitive function in psychiatric and neurological disorders.

Jon Evans is Professor of Applied Neuropsychology at the University of Glasgow and honorary Consultant Clinical Psychologist with NHS Greater Glasgow and Clyde. Jon was the first Clinical Director of the Oliver Zangwill Centre for Neuropsychological Rehabilitation in Ely, Cambridgeshire. He is now Programme Director for the MSc in Clinical Neuropsychology programme at the University of Glasgow. Jon has published more than 140 papers, books and book chapters in the field of cognitive neuropsychology, neuropsychological assessment and rehabilitation. He is an Executive Editor of the journal *Neuropsychological Rehabilitation* and is a co-author of the *Behavioural Assessment of the Dysexecutive Syndrome* and the *Cambridge Prospective Memory Test*.

Simon Fleminger qualified from Cambridge University and St George's Medical School in 1978, and subsequently undertook periods of research in Professor David Marsden's department of neurology and Professor Lishman's department of neuropsychiatry, both at the institute of Psychiatry. He was appointed Consultant Neuropsychiatrist at the Maudsley Hospital in 1996 where he set up the Lishman Brain Injury Unit. He has published over 100 peer reviewed research papers, reviews and chapters, largely in the field of brain injury. An RCT of CBT for patients with persistent post concussional symptoms has recently been accepted for publication.

Caron Gan is an RN, Registered Marriage and Family Therapist, and Registered Psychotherapist. For the past 25 years, she has worked at Holland Bloorview Kids Rehabilitation Hospital providing family therapy intervention to children, youth, and families living with the effects of acquired brain injury. As a Clinical Team Investigator with the Bloorview Research Institute, she is currently leading a validation study of the newly developed Pediatric Family Needs Questionnaire with four international collaborators. She is also the primary developer of the Brain Injury Family Intervention for Adolescents (BIFI-A), which has been designated a leading practice by Accreditation Canada.

Alex Gillespie is Associate Professor in Social Psychology at the London School of Economics, Deputy Head of Department, and an Editor of *Journal for the Theory of Social Behaviour*. His research focuses on communication, divergences of perspective, misunderstandings and listening especially in the field of healthcare. His research aims to develop useful social psychological tools and methods. With Dr Brian O'Neill he developed a microprompting device (GUIDE) and with Dr Tom Reader he has developed the Healthcare Complaints Analysis Tool (HCAT).

Richard Greenwood is Consultant Neurologist at the National Hospital for Neurology and Neurosurgery, and Homerton University Hospital, and Lead Clinician to the Acute Brain Injury Service at the National Hospital and UCLH, and the Homerton Regional Neurological Rehabilitation Unit (RNRU), and initiated the RNRU Outreach team and Headway East London. He has focussed on the development of acute and early inpatient and late outpatient rehabilitation services for patients after traumatic and vascular brain injury, and has reflected this in his research output at the level of pathology, impairment and function.

His research collaborations have focussed on the mechanism and management of neurological recovery and have become increasingly impairment based. They particularly relate to the ways in which the behavioural interventions and skill learning of physio-, occupational and speech therapy drive brain plasticity, and thus enhance recovery of motor, cognitive and independent living skills, and how combining electrical and magnetic cortical stimulation, and drugs with therapist guided practice, may be of additional use. He has also contributed to research investigating how advanced imaging techniques define the network injuries that occur after traumatic brain injury, and increase knowledge of the clinical effects and treatment of patients after TBI.

Jeffrey S. Kreutzer is a Professor of Physical Medicine and Rehabilitation at Virginia Commonwealth University (VCU), Medical College of Virginia Campus. Dr Kreutzer is a neuropsychologist and family therapist with three decades' experience developing, providing, and evaluating brain injury services. He serves as Director of Virginia's federally designated Traumatic Brain Injury Model System and coordinates VCU Health System outpatient services for families and persons with brain injury. He has published more than 160 peer reviewed papers and is the primary developer of the Brain Injury Family Intervention, an empirically based education, skill building, and psychotherapeutic program for families.

Jennifer H. Marwitz is an Associate Professor in Virginia Commonwealth University's Department of Physical Medicine and Rehabilitation. She has experience coordinating research and demonstration projects and serves as Project Coordinator for the VCU Traumatic Brain Injury Model System. In addition to developing the Neurobehavioral Functioning Inventory with Jeffrey Kreutzer and Ronald Seel, Ms. Marwitz has co-authored over 50 journal articles and book chapters related to brain injury. She serves as managing editor for *Brain Injury*, an international journal focused on research findings and program development in the field of brain injury. Research interests include emotional adjustment, community reintegration, and family functioning.

Hamish McLeod, PhD is Director of the Doctorate in Clinical Psychology at the University of Glasgow and an Honorary Consultant Clinical Psychologist with NHS Greater Glasgow and Clyde. He completed his clinical psychology training in New Zealand and his PhD at Imperial College, London, where his research examined neuropsychological aspects of autobiographical memory functioning in people experiencing psychosis. Since then, his clinical and research work has been focused on improving psychological therapies for people whose emotional and behavioural problems are accompanied by significant neuropsychological impairments. A major theme of his current work is the psychological understanding and effective treatment of apathy, anhedonia, and problems arising from diminished or distorted self-awareness. He also conducts studies focused on improving the implementation fidelity and reach of psychological interventions for complex psychiatric and neurological conditions.

Tom M. McMillan obtained a PhD in psychopharmacology in 1981 and qualified in clinical psychology in 1983. He worked at the Institute of Psychiatry in London for 10 years and later became the Head of Clinical Neuropsychology for the South West Thames Region of London and Professor of Clinical Psychology at the University of Surrey. He returned to Glasgow in 1999 where he is the Professor of Clinical Neuropsychology at the University of Glasgow. He has published over 170 articles and three books. He has worked clinically throughout his career in the NHS in the area of neurorehabilitation of head injury.

Michael Oddy is a clinical neuropsychologist who has spent more than 40 years working in brain injury rehabilitation. He worked in the NHS from 1972 until 2007. From 1989 he was director of brain injury rehabilitation units at Ticehurst and Unsted Park Hospitals before becoming clinical director of the Brain Injury Rehabilitation Trust in 2001. He is a former Chair of the British Psychological Society Division of Neuropsychology and was the first recipient of the DoN Barbara Wilson award for his contribution to UK clinical neuropsychology. He has been publishing in areas related to brain injury since the 1970s and, despite retirement, remains active in research.

Brian O'Neill is the Consultant in Neuropsychology and Rehabilitation at Graham Anderson House, a neurobehavioural rehabilitation centre in Glasgow, Scotland. He studied at Trinity College, Dublin (B.A. Psychology, 1997) and at the University of Glasgow (D.Clin.Psy. 2002; MSc Clin.Neuropsychol. 2006). His research interests focus on ways to ameliorate cognitive and emotional difficulties after acquired brain injury. He has also examined cognitive ability as a mediator of independent activity and the use of assistive technology for cognition to surmount these difficulties. He co-edited, with Alex Gillespie (2015), *Assistive Technology for Cognition* (Hove: Psychology Press).

Jennie Ponsford, BA (Hons), MA (Clin Neuropsych), PhD, MAPsS, is a Professor of Neuropsychology in the School of Psychological Sciences at Monash University and Director of the Monash-Epworth Rehabilitation Research Centre at Epworth Hospital in Melbourne, Australia. She has spent the past 35 years engaged in clinical work and research with individuals with brain injury. Her research has investigated outcomes following mild, moderate and severe traumatic brain injury (TBI), factors predicting outcome, including return to work and study and the efficacy of rehabilitative interventions to improve outcome, with current intervention studies focusing specifically on fatigue and sleep changes, anxiety and depression and substance use following TBI. She has published over 230 journal articles and book chapters on these subjects, as well as two books on rehabilitation following traumatic brain injury. She also directs a doctoral training program in Clinical Neuropsychology at Monash University and her students are actively engaged with her research program.

George P. Prigatano, PhD is presently Emeritus Chair of the Department of Clinical Neuropsychology and Newsome Chair of Neuropsychology at the Barrow Neurological Institute. His clinical and research interests have been in understanding disorders of self-awareness in various groups of patients and applying that information to neuropsychological rehabilitation. He has also been interested in the psychological adjustment issues of neurological patients and the role of psychoanalytic psychotherapies in assisting them to cope with the permanent effects of a brain disorder throughout the life span.

Sara Ramos is a Chartered Psychologist. She started her career in Portugal, in a hospital with a long-standing tradition in neuropsychological practice and research (Language Research Laboratory, Lisbon). She then moved to England where she completed a Masters in Cognitive Neuropsychology and a PhD investigating the interaction between language and cognition. Before joining BIRT in 2011 from Heriot-Watt University (Edinburgh), she was involved in research looking into language and memory functioning in bilingual children and adults at the National University of Singapore. Her current work focuses on evaluating the outcomes and cost-benefits of acquired brain injury rehabilitation.

Christian Salas is a clinical neuropsychologist and a psychoanalytic psychotherapist from Chile. His main interest is to understand emotional and personality changes after brain injury and how psychoanalytic tools can be adapted to facilitate socio-emotional adjustment and well-being. He obtained a PhD in Psychology at Bangor University (Wales, UK) with a thesis entitled 'Emotion Regulation after Acquired Brain Injury'. From 2013 to 2016 he worked as Program Director of the Head Forward Centre (Manchester, UK), a social rehabilitation facility for individuals with chronic TBI. Today, he is a Reader at the Faculty of Psychology of the Diego Portales University (Santiago, Chile).

Claire Williams BSc (Hons), MSc, PhD is a Senior Lecturer in the Department of Psychology at Swansea University. She has a strong track record of applied and translational research, leadership experience of delivering research projects with clinical impact, and experience of developing specialist neurobehavioural assessment tools for use in brain injury. She has a particular interest in emotion deficit disorders after traumatic brain injury, focusing predominantly on alexithymia, nonverbal communication, and emotional empathy. Other principal research interests include neurobehavioural disability, dysregulated behaviours, and outcome measurement.

Huw Williams is an Associate Professor of Clinical Neuropsychology and Co-Director of the Centre for Clinical Neuropsychology Research (CCNR) at Exeter University. He was on the founding staff team of the Oliver Zangwill Centre (OZC). He has honorary positions with the OZC and the Royal Devon and Exeter Hospital's Emergency Department. He has published papers and books and held grants in a range of areas of Clinical Neuropsychology relevant to children, young adults and adults. Including guest editor of the *Journal of Head Trauma Rehabilitation* on brain injury and crime in young and youth offenders and special issues of the journal *Neuropsychological Rehabilitation* on neuropsychiatric consequences of brain injury. He is the past Chair of the Division of Neuropsychology (DON) of the British Psychological Society (BPS), and is currently Vice Chair of the DON Policy Group, Chair of the BPS working group on Neurodisability and Offending Behaviour, and Vice Chair of the Criminal Justice and Acquired Brain Injury Group (CJAABIG) (established with Child Brain Injury Trust (CBIT) and General Lord Ramsbotham).

Rodger Ll. Wood began working in brain injury rehabilitation at the Kemsley Unit, St Andrew's Hospital, in 1979. In 1985 he was appointed Clinical Director, Brain Injury Rehabilitation Services, Casa Colina Hospital, Los Angeles, and Visiting Professor in Rehabilitation Medicine at the State University of New York. In 1991 he took up an appointment as Clinical Director of the newly formed Brain Injury Rehabilitation Trust in the UK. He is currently Emeritus Professor, Clinical Neuropsychology, College of Medicine, Swansea University, Wales. He has published over 100 research papers, plus various book chapters, five edited volumes and one single author book.

Andrew Worthington is a consultant in neuropsychology and rehabilitation and is director of Headwise, an independent provider of consultancy, medico-legal and rehabilitation services in the UK. Dr Worthington has over 25 years' experience as a clinician, teacher and academic and has particular expertise in neurobehavioural rehabilitation. He has published widely, his research interests reflecting his clinical practice, focussing on executive dysfunction, behaviour management, outcome measurement and cost–effectiveness.

PREFACE

Since the publication of the first edition of this book in 2001, there have been significant advances in science that have implications for our understanding of brain behaviour relationships, and the impact of damage to the brain. In this book we update and expand upon the first edition to take account of some of these developments. The book addresses the range of cognitive emotional and behavioural effects of brain damage that are most commonly associated with damage to the frontal and associated structures of the brain that in concert govern social behaviour. As in the first edition, traumatic brain injury is used as a model given its high incidence and prevalence in young adults who can often face a lifetime of disability. However, the book is relevant to those with other forms of brain damage including cerebral hypoxia, brain infection, intracerebral haemorrhage and some forms of brain tumour.

In this book we explore the nature of neurobehavioural disability (NBD) and how this has an impact on social roles in adults, and what is known about assessment methods and the effectiveness of interventions. The chapters are largely written by clinicians who have considerable research and clinical experience with people who have suffered from traumatic brain injury and who have been engaged in neurorehabilitation.

In order to reflect current clinical and scientific interest, we have expanded the second edition with five additional chapters, and there is an increased emphasis on psychological interventions. We also have new chapters on brain imaging, pharmacotherapy and assistive technology for disability.

In the first section of the book, Chapters 1 and 2 provide an account of the historical development of the neurobehavioural paradigm, its conceptualisation, recent insights and developments and an indication of challenges that the paradigm faces in the future. Cardinal features of NBD, namely disorders of emotion and impulse control, are detailed in Chapters 3 and 4. In Chapter 5, evidence for a potential consequence of these disorders, namely offending and involvement with the criminal justice system, is discussed. Finally, in Chapter 6 the pervasive effects of NBD on the family and carers is presented.

Part II deals with assessment methodologies. There continues to be limitations in tools available for the assessment of NBD, including cognitive assessment and this problem is discussed in Chapter 7. In Chapter 8, the current and potential contribution of neuroimaging to the identification and assessment of NBD is summarised.

In the second edition, there is particular emphasis on interventions for NBD, and most chapters in the book give information about treatment. However, in Part III there are *eight* chapters that specifically focus on interventions to ameliorate particular effects of traumatic brain injury that are at the heart of NBD, including for disorders of executive function, awareness, adjustment, empathy, anxiety, depression, sleep, fatigue and challenging behaviour. The section concludes with two chapters that, in broader terms, indicate roles for psychodynamic and pharmacological approaches and of assistive technology in reducing disability and social handicap. These chapters not only reference progress in our understanding of these problem areas and of potential solutions, but also make clear the limitations of the evidence base for psychological and pharmacological therapies currently.

In the final section of the book, service provision for people with brain injury and the effectiveness and cost-effectiveness of neurobehavioural rehabilitation is reviewed in Chapter 17. The final chapter looks to the future and from where we may expect further developments in forthcoming decades. It also highlights the new horizons of a growing incidence of traumatic brain injury in low and middle economy nations and the increasing incidence of traumatic brain injury in adults in the West who are living to older ages.

Implicit throughout the book is a need for an understanding of the nature of brain behaviour relationships that is fundamental to the science and practice of neuropsychology. The editors hope that this book will lead to greater awareness of the need for specialist post-acute neurorehabilitation, that it will encourage students to work in the area of brain injury, that it will stimulate researchers to contribute to our knowledge base and will inform and strengthen the guiding hands of clinicians. We also hope that the book will be of interest to lawyers and relatives of people with brain injury and support workers who seek to broaden their knowledge base.

T.M. McMillan and R.Ll. Wood
May 2016

PART I
Nature and impact

1

NEUROBEHAVIOURAL DISABILITY OVER THE PAST FOUR DECADES

Andrew Worthington, Rodger Ll. Wood and Tom M. McMillan

Origins and early development

The concept of neurobehavioural disability developed from early pioneering efforts to find better ways of understanding and treating the more debilitating and chronic behavioural consequences of serious brain injury. Although the origins of this approach can be traced back at least as far as the First World War it was not until the final decades of the twentieth century that significant advances were made. Prior to this it had been left to one or two gifted and enlightened clinicians to prepare the hinterland from which later practitioners benefitted. Key figures in an approach that would develop into neurobehavioural rehabilitation were Kurt Goldstein and Alexander Luria, both of whom recognised the importance of the frontal lobes in the regulation of human social behaviour.

Goldstein's recognition of the importance of injury to the frontal lobes is evident in the distinction he drew between the impact of injury on new learning as opposed to established habit patterns – 'in patients with lesions of the frontal lobe, active (abstract) behaviour is lacking, but the concrete behaviour may be very well preserved' (Goldstein, 1936, p. 38). About the same time Luria developed his theory of frontal lobe functioning, which was most comprehensively set out in English in his 1973 work, *The Working Brain*:

> For any mental process to take place a certain level of cortical tone is necessary and this cortical tone must be modified in accordance both with the task to be accomplished and the stage of the activity reached. The first important function of the frontal lobes is to regulate this state of activity.

> *(p. 188)*

Luria then emphasised the role of the frontal lobes in the regulation of attention control and social cognition:

> Maintenance of the optimal cortical tone is absolutely essential for the basic condition of all forms of conscious activity, namely the formation of plans and intentions that are stable enough to become dominant and to withstand any distracting or irrelevant stimulus . . . capable of controlling the subject's subsequent conscious behaviour.
>
> *(pp. 197–198)*

Here is an explicit statement of the importance of a region of the brain, often thought at that time to be silent, in regulating thought and action. It followed that frontal brain damage led to disruption of complex forms of behaviour and, especially, 'activity which is controlled by motives formulated with the aid of speech' (p. 199). This has, in turn, provided an important neurological rationale for recruiting speech processes in neurobehavioural rehabilitation (Vocate, 1987).

More recent descriptions of disability have developed from these early concepts by focussing on the role of the prefrontal cortex in the self-regulation of behaviour (Stuss and Benson, 1987; Damasio et al., 1991). Diminished self-regulation is a major legacy of traumatic brain injury and central to the concept of 'neurobehavioural disability' (Wood, 1987). This new concept of disability pointed to patterns of maladaptive behaviour characterised by impulsivity; inappropriate social or sexual behaviour; lack of tact and discretion during interpersonal activities; diminished self or social awareness; an egocentric attitude lacking in warmth and empathy towards others; labile mood with shallow irritability that can escalate into impulsive aggression; poor attention control resulting in an inability to maintain goal directed behaviour; a lack of ability to spontaneously initiate purposeful behaviour; and fatigue, often associated with a lack of drive and motivation.

The pattern of disability exhibited by individuals can vary considerably depending upon the nature, location, and severity of their brain injury; pre-injury behaviour and personality, and post-injury circumstances. In many cases the disability can be subtle but still have a pervasive psychosocial impact because of problems with interpersonal relationships, an inability to adapt behaviour to changing situations, and poor temper control.

The neurobehavioural rehabilitation paradigm

Goldstein's approach to rehabilitation was influenced by the Gestalt psychology movement (see Prigatano and Salas, Chapter 14, this volume) and included an appreciation of context in driving behaviour. His approach recognised that effective rehabilitation required a change from focusing on physical and cognitive symptoms to addressing long-term behavioural and personality change (Goldstein, 1952). Challenges of caring humanely for those with disordered behaviour came to the fore in the 1960s and 1970s, initially for people with psychiatric conditions, what were then called 'mental handicaps', and latterly for acquired brain injury. From the 1970s this gave rise to two streams of rehabilitation. Although both were to consider rehabilitation in a 'holistic' sense and embrace the role of the family and of the environment as a milieu for intervention, one focused on higher functioning adults with predominantly emotional and adjustment problems, epitomised by Prigatano et al. (1984) and Ben-Yishay (Ben-Yishay et al., 1985). The other was a neurobehavioural approach that initially developed in response to the needs of a very severely injured, challenging population who were otherwise excluded from treatment on the basis of their disturbed behaviour (Wood and Eames, 1981; Eames and Wood, 1985). Left untreated, or inappropriately medicated, the disproportionate impact of this population had become increasingly apparent in terms of the effects on the wider family. Panting and Merry (1972) for example noted

> the majority of our patients suffered from outbursts of very vivid emotional rage . . . the patient's accident had been a great strain on all relatives, especially to wives and mothers, and 61% had needed supportive treatment with tranquillisers and sleeping tablets which had not been necessary previously.
>
> *(p. 35)*

It was these personality changes rather than injury severity per se that were linked to stress amongst relatives (Oddy et al., 1978; McKinlay et al., 1981). The emerging awareness of the impact of behaviour and personality problems led Bond (1979) to comment that

> the nature of rehabilitation techniques for patients over and above those required to prevent secondary complications of physical disabilities, which have formed the basis of most rehabilitation to date, will entail various psychological and social therapies, and excursions into the fields of occupational training.
>
> *(p. 158)*

There was clearly a need for a new type of rehabilitation and in the same year the management of St Andrews Hospital, an independent psychiatric institution in Northampton, England, was persuaded to run an experimental programme at the Kemsley Unit, using behaviour modification techniques already in use elsewhere in the hospital, to treat adults with severe brain injury (Wood and Eames, 1981). Chief amongst behavioural methods in vogue at the time was the token economy system, which was an all-encompassing system of rewards contingent upon certain behaviours that had proved effective in its application to a wide range of conditions (Kazdin, 1977). It is easy now to forget that this was very much unchartered territory in rehabilitation, as epitomised in Lishman's (1984) comments on 'the brave attempts underway to tackle the more disruptive behavioural aftermaths in severely damaged patients by behaviour modification techniques – pioneering work at the rehabilitation unit of St. Andrew's Hospital Northampton' (p. 1148). Underpinning this new approach was a shift from a primarily psychiatric perspective on behaviour disorders at that time to a psychological model of learning. The traditional medical model had been syndrome-based, viewing disordered behaviour as dispositional rather than situational, enduring rather than transitory, and consequently treatments were largely drug-based. In contrast, learning theory promoted a more dynamic approach whereby behaviour was largely situationally determined, accessible to functional analysis and amenable to modification by altering contingencies of reinforcement in the environment. The initial outcomes for those with severe brain injury were said to be surprisingly good (Eames and Wood, 1985). A cohort treated approximately four years post-injury (i.e. beyond the period of likely natural resolution of their behaviour disturbance) showed that clear gains from treatment were still evident at follow-up, an average of 18 months later. Better outcomes were associated with longer periods of intervention but longer admissions were not necessary to achieve good outcomes. Token economy programmes began to be used elsewhere with reports of improved efficacy over drug treatment in the so-called 'frontal lobe syndrome' (Whale et al., 1986; Tate, 1986).

However, it gradually became evident that the particular kind of cognitive impairment associated with TBI imposed constraints on associational learning that was fundamental to operant learning methods intrinsic to a behaviour management approach (Wood, 1987; 1989). The principal deficits were (a) a loss of attention control, which prevented the patient making consistent/frequent associations between stimulus and response, or response and reinforcement; (b) lack of awareness of the target behaviour being a problem and therefore rejecting reinforcement as a response contingency, and (c) indifference to reinforcement itself, such that it had neither rewarding or aversive/punishing properties (Wood, 1992). A final limitation of behaviour management with these patients was a recognition that conditioned responses often failed to generalise outside the narrow and highly structured context in which the reinforcement contingencies took place (Wood, 1990).

These constraints on association learning, as a vehicle for developing better self-control and socially appropriate or constructive behaviours, changed the narrow focus of behaviour management to one of cognitive-behaviour management which recognised the organically mediated constraints on learning and response generalisation. In order to accommodate deficits in attention control and other neuropsychological factors that interfere with associational learning (which is the basis of behaviour modification) Wood (1984) argued that it was important to administer reinforcement as *immediately* as possible, in an *obvious* way to ensure correct associations are made, as *frequently* as possible, and over an *extended* period to promote overlearning, which would help generalisation to other less structured situations.

A neurobehavioural paradigm for brain injury rehabilitation (Wood, 1987; 1990; 1992; Wood and Worthington, 2001a; 2001b) evolved out of this behaviour management approach. The 'neuro' prefix was intended to remind rehabilitation practitioners that some aspects of disturbed or otherwise socially inappropriate behaviour was a result of cerebral injury, over which the individual had little or no control and, often, incomplete awareness, rather than being gratuitous or pre-planned, or directly under the control of (external) environmental events (Wood, 1987; Wood and Cope, 1989). Some of the techniques have changed over time as the focus of neurobehavioural approaches to TBI rehabilitation therefore gradually shifted from control over inappropriate and challenging behaviour to the development of effective learning strategies to promote the acquisition of functional abilities likely to lead to greater social independence (Wood, 1989; Manchester and Wood, 2001). This in turn has opened up neurobehavioural rehabilitation to a range of awareness-based and insight-oriented therapies (see Chapters 4 and 11 this volume). This development was anticipated by Wood (1987) who noted:

> A neurobehavioural approach also avoids the conflict of whether to use a predominantly behavioural or cognitive method of treatment. This is because it combines elements of both, emphasising the objective characteristics of cognitive processes which are reflected in the behaviour of an individual.
>
> *(p. 155)*

It is worth noting that the term 'neurobehavioural' had previously been in use but lacked any coherence and conceptual validity, being applied either specifically to psychiatric symptoms or in general terms to any form of behaviour without any clear link to underlying brain function. There was no notion of neurobehavioural disability encapsulating diverse functional and behavioural consequences of the breakdown of frontally-mediated regulatory control processes, and no theoretical link to intervention. Thus an early text entitled *Neurobehavioural Consequences of Closed Head Injury* (Levin et al., 1982) focused on psychotherapy and does not even mention 'behaviour' or 'behaviour management' in the index, stating in a single reference to this aspect of rehabilitation: 'behavioural management is facilitated by providing a supportive, calm environment and encouraging the participation of the patient's family in achieving a sense of security and reorientation' (p. 210).

The neurobehavioural approach in TBI rehabilitation became distinguished from the traditional neurorehabilitation approach (that primarily addressed problems associated with cerebrovascular accident) by its organisational structure of staff as well as procedural methods in the way rehabilitation interventions were employed (Eames and Wood, 1985; 1989; Wood, 1989). The organisational structure primarily involved the working relationships between different therapy disciplines which, in a neurobehavioural context, needed to be inter-disciplinary rather than multi-disciplinary (Wood, 1990; 1993). Therapy interventions in every discipline placed an emphasis on psychological methods of intervention that, through careful assessment and structured observation (Wood, 1987), recognised how problems of attention, awareness, and executive function undermined many aspects of everyday behaviour, either social or functional, and did not respond to conventional methods of therapy management (e.g. Worthington et al., 1997; Worthington and Waller, 2009). Eames (1988) described the importance of staff embracing 'a general atmosphere of positivity' and of adopting 'a slightly over-effusive social demeanour' in order that contingencies of positive reinforcement would be more salient.

This post-acute phase of rehabilitation becomes less medical, more broadly clinical and, ultimately, a social endeavour. To promote these aims and counter neurobehavioural problems, practitioners needed to have knowledge of associational learning methods to devise effective rehabilitation interventions (Burgess and Wood, 1990). This meant that rehabilitation programmes and services were more often led by psychologists (preferably clinical neuropsychologists) rather than by medical doctors (Wood, 2003; Worthington and Merriman, 2008). Furthermore therapy did not take place in time-limited formal *sessions* and only with qualified *therapists* during the nine-to-five working day but was continually being reinforced through every interaction with every member of the team. Rehabilitation was no longer the sole province of professional therapists but the whole team was empowered to regard their role as that of agent for behaviour change. In practice this meant that while therapists often conducted assessments and prescribed ways of doing things, the majority of rehabilitation was actually practised by a host of therapy care assistants, rehabilitation support workers and similarly designated groups who worked under the guidance of clinicians. This was quite distinct from the traditional division of hospital labour between doctors, nurses, therapists, and auxiliaries or healthcare assistants with more domestic responsibilities.

The neurobehavioural paradigm recognised that even the hospital environment itself can be counter-productive for rehabilitation. In part this is because the needs of the rehabilitation facility are subordinate to those of the larger hospital, with its medical hierarchy, therapists having to work across wards with very different types of patients, and nursing staff often being transferred in and out of the facility at short notice with neither the time or inclination to understand the unique neurobehavioural approach. The other reason is more endemic: hospitals are for ill people to be cared for; rehabilitation is about learning to do things for yourself. As the late Sheldon Berrol remarked, one of the first things a child learns is that when you're sick you don't have to go to school (Eames, personal communication). Consequently Eames (1989) proposed that 'rehabilitation units for the head-injured should be developed separately from patients with other sorts of disorders and should be located, as far as possible, away from hospitals' (p. 51).

The organisational constraints on delivering neurobehavioural rehabilitation in its pure form led to a the subsequent development of a stand-alone service in 1985 at Grafton Manor, a few miles from St Andrews Hospital, by several of the original Kemsley Unit pioneers. Eames et al. (1996) reported outcomes for 55 of the first 71 admissions for residential rehabilitation in the unit's first seven years of operation. The profile of brain damage and clinical presentation was very similar to the Kemsley cohort (Eames and Wood, 1985) with 51 of the 55 having been involved in road accidents. Mean time post injury was almost 29 months and average length of stay was 11 months. Prior to admission 95 per cent had needed significant care; upon discharge 63 per cent had improved placement which increased to 78 per cent at follow up. Only 55 per cent required professional care after rehabilitation compared with 87 per cent on admission. However, only 26 cases completed their rehabilitation as planned meaning that the majority either had insufficient funding, were withdrawn prematurely (usually by their family) or were considered inappropriate.

In 1990 the first of a network of community-based post-acute rehabilitation units in the UK was established by the Brain Injury Rehabilitation Trust. By siting these facilities away from hospitals and within the community a greater range of social learning opportunities was immediately available, which helped consolidate learning and overcome some of the difficulties of generalising gains made in special units back into the community. In that sense it reflected increasing awareness of the limitations of hospital-based approaches for these kinds of disorders, exemplified by Greenwood and McMillan (1993, p. 253):

> The learning difficulties and other neuropsychological deficits that these patients have means that many elements [of rehabilitation] should not be sited at institutions, but in a natural community setting, to emphasise a move towards independence, minimise problems with generalisation to everyday routine and emphasise the educational and training nature of the service.

Neurobehavioural rehabilitation in practice

The complex and pervasive nature of neurobehavioural disability has continued to present challenges to clinicians and researchers, requiring reliable tools that are ecologically valid and meaningful and which are sensitive to neuropsychological systems that underpin cognitive abilities, behaviour patterns and personality traits (Powell and Wood, 2001). This has required a different approach to assessment because even standardised psychometric tests of executive functions may fail to identify significant deficiencies in adaptive functioning (Shallice and Burgess, 1991; Bennett et al., 2005; Wood and Bigler, Chapter 7 this volume), necessitating a greater emphasis on structured behavioural observations of function (Wood and Worthington, 1999). Significantly, since the first edition of this book, further progress has been made in developing instruments to encapsulate the nature of neurobehavioural disability (Alderman et al., 2011), specific underlying behaviours (e.g. Knight et al., 2008) and ecological evaluation of executive function (Knight et al., 2002). The clinical application of neurobehavioural principles has been outlined by Wood and Worthington (2001b). Although over time factors such as population need, legislation and new technologies may affect the day-to-day practicalities of service delivery, this framework remains as a useful guide for clinicians with the additional benefit of improved tools and a growing evidence base.

Effectiveness of neurobehavioural rehabilitation

With an emphasis on structured design, systematic recordings and analysis underpinning this approach there is a wealth of empirical support for neurobehavioural rehabilitation at the level of specific interventions and service organisation. An analysis of the outcomes of the first two such centres was published by Wood et al.

(1999) which established the credibility of a community based neurobehavioural approach many years post injury in ameliorating significant challenging behaviour. Standard clinical outcome measures are ill-suited to measuring neurobehavioural disability (Wood and Worthington, 1999; Wood, Alderman and Williams, 2008) and progress until recently has had to be measured descriptively. For example, a cohort of 76 adults, an average of six years post injury, underwent at least six months' rehabilitation (mean: 14 months) and were followed up 1–5 years after discharge. Improvements were described in type of living arrangements, significant reductions in hours of care, and 61 per cent were in some form of work placement or education compared with only 4 per cent before rehabilitation. Gains were larger for people admitted within two years of injury but were still evident if rehabilitation began five years or more post-injury. Importantly, given the significant costs of residential rehabilitation, care costs after treatment were much lower, and reduced further upon follow-up. Wood et al. (1999) calculated a notional saving in lifetime care costs for each individual of between £0.5M and £1.1M depending on how soon after injury neurobehavioural rehabilitation commenced. Worthington (2003) described the evolution of a third such facility, developed in close relationship with local hospitals, in which many more admissions took place within one year of injury, resulting in 56 per cent being discharged home with support and one-quarter to longer term residential facilities previously inaccessible to them due to their behaviour disorder.

Worthington et al. (2006) reported a larger UK study of 133 cases across four sites providing the same community-based neurobehavioural programme. This research replicated the benefits in terms of functional gains and cost-savings of early intervention whilst confirming the value of neurobehavioural rehabilitation to make significant inroads into chronic behaviour disorders many years post injury. This study also factored in the costs of rehabilitation and demonstrated that these had a negligible effect on overall lifetime cost savings, sensitivity analysis confirming estimated savings of £0.8–£1.1M for adults admitted within a year of injury and £0.4–£0.5 for those admitted more than two years after. These figures are remarkably similar to those previously reported by Wood et al. (1999). Importantly both studies demonstrated that functional gains continued to be made beyond the period of residential rehabilitation, reflecting sustainable behaviour change that translated into long-term amelioration of neurobehavioural disability.

Most recently Oddy and da Silva Ramos (2013a) reported an updated analysis of the same neurobehavioural programme across 10 sites using much the same cost-benefit methodology employed by Worthington et al. (2006). They showed that more than 80 per cent of adults previously requiring hospital or residential care did not do so after rehabilitation, and a similar proportion requiring full time supervision at discharge no longer needed this level of support. The average duration of rehabilitation was again around six months but evidence suggests that it is becoming more difficult to sustain gains, perhaps – as the authors acknowledge – because it is difficult to access longer-term assistance in the current economic climate. At discharge 21.5 per cent had no productive activity (54 out of 251) whereas six months later at follow up 35.6 per cent (31/87) had no productive activity, although the proportion in education or employment also went up slightly from 6 per cent to 8 per cent. There are financial constraints to which no service relying on public expenditure is immune, but nonetheless, even with a more conservative discount rate of 1.5 per cent economic analysis showed estimated lifetime cost savings of £0.57M – £1.13M for those admitted within 12 months of injury, which are similar to previous estimates for neurobehavioural rehabilitation, in the UK at least. Although it takes longer to recoup costs for those admitted beyond this period, savings in care costs of £0.19M–£0.86M were reported. Taking into account the lower discount rate applied to take account of recent economic conditions these figures are comparable with those reported by Worthington et al. (2006).

Future developments

Of particular interest is the prospect for emerging technologies to be incorporated into neurobehavioural rehabilitation, which to date has been rather more reliant on a ready supply of skilled support workers than has the traditional medical model of intervention. It can be challenging to ensure access to properly trained personnel in the community other than via specialist units. However, as mainstream technology becomes more versatile and accessible it provides a means to augment the prosthetic environment typically provided by rehabilitation staff to overcome deficiencies in self-regulation. For those able to take advantage new micro-technologies are being developed that provide consistent step-by-step prompting to assist in planning, initiation and sequencing of daily living tasks that would otherwise need the labour-intensive and somewhat intrusive presence of therapist or 'buddy' (Oddy and da Silva Ramos, 2013b; Jamieson and Evans, 2015). This should be welcomed as another intervention modality which, if applied appropriately under skilled supervision, will help ensure that neurobehavioural rehabilitation remains relevant and optimally effective.

Conclusion

Significant progress has been made in understanding neurobehavioural disability over the past four decades, following from the clinical insights of Goldstein, Luria and others, given urgency by early research into the impact of personality and behaviour change after severe brain injury, and building on the successes and failures of pioneering neurobehavioural services. Neurobehavioural interventions have evolved both theoretically and practically, keeping pace with a changing healthcare system. Financial, social and political imperatives will always affect how principles are put into practice. However, there is little doubt that neurobehavioural rehabilitation is socially and economically beneficial. Recent clinical innovations have seen the development of sophisticated tools for characterising neurobehavioural disability (Alderman et al., 2011), that have demonstrated cost-effectiveness and the advantage of integrating technology to augment and enhance the work of practitioners. It is very likely that these developments will shape the way neurobehavioural disability is conceptualised and managed in future.

References

Alderman N, Wood R Ll & Williams, C (2011) The development of the St Andrews–Swansea Neurobehavioural Outcome Scale: Validity and reliability of a new measure of neurobehavioural disability and social handicap. *Brain Injury* 25 (1): 83–100.

Bennett, P C, Ong, B & Ponsford, J (2005) Assessment of executive dysfunction following traumatic brain injury: Comparison of the BADS with other clinical neuropsychological measures. *Journal of the International Neuropsychological Society* 11 (5): 606–613.

Ben-Yishay, Y, Rattock, J, Lakin, P, Piasetsky, E, Ross, B, Silver, S M, Zide, E & Ezrachi, O (1985) Neuropsychological rehabilitation: The quest for a holistic approach. *Seminars in Neurology* 5: 252–259.

Bond, M (1979) The stages of recovery from severe head injury with special reference to late outcome. *Disability and Rehabilitation* 1 (4): 155–159.

Burgess, P W & Wood, R Ll (1990) Neuropsychology of behaviour disorders following brain injury. In: Wood, R. Ll (Ed.) *Neurobehavioural Sequelae of Traumatic Brain Injury.* London: Taylor Francis, 110–133.

Damasio, A R, Tranel, D & Damasio, H R (1991) Somatic markers and the guidance of behavior: Theory and preliminary testing. In: Levin, H S, Eisenberg, H M & Benton, A L (Eds) *Frontal Lobe Function and Dysfunction.* New York: Oxford University Press, 217–229.

Eames, P (1988) Some aspects of the management of difficult behaviour. In: Hall, P & Stonier, P D (Eds) *Perspectives in Psychiatry: The Worcester Lectures.* London: J Wiley & Sons, 41–58.

Eames, P (1989) Head injury rehabilitation: Towards a 'model' service. In Wood, R Ll & Eames, P (Eds) *Models of Brain Injury Rehabilitation.* London: Chapman Hall, 48–58.

Eames, P and Wood, R Ll (1985) Rehabilitation after severe brain injury: A special unit approach to behaviour disorders. *Disability and Rehabilitation* 7 (3): 130–133.

Eames, P G & Wood, R Ll (1989) The structure and content of a head injury rehabilitation service. In: Wood, R Ll & Eames, P (Eds) *Models of Brain Injury Rehabilitation.* London: Chapman Hall, 31–47.

Eames, P, Cotterill, G, Kneale, T A, Storrar, A L & Yeomans, P (1995) Outcome of intensive rehabilitation after severe brain injury: A long-term follow-up study. *Brain Injury* 10 (9): 631–650.

Goldstein, K (1936) The significance of the frontal lobes for mental performances. *Journal of Neurology and Psychopathology* 17 (65): 27–40.

Goldstein, K (1952) The effect of brain damage on the personality. *Psychiatry: Interpersonal and Biological Processes* 15 (3): 245–260.

Greenwood, R J & McMillan, T M (1993) Models of rehabilitation programmes for the brain injured adult. I: Current provision, efficacy and good practice. *Clinical Rehabilitation* 7 (3): 248–255.

Jamieson, M & Evans, J J (2015) Assistive technology for executive functions. In: O'Neill, B & Gillespie, A (Eds) *Assistive Technology for Cognition.* Hove: Psychology Press, 81–96.

Kazdin, A E (1977) *The Token Economy. A Review and Evaluation.* New York: Plenum Press.

Knight, C, Alderman, N & Burgess, P W (2002) Development of a simplified version of the multiple errands test for use in hospital settings. *Neuropsychological Rehabilitation* 12 (3): 231–255.

Knight, C, Alderman, N, Johnson, C, Green, S, Birkett-Swan, L & Yorstan, G (2008) The St Andrew's Sexual Behaviour Assessment (SASBA): Development of a standardised recording instrument for the measurement and assessment of challenging sexual behaviour in people with progressive and acquired neurological impairment. *Neuropsychological Rehabilitation* 18 (2): 129–159.

Levin, H S, Benton, A L & Grossman, R G (1982) *Neurobehavioral Consequences of Closed Head Injury.* New York: Oxford University Press.

Lishman, W A (1984) Book review of Brooks, N (Ed.) *Closed Head Injury: Psychological, Social and Family Consequences. Journal of Neurology Neurosurgery and Psychiatry* 47: 1148.

Luria, A R (1973) *The Working Brain.* Harmondsworth, Middlesex: Penguin.

Manchester, D & Wood, R Ll (2001) Applying cognitive therapy in neurobehavioural rehabilitation. In: Wood, R Ll & McMillan, T M (Eds) *Neurobehavioural Disability and Social Handicap Following Traumatic Brain Injury.* Hove: Psychology Press, 157–174.

McKinlay, W W, Brooks, D N, Bond, M R, Martinage, D P & Marshall, M M (1981) The short term outcome of severe blunt head injury as reported by relatives of the injured persons. *Journal of Neurology, Neurosurgery and Psychiatry* 44: 527–533.

Oddy, M, Humphrey, M & Uttley, D (1978) Stress upon the relatives of head-injured patients. *British Journal of Psychiatry* 133: 507–513.

Oddy, M & da Silva Ramos, S (2013a) The clinical and cost-benefits of investing in neurobehavioural rehabilitation: A multi-centre study. *Brain Injury* 27: 1500–1507.

Oddy, M & da Silva Ramos, S (2013b) Cost effective ways of facilitating home based rehabilitation and support. *NeuroRehabilitation* 32: 781–701.

Panting, A & Merry, P H (1972) The long-term rehabilitation of severe head injuries with particular reference to the need for social and medical support for the patient's family. *Rehabilitation* 38: 33–37.

Powell, G E & Wood, R Ll (2001) Assessing the nature and extent of neurobehavioural disability. In: Wood, R Ll & McMillan, T M (Eds) *Neurobehavioural Disability and Social Handicap Following Traumatic Brain Injury.* Hove: Psychology Press, 65–90.

Prigatano, G P, Fordyce, D J, Zeiner, H K, Roueche, J R, Pepping, M & Wood, B C (1984) Neuropsychological rehabilitation after closed head injury in young adults. *Journal of Neurology, Neurosurgery and Psychiatry* 47: 505–512.

Shallice, T & Burgess, P W (1991) Deficits in strategy application following frontal lobe damage in man. *Brain* 114: 727–741.

Stuss, D T & Benson, F D (1987) The frontal lobes and control of cognition and memory. In: Perecman, E (Ed.) *The Frontal Lobes Revisited.* New York: The IRBN Press, 141–158.

Tate, R L (1986) Issues in the management of behaviour disturbance as a consequence of severe head injury. *Scandanavian Journal of Rehabilitation Medicine* 19: 13–17.

Vocate, D R (1987) *The Theory of A R Luria: Functions of Spoken Language in the Development of Higher Mental Processes.* Hillsdale, N.J.: Lawrence Erlbaum.

Whale, A L, Stanford, C B & Pollack, I W (1986) The effects of behaviour modification vs lithium therapy on frontal lobe syndrome. *Journal of Behavior Therapy and Experimental Psychiatry* 17 (2): 111–115.

Wood, R Ll (1984) Behaviour disorders following severe brain injury: Their presentation and psychological management. In: Brooks, D N (Ed.) *Closed Head Injury: Psychological, Social and Family Consequences.* New York: Oxford University Press.

Wood, R Ll (1987) *Brain Injury Rehabilitation: A Neurobehavioural Approach.* London: Croom Helm.

Wood, R Ll (1989) Salient factors approach to rehabilitation. In: Wood, R Ll & Eames, P (Eds) *Models of Brain Injury Rehabilitation.* London: Chapman and Hall, 75–99.

Wood, R Ll (1990) A neurobehavioural paradigm for brain injury rehabilitation. In: Wood, R Ll (Ed.) *Neurobehavioural Sequelae of Traumatic Brain Injury*. London: Taylor and Francis, 3–17.

Wood, R Ll (1992) A neurobehavioural approach to brain injury rehabilitation. In: Stein, D G (Ed.) *Controversial Concepts of Rehabilitation*. Heidelberg: Springer-Verlag, 49–54.

Wood, R Ll (1993) The rehabilitation team. In: Greenwood, R & McMillan, T (Eds) *Neurological Rehabilitation*. London: Churchill Livingstone.

Wood, R Ll (2003) The rehabilitation team. In: Greenwood, R J, Barnes, M P, McMillan, T M & Ward, C D (Eds) *Handbook of Neurological Rehabilitation*. London: Churchill Livingstone, 41–50.

Wood, R Ll & Eames, P G (1981) Application of behaviour modification in the rehabilitation of traumatically brain-injured patients. In: Davey, G (Ed.) *Applications of Conditioning Theory*. London: Methuen, 81–101.

Wood, R Ll & Cope, N. (1989) Behavior problems and treatment after head injury. In: Horn, L & Cope, N (Eds) *Rehabilitation Reviews*. New York: Hanley and Belfus, 123–143.

Wood, R Ll & Worthington, A D (1999) Outcome in community rehabilitation: Measuring the social impact of disability. *Neuropsychological Rehabilitation* 9 (3/4): 505–516.

Wood, R Ll & Worthington, A D (2001a) Neurobehavioural rehabilitation: A conceptual paradigm. In Wood, R Ll & McMillan, T M (Eds) *Neurobehavioural Disability and social handicap following traumatic brain injury*. Hove: Psychology Press, 107–131.

Wood, R Ll & Worthington, A D (2001b) Neurobehavioural rehabilitation in practice. In Wood, R Ll & McMillan, T M (Eds) *Neurobehavioural Disability and social handicap following traumatic brain injury*. Hove: Psychology Press, 133–155.

Wood, R Ll, McCrea, J D, Wood, L M & Merriment, R N (1999) Clinical and cost-effectiveness of post-acute neurobehavioural rehabilitation. *Brain Injury* 13 (2): 69–88.

Wood, R Ll, Alderman, N & Williams, C (2008) Assessment of neurobehavioural disability: A review of existing measures and recommendations for a comprehensive assessment tool. *Brain Injury* 22 (12): 905–918.

Worthington, A (2003) Out on a limb? Developing an integrated rehabilitation service for adults with acquired brain injury. *Clinical Psychology* 23: 14–18.

Worthington, A D & Merriman, R N (2008) Residential services. In Tyerman, A & King, N (Eds) *Psychological Approaches to rehabilitation after traumatic brain injury*. Oxford: BPS Blackwell, 91–110.

Worthington, A & Waller, J (2009) Rehabilitation of everyday living skills in the context of executive disorders. In: Oddy, M & Worthington, A (Eds) *The rehabilitation of executive disorders*. New York; Oxford University Press, 195–210.

Worthington, A, Williams, C, Young, K & Pownall, J (1997) Retraining gait components for walking in the context of abulia. *Physiotherapy Theory and Practice* 13: 247–256.

Worthington, A D, Matthews, S, Melia, Y & Oddy, M (2006) Cost-benefits associated with social outcome from neurobehavioural rehabilitation. *Brain Injury* 20 (9): 947–957.

2

NEUROBEHAVIOURAL REHABILITATION: A DEVELOPING PARADIGM

Andrew Worthington and Nick Alderman

Introduction

The conceptual basis of neurobehavioural rehabilitation was explained in Chapter 1 as a treatment paradigm for people with challenging behaviour after TBI who were refractory to drug treatments and psychological therapies available in a neurorehabilitation setting in the 1970s. A behavioural management approach, largely based on operant learning theory, provided the main framework for this new way of delivering rehabilitation. The approach, which evolved into what is now called 'neurobehavioural rehabilitation' considered characteristics of neurobehavioural disability (NBD) as dynamic, functional phenomena, which could change over time, rather than being fixed from time of injury. The original paradigm has continued to evolve, leading to new ways of organising and implementing rehabilitation to address long term neurobehavioural disability.

This chapter reflects the authors' experience of leading neurobehavioural services, involving managing staff teams, delivering interventions and conducting research in this setting. We first review the conceptual basis for this specialist type of rehabilitation and focus on three approaches to behaviour as distinct but complementary strands that have been woven into the current fabric of neurobehavioural rehabilitation: operant conditioning, neuropsychology, and social learning theory. We then consider how this translates into clinical practice in terms of core features of service organisation and therapeutic procedures. In so doing we also reflect on factors that can facilitate or undermine effective neurobehavioural intervention. We conclude with a review of the way neurobehavioural rehabilitation has developed in the past two decades with a view to how this is likely to influence future service provision.

What is neurobehavioural rehabilitation?

The 'organic' basis of symptoms representing neurobehavioural disability, including challenging behaviour, has always been central but over time the conceptual basis of neurobehavioural rehabilitation evolved to incorporate constructs, theories and procedures from cognitive, behavioural and social psychology. However, against this shifting background, core concepts underpinning service delivery have remained constant. These comprise a learning process that re-equips the person, as far as possible, with functional skills, abilities and social behaviours to maximise personal autonomy and then establishing these as habit patterns to enhance the person's ability to apply skills spontaneously and (ideally) adaptively (Wood & Worthington, 2001). Structure is sustained through the physical environment, a daily routine, and interventions derived from learning theory, delivered as far as possible by a team that works across traditional disciplinary boundaries – a transdisciplinary team (TDT). The net effect is to create a prosthetic environment that increases awareness and motivation, whilst shaping behavioural responses into acceptable forms, and optimising capacity for social learning.

Conceptual background

Operant conditioning

Theories about what drives human behaviour have underpinned neurobehavioural rehabilitation from the outset, especially those regarding new learning, including operant conditioning. The basic premise of operant conditioning is that the response experienced following an action will influence future behaviour.

Operant conditioning asserts that behaviour 'operates' on the environment and is maintained by its consequences. The probability that behaviour will occur again is dependent on whether it is a) rewarded (positive and negative reinforcement), b) not rewarded, c) if an expected reward has been withheld (extinction), or d) if behaviour is punished (positive punishment). The positive reinforcement principle states that behaviours are maintained through contingent delivery of reinforcement, including social attention and preferred activities. Likelihood of behaviours maintaining or increasing also occurs through negative reinforcement, when they serve a function that removes, postpones, or reduces aversive stimuli (such as demanding activities). These are often conceptualised as escape or avoidance behaviours. Behaviour that results in some aversive consequence or withdrawing a reinforcer that is maintaining it will do likewise, and may result in permanent change to a person's behavioural repertoire.

Operant conditioning provides a conceptual framework for understanding how reinforcement, through environmental factors, contributes to development and maintenance of challenging behaviour, enabling design of effective interventions, providing a seamless link between assessment and treatment. This enables a systematic, structured approach to be taken, including (1) designation of a clear set of procedures to follow, ensuring a consistent, objective approach; (2) detailed assessment of social and environmental factors impacting on behaviour; (3) individually designed interventions based on a functional analysis of contingencies and antecedents that trigger or maintain behaviour; (4) continuous monitoring using operational criteria; (5) attempts to generalise modified behaviour to other environments; and (6) if not successful, further functional analysis to re-evaluate the original formulation.

Other influences on neurobehavioural rehabilitation

Complete reliance on an operant approach in neurobehavioural rehabilitation will not succeed because of the complexity and multivariate nature of neurobehavioural disability. Nevertheless, it provides an overall framework within which rehabilitation is delivered, and a means of capturing and utilising environmental factors. Damage to the brain causes disruption to neural circuits, processes and cognitive functions. Whilst these cannot be directly observed in situ, they nevertheless exert a mediating influence between environmental events and behaviours, which may explain some unexpected responses to operant learning interventions.

Neurobehavioural rehabilitation recognises the importance of considering mediational processes in the form of internal events to the person with brain injury. Whilst, as a concept, operant conditioning provides a fundamental framework to underpin rehabilitation, neurobehavioural disability and social handicap are ultimately the product of complex interactions between a range of factors which, if not taken into account, can lead to failure of a purely 'behavioural' approach. Recognition that internal events that cannot be directly observed has enriched the paradigm further through incorporation of a range of concepts within the overall framework provided by learning theory. For example, behaviour can be 'automatically' reinforced by internal factors, including perceptual feedback, modulation of arousal and pain attenuation, none of which can be directly observed. It is therefore important to consider some of the principal mediators.

Neuropsychological explanations of behaviour

Central amongst these internal mediators of behaviour is neurocognitive impairment, which is an enduring legacy of TBI, one which imposes constraints on learning ability. Cognitive impairment cannot be directly observed, but neuropsychological theories and models help explain behaviour change (often when a functional analysis of observable behaviour cannot), as well as providing assessment tools to quantify and measure 'hidden' disability (however, the limitations of neuropsychological assessment methods as described in Chapter 7 should not be overlooked).

Neuropsychological perspectives in understanding constraints on new learning require clinicians to take account of the mediating influence of arousal, alertness and attention (Wood, 1988). For example, Alderman (1996) demonstrated poor response to conventional operant conditioning methods (reinforcement, extinction and time-out) was related to difficulties on a dual-task exercise, but not to tests of intelligence, memory or executive function. It was proposed that deficits in the central executive component of working memory interfered with allocation of attentional resources and undermined learning. Consequently, methods such as response-cost, involving immediate feedback, provide more effective treatment. This approach to understanding behaviour, the poor response to some operant interventions, and identification of effective means of managing disability, was highly influenced by the working memory model of Baddeley and Hitch (1974). Other examples of how theoretical neuropsychological models explain both the root causes of neurobehavioural disorders and their rehabilitation have been notable, especially those concerning frontal lobe regulation of attention to action. In particular, Norman and Shallice's model of a Supervisory Attentional System has proved influential in directing and describing outcomes from neurobehavioural intervention (Alderman & Burgess, 1990).

Influence of social learning theory

Another highly influential concept on the development of neurobehavioural rehabilitation is social learning theory, which has provided a further means of understanding and addressing social psychological aspects of rehabilitation and behavioural approaches (Eames & Wood, 1989). Bandura (1977) advocated the view that humans are active information processors and think about relationships between behaviour and its consequences; observational learning, for instance, could not occur unless cognitive processes were at work. They constitute a set of internal factors that mediate the learning process to determine if a new response is acquired.

A good example of this mediational role in determining behaviour was provided by Seligman and Maier (1967) who demonstrated that spontaneous escape/avoidance responses in animals could be suppressed through learned helplessness, leading others to propose that expectations of efficacy determine how much effort and persistence people demonstrate to achieve an objective (Bandura, 1977). This introduces the idea that incentives, as well as reinforcement, can mediate behaviour change, introducing the relevance of subjective value into the matrix of things to be considered. Moreover, by arguing that behaviour is governed by an expectation that engagement in behaviour will achieve an outcome, social learning theorists shifted the emphasis from response-outcome expectancies to self-efficacy expectancies (the idea that behaviour is not simply an outcome of reinforcement contingencies per se but also perceived reinforcement). Such factors emphasise that behaviour is the product of complex interactions between internal and environmental events, such that 'thinking' and internal mental processes must be taken into account to fully understand disability and handicap after TBI. This has further expanded the scope of neurobehavioural rehabilitation to include interventions such as modelling, self-instruction, and cognitive challenges to attributional style.

Self-instruction training and metacognition

Self-instruction training, as developed by Meichenbaum and Goodman (1971), provides an important bridge between different elements central to neurobehavioural rehabilitation. It links the self-efficacy/social learning approach to the more traditional behavioural landscape by integrating notions of self-regulation with the idea that behaviour is predicted by outcome expectancies. It also links neuropsychological perspectives to the behavioural literature through ideas such as the role of the frontal lobes in verbal regulation of behaviour, addressing some of the attentional constraints on learning. This approach was developed further by Ylvisaker and colleagues with their emphasis on strategies to support positive behavioural change in specific learning environments (Feeney & Ylvisaker, 2003; Ylvisaker, Turkstra & Coelho, 2005). Essentially social learning, or social cognitive theories as they have become known, view behavioural self-regulation as a complex cognitive operation mediated by self-efficacy (Bandura, 1991). Their neobehavioural origins are evident in the emphasis on a proactive anticipatory system as opposed to a stimulus reactive model which also allows for a wider range of therapeutic interventions involving cognitive and social constructs.

The practical application of neurobehavioural principles

Neurobehavioural rehabilitation is distinguishable from other forms of neurorehabilitation because a) it addresses problems that emerge at a post-acute stage of recovery; b) there is no requirement that services are hospital based, in fact most are in community settings; c) it is not medical but a psychosocial (neuropsychological) form of intervention; and d) rehabilitation goals are social, functional, and client-centred.

The rehabilitation team is at the heart of any neurobehavioural service, the training and organisation of which is critical to its effectiveness. Structure is sustained through the physical environment, a daily routine, and interventions derived from learning theory, delivered by a transdisciplinary team (TDT). The net effect is to create a prosthetic environment that increases awareness and motivation, whilst shaping behavioural responses into acceptable forms, and optimising capacity for social learning.

Team members are responsible for attainment of rehabilitation goals by delivering a consistent treatment programme that is not 'session bound', providing multiple opportunities to encourage and reinforce new skills and abilities. The aim of rehabilitation is not simply to achieve socially functional behaviours but to establish these as social habit patterns that increase the likelihood of being generalised to other environments, thereby maximising autonomy.

Interventions implemented within this therapeutic milieu rely heavily on methods from learning theory, especially operant conditioning, in the form of multicomponent programmes utilising both contingency management and positive behaviour support (Alderman & Wood, 2013; Alderman, Knight & Brooks, 2013). Behavioural methodologies are especially relevant as they create prosthetic structures that circumvent two major contributing factors that drive challenging behaviour, neurocognitive impairment and the environment.

The combination of methods employed by neurobehavioural rehabilitation is ideally suited to meeting the complex problems of neurobehavioural disability the evidence base for which is principally drawn from single case studies (Alderman & Wood, 2013; Alderman et al., 2013), although research using group cohorts support longer-term benefits, including savings in care costs (Worthington et al., 2006; Oddy & Ramos, 2013; see also Chapter 17).

A transdisciplinary approach

The transdisciplinary approach has been recognised as best practice for optimising service delivery in a range of contexts (Guralnick, 2001) and the complex, hetero-geneous needs of people with traumatic brain injury are often best met through input from multiple disciplines working together, rather than separately. A TDT shares roles across disciplinary boundaries so that communication, interaction and cooperation are maximised among team members. It is characterised by the com-mitment of its members to teach, learn and work together to implement coordi-nated services. A key outcome of transdisciplinary working is the development of a mutual vision or 'shared meaning' among the team (Davies, 2007). King et al. (2009) defined three essential and unique operational features. The first is arena assessment, where professionals from multiple disciplines come together to under-take simultaneous assessment, using both standardised measures and informal methods. Data is analysed and reflected on by the TDT and joint formulations are made regarding goals. The second feature is ongoing interaction among team members from different disciplines, enabling them to pool and exchange informa-tion, knowledge and skills, and work together cooperatively. The third defining feature is 'role release', the most crucial and challenging component in TDT devel-opment. When fully embraced, members give up or 'release' intervention strategies from their disciplines, under the supervision and support of team members whose disciplines are accountable for those practices. The role release process involves sharing of expertise; valuing perspectives, knowledge and skills of those from other disciplines; and trust, evidenced by being able to 'let go' of one's specific role when appropriate.

Transdisciplinary working in cognitive and behavioural rehabilitation has been previously endorsed in the UK, Australia and the USA, including in a compre-hensive day treatment program (Malec, 2001) and in enhancing goal setting in both residential and community rehabilitation environments (Todd, 2014). The advantages of this team structure in neurobehavioural rehabilitation have also been previously supported, including in the first edition of this book (Wood & Worthington, 2001) and very recently (Alderman & Knight, in press). The approach fosters consistency (especially important when behavioural approaches are used), pursuit of functional goals that are meaningful to the patient, delivery of rehabilitation 24/7, and encourages generalisation of gains.

Whilst delivery of neurobehavioural rehabilitation through a TDT represents the ideal, it is recognised that there are considerable challenges in doing so that may render this unreachable in some services (King et al., 2009). Examples of impediments to transdisciplinary working include the time required for teams to plan, practise and critique their work together, which may not be affordable if cost-effective services are to be maintained. Another example is loss of professional identity, with potential for team members to feel threatened by sharing knowledge with others, undermining the crucial feature that is 'role release' (Long et al., 2003; Hall, 2005).

All team members are responsible for attainment of these goals by delivering a consistent treatment programme that is not 'session bound', providing multiple opportunities to encourage and reinforce new skills and abilities. The aim of rehabilitation is not simply to achieve socially functional behaviours but to establish these as social habit patterns that increase the likelihood of being generalised to other environments, thereby maximising autonomy.

Interventions implemented within this therapeutic milieu rely heavily on methods from learning theory, especially operant conditioning, in the form of multicomponent programmes utilising both contingency management and positive behaviour support (Alderman & Wood, 2013; Alderman, Knight & Brooks, 2013). Behavioural methodologies are especially relevant as they create prosthetic structures that circumvent two major contributing factors that drive challenging behaviour, neurocognitive impairment and the environment.

Challenges to neurobehavioural rehabilitation

If neurobehavioural rehabilitation is to prosper beyond the walls of a few specialist centres in relatively wealthy countries then not only must the fundamental principles translate into realistic ways of working elsewhere but it must also resist efforts to impose wholly inappropriate structures and methods. The threats to neurobehavioural rehabilitation come from two different directions. One of these is due to the success of the paradigm in that over the past 20 years many of the principles of neurobehavioural rehabilitation have been more widely embraced in other forms of rehabilitation. These include core concepts such as cross-disciplinary team working, non-medical team leaders, blurred boundaries between job roles, and functional rather than impairment-based outcome measures which are all now commonplace (Ward et al., 2009). A degree of compromise is often involved when the principles are adopted more broadly however, which risks undermining the whole edifice. For example the idea that staff work more effectively when professional roles are shared often conflicts with departmental identities that many institutions uphold. Rehabilitation goals frequently remain discipline-specific and do not facilitate joint-working. Some services, especially in hospitals maintain an unhelpful distinction between staff who carry out therapy and those who provide care, creating divisions within the workplace that can hinder communication and the continuity of therapeutic interventions. Under such circumstances it is very difficult to deliver effective neurobehavioural rehabilitation.

This situation is exacerbated by the limited numbers of clinical psychologists and neuropsychiatrists trained in this field. Even in the comparatively well resourced environs of the UK, many rehabilitation teams lack expert clinical psychology input (McMillan & Ledder, 2001; BSRM, 2008). Inter-professional working is challenging and requires appropriate representation of relevant expertise. Yet with resources scarce, services may resort to piecemeal contributions from therapists, with rehabilitation being relegated to carefully packaged hour-long sessions from individual practitioners. Such a model is more akin to services for stroke or elderly care (Monaghan et al., 2005) with clinical psychologists and neuropsychiatrists being regarded as liaison professionals rather than essential personnel to build a team around. In order to remain relevant and effective neurobehavioural rehabilitation must retain the core concepts that distinguish it from other approaches. In this regard there remains a considerable need for training and education.

Developments in neurobehavioural rehabilitation

Over the past 20 years neurobehavioural rehabilitation has continued to evolve by incorporating new insights (in particular from psychology, cognitive neuroscience and technology). Its central strength is that it remains conceptually driven, which provides a bulwark to ensure its survival as a distinct approach. Practitioners must not ignore the theoretical foundation that underpins neurobehavioural rehabilitation. However, it must also be recognised that its longevity depends on adaptation to new ideas and technologies.

Legislative changes

There is considerable variation in the legislative background to healthcare practice from country to country and, in places, from state to state. It is therefore difficult to generalise or do justice to the many possible ways this can affect clinical practice, from how services are organised and paid for to the responsibilities of individual practitioners. For example, the level of autonomy accorded to non-medical team leaders may vary, which may make it difficult to develop psychology-led therapy teams. In the UK there is still resistance to clinicians other than medical doctors taking clinical responsibility for patients legally detained, a role introduced by changes in mental health legislation. For the non-detained (informal) patient, which is the majority of cases, the Adults with Incapacity (Scotland) Act (2000) and in England and Wales, the Mental Capacity Act (2005) placed capacity to make decisions for oneself within a legal framework outside mental health law for the first time. This has instigated a welcome focus on individual autonomy and personal choice, including the right to make unwise decisions, but has also introduced major challenges for clinicians and others obliged to carry out formal evaluations of capacity in adults who may lack insight and judgement due to severe brain injury. In response services have developed protocols and procedures as part of the rehabilitation process. As a result clinicians can become embroiled in disputes on contentious issues and at times have to accept a person's right to refuse a treatment from which they would probably benefit.

Cognitive behavioural therapy (CBT) and neurobehavioural rehabilitation

Cognitive treatment approaches and CBT in particular have formed the basis of much of the evidence base for treatment in clinical psychology and psychiatry. Whilst there is a case for using CBT in treating specific mental health problems that occur in the context of TBI (see Chapters 11–14) the current evidence base for the efficacy of the approach with this clinical population remains limited (Alderman et al., 2013; Waldron et al., 2013). As techniques develop more evidence may accrue but ultimately there will always be restrictions on how effectively this approach can be applied. To work well CBT demands the ability to comprehend novel and abstract ideas, which requires introspection and a certain level of intellectual and emotional detachment, not to mention the ability to reflect on and articulate thoughts and feelings. It works well with motivated people who can complete homework assignments and report back diligently at the next session. In contrast, neurocognitive impairment, which includes characteristics such as concrete thinking, diminished levels of self-awareness, impaired reasoning and judgement, concentration and memory problems, all mitigate against successful engagement in CBT. Cumulative effects of these and other aspects of neurobehavioural disability, including emotional volatility, awareness disorders, and presence of challenging behaviour itself, conspire to reduce ability to engage in CBT.

Reduced awareness

In contrast to CBT, neurobehavioural rehabilitation is uniquely designed to address the organic constraints on insight and learning which, in many cases, are permanent. Attempts to manage this through first developing insight are often futile; instead, a more conventional behavioural manipulation of environmental contingencies is more effective.

Rehabilitation is ultimately about learning and, when applied to behaviour, works by modifying schedules of reinforcement. As virtually all behaviour elicits a reaction from someone, all responses are potentially reinforcing. Clinicians cannot opt out of this process of reinforcement – they are either doing it right or they must be doing it wrong. Therapists must understand what is driving the behaviour and be aware of their impact in light of this. Hence, where a challenging behaviour is reinforced by an outcome desired by the individual rather than the therapist, drawing attention to this is likely to prove ineffective. Cognitively minded practitioners must be sure there is scope for reflection and a willingness to consider alterative actions, as well as potential to prioritise longer-term benefit over short-term gains, in order to justify an approach that might otherwise exacerbate the problem.

Motivation for change

In the absence of insight it is very difficult to generate the conditions necessary for engagement in treatment. It has been recognised that readiness for change is a key determinant of progress in addressing chronic habitual patterns of behaviour such as taking illegal substances and alcohol abuse. Much work has been focussed in recent years on exploring whether preparing people for change helps to address one of the common barriers to engagement (reviewed by Medley & Powell, 2010). There is some suggestion that this approach may be useful for adults presenting with serious brain injury and alcohol/substance misuse. Bombardier and Rimmele (1999), for example, showed this was helpful in reducing alcohol in inpatient settings as did Cox et al. (2003) in terms of substance misuse, but the evidence to date is limited. This kind of approach, borrowing methods from other areas and adapting them for brain injury, is likely to be increasingly important in future as neurobehavioural series expand their services into sub-specialisms concerned with specific populations such as offenders, drug addicts, adolescents and the homeless,

Inertia and avoidance

Enhancing insight may well improve motivation but this will not guarantee behaviour change. One of the principal constraints on learning in neurobehavioural disorders is the inability or reluctance to act in accordance with stated intentions, without which experiential learning cannot occur. This is why so much emphasis is placed on structure and implicit cueing and feedback in order that behaviours will be triggered or activated by the prosthetic rehabilitative environment. This idea of behavioural activation is also a crucial component in CBT, one that has been shown to be better or equivalent to more cognitively elaborate therapies (Coffman et al., 2007). Indeed, in their review, Longmore and Worrell (2007: p. 173) concluded that 'there is little empirical support for the role of cognitive change as causal in the symptomatic improvements achieved in CBT'.

Activation is key

Behavioural activation targets inertia and avoidance. It is ideally suited to TBI where lack of initiative and planning can be a major barrier to therapeutic engagement. It works from the 'outside in', utilising scheduling activities and graded exercises that promote the acquisition of skills and self-efficacy, by maximising the opportunity to positively reinforce constructive activities. It is a transdisciplinary technique that can readily be taught to non-specialists (Ekers et al., 2011). From a neuropsychological perspective, such methods may target Gray's Behavioural Activation System (BAS), a mesolimbic dopamine-driven mechanism that processes rewarding stimuli (Pickering & Gray, 1999). According to Gray's theory of reinforcement sensitivity, an over-reactive BAS leads to impulsive behaviour when faced with conditioned stimuli signalling reward. It follows that a deficient system should be treated with repeated exposure to such events.

In neurobehavioural rehabilitation behavioural activation can be achieved by substituting a less desirable behavioural response with a more desirable one through operant conditioning. According to cognitive neuropsychological models this involves preferential activation of a selected action schema (Cooper & Shallice, 2000; Kumada & Humphreys, 2002) possibly through a process of reciprocal inhibition. There is no reason why this operation should not apply as equally to cognitive schemas as behavioural schemas. A good example is Brewin's (2006) model of how CBT works. Brewin proposed that representations in long-term memory contain negative or positive representations of the Self and these compete for conscious attention, with negative self-schemas being more readily brought to mind in emotional disorders. Therapy serves not to modify negative information in memory but to change the relative accessibility of positive and negative representations. Accordingly new learning deactivates problematic representations rather than changes them, and can be undertaken either by associational (behavioural) methods or logical (cognitive) analysis.

This framework involves teaching people to think more logically by providing them with the means and opportunity to develop increased behavioural repertoires that lead to greater self-efficacy. In turn, this should lead to greater behavioural initiation and increased accessibility of positively reinforcing events (to which the Behavioural Activation System is uniquely sensitive).

The future of neurobehavioural rehabilitation

In this chapter we have discussed the conceptual background to and the practical implementation of neurobehavioural rehabilitation. We have also considered challenges to developing services and threats that risk undermining the essence of a neurobehavioural approach. In rehabilitation, progress is rarely accompanied by the kinds of publicity that heralds a new medical advance or development of a new 'wonder drug'. In rehabilitation advances are typically slow and steady, and are generally achieved by gradual accumulation of evidence. For practitioners of neurobehavioural rehabilitation it is no easy task to maintain a steady course though the multiple professional, bureaucratic, political and economic vagaries that constitute the backdrop to clinical practice. Despite this we have reviewed trends that indicate there is considerable potential for neurobehavioural rehabilitation if it can resist dilution of key principles and retain a distinct identity.

Improved measures

In terms of conceptual advances, new methods of characterising and measuring neurobehavioural disorders, discussed elsewhere in this volume, are leading to improved understanding of disability and more sensitive evaluation of clinical outcomes. Until recently practitioners have been hampered by inadequate tools (Wood, 2013). An improved ability to identify neurobehavioural disability and social handicap will improve intervention outcomes.

Improved methods

With more sensitive means of assessment come better methods of evaluating interventions, which in turn leads to new and more effective treatment techniques. In recent years there has been a steady growth of evidence from single cases, case series and cohort studies that we are able to deliver empirically validated, theoretically informed rehabilitation that produces meaningful and sustainable changes in function and behaviour for some of the most challenging and disadvantaged sections of society. This improves the lives not only of the individual recipient but of the many family members, friends, colleagues and others that comprise their wider social network.

Improved efficiency

In the past 15 years there has been a growing recognition, with evidence to support this, that neurobehavioural rehabilitation is not just clinically effective but also cost-effective. Economic conditions change but studies undertaken at different times in different services have confirmed that investment in neurobehavioural rehabilitation remains worthwhile. Whilst a properly organised and resourced neurobehavioural service requires sufficient funding numerous studies have shown that costs are generally recouped within a relatively brief time-span when one considers overall life expectancy. If neurobehavioural services are to thrive in future policy makers and payers need to be made aware of the long term economic as well as clinical benefits.

New technologies

Compared with the situation at the time of the first edition of this book there has been a gradual but increasing use of technological aids to overcome disability. In particular, mainstream technology can be tailored to meet individual needs. Interventions utilising technology to address some of the cognitive deficits underpinning neurobehavioural disability are reported elsewhere in this volume (see Chapter 16). This is a rapidly developing area; attentional alerts, memory cueing devices, communication aids and micro-prompting systems for carrying out multi-step actions are all likely to play a greater role in future in addressing chronic handicap arising from neurobehavioural disability. Where behavioural, attentional and physical constraints prevent this, whole systems can be created in the form of Smart homes that provide a prosthetic living environment (Gentry, 2009) and can assist the provision of round the clock support (Oddy & Ramos, 2013).

Concluding comments

Neurobehavioural rehabilitation developed to meet the challenge of complex patterns of neurobehavioral disability and maximise personal autonomy. It provided an alternative means of conceptualising and managing emotional and behavioural legacies of TBI, and many of the original tenets have since been adopted by the wider rehabilitation community. The question of whether neurobehavioural rehabilitation remains sufficiently distinct from other forms of rehabilitation has perhaps become less relevant over time than the need to retain a clear conceptual framework, one that evolves alongside developments in neuroscience, and assistive technology, without losing its underlying roots in learning theory. Future practitioners and researchers will increasingly need to integrate multiple theoretical and technological advances to ensure continued evolution of the paradigm.

References

Alderman, N (1996) Central executive deficit and response to operant conditioning methods. *Neuropsychological Rehabilitation* 6(3): 161–186.

Alderman, N & Burgess, P W (1990) Integrating cognition and behaviour: A pragmatic approach to brain injury rehabilitation. In: Wood, R Ll & Fussey, I (Eds) *Cognitive Rehabilitation in Perspective*. London: Taylor & Francis, 204–228

Alderman, N & Wood, R Ll (2013) Neurobehavioural approaches to the rehabilitation of challenging behaviour. *NeuroRehabilitation* 32: 761–770.

Alderman, N & Knight, C (in press) Managing disorders of social and behavioural control and disorders of apathy. In: Wilson, B A, van Heugten, C, Winegardner, J & Ownsworth T (Eds) *The International Handbook of Neuropsychological Rehabilitation*. Psychology Press.

Alderman, N, Knight, C & Brooks, J (2013) Rehabilitation approaches to the management of aggressive behaviour disorders after acquired brain injury. *Brain Impairment* 14(1): 5–20.

Baddeley, A D & Hitch, G J (1974). Working memory. In: Bower, G. (Ed.) *Recent Advances in Learning and Motivation, Vol. VIII*. New York: Academic Press, 47–90.

Bandura, A (1977) Self-efficacy: Toward a unifying theory of behavioral change. *Psychological Review* 84(2): 191–215.

Bandura, A (1991) Social cognitive theory of self-regulation. *Organizational Behavior and Human Decision Processes* 50: 248–287.

Bombardier, C H & Rimmele, C T (1999) Motivation interviewing to prevent alcohol abuse after traumatic brain injury: A case series. *Rehabilitation Psychology* 44(10): 52–67.

Brewin, C (2006) Understanding cognitive behaviour therapy: A retrieval competition account. *Behaviour Research and Therapy* 44: 765–784.

British Society of Rehabilitation Medicine (2008) *Neurological Rehabilitation: A Briefing Paper for Commissioners of Clinical Neurosciences*. London: BSRM/RCP.

Coffman, S J, Martell, C R, Dimidjian, S, Gallop, R & Hollon, S D (2007) Extreme nonresponse in cognitive therapy: Can behavioral activation succeed where cognitive therapy fails? *Journal of Consulting and Clinical Psychology* 75(4): 531–541.

Cooper, R & Shallice, T (2000) Contention scheduling and the control of routine activities. *Cognitive Neuropsychology* 17(4): 297–338.

Cox, W M, Heinemann, A W, Miranti, S V, Schmidt, M, Klinger, E & Blount, J (2003) Outcomes of systematic motivational counselling for substance use following traumatic brain injury. *Journal of Addictive Diseases* 22(1): 93–110.

Davies, S (Ed.) (2007) *Team Around the Child: Working Together in Early Childhood Education*. Wagga Wagga, New South Wales, Australia: Kurrajong Early Intervention Service.

Eames, P & Wood, R Ll (1989) The structure and content of a head injury rehabilitation service. In: Wood, R Ll & Eames, P (Eds) *Models of Brain Injury Rehabilitation*. London: Chapman & Hall, 31–47.

Ekers, D, Richards, D, McMillan, D, Bland, J M & Gilbody, S (2011) Behavioural activation delivered by the non-specialist: Phase II randomised controlled trial. *The British Journal of Psychiatry* 198(1): 66–72.

Feeney, T and Ylvisaker, M (2003) Context-sensitive behavioural supports for young children with TBI: Short-term effects and long-term outcomes. *Journal of Head Trauma Rehabilitation* 18(1): 33–31.

Gentry, T (2009) Smart homes for people with neurological disability: State of the art. *NeuroRehabilitation* 25: 209–217.

Guralnick, M J (2001) A developmental systems model for early intervention. *Infants and Young Children* 14(2): 1–18.

Hall, P (2005) Interprofessional teamwork: Professional cultures as barriers. *Journal of Interprofessional Care Supp* 1: 188–196.

King, G, Strachan, D, Tucker, M, Duwyn, B, Desserud, S & Shillington, M (2009) The application of a transdisciplinary model for early intervention services. *Infants and Young Children* 22(3): 211–223.

Kumada, T & Humphreys, G W (2002) Early selection induced by perceptual load in a patient with frontal lobe damage: External vs. internal modulation of processing control. *Cognitive Neuropsychology* 19(1): 49–65.

Long, A F, Kneafsey, R & Ryan, J (2003) Rehabilitation practice: Challenges to effective team working. *International Journal or Nursing Studies* 40(6): 663–673.

Longmore, R J and Worrell, M (2007) Do we need to challenge thoughts in cognitive behaviour therapy? *Clinical Psychology Review* 27: 173–187.

Malec, J F (2001) Impact of comprehensive day treatment on societal participation for persons with acquired brain injury. *Archives of Physical Medicine and Rehabilitation* 82(7): 885–895.

McMillan, T M & Ledder, H (2001) A survey of services provided by community neurorehabilitation teams in South East England. *Clinical Rehabilitation* 15(6): 582–588.

Medley, A R & Powell, T (2010) Motivational interviewing to promote self-awareness and engagement in rehabilitation following acquired brain injury: A conceptual review. *Neuropsychological Rehabilitation* 20(4): 481–508.

Meichenbaum, D & Goodman, J (1971) Training impulsive children to talk to themselves: A means of developing self-control. *Journal of Abnormal Psychology* 77(2): 115–126.

Monaghan, J, Channell, K, Mcdowell, D & Sharma, A K (2005) Improving patient and carer communication, multidisciplinary team working and goal-setting in stroke rehabilitation. *Clinical Rehabilitation* 19(20): 194–199.

Oddy, M & Ramos, D S (2013) Cost effective ways of facilitating home based rehabilitation and support. *NeuroRehabilitation* 32: 781–701.

O'Neill, B & Gillespie, A (Eds) (2015) *Assistive Technology for Cognition.* Hove: Psychology Press.

Pickering, A D & Gray, J A (1999) The neuroscience of personality. *Handbook of personality: Theory and research* 2: 277–299.

Seligman, M E P & Maier, S F (1967) Failure to escape traumatic shock. *Journal of Experimental Psychology* 74(1): 1–9.

Todd, D (2014) Narrative approaches to goal setting. In: Weatherhead, S & Todd, D (Eds) *Narrative Approaches to Brain Injury.* London: Karnac Books Ltd, 51–76.

Waldron, B, Casserly, L M & O'Sullivan, C (2013) Cognitive behavioural therapy for depression and anxiety in adults with acquired brain injury. What works for whom? *Neuropsychological Rehabilitation* 23(1): 64–101.

Ward, A B, Barnes, M P, Stark, S C & Ryan, S (Eds) (2009) *Oxford Handbook of Clinical Rehabilitation (2nd edition).* New York: Oxford University Press.

Wood, R Ll (1988) Clinical constraints affecting human conditioning. In: Davey, G & Cullen, C (Eds) *Human Operant Conditioning and Behavior Modification.* Chichester: John Wiley & Sons Ltd, 87–118.

Wood, R Ll (2013) Recognising and assessing neurobehavioural disability after traumatic brain injury. *NeuroRehabilitation* 32(4): 699–706.

Wood, R Ll & Worthington, A D (2001) Neurobehavioural rehabilitation: A conceptual paradigm. In: Wood, R Ll & McMillan, T (Eds) *Neurobehavioural Disability and Social Handicap Following Traumatic Brain Injury.* Hove: East Sussex, UK: Psychology Press, 107–131.

Worthington, A D, Matthews, S, Melia, Y & Oddy, M (2006) Cost-benefits associated with social outcome from neurobehavioural rehabilitation. *Brain Injury* 20(9): 947–957.

Ylvisaker, M, Turkstra, L S & Coelho, C (2005) Behavioral and social interventions for individuals with traumatic brain injury: A summary of the research with clinical implications. *Seminars in Speech and Language* 26(4): 256–267.

3

DISORDERS OF EMOTION RECOGNITION AND EXPRESSION

Claire Williams and Rodger Ll. Wood

Dolan (2002) has described emotion as 'the principal currency in human relationships as well as the motivational force for what is best and worst in human behaviour' (p. 1191). The central role played by emotion in human social behaviour has made this an important topic in neuroscience research with growing awareness of how deficits in emotion perception can have a major influence on psychosocial outcome following traumatic brain injury (TBI). Successful social interaction depends on the ability to perceive, discriminate, and regulate emotion expression in oneself and in others. This however, is by no means an easy task. Emotions represent a complex amalgam of cognitions, physiological changes, and sensations that fluctuate over time according to changing events, as well as our changing cognitive appraisal of those events (Panskepp, 1998). The resulting emotion tends to be either positive or negative in direction and each has its own characteristic *'feeling tone'*, which allows individuals to discriminate subtle, and often contradictory feelings about a person or object. Changes in our emotional state are conveyed to others through a variety of powerful indicators that have been shown to be universal in character, such as facial expression, body language, posture and tone of voice (Ekman & Davidson, 1994). Our ability to recognise and respond appropriately to such indicators provides a framework for decision making, human communication and successful social interaction. The loss or impairment of this ability can have serious psychosocial consequences. This was recognised as early as 1902 by William James:

> Conceive yourself, if possible, suddenly stripped of all of the emotion with which our world now inspires you . . . no one portion of the universe would then have importance beyond another, and the whole character of its things and series of its events would be without significance, character, expression, or perspective.

(p. 150)

This chapter will therefore consider those systems and structures mediating emotion, how they are affected by traumatic brain injury, and the psychosocial implications of impaired emotion perception.

Neurobiology of emotion recognition and the effects of traumatic brain injury

The perception of emotionally salient information involves a complex and diverse neural system that includes the ventral striatum, specific thalamic nuclei, the amygdala, the anterior insula and regions of the prefrontal cortex (Davidson, 2000). With regard to subcortical structures, the ventral striatum, dorsomedial nucleus of the thalamus, anterior insula and amygdala appear to be important for the identification of emotionally salient stimuli. The amygdala is one of the primary structures involved in threat-related emotions such as fear, but also sadness and happiness (Adolphs et al., 2000; Calder, Lawrence & Young, 2001). The role of the anterior insula is particularly important in the autonomic response to aversive stimuli, fear reactivity and anticipatory anxiety, as well as reactions to unpleasant taste, pain perception, anxiety and nausea (Calder, Lawrence & Young, 2001).

At a cortical level, the ventromedial and ventrolateral prefrontal regions appear to be of particular importance for the generation of emotional experience and behaviour regulation in response to these stimuli. The ventrolateral prefrontal cortex responds to emotional information, including the induction of sad mood and the recall of personal memories and emotional material (Drevets, 2000). Functional neuroimaging in humans has also identified dorsal regions of the anterior cingulate gyrus and dorsomedial and dorsolateral prefrontal cortices in the selective attention, planning, and motor responses to emotional stimuli, and the integration of these processes with emotional input (Ochsner, Bunge, Gross & Gabrieli, 2002; Phillips, 2003). The ventral anterior cingulate gyrus, in combination with the ventromedial and ventrolateral prefrontal regions, also appears to mediate autonomic functions associated with emotional behaviour and anxiety associated with the anticipation of pain (Drevets, 2000). The orbitofrontal cortex (OFC), which has direct reciprocal connections with the amygdala, has been shown to play an important role in the perception of pleasant and unpleasant odours, flavours and tactile stimuli. The OFC also determines the reward value of a stimulus and the way in which this representation guides goal-directed social behaviour (Damasio, 1996). Patients with orbitofrontal and inferior frontal regions, experience difficulty not only recognising social and emotional signals derived from face and voice expression but also nonverbal vocal expressions of emotion (Hornak, Rolls & Wade, 1996; Straube & Mitner, 2011).

These systems and structures are vulnerable to TBI because of the mechanical forces associated with many forms of head trauma. The structure of the brain combined with the internal architecture of the skull means that deccelerative forces have a direct impact on prefrontal systems (which includes the subcortical limbic system) which is why prefrontal dysfunction is the most frequent legacy of TBI

(Bigler, 2007). It is therefore unsurprising that studies of individuals with TBI have identified emotion recognition difficulties as a major legacy of head trauma, one which potentially has a prominent impact on psychosocial outcome.

Allerdings and Alfano (2006), as well as Spikman et al. (2013), found that after TBI individuals identified significantly fewer emotional stimuli than demographically matched controls. Consistent with these findings, Babbage et al. (2011) in their meta-analysis concluded that as many as 13–39 per cent of people with moderate to severe TBI may experience significant difficulties with affect recognition. However, whilst the extent of emotion perception and recognition difficulties after TBI is now reasonably well established, it has been noted that the nature of these difficulties may vary depending on the emotional valence of stimuli. For example, Croker and McDonald (2005) compared emotion labelling and expression in a group of individuals after TBI with matched controls, finding that both groups were more accurate recognising positive versus negative emotions. However, the TBI group experienced greater difficulty overall, a finding later replicated by Williams and Wood (2010a).

Emotion disorder and social cognition

Emotions serve to communicate social information about people's thoughts and intentions, thereby helping to mediate social encounters. Social cognition is the ability to interpret signals, expressions, gestures, etc., in a way that helps us not only share the emotional state of others, but also to understand and potentially predict their behaviour. It follows therefore that individuals who lack the ability to correctly recognise their own emotion may not only experience difficulty regulating and gauging the appropriateness of their behaviour but may not fully understand the behaviour of others if communicated by expressions of emotion.

McDonald (2013) divided the process of social cognition into 'hot' processes, which involve emotion perception and emotional empathy, and 'cold' processes, which reflect the ability to infer the beliefs, feelings and intentions of others (theory of mind), to see their point of view (cognitive empathy), and what they mean when communicating (pragmatic inference). Whilst the notion of a modular structure has been debated, the role of context as a mediating influence is more easily understood. For example, showing anger or elation on the stand of one's sports club is understandable. However, similar expressions of emotion outside one's local supermarket may be interpreted less favourably. Emotional states (moods and reactions) need to be proportional to the precipitating stimuli, and therefore, recognising the context appropriate to the expression of emotion is a pivotal component of emotional self-regulation and successful human interaction.

If the ability to communicate emotion effectively is fundamental to establishing and maintaining social relationships, deficits of emotion recognition may help to explain why a high proportion of individuals with TBI experience a decline in social and leisure activities, leading to high levels of social isolation (Morton & Wehman, 1995). Consistent with this line of thinking, numerous studies have highlighted an association between emotion recognition abilities and either social competence itself, or characteristics that can undermine social competence after TBI, specifically social immaturity and a general lack of social tact (e.g., Watts & Douglas, 2006). A lack of emotional awareness after TBI can have an adverse impact on the size or quality of a person's social network. In such circumstances individuals have fewer opportunities to observe or practise appropriate social communication. This may contribute to poor emotional awareness persisting over a long period post injury. If the availability of meaningful social feedback is reduced it will result in lost opportunities to learn from experience, adding to the risk of social isolation. It also means that many individuals become increasingly dependent on family members for social interaction and access to community and recreational activities. In turn, this imposes an additional burden on family relationships after TBI, which are already prone to strain and breakdown (Godwin, Kreutzer, Arango-Laspirilla & Lehan, 2011). Therefore, in situations where close personal relationships dissolve after injury, the individual may not only have to come to terms with the loss of a partner, but also their last remaining source of emotional and social support. This is then likely to have further profound psychological implications, potentially increasing the risk of alcohol or drug dependency to compensate for the loss of meaningful social contact.

The role of empathy

The ability to recognise emotion in oneself is usually a prerequisite for understanding other people's thoughts, intentions and feelings, a process intrinsic to social cognition. Consequently, deficits of emotional recognition after TBI can also lead to a reduction in empathy, associated with a lack of tact and social discretion, poor awareness of the emotional needs and sensitivities of others, and an egocentric, self-centred attitude that is insensitive to, or neglectful of, the needs of others (Wood, 2001). Empathy has been described as the 'binding force' of social cognition, allowing individuals to share experiences and understand each other's perspectives (Eslinger, 1998). Unsurprisingly therefore, a lack of empathy can contribute to the fragility of relationships when a partner, who was previously loving and affectionate, becomes, after TBI, emotionally withdrawn and aloof. In turn, this further serves to magnify the feelings of social isolation and loneliness described above that are all too common after TBI.

Empathy involves three primary components: *emotional empathy*; an affective response to another person, which often, but not always, entails sharing a person's emotional state; *cognitive empathy;* reflecting the capacity to understand how and why a person exhibits an emotional state without sharing the emotion itself; and *compassionate empathy*; a regulatory mechanism that keeps track of feelings experienced by oneself and others, allowing one to decide whether it is appropriate to respond compassionately to another person's distress (Decety & Jackson, 2004). Thus, empathy requires both the ability to vicariously experience the emotional state of others (emotional empathy), and an understanding of others' experience (cognitive empathy).

The capacity to empathise seems to be underpinned by a complex network of neural structures and networks, including the dorsolateral, orbital and ventromedial regions of the PFC (Grattan, Bloomer, Archamault & Eslinger, 1994; Shamay-Tsoory, Tomer, Berger & Aharon-Peretz, 2004), the anterior cingulate cortex (ACC) (Singer et al., 2004), and the left anterior middle temporal and left inferior frontal gyri (Farrow et al., 2001). Consequently, impairment in emotional and cognitive empathy after TBI would be unsurprising given that both have been associated with the neural systems and structures typically disrupted after such trauma.

However, despite this recognition, there have been few attempts to examine the capacity for empathy in individuals who have suffered TBI. In one of the most comprehensive studies of this topic to date, Wood and Williams (2008) explored the capacity for emotional empathy in a cohort of 89 head injured patients, 59 of whom were male. In total 60.7 per cent of patients recorded low levels of emotional empathy, compared with 31 per cent of a demographically matched control group drawn from the general population. Males reported higher rates of low emotional empathy than females in both TBI and control groups, consistent with gender bias for empathy. However, the group with TBI reported significantly higher rates of low empathy for both males and females, suggesting that this important aspect of social cognition is vulnerable to head trauma, irrespective of gender. Subsequent research (Williams & Wood, 2010b) confirmed this finding. Interestingly, there was no relationship between emotional empathy and severity of TBI, implying that even relatively minor head injury (presumably in vulnerable individuals) has the potential to alter some emotional functions important to social cognition. Neither was there any relationship between emotional empathy and cognitive abilities, including tests of cognitive flexibility and ecologically relevant executive tests. This suggests that emotional empathy, as a component of social cognition, may operate in a manner that is relatively independent of cognitive ability per se. Further, there was no obvious relationship between emotional empathy and measures of depression and anxiety.

The role of alexithymia

Alexithymia is a personality construct that has been linked to deficits of emotional perception and expression in clinical and non-clinical populations and therefore may help explain deficits of emotion recognition and empathy after TBI. Alexithymia is a multifaceted construct comprising the following salient features: (a) difficulty identifying feelings; (b) difficulty distinguishing between feelings and bodily sensations of emotional arousal; (c) difficulty describing feelings to other people; (d) constricted imaginal processes evidenced by paucity of fantasies; and (e) a stimulus-bound, externally-oriented thinking style (Taylor, Bagby & Parker, 1997, p. 29). Clinically, patients exhibiting alexithymia demonstrate little knowledge about their own feelings and, in most instances, are unable to link them with memories, fantasies, higher level affects or specific situations. In addition, alexithymia has also been associated clinically with a tendency towards social conformity, a tendency to avoid conflicts, a repressive and avoidant coping style, a paucity of facial and gestural expressions, a preoccupation with one's body and the adequacy of its physiological functions (De Gucht, Fischler & Heiser, 2004; Wood & Doughty, 2013).

Given the impaired emotion processing and regulating capacities thought to underpin alexithymia, it is not surprising that it has been conceptualised as one of several possible personality risk factors for a variety of medical and psychiatric disorders involving problems in affect regulation. For example, an inability to modulate emotions through cognitive processing might explain the tendency of alexithymic individuals to discharge tension arising from unpleasant emotions through impulsive acts or compulsive behaviours such as binge eating and substance misuse. Indeed, alexithymia has been associated with a variety of medical and psychiatric disorders (for a review, see Taylor et al., 1997), although it remains unclear whether alexithymia manifests itself similarly in these various clinical contexts.

Early neurobiological models of alexithymia focused on the functioning of the corpus callosum (Houtveen, Bermond & Elton, 1997), but more recent research has highlighted associations between alexithymic characteristics and dysfunction of the anterior cingulate cortex (ACC), right cerebral hemisphere, inferior and middle gyrus, and orbitofrontal cortex (Kano & Fukudo, 2013). Alexithymia should therefore be prevalent after TBI because all these structures are vulnerable in TBI, either directly or because of reciprocal connections with the prefrontal cortex. In support of this hypothesis Williams et al. (2001) examined the potential comorbidity of head injury and alexithymia in a family practice setting, finding that patients with a history of head injury (elicited via a self-report questionnaire) reported higher levels of alexithymia than their non-injured counterparts. In response to these findings, Becerra, Amos and Jongenelis (2002) introduced the concept of 'organic alexithymia' to distinguish the constitutional deficits associated with a developmental history of affective, somatoform, and personality disorders, from an acquired disorder following TBI. Based on data from a single case study, in which the individual with TBI presented with a syndrome considerably similar to alexithymia, they argued that characteristics of organic alexithymia may present in ways that are similar to 'non-organic' alexithymia, but are usually more circumscribed in character and do not manifest until after brain injury, implying a causal role for head trauma.

Wood and Williams (2007) therefore conducted a large scale study to determine whether the proportion of individuals with TBI reporting alexithymia would exceed (a) the general population rate, and (b) the number of cases in a matched control group of orthopaedic patients (N=52), included to control for demographic, familial and social differences that might exist between individuals with TBI and the general population. On the premise that alexithymia reflects a deficit in the regulation of emotions and a syndrome that may limit the extent to which individuals can modulate emotions by fantasy and dreams, the relationship between alexithymia, depression and anxiety was also explored. They found a much higher rate of alexithymia in their sample of 121 cases with TBI (57.9 per cent), relative to both the reported general population rate (7–10 per cent; Pasini, Chiaie & Serpia, 1992), and the orthopaedic control group (15.4 per cent). There was no relationship between injury severity and presence or degree of alexithymia. Hendryx, Haviland and Shaw (1991) suggested that measures of alexithymia may reflect aspects of depression and anxiety, rather than it being a unique personality construct that could increase the risk of secondary affective disturbance. However, the Wood and Williams (2007) study revealed that affective disturbance accounted for only 12 per cent of the variance in alexithymia scores. Neither depression nor anxiety made a unique contribution to alexithymia scores, indicating that even though there is a relationship between affective disturbance and alexithymia, they should be considered as distinct constructs.

Similarly high rates of alexithymia have since been documented in other samples with TBI; raising the possibility that alexithymia may be 'a marker of a more generalised impairment in the capacity for emotion processing' (Lane et al., 1996, p. 203). Specifically, the presence of alexithymia may help to explain why many individuals with TBI exhibit impaired emotion recognition as discussed earlier, on the basis that the ability to identify and understand one's own emotions is a pre-requisite to understanding others' emotions. Consistent with this line of reasoning, Neumann, Zupan, Malec and Hammond (2014), in a sample of 60 individuals with TBI, found that alexithymia significantly explained 12 per cent and 8 per cent of the variance in facial and vocal affect recognition performance respectively. They concluded that people with TBI are more likely to experience problems recognising others' emotions when they have a tendency to minimise emotional experience, avoid affective thinking, and focus attention externally.

In addition to emotion recognition, the presence of alexithymia after TBI may also render an individual unable to vicariously experience the emotions of others, offering a framework from which to understand why so many individuals with TBI experience deficits of empathic processing. On this premise, Williams and Wood (2010b) explored the relationship between alexithymia and emotional empathy in 64 cases with TBI and 64 demographically matched healthy controls, finding a significant inverse relationship between alexithymia and emotional empathy in both groups. Overall, alexithymia scores explained 21.1 per cent of the variance in emotional empathy scores in the control group, and 9 per cent in the group with TBI, suggesting that the relationship between the two emotional constructs was strongest in the absence of head trauma.

Research into the psychosocial consequences of alexithymia has shown that an inability to recognise and express emotions not only has a detrimental impact on the quality of inter-personal relationships (Williams & Wood, 2013), with attendant risks of social isolation and depression, but can also lead to poor emotional coping skills (Wood & Doughty, 2013). Further research has shown that alexithymia increases the risk of post traumatic psychosomatic reactions that can develop into somatoform states (Wood, Williams & Kaylani, 2009), and also increase the risk of suicidal ideation (Wood, Williams & Lewis, 2010). More recently, Williams and Wood (in submission) also demonstrated for the first time that the presence of alexithymia increases the risk of aggressive behaviour after TBI. In a large sample of individuals with TBI and a demographically matched control group, they found significant positive relationships between alexithymia (total and sub-scale scores) and self and proxy reports of physical and verbal aggression, as well as ratings of anger and hostility as measured by the Buss Perry Aggression Questionnaire (Buss & Perry, 1992). They also found that alexithymia, particularly difficulties identifying and describing feelings, explained a significant amount of variance in aggression ratings in both groups.

Emotional decision making

Many of the decisions we make are mediated not by logic but by how we feel about a situation. The emotions aroused by circumstances in which decisions have to be made help us balance the pros and cons of the consequences of our decisions. However, following TBI poor emotional decision making frequently undermines a person's capacity for community independence. Many such individuals are able to describe what they should be doing in logical terms when asked in the abstract, yet in practice fail to use this knowledge to guide their actions. These individuals often have difficulty making even simple decisions, especially when there is no rational way to decide how to act. This can lead to impulsive and often irrational behaviour that is inconsistent with their known (measured) level of cognitive ability (see Chapters 3 and 7).

When a person cannot regulate their emotions, such as when in a fit of temper, judgement may be lost, leading to an individual lashing out with no thought of the potential detrimental consequences of their action. Similarly, the desire to acquire something may lead to an emotional urge to spend money one does not have, for an item one does not really need. This has important implications for judgements on mental capacity especially in the context of neuropsychological assessment because poor emotional decision making does not necessarily manifest itself as a deficit in conventional intellectual functions. Such individuals can even perform normally on many so-called frontal lobe tests which place demands on abstract thinking and flexible responding (see Chapter 7).

Therefore it appears that too little emotion may be just as detrimental for good decision making as too much emotion. This was the basis of the somatic marker hypothesis (Damasio, 1996), developed to explain how emotions can guide decision making. Damasio postulated that somatic signals associated with emotion can enhance attention and working memory that relate to conditions relevant to the decision making process. This occurs when sensory representations of a decision-making situation activate neural systems associated with dispositional knowledge about one's previous emotional experience in similar situations. Specific events activate somatosensory structures such as the amygdala, hypothalamus and brain stem, to reconstruct the kind of somatic state that was part of the original experience, prompting appetitive or aversive. An event will activate autonomic and transmitter nuclei that mediate cognitive evaluation and reasoning to generate potential response options and associated outcomes. In turn this imposes limitations on reasoning and decision-making activities by marking potential outcomes as good or bad. Therefore, somatic markers, whether they are perceived consciously in the form of feelings or unconsciously in the regulation of homeostatic states, provide critical signals needed for reasoning and decision making, especially for activities that occur in a social context.

Evidence to support the somatic marker hypothesis was derived from studies of people with ventromedial prefrontal (VMPF) damage. These individuals exhibit many of the following characteristics: a lack of insight, poor initiative, poor judgement, indecisiveness, inflexibility, blunted emotional awareness, poor empathy, inappropriate affect, poor frustration tolerance, shallow irritability, emotional lability and socially irresponsible behaviour. Many of these features are associated with developmental psychopathology found in conduct disorders and later in antisocial personality disorders. However, after TBI, the emergence of these characteristics in a person with an otherwise normal developmental history has been referred to as *acquired sociopathy* (Eslinger & Damasio, 1985; Blair & Cipolotti, 2000; Blumer & Benson, 1975; see also Chapter 3 this volume). One prominent feature of these individuals is a lack of empathy or concern about close friends and family, which is out of character to the individual's pre-accident behaviour.

Rehabilitation

Whilst the nature and extent of emotion recognition deficits, and their impact on neurobehavioural disability after TBI has been clearly established, less progress has been made in the treatment/rehabilitation of such deficits, or the social handicap consequent upon this type of disability. Where research has taken place the results are mixed. Bornhofen and McDonald (2008) compared the efficacy of two strategies, a static photograph-based emotion recognition tasks, and The Awareness of Social Inferences Test for remediating emotion perception deficits in individuals with TBI. Both treatment groups showed modest improvement in emotion perception ability but this was at six months post injury when further spontaneous recovery was still possible. Better emotion perception was not obtained from viewing static faces yet benefits were recorded from viewing dynamic videos, in contrast to findings by Radice-Neumann, Zupan, Tomita and Willer (2009). They used face affect recognition training over 6–9 sessions with 19 participants several years post injury, finding improved recognition of affect from training with static faces but not dynamic video. They also reported improved ability to infer emotion from context, and socio-emotional behaviour at the end of training with some signs that improved emotion perception translated into better inter-personal relationships.

In a recent review, Yeates (2014) noted that gains have been reported from the training of cognitive control operations that underpin mentalising and emotion recognition, such as attending to certain facial areas or social problem solving. Spikman et al. (2013) instructed participants in facial mimicry with cues to understand proprioception of facial expression with memory of previous sensations, but only modest results were obtained. Yeates points to a combination of explicit skills training, affective recognition training, and interventions targeting social interaction processes as having the greatest promise.

Conclusions

The presence of deficits in emotional awareness can be subtle yet they often have a pervasive and detrimental influence on psychosocial outcome. The emotionally blunted and aloof character that emerges after TBI is alien to relatives and friends who cannot, or will not adjust to a change in personality that makes them feel unloved and unwanted. This can lead to the person becoming socially isolated and vulnerable to alcohol or drug dependency. Research has shown that a loss of emotional awareness associated with alexithymia can have an adverse impact of coping skills, increase the likelihood of a somatoform reaction, lead to increased aggressiveness and result in suicide ideation. People who lack emotional awareness often exhibit profound impairment in real-life decision making, especially in situations involving ambiguity, response conflict and social contingencies, for example, when trying to choose a course of action that leads to an unpredictable blend of short-term reward and long-term punishment, or vice versa. Examples of such uncertainties in everyday life include – a female who accepts a lift home from someone who has been drinking and who she has only just met; deciding not to go out to meet friends and stay home to finish an overdue assignment, a decision which may be onerous at the time but highly rewarding later on. In such cases, VMPF individuals repeatedly engage in courses of action that are detrimental to their best long-term interest. Damasio's theory that deficits in bio-regulatory responses provides a plausible explanation because the ventral prefrontal cortex is necessary for learning associations between complex stimuli and internal states of the organism, such as emotions.

References

Adolphs, R., Damasio, H., Tranel, D., Cooper, G. & Damasio, A. R. (2000). A role for the somatosensory cortices in the visual recognition of emotions as revealed by three dimensional lesion mapping. *Journal of Neuroscience, 20*, 2683–2690.

Allerdings, M. D. & Alfano, D. P. (2006). Neuropsychological correlates of impaired emotion recognition following traumatic brain injury. *Brain and Cognition, 60*(2), 193–194.

Babbage, D., Yim, J., Zupan, B., Neumann, D., Tomita, M. & Willer, B. (2011). Meta-analysis of facial affect recognition difficulties after traumatic brain injury. *Neuropsychology, 25*, 277–285.

Becerra, R., Amos, A. & Jongenelis, S. (2002). Case study. Organic alexithymia: A study of acquired emotional blindness. *Brain Injury, 16*(7), 633–645.

Bigler, E. D. (2007). Anterior and middle cranial fossa in traumatic brain injury: Relevant neuroanatomy and neuropathology in the study of neuropsychological outcome. *Neuropsychology, 21*, 515–531.

Blair, R. J. R. & Cipolotti, L. (2000). Impaired social response reversal: A case of acquired 'sociopathy'. *Brain, 123*, 1122–1141.

Blumer, D. & Benson, D. F. (1975). Personality changes with frontal lobe lesions. In: D. F. Benson & D. Blumer (Eds.), *Psychiatric Aspects of Neurological Disease* (pp. 151–170). New York: Grune & Stratton.

Bornhoffen, C. & McDonald, S. (2008). Comparing strategies in emotion perception following TBI. *Journal of Head Trauma Rehabilitation, 23*(2), 103–113.

Buss, A. H. & Perry, M. (1992). The aggression questionnaire. *Journal of Personality and Social Psychology, 63*(3), 452–459.

Calder, A. J., Lawrence, A. D. & Young, A. W. (2001). Neuropsychology of fear and loathing. *Nature Reviews Neuroscience, 2*, 352–363.

Croker, V. & McDonald, S. (2005). Recognition of emotion from facial expressions following traumatic brain injury. *Brain Injury, 19*, 787–799.

Damasio, A. R. (1996). The somatic marker hypothesis and the possible functions of the prefrontal cortex. *Philosophical Transactions of the Royal Society of London, 351*(1346), 1413–1420.

Davidson, R. J. (2000). Dysfunction in the neural circuitry of emotion regulation – a possible prelude to violence. *Science, 289*(5479), 591–594.

De Gucht, V., Fischler, B. & Heiser, W. (2004). Neuroticism, alexithymia, negative affect, and positive affect as determinants of medically unexplained symptoms. *Personality and Individual Differences, 36*, 1655–1667.

Decety, J. & Jackson, P. L. (2004). The functional architecture of human empathy. *Behavioral and Cognitive Neuroscience Reviews, 3*, 71–100.

Dolan, R. J. (2002). Emotion, cognition and behaviour. *Science, 298*(5596), 1191–1194.

Drevets, W. C. (2000). Neuroimaging studies of mood disorders. *Biological Psychiatry, 48*, 813–829.

Ekman, P. & Davidson, R. J. (1994). *Nature of Emotion: Fundamental Questions*. Oxford: Oxford University Press.

Eslinger, P. J. (1998). Neurological and neuropsychological bases of empathy. *European Neurology, 39*, 193–199.

Eslinger, P. J. & Damasio, A. R. (1985). Severe disturbance of higher cognition after bilateral frontal lobe ablation. *Neurology, 35*(12), 1731–1741.

Farrow, T. F., Zheng, Y., Wilkinson, I. D., Spence, S. A., Deakin, J. F., Tarrier, N., Griffiths, P. D. & Woodruff, P. W. R. (2001). Investigating the functional anatomy of empathy and forgiveness. *NeuroReport, 12*, 2433–2438.

Godwin, E., Kreutzer, J. S., Arango-Laspiralla, J. C. & Lehan, T. (2011). Marriage after brain injury: Review, analysis, and research recommendations. *Journal of Head Trauma Rehabilitation, 26*(1), 43–55.

Grattan, L. L., Bloomer, R. H., Archambault, F. X. & Eslinger, P. J. (1994). Cognitive flexibility and empathy after frontal lobe lesion. *Neuropsychiatry, neuropsychology and Behavioral Neurology, 7*(4), 251–259.

Hendryx, M. S., Haviland, M. G. & Shaw, D. G. (1991). Dimensions of alexithymia and their relationships to anxiety and depression. *Journal of Personality Assessment, 56*, 227–237.

Hornak, J., Rolls, E. T. & Wade, D. (1996). Face and voice expression identification in patients with emotional and behavioural changes following ventral frontal lobe damage. *Neuropsychologia, 34*, 247–261.

Houtveen, J. H., Bermond, B. & Elton, M. R. (1997). Alexithymia: A disruption in a cortical network? An EEG power and coherence analysis. *Journal of Psychophysiology, 11*, 147–157.

James, W. (1902). *The Varieties of Religious Experience* (pp. 150). New York: Longmans, Green & Co.

Kano, M. & Fukudo, S. (2013). The alexithymia brain: The neural pathways linking alexithymia to physical disorders. *BioPsychSocial Medicine, 7*, 1.

Lane, R., Sechrest, L., Reidel, R., Weldon, V., Kaszniak, A. & Schwartz, G. (1996). Impaired verbal and nonverbal emotion recognition in alexithymia. *Psychosomatic Medicine, 58*, 203–210.

McDonald, S. (2013). Impairments in social cognition following severe traumatic brain injury. *Journal of the International Neuropsychological Society, 19*(3), 231–246.

Morton, M. V. & Wehman, P. (1995). Psychosocial and emotional sequelae of individuals with traumatic brain injury: A literature review and recommendations. *Brain Injury, 9*(1), 81–92.

Neumann, D., Zupan, B., Malec, J. F. & Hammond, F. (2014). Relationship between alexithymia, affect recognition, and empathy after traumatic brain injury. *Journal of Head Trauma Rehabilitation, 29*(1), E18–27.

Ochsner, K. N., Bunge, S. A., Gross, J. J. & Gabrieli, J. D. E. (2002). Rethinking feelings: An fMRI study of the cognitive regulation of emotion. *Journal of Cognitive Neuroscience, 14*(8), 1215–1229.

Panskepp, J. (1998). *Affective Neuroscience: The Foundations of Human and Animal Emotions.* Oxford: Oxford University Press.

Pasini, A., Chiaie, D. & Serpia, S. (1992). Alexithymia as related to sex, age, and educational level: results of the Toronto Alexithymia Scale in 417 normal subjects. *Comprehensive Psychiatry, 33*, 42–46.

Phillips, M. L. (2003). Understanding the neurobiology of emotion perception: Implications for psychiatry. *The British Journal of Psychiatry, 182*(3), 190–192.

Radice-Neumann, D., Zupan, B., Tomita, M. & Willer. B. (2009). Training emotion processing in persons with traumatic brain injury. *Journal of Head Trauma Rehabilitation, 24*(5), 31–323.

Shamay-Tsoory, S. G., Tomer, R., Berger, B. D. & Aharon-Peretz, J. (2004). Characterization of empathy deficits following prefrontal brain damage: The role of the right ventromedial prefrontal cortex. *Journal of Cognitive Neuroscience, 15*(3), 324–337.

Singer, T., Seymour, B., O'Doherty, J., Kaube, H., Dolan, R. J. & Frith, C. D. (2004). Empathy for pain involves the affective but not sensory components of pain. *Science, 303*(5661), 1157–1162.

Spikman, J. M., Milders, M. V., Visser-Keizer, A. C., Westerhof-Evers, H. J., Herben-Dekker, M. & van der Nallt, J. (2013). Deficits in facial emotion recognition indicate behavioural changes and impaired self-awareness after moderate to severe traumatic brain injury. *PLoS ONE, 8*(6), e65581.

Spikman, J. M., Westerhof-Evers, H. J. & Visser-Keizer, A. C. (2013). Neuropsychological rehabilitation of social cognitive impairment resulting in behaviour changes. Workshop presented at the Mid-Year meeting of the International Neuropsychological Society. Amsterdam, Netherlands.

Straube, T. & Mitner, W. H. R. (2011). Attention to aversive emotion and specific activation of the right insula and right somatosensory cortex. *NeuroImage, 54*(3), 2534–2538.

Taylor, G. J., Bagby, R. M. & Parker, J. D. A. (1997). *Disorders of Affect Regulation: Alexithymia in Medical and Psychiatric Illness.* Cambridge: Cambridge University Press.

Watts, A. J. & Douglas, J. M. (2006). Interpreting facial expression and communication competence following severe traumatic brain injury. *Aphasiology, 20*(8), 707–722.

Williams, C. & Wood, R. Ll. (2010a). Impairment in the recognition of emotion across different media following traumatic brain injury. *Journal of Clinical and Experimental Neuropsychology, 32*(2), 113–122.

Williams, C. & Wood, R. Ll. (2010b). Alexithymia and emotional empathy following traumatic brain injury. *Journal of Clinical and Experimental Neuropsychology, 32*(3), 259–267.

Williams, C. & Wood, R. Ll. (2013). The impact of alexithymia on relationship quality and satisfaction following traumatic brain injury. *Journal of Head Trauma Rehabilitation, 28*(5), E21–E30.

Williams, C. & Wood, R. Ll. The role of alexithymia in the expression of aggression following traumatic brain injury. Manuscript submitted for publication.

Williams, K. R., Jeffrey, G., Light, D., Pepper, C., Ryan, C., Kleinmann, A. E., Burright, R. & Donovick, P. (2001). Head injury and alexithymia: Implications for family practice care. *Brain Injury*, *15*, 349–356.

Wood, R. Ll. (2001). Understanding neurobehavioural disability. In: R. Ll. Wood & T. M. McMillan (Eds), *Neurobehavioural Disability and Social Handicap Following Traumatic Brain Injury* (pp. 3–28). Hove: Psychology Press Ltd.

Wood, R. Ll. & Doughty, C. (2013). Alexithymia and avoidance coping following traumatic brain injury. *Journal of Head Trauma Rehabilitation*, *28*(2), 98–105.

Wood, R. Ll. & Williams, C. (2007). Neuropsychological correlates of organic alexithymia. *Journal of the International Neuropsychological Society*, *13*(3), 471–479.

Wood, R. Ll. & Williams, C. (2008). Inability to empathize following traumatic brain injury. *Journal of the International Neuropsychological Society*, *14*, 289–296.

Wood, R. Ll., Williams, C. & Kalyani, T. (2009). Alexithymia and somatisation in a traumatic brain injury sample. *Brain Injury*, *23*(7), 649–654.

Wood, R. Ll., Williams, C. & Lewis, R. (2010). The role of alexithymia in suicide ideation after traumatic brain injury. *Journal of the International Neuropsychological Society*, *16*(6), 1108–1114.

Yeates, G. (2014). Social cognitive interventions in neurorehabilitation: An overview. *Advances in Clinical Neuroscience and Rehabilitation*, *14*(1), 12–13.

4

DISORDERS OF IMPULSE CONTROL AFTER TBI

Rodger Ll. Wood

Inhibitory control is a neuropsychological construct that explains a person's capacity to control (inhibit) harmful or inappropriate emotions, cognitions, or behaviour. It has been described by Fuster (2002) as a key component of behavioural self-regulation that interacts with executive–cognitive processes, such as working memory, to guide adaptive interactions with the environment. In the context of traumatic brain injury (TBI) the term *poor impulse control* has been used interchangeably with disinhibition, which Grafman et al. (1996) defined as a lack of restraint affecting motor, instinctual, emotional, cognitive, and perceptual abilities and, as such, is a cardinal feature of neurobehavioural disability. Actions referred to as '*impulsive*', represent a *predisposition* toward rapid, unplanned reactions to internal or external stimuli without regard to their potential negative consequences, either to the impulsive individual or others (Moeller et al., 2001).

The term *predisposition* implies a personality trait, such as described by Eysenck and Eysenck (1977) – one that underpins a pattern of behaviour related to people who engage in risk taking behaviour, with a lack of planning, often adopting a narrow perspective of options, and a tendency to jump to conclusions. Within this conceptual framework impulsivity is only construed as pathological when a person's actions are maladaptive and dangerous to self and/or others. Pathological forms of impulsivity are found in numerous psychiatric illnesses, including attention deficit/hyperactivity disorder (ADHD), mania, alcohol and substance abuse. However, Moeller et al. (2001) pointed out that whilst impulsive behaviour is present in many forms of psychiatric disorder the nature of impulsivity and its precise role in each disorder has not been explicitly defined.

The lack of clarity may be explained by the nomenclature associated with this condition. *Inhibitory control* is considered to be a neural process largely mediated by fronto–limbic systems. *Impulsivity* refers to a personality trait presumed to underpin a certain style of behaviour. *Impulsive* is a term that refers to some observable act of behaviour that is likely to have a negative outcome for the individual. Therefore, throughout this chapter behaviour reflected by certain forms of neurobehavioural disability will be referred to as *impulsive* and the notion of *poor inhibitory control* will refer to the neural process presumed to underlie impulsive behaviours, whilst *impulsivity* will be restricted to a presumed trait of personality.

Psychological models of impulsivity

Barratt (1959) proposed a Three Factor Model of impulsivity. The three dimensions include: *motor impulsivity*, which refers to acting without thinking; *cognitive impulsivity,* reflecting quick decision making; and *non-planning impulsivity*, which is largely a combination of the cognitive and motor components that represents a reactive form of behaviour. This was reflected in the attempt by Patton, Stanford and Barratt (1995) to separate the motor activation component of impulsivity (acting on the spur of the moment) from two cognitive components: *attention failure* (not focusing on the task at hand), and an *executive deficit* involving lack of planning (not thinking carefully about options). More recently the UPPS four-dimensional model of impulsivity (Urgency, Perseverance, Premeditation and Sensation-seeking) based on a Five Factor Model of personality, has been introduced into the TBI literature by Whiteside and Lynam (2001). *Urgency* refers to the tendency to experience and act on strong impulses, frequently under conditions of negative affect. *Perseverance* (lack of) refers to an individual's inability to remain focused on a task that may be boring or difficult. *Premeditation* (lack of) refers to the inability to think and reflect on the consequences of an act before engaging in that act. *Sensation seeking* refers to the tendency to enjoy activities that are exciting and the willingness to try new experiences.

Barratt's self-report questionnaire based on a three dimension model has been the most commonly used to assess impulsivity in TBI populations, probably because of its longevity. Some examples include research by Floden et al. (2008) who used the BIS-11 motor and non-planning component to distinguish impulsivity from risk-taking. Wood and McHugh (2013) used the BIS-11 to examine the relation between impulsivity and decision making after brain injury, demonstrating that the TBI group's decision-making was more impulsive than a matched control group, with TBI participants scoring higher on all three dimensions of the BIS-11. Greve and colleagues (2002) have used the BIS-11 to differentiate TBI patients at risk for impulsive aggression from those who were not. Ferguson (2009) and Coccaro (2011) also used the BIS-11 to determine if a history of mild or moderate TBI was associated with impulsivity and aggression. However, the UPPS is beginning to show that it has versatility in TBI research. Rochat et al. (2011) demonstrated that the relative-reported version of this questionnaire had adequate factor structure in a TBI sample, with urgency, lack of premeditation, and lack of perseverance showing an increase following brain injury, with a decrease in sensation seeking. It has been used by Nellaney (2012) to examine the validity of a new virtual reality task developed to measure impulsivity after TBI. Kocka and Gagnon (2014) in their review of the literature conclude that the UPPS model seems to have a moderately good fit with the main concepts that define impulsivity.

Behavioural measures of impulsivity broadly fall into three categories: those based on punishment paradigms, when a response is maintained even when punished or unrewarded (Matthys et al., 1998); reward-choice paradigms, reflected by preference for small immediate reward rather than larger delayed reward (Ainslie, 1975); and response-disinhibition paradigms, reflected by an inability to withhold a response (Doherty et al., 1999). Reynolds et al. (2006) employed behavioural tasks to distinguish different types of impulsivity and concluded that behavioural tasks probably measure different constructs of impulsivity to self-report questionnaires and that even among the behavioural measures different tasks measure different, perhaps unrelated, components of impulsive behaviour. The range of behaviours reflected by these different theories and measurement approaches therefore suggests that impulsivity should be viewed as a multidimensional construct (Evenden, 1999; Rochat et al., 2011) encompassing a variety of related phenomena that differ according to underlying neurobiological dysfunction.

Following TBI Winstanley, Eagle and Robbins (2006) pointed to the role played by frontal dysfunction as the most credible explanation for different forms of impulsive behaviour. However, there appear to be several substrates of inhibitory control that mediate impulsive behaviour linked to different regions of the prefrontal cortex (Bechara, 2003). The ventromedial prefrontal cortex (VMF) and orbito-frontal cortex (OFC) are generally considered the principal regions controlling self-regulated behaviour. VMF dysfunction influences how inhibitory control mediates decision making – such as preparing to act, (Brass & Von Cramon, 2002), adaptive thinking – to switch between response alternatives (Dove et al., 2000), and inhibiting inappropriate responses during strategy tasks (Rogers et al., 1998; Shallice & Burgess, 1991a, b). Fuster (1999) proposed that patients with orbitofrontal damage lack the capacity for *response inhibition*, a process that normally helps maintain goal-directed behaviour. He considered an impairment of response inhibition as something reflected by distractibility, which may result in impulsive responding to random environmental stimuli, undermining planned, goal-directed behaviour. Sohlberg and Mateer (2001) regard *impulse control* as an ability mediated primarily by the OFC to inhibit automatic response tendencies to allow flexible goal-directed behaviour. They propose that an impairment of response inhibition may result in impulsive responding, stimulus-boundedness and perseveration that can have an adverse impact on various forms of decision making.

Emotional decision making

Decision making deficits are often blatant in the everyday lives of such individuals but difficult to measure by conventional neuropsychological tests (see Chapter 7) or standardised personality inventories. Maladaptive decision-making and aberrant social behaviour has been linked to damage in the right inferior frontal gyrus (Aron et al., 2003) as well as the VMF and OFC, based on making risky choices on the Iowa Gambling Task (Bechara et al., 1994; 1999) and increased betting in the presence of normal probability judgements (Manes et al., 2002). Bechara et al. (1997) and Damasio (1996) proposed the *somatic marker hypothesis*, which implicates both the VMF and the amygdala as components of a neural system underpinning emotional decision making examined by performance on the Iowa Gambling Task. This has been employed as a paradigm to simulate real-life decision making when consequences of reward and punishment are ambiguous. Subjects have to choose between decks of cards that yield high immediate gain but larger future loss and decks that yield lower immediate gain but a smaller future loss. Skin conductance responses (SCRs) have been used as an index of somatic state activation. Choosing advantageously in the gambling task is correlated with the development of anti-cipatory SCRs, which normal subjects begin to generate before choosing from a risky deck. Individuals with VMF cortex lesions choose disadvantageously on this task and usually exhibit impulsive behaviour in everyday situations.

The amygdala is considered by Bechara et al. (1999) and Winstanley et al. (2004) to be a critical structure in a neural system necessary for somatic state activa-tion mediating advantageous decision making. It becomes active when efforts are made to reappraise events in a way that could generate emotional awareness of our actions. Impulsive decision-making after amygdala damage is attributed to a lack of ability to experience the emotional attributes of a situation, precluding the possibility to evoke somatic states that help an individual anticipate the future consequences of a decision. On the other hand, the decision-making impairment after VMF damage is related to an inability to integrate effectively all of the somatic state information triggered by the amygdala as well as other somatic effectors, such as the hypothalamus and brainstem nuclei. When faced with the need to make a decision, the neural activity pertaining to outcome is signalled to VMF cortices, which in turn activate the amygdala. This latter activity would reconstitute a somatic state that integrates the numerous and conflicting instances of reward and punishment related to that decision. The final somatic state, reflected by anticipatory SCRs, would then influence the decision to act or alternatively abandon a decision in favour of some alternative action. VMF damage precludes this process and contributes to impulsive decision making and actions that can be maladaptive and antisocial.

Acquired sociopathy

Whilst different forms of poor impulse control can be attributed to different prefrontal abnormalities, impulsivity as a personality predisposition, and impulsive behaviours, remain major legacies of TBI, fuelling a broad range of problem behav-iours, comprising poor tolerance, irritability, impulsive aggression, social and/or sexual irresponsibility, oppositional behaviour, a disregard for social norms, indif-ference about the well-being of others, and poor decision making, leading to risk taking behaviours. These aspects of impulsivity are usually interpreted as alterations to personality that can have serious psychosocial implications.

Acting without thought of the consequences is considered by many to be a cardinal feature of altered personality after TBI. Impulsive decision making and poor social judgement are often accompanied by shallow affect and a lack of concern for social values, a condition that has been referred to as *pseudo-psychopathy* (Blumer & Benson, 1975). In contrast to conventional psychopathy, in which psychopathic traits emerge in childhood and adolescence with no gross structural brain lesion, *pseudo-psychopathy* is a post-accident feature, usually associated with right hemisphere prefrontal injury. Such individuals exhibit a tendency to hold an unrealistically favourable view of themselves. They exhibit a jocular, often puerile sense of humour, making facetious comments or acting in a manner that reflects a lack of tact and restraint, usually interpreted as social and/or sexual disinhibition. Whilst maintaining a social and emotional veneer, their behaviour towards close friends and family is emotionally indifferent, reflecting a lack of empathy combined with a self-indulgent attitude and an amoral disposition that is out of character with the individual's pre-accident behaviour. This pattern of behaviour after TBI has been called *acquired sociopathy* (Eslinger & Damasio, 1985; Blair & Cipolotti, 2000). It is usually seen in association with poor social judgement and short-lived enthusiasm for ill-judged projects, euphoric mood, sometimes accompanied by emotionally labile and erratic behaviour, with low tolerance of frustration, leading to irritability and impulsive aggression.

Aggression

Aggressive behaviour is a frequent legacy of TBI (Rao, 2009) with prevalence estimates ranging from 11% (Brooke et al., 1992) to 34% (Tateno, Jorge and Robinson, 2003) depending upon the samples studies and how aggression is defined. At an early stage post injury 30–70% of patients with frontal injury exhibit 'confused-agitated' behaviour that evolves into 'shallow irritability' (Brooks et al., 1987; Tateno et al., 2003), 20% of which includes violent behaviour. Brooks et al. (1987) and Baguley et al. (2006) have noted that early irritability matures into impulsive aggression characterised by a querulous, intolerant personality, one in which an individual is primed to react sharply to frustration. Baguley et al. point to this being a long-term problem, covering at least a five-year interval post injury but can be a life-long problem, one that can lead to domestic violence (Thomsen, 1984; Brooks et al., 1987) that alienates family members and caregivers (Eslinger, Grattan & Geder, 1995; Wood & Yurdakul, 1997) as well as contributing to high rates of unemployment (Schönberger et al., 2011) and criminality (Grafman et al., 1996; Williams et al., 2010). The study by Williams reported that 60% of criminals in British prisons have a history of head trauma.

Given its frequency and intrusive nature it is surprising that little attempt has been made to distinguish characteristics of aggressive behaviour that might suggest differences in aetiology and offer alternative approaches to treatment (see the Cochrane Review by Fleminger, Greenwood & Oliver, 2006). For example, there is no classification to distinguish aggressive disorders in either ICD-10 (1992) or

DSM V (APA, 2015). One potentially important aetiological distinction of aggression after TBI was, however, offered by Lishman (1968; 1987). He described two forms, one of which involved *impulsive aggression*, linked to a loss of inhibitory control, whilst the other was associated with spontaneous electrical disturbances, usually implicating the temporolimbic system, referred to as *episodic dyscontrol*.

Impulsive aggression

Impulsive aggression reflects a disorder of self-regulatory behaviour involving verbal or physical aggression distinguished by a hair-trigger response following minimal provocation, usually out of proportion to the event that triggered it (Barratt et al., 1997). In its verbal form it has been described by Dyer et al. (2006) as the principal aggressive trait after brain injury. Impulsive acts of violent and aggressive behaviour have been associated with flawed inhibitory control at the level of the orbitofrontal cortex and medial prefrontal cortex resulting in an inability to control emotions generated by limbic structures such as the amygdala (Coccaro et al., 1997; Davidson, et al., 2000). Blair (2001) noted that the brainstem threat-response system, mediated by the hypothalamus and periaqueductal grey matter, is linked to both the amygdala, which feeds the response, and the orbitofrontal cortex, which has an inhibitory role, implying that damage to the latter potentiates the former and releases the 'fight' response. Eslinger et al. (1995) also suggest that damage to, or dysfunction of, orbital and ventro-medial structures limits awareness of, and response to, social cues that normally guide our reactions and inhibit extremes of behaviour. Grafman et al. (1996) further noted that many individuals with orbito-frontal injuries seemed unaware of their level of aggression and violence, reducing awareness of, or empathy for, the consequences of their actions (Best et al., 2002; Bechara, 2003).

In clinical interviews, family members often remark on the relentless nature of tension experienced when living with relatives who exhibit irritability and impulsive aggression. The aggressive reaction usually emerges when the protagonist perceives a threat, in the form of being challenged, criticised, or otherwise frustrated in some way. The emotional element associated with this form of poor temper control explains why it is sometimes referred to as '*affective aggression*', a form of reactive behaviour which, builds in momentum then escalates out of control, often lacking direction or any clear sense of purpose. The state of agitated irritability that usually accompanies the angry outburst often renders information processing inefficient, making intervention via some form of interpersonal communication ineffective.

Impulsive aggression is not specific to TBI and has been associated with various psychosocial risk factors prevalent in the general population. Idiopathic forms of impulsive aggression have been described in people with low intelligence (especially poor verbal skills), low socioeconomic status, poor social functioning, low mood, and alcohol or substance abuse (Stanford, Greve & Gerstle, 1997; Greve et al., 2002). The demographics of TBI indicate that young males who suffer head injury often conform to many of these risk factors. For example, Greve et al. (2002) compared a TBI sample who exhibited impulsive aggression with a TBI control matched for injury severity but without aggressive behaviour. They found that those exhibiting impulsive aggression were younger, had a pre-accident history of aggressive behaviour, and had generally been more irritable and antisocial. Kerr et al. (2011) focused on post-accident characteristics and found that impulsive aggression could potentially be predicted on the basis of four factors: an education of 10 years or less, a pre-accident history of aggression, post-accident dependence on hospital staff for assistance with activities of daily living, and a hospitalisation period of 51 days or more. Hawkins and Trobst (2000) also noted an association between weak cognition, executive ability, and aggressive tendencies after TBI. However, no differences were reported in the Greve et al. study or by Blair (2001), a finding that Wood and Liossi (2006) attributed to a lack of sensitivity and weak ecological validity in many executive tests used in those studies (see Chapter 7, this volume).

Episodic aggression

Episodic aggression is often used synonymously with the term '*episodic dyscontrol*', a condition first described by Meninger and Mayman (1956) to explain recurrent acts of rage in response to minor provocation. Elliott (1982) defined the disorder based on characteristics identified by Bach-Y-Rita et al. (1971). However, these authors did not restrict the term episodic aggression to aggressive acts following head trauma. Indeed, throughout the 1970s it was applied to a broad range of violent or aggressive behaviours in association with a variety of diagnostic categories (Maletsky, 1973; Monroe, 1974). In its idiopathic form, episodic dyscontrol tends to emerge during the early teens, often in association with exposure to violence as a child, low socioeconomic status, a history of birth trauma, and minimal brain damage. Post traumatic episodic aggression can emerge weeks or months following TBI, reminiscent of the onset of seizures seen in post-traumatic epilepsy (Eames & Wood, 2003).

The developmental history of the idiopathic group is characterised by violent physical assaults often associated with characteristics of antisocial personality disorder, pathological intoxication, serious road traffic violations, and impulsive sexual behaviour (Elliott, 1984). These characteristics are not usually seen premorbidly in those who exhibit episodic aggression after TBI. However, some characteristics are shared by both idiopathic and post traumatic episodic aggression:

a) *Abrupt onset*: Aggression occurs with little or no warning, sometimes in response to very minor frustration but often without any precipitating stimulus.

b) *Explosive rage*: The outburst itself is characterised by an *explosive rage* that can be verbal or physical. As early as 1899 Kaplan used the term "*explosive diathesis*" to describe this form of aggression in the genesis of mental disorders after head injury. Hooper et al. (1945) also described an "*explosive*" element associated with "*aggressive rage*" after head injury, which they felt distinguished this form of aggression from general irritability.

c) *Loss of control*: This reflects an inability to prevent the outburst itself, not necessarily the behaviour that accompanies the outburst (for example, there is a tendency to punch walls or smash furniture rather than attack people).

d) *Duration*: The outburst itself is usually measured in minutes but for some hours prior to the outburst itself relatives observe what may be described as 'prodromal signs', such as changes in facial expression, alterations in tone of voice, or an argumentative, unreasonable, and (often) suspicious manner.

e) *Withdrawal*: Many individuals appear unable (or unwilling) to engage meaningfully with relatives in the period preceding the outburst and withdraw to a bedroom or seek seclusion in some other way.

f) *Frequency*: Outbursts occur with variable frequency. In some cases they occur more or less daily whilst others can have episodes separated by several weeks, even months.

Memory for the aggressive event during these episodes is often imperfect but total amnesia is rare. However, following each outburst many individuals exhibit fatigue; some express a sense of relief, others remorse, which points to the possibility of such events being epileptogenic (Wood, 1987), a form of seizure activity which Lishman (1987) speculated could be temporolimbic in origin. Ictal violence has been found to be extremely uncommon in cases of *idiopathic* epilepsy. However, Wood and Thomas (2013) comment on case reports of seemingly directed ictal aggressive behaviour, predominantly in *focal* epilepsies. Mark and Ervin (1970) reported a patient who became violent during a focal seizure and depth electrodes showed that this behaviour coincided with an ictal discharge from the amygdala. Weiser (1983) was also able to establish a correlation between an aggressive attack and a sub-cortical discharge pattern in limbic structures. Discharges of this kind would be undetectable via surface electrodes. This has received support from Valzelli (1978) who argued that spontaneous abnormal firing in the temporal lobe can result in feelings of irritation, anger or rage, giving rise to actual violence when this firing activity is sufficiently intense. McElroy et al. (1998) noted that many patients diagnosed with intermittent explosive disorder (IED), a related condition to episodic aggression, report physiological anomalies, such as tingling, tremors, palpitations, chest tightness, head pressure, or hearing an echo, as prodromal characteristics to aggressive outbursts. It was speculated that these features could be associated with hypothalamic pituitary activation and the 'adrenaline rush' of the fight or flight response. Over half their participants reported an alteration in awareness during the episode but none reported amnesia for the event. An inability to resist the impulse to violence was common and a feeling of relief, even pleasure was reported. However, after the outburst a feeling of remorse was most common. The description of the event suggested that aggression reflected a force beyond the person's control, even though the actions were recognised as their own responsibility. There has been no attempt to systematically examine these phenomena in cases who have suffered TBI.

Distinguishing impulsive from episodic aggression

The ICD 10 and DSM IV and V handbooks have failed to make a distinction between impulsive and episodic aggression and incorporate both forms into one class, that of "*intermittent explosive disorder*" – IED (ICD 10 F63.8; DSM-IV 312.34). IED is classed as an impulse-control disorder alongside other habit and impulse disorders such as kleptomania and pyromania. However, as Eames and Wood (2003) have pointed out, IED criteria fail to clearly distinguish between impulsive and episodic conditions because characteristics of IED, such as – *several discreet episodes of loss of control*, or *aggressive impulses resulting in serious assault*, or *behaviour that is grossly out of proportion to any precipitating psycho-social stressor* – are associated with both impulsive and episodic aggression. Also, a diagnosis of IED can only be made when there is no associated general medical condition, such as head trauma. Therefore, the diagnosis is unusable as an explanation of either impulsive or episodic aggression in the context of TBI. Other efforts to provide a clinical typology of aggression also lack discrete criteria that distinguish impulsive from episodic sub-types (Ahmed et al., 2012). Coccaro (1998) noted that characteristics of impulsive-aggression overlapped with criteria for intermittent explosive disorder (IED-R). Coccaro (2011) therefore proposed new criteria to clarify and distinguish cases with recurrent, problematic, impulsive aggression but did not include information that might distinguish impulsive from episodic aggression.

Clinical observations in the context of TBI suggest that episodic aggression can usually be distinguished from impulsive aggression by the time of onset in relation to injury. Impulsive aggression seems to evolve out of a confused-agitated stage in the very early recovery period, through irritability, finally evolving into impulsive aggression. In contrast, there seems to be a delay of several months before episodic aggression is first observed (Eames & Wood, 2003). The emotional background is also different. Individuals with impulsive aggression are described as being constantly intolerant, irritable, and emotionally fragile, leading relatives to describe life as characterised by having to "*walk on eggshells*". In contrast, those who exhibit episodic aggression have transient swings of mood (which includes the angry outburst) but then resume their 'normal' pre-accident disposition, often leading families to state that "*it's like living with Jekyll and Hyde*". In between the episodes there is no evidence of personality disorder, and social interaction appears to be on a par with the person's pre-injury character. Another distinguishing feature is the way individuals react to the consequences of their aggression. Those with impulsive aggression usually attempt to attribute blame for their actions onto others, in an attempt to justify their angry behaviour, whereas people who exhibit episodic aggression usually express remorse for their behaviour. Therefore, careful observation over time, or semi-structured and detailed interviews with relatives should provide a framework for interpreting and distinguishing between these different forms of aggression which has direct implications for treatment approaches (see Wood and Thomas, 2013).

Conclusions

Disorders of impulse control, whilst a major feature of neurobehavioural disability, are not confined to a class of disorders represented by TBI. The DSM-5 describes poor impulse-control as a problem of emotional and behavioural self-control that includes such diverse conditions as intermittent explosive disorder, pyromania, and kleptomania. In the context of TBI impulsivity usually reflects an abnormality of those brain functions that mediate self-regulation, leading to impulsive behaviour that contributes to such diverse deficits as poor temper control and impulsive aggression, as well as poor emotional decision making and an amoral (pseudopsychopathic) disposition which, in combination, have implications for mental capacity. However, even though disorders of impulse control represent a frequent legacy of TBI they remain poorly understood and not always easy to recognise. Hopefully, within the limited scope of this chapter, there is some clarification of how damaged mechanisms of inhibitory control manifest as disorders of behaviour leading to improved rehabilitation interventions.

References

Ahmed, AG, Kingston, DA, DiGiuseppe, R, Bradford, JM and Seto, MC. Developing a clinical typology of dysfunctional anger. *Journal of Affective Disorders*. 2012; 136: 139–148.

Ainslie, G. A behavioral theory of impulsiveness and impulse control. *Psychological Bulletin*. 1975; 82(4): 463–496.

American Psychiatric Association. *Diagnostic and Statistical Manual of Mental Disorders*. 5th ed. Washingon, DC: American Psychiatric Association; 2015.

Aron, AR, Fletcher, PC, Bullmore, ET, Sahakian, BJ and Robbins, TW. Stop-signal inhibition disrupted by damage to right inferior frontal gyrus in humans. *Nature Neuroscience*. 2003; 6(2): 115–116.

Bach-Y-Rita, G, Lion, JR, Climentand, CE and Ervin, FR. Episodic dyscontrol: A study of 130 violent patients. *Am J Psychiatry*. 1971; 127: 1473–1478.

Baguley, IJ, Cooper, J and Felmingham, K. Aggressive behavior following traumatic brain injury: How common is common? *Journal of Head Trauma Rehabilitation. Focus on Clinical Research and Practice*. 2006; 21(1): 45–56.

Barratt, ES. Anxiety and impulsiveness related to psychomotor efficiency. *Percept. Mot. Skills*. 1959; 9: 191–198.

Barratt, ES, Stanford, MS, Kent, TA and Felthous, A. Neuropsychological and cognitive psychophysiological substrates of impulsive aggression. *Biol Psychiatry*. 1997; 41: 1045–1047.

Bechara, A. The role of emotion in decision making. *Brain and Cognition*. 2004; 55: 30–40.

Bechara, A, Damasio, AR, Damasio, H and Anderson SW. Insensitivity to future consequences following damage to human prefrontal cortex. *Cognition*. 1994; 50: 7–15.

Bechara, A, Damasio, H, Tranel, D and Damasio, AR. Deciding advantageously before knowing the advantageous strategy. *Science*. 1997; 275: 1293–1295.

Bechara, A, Damasio, H, Damasio, AR and Lee, GP. Different contributions of the human amygdala and ventromedial prefrontal cortex to decision-making. *Journal of Neuroscience*. 1999; 19(13): 5473–5481.

Best, M, Williams, JM and Coccaro, EF. Evidence for a dysfunctional prefrontal circuit in patients with an impulsive aggressive disorder. *Proc. Natl. Acad. Sci. U.S.A.* 2002; 99: 8448–8453.

Blair, RJR. Neurocognitive models of aggression, the antisocial personality disorders, and psychopathy. *J Neurol Neurosurg Psychiatry.* 2001; 71: 727–731.

Blair, RJ and Cipolotti, L. Impaired social response reversal. A case of 'acquired sociopathy'. *Brain.* 2000 Jun; 123(6): 1122–1141.

Blumer, D and Benson, DF. Personality change with frontal and temporal lobe lesions. In: Benson, DF and Blumer, D, (eds), *Psychiatric Aspects of Neurological Disease.* New York: Grune & Stratton; 1975.

Brass, M. and Von Cramon, D.Y. The role of the frontal cortex in task preparation. *Cerebral Cortex.* 2002; 12: 908–914.

Brooke, MM, Questad, KA, Patterson, DR and Bashak, KJ. Agitation and restlessness after closed head injury: A prospective study of 100 consecutive admissions. *Arch Phys Med Rehabil.* 1992; 73(4): 320–323.

Brooks, N, Campsie, L, Symington, C, Beattie, A and McKinlay, W. The effects of severe head injury on patient and relative within seven years of injury. *Journal of Head Trauma and Rehabilitation.* 1987; 2: 1–13.

Coccaro, EF. Impulsive aggression: a behaviour in search of a definition. *Harvard Review of Psychiatry.* 1998; 5, 1–4.

Coccaro, EF. Amygdala and orbitofrontal reactivity to social threat in individuals with impulsive aggression. *Biol Psychiatry.* 2007 Jul 15; 62(2): 168–178.

Coccaro, EF. Intermittent explosive disorder: Development of integrated research criteria for diagnostic and statistical manual of mental disorders. *Compr Psychiatry.* 2011; 52: 119–125.

Coccaro, EF, Berman, ME, Kavoussi, RJ. Assessment of life history of aggression: development and psychometric characteristics. *Psychiatry Res.* 1997; 73: 147–157.

Damasio, AR. The somatic marker hypothesis and the possible functions of the prefrontal cortex. *Philos Trans R Soc Lond B Biol Sci.* 1996 Oct 29; 351(1346): 1413–1420.

Davidson, RJ, Putnam, KM and Larson, CL. Dysfunction in the neural circuitry of emotion regulation – a possible prelude to violence. *Science.* 2000; 289: 591–594.

Doherty, DM, Bjork, JM, Huckabee, HC, Moeller, FG and Swann, AC. Laboratory measures of aggression and impulsivity in women with borderline personality disorder. *Psychiatry Res.* 1999; 85: 315–326.

Dove, A, Pollman, S, Schubert, T, Wiggins, CJ, Von Cramon, DY. Prefrontal cortex activation in task switching: An event related fMRI study. *Brain Research: Cognition and Brain Research.* 2000; 9: 103–109.

Dyer, K, Bell, R, McCann, J and Rauch, R. Aggression after traumatic brain injury: Analysing socially desirable responses and the nature of aggressive traits. *Brain Injury.* 2006; 20(11): 1163–1173.

Eames, PE and Wood, RL. Episodic disorders of behaviour and affect after acquired brain injury. *Neuropsychol Rehabil.* 2003; 13: 241–258.

Elliott, FA. The episodic dyscontrol syndrome and aggression. *Neurologic Clinics.* 1984; 2: 113–125.

Eslinger, PJ and Damasio, AR. Severe disturbance of higher cognition after bilateral frontal lobe ablation: Patient EVR. *Neurology.* 1985; 35(12): 1731–1741.

Eslinger, PJ, Grattan, LM and Geder, L. Impact of frontal lobe lesions on rehabilitation and recovery from acute brain injury. *Neurorehabilitation.* 1995; 5: 161–185.

Evenden, JL. Varieties of impulsivity. *Psychopharmacology.* 1999; 146: 348–361.

Eysenck, SBG and Eysenck, HJ. The place of impulsiveness in a dimensional system of personality description. *British Journal of Social and Clinical Psychology*. February 1977; 16(1): 57–68.

Ferguson, SD and Coccaro, EF. History of mild to moderate traumatic brain injury and aggression in physically healthy participants with and without personality disorder. *J. Personal. Disord*. 2009; 23: 230–239.

Fleminger, S, Greenwood, RJ and Oliver, DL. Pharmacological management for agitation and aggression in people with acquired brain injury. *Cochrane Database Syst Rev*. 2006; 4.

Floden, D, Alexander, MP, Kubu, CS, Katz, D and Stuss, DT. Impulsivity and risk-taking behavior in focal frontal lobe lesions. *Neuropsychologia*. 2008; 46: 213–223.

Fuster, JM. Cognitive functions of the frontal lobes. In: Miller, B and Cummings, J (eds) *The Human Frontal Lobes*. New York, NY, USA: The Guilford Press; 1999, pp. 187–195.

Fuster, JM. Frontal lobe and cognitive development. *Journal of Neurocytology*. 2002; 31: 373–385.

Grafman, J, Schwab, K, Warden, D, Pridgen, A, Brown, HR and Salazar, AM. Frontal lobe injuries, violence, and aggression: A report of the Vietnam Head Injury Study. *Neurology*. 1996; 46: 1231–1238.

Greve, KW, Love, J, Sherwin, E, Stanford, MS, Mathias, C and Houston, R. Cognitive strategy usage in long-term survivors of severe traumatic brain injury with persisting impulsive aggression. *Personal. Individ. Differ*. 2002; 32: 639–647.

Hawkins, KA and Trobst, K. Frontal lobe dysfunction and aggression: conceptual issues and research findings. *Aggression and Violent Behavior*. 2000; 5(2): 147–157.

Hooper, RS, McGregor, JM and Nathan, PW. Explosive rage following head injury. *Proceedings of the Royal Society of Medicine*. 1945; 2: 458–471.

Kaplan, K. 1899: cited by Hooper, RS, McGregor, JM and Nathan PW. Explosive rage following head injury. *Proceeding of the Royal Society of Medicine*. 1945; 2: 58–471.

Kerr, K, Oram, J, Tinson, H and Shum, D. The correlates of aggression in people with acquired brain injury: A preliminary retrospective study. *Brain Injury*. July 2011; 25(7–8): 729–741.

Kocka, A and Gagnon, J. Definition of impulsivity and related terms following traumatic brain injury: A review of the different concepts and measures used to assess impulsivity, disinhibition and other related concepts. *Behav Sci (Basel)*. 2014 Dec; 4(4): 352–370.

Lishman, WA. Brain damage in relation to psychiatric disability after head injury. *British Journal of Psychiatry*. 1968; 114: 373–410.

Lishman, WA. *Organic Psychiatry*. 2nd ed. Oxford: Blackwell Scientific Publications; 1987.

Mark, VH and Ervin, F. *Violence and the Brain*. New York: Harper and Rowe; 1970.

McElroy, SL, Soutullo, CA, Beckman, DA, Taylor, P, Jr and Keck, PE, Jr. DSM-IV intermittent explosive disorder: a report of 27 cases. *J. Clin. Psychol*. 1998; 59: 203.

Maletsky, BM. The episodic dyscontrol syndrome. *Disorders of the Nervous System*. 1973; 34: 178–185.

Manes, F, Sahakian, BJ, Clark, L, Rogers, RD, Antoun, N and Aitken, M. Decision-making processes following damage to prefrontal cortex. *Brain*. 2002; 125: 624–639.

Matthys, W, van Goozen, SHM, de Vries, H, Cohen-Kettenis, PT and van Engeland, H. The dominance of behavioural activation over behavioural inhibition in conduct disordered boys with our without attention deficit hyperactivity disorder. *Journal of Child Psychology and Psychiatry*. 1998; 39: 643–651.

Meninger, K and Mayman, M. Episodic dyscontrol: A third order of stress adaptation. *Bull Menninger Clin*. 1956; 20: 153–165.

Moeller, FG, Barratt, ES, Dougherty, DM, Schmitz, JM and Swann, AC. Psychiatric aspects of impulsivity. *Am J Psychiatry*. Nov 2001; 158(11): 1783–1793.

Monroe, RR. *Behavioral Disorders*. Cambridge, Mass.: Harvard University Press; 1970.

Monroe, R. Episodic behavioural disorders: An unclassified syndrome. In: Arieti, S (ed.) *American Handbook of Psychiatry*. 2nd ed. New York: Basic Books; 1974.

Nellaney, J. *Assessment of decision making following traumatic brain injury*. D Clin Psy thesis, University of Glasgow; 2012.

Patton, JH, Stanford, MS and Barratt, ES. Factor structure of the Barratt impulsiveness scale. *J. Clin. Psychol*. 1995; 51: 768–774.

Rao, V, Rosenberg, P, Bertrand, M, Salehinia, S, Spiro, J, Vaishnavi, S, Rastogi, P, Noll, K, Schretlen, DJ, Brandt, J, Cornwell, E, Makley, M and Miles, QS. Aggression after traumatic brain injury: prevalence and correlates. *J Neuropsychiatry Clin Neurosci*. 2009 Fall; 21(4): 420–429. doi: 10.1176/appi.neuropsych.21.4.420.

Reynolds, B, Ortengren, A, Richards, JB and de Wit, H. Dimensions of impulsive behavior: Personality and behavioral measures. *Personality and Individual Differences*. January 2006; 40(2): 305–315.

Rochat, L, Beni, C, Billieux, J, Annoni, J-M and van der Linden, M. How impulsivity relates to compulsive buying and the burden perceived by caregivers after moderate-to-severe traumatic brain injury. *Psychopathology*. 2011; 44: 158–164.

Rogers, RD, Sahakian, BJ, Hodges, JR, Polkey, CE, Kennard, C and Robbins, TW. Dissociating executive mechanisms for task control following frontal lobe damage and Parkinson's disease. *Brain*. 1998; 121: 815–842.

Schönberger, M, Ponsford, J, Olver, J, Ponsford, M and Wirtz, M. Prediction of functional and employment outcome 1 year after traumatic brain injury: a structural equation modelling approach. *J Neurol Neurosurg Psychiatry*. 2011; 82: 936–941.

Shallice, T and Burgess, PW. Deficits in strategy applications following frontal lobe damage in man. *Brain*. 1991a; 114: 727–741.

Shallice, T and Burgess, PW. Higher-order cognitive impairments and frontal lobe lesions in man. In: Levin, HS, Eisenberg, HM, Benton, AL (eds) *Frontal Lobe and Injury*. Oxford University Press: New York; 1991b, pp. 125–138.

Sohlberg, MM and Mateer, CM. *Cognitive Rehabilitation: An Integrative Neuropsychological Approach*. New York, NY, USA: Guilford Press; 2001.

Stanford, MS, Greve, KW and Gerstle, JE. Neuropsychological correlates of self-reported impulsive aggression in a college sample. *Personality and Individual Differences*. 1997; 23: 961–966.

Tateno, A, Jorge, RE and Robinson, RG. Clinical correlates of aggressive behavior after traumatic brain injury. *Journal of Neuropsychiatry & Clinical Neurosciences*. 2003; 15: 155–160.

Thomsen, IV. Late outcome of very severe blunt head trauma: A 10–15 year second follow-up. *Journal of Neurology, Neurosurgery and Psychiatry*. 1984; 47: 260–268.

Valzelli, L. Human and animal studies on the neuropharmacology of aggression. *Prog Neuro-Psychopharmacol Biol Psychiat*. 1978; 2: 591–610.

Weiser, HG. Depth recorded limbic seizures and psychopathology. *Neurosci Biobehav Rev*. 1983; 7: 427–440.

Winstanley, CA, Theobald, DE, Cardinal, RN and Robbins, TW. Contrasting roles for basolateral amygdala and orbitofrontal cortex in impulsive choice. *Journal of Neuroscience*. 2004; 24: 4718–4722.

Winstanley, CA, Eagle, DM, and Robbins, TW. Behavioral models of impulsivity in relation to ADHD: Translation between clinical and preclinical studies. *Clin Psychol Rev*. 2006 Aug; 26(4): 379–395.

Whiteside, SP and Lynam, DR. The Five Factor Model and impulsivity: using a structural model of personality to understand impulsivity. *Personality and Individual Differences*. 2001; 30(4), 669–689.

Williams, WH, Mewse, AJ, Tonks, J and Mills, S. Traumatic brain injury in a prison population: Prevalence and risk for re-offending. *Brain Injury*. 2010; 24(10): 1184–1188.

Wood, RL. *Brain Injury Rehabilitation: A Neurobehavioural Approach*. London: Croom Helm; 1987.

Wood, RL and McHugh, L. Decision making after traumatic brain injury: a temporal discounting paradigm. *Journal of the International Neuropsychological Society*. 2013; 19: 1–8.

Wood, RL and Yurdakul, LK. Change in relationship status following traumatic brain injury. *Brain Inj*. 1997; 11: 491–495.

Wood, RL and Liossi, C. Neuropsychological and neurobehavioural correlates of aggression following traumatic brain injury. *The Journal of Neuropsychiatry and Clinical Neurosciences*. 2006; 21: 429–437.

Wood, RL and Thomas, R. Impulsive and episodic disorders of aggressive behaviour following traumatic brain injury. *Brain Injury*. 2013; 27(3): 253–261.

5

NEUROBEHAVIOURAL DISABILITY AND THE CRIMINAL JUSTICE SYSTEM

Tom M. McMillan and Huw Williams

Introduction

The risk of having a head injury is higher in young males and in those who have a background of social deprivation and alcohol abuse (Tagliaferri et al. 2006; Langlois et al. 2006). These factors are also predominant in offenders and it is easy to envisage that many of the neurobehavioural impairments that are associated with head injury can lead to antisocial behaviour which, in turn, could lead to involvement with the Criminal Justice System. It can be envisaged that risk taking will be greater following a severe head injury as a result of impatience, intolerance, impulsivity, and irritability associated with aggression and violence (Wood 2001; Baguley et al. 2006). Furthermore, as severe head injury is also often associated with egocentricity, impaired insight, low empathy and lack of concern for others (Wood and Williams 2010), it can be seen that antisocial acts may not only be more likely to occur, but are more likely to be repeated (McMillan 2010). Deficits in concentration, memory, flexibility of thinking, problem solving, and planning, can further contribute to poor judgement, leading not only to an increased likelihood of offending, but to a higher probability of being caught. Indeed there is evidence to support this tenet. In addition to increasingly sophisticated neuroimaging evidence that links neuropathology and neurobehavioural disability (see Chapter 8), epidemiological studies of the general population in Sweden, found that the risk of violent crime (convictions for homicide, assault, robbery, arson, any sexual offence, illegal threats or intimidation) was more than three times higher in people with head injury than in age and gender matched controls (Fazel et al. 2011). A study on the general population in Western Australia also found a significant, but more modest association between a history of head injury and criminal convictions, including for violent crime (Schofield et al. 2015).

Within a few weeks or months after a head injury there is often no obvious outward sign of physical injury and both the individual concerned and those involved with them may not attribute their behaviour to the brain injury, and may not seek support or make adjustments or allowances for neurobehavioural legacies. Given this background, it is perhaps not surprising that there is limited awareness of the potential psychosocial impact of a head injury in the Criminal Justice System (McMillan 2010). Therefore, there is clearly a need to understand more about the potential links between neurobehavioural effects of brain injury and offending.

The prevalence of brain injury in offenders

Studies on the prevalence of head injury, its severity, neurobehavioural effects and relationships with offending and reoffending are largely based on self-report (Moynan and McMillan submitted). Three meta-analyses of the literature on offenders included studies covering a broad range of injury severity, suggesting that the prevalence of head injury is very high, at about 50–60% (Farrer and Hedges 2011; Shiroma et al. 2010) and somewhat lower in juvenile offenders, at 30% (Farrer et al. 2013). As mild head injury accounts for over 90% of the incidence of head injury, the majority of cases would be expected to make a good recovery and this could lead to an over-statement of the relationship between brain injury and offending. If taking moderate-severe head injury (defined as loss of consciousness of more than 30 minutes) as more likely to result in persisting disability (Carroll et al. 2004) and more relevant to any estimates of studies of prison inmates. If using this definition, studies on the prevalence of brain injury in prison inmates estimate the prevalence in adults to range between 7% and 37% (Moynan and McMillan in submission).

Existing studies on prevalence of head injury in prisoners contain weaknesses that make interpretation difficult. For example, they do not address the impact of brain injury on day to day life, making it difficult to estimate the health service need in prisoners. A recent systematic review indicates that (i) all of the prevalence studies are based on self-report of the occurrence of head injury; (ii) a 'gold standard' assessment of the occurrence of brain injury by self-report has not been established; (iii) classification of the severity of brain injury, when reported, often does not utilise standard criteria, and (iv) most studies present data on a sample of the prison population which is not, or may not, be representative of that population, making generalisation difficult (Moynan and McMillan in submission).

Although there needs to be caution in arguing that antisocial behaviour in offenders is frequently associated with head injury, on the basis of prevalence data that largely comprise mild head injury, this view needs to be tempered by consideration of cumulative effects of multiple mild head injuries that can be associated with long-term functional deficits (McKee et al. 2009; Guskiewicz et al. 2005), and this may be particularly relevant in the case of prisoners where repeated head injuries can be common (Schofield et al. 2006a; Williams et al. 2010; Moore et al. 2014). Overall, however, the evidence base for the impact of cumulative effects of concussion is limited and further research is required (Karr et al. 2014).

A second issue in accurately determining the prevalence of head injury is establishing a 'gold standard' means of assessment. This requires consideration of the validity of self-report in comparison to hospital records of head injury. Currently, however, the evidence base is very limited and has suffered from many methodological weaknesses. For example, Schofield et al. (2011) compared hospital records and prisoner self-report of head injury in 200 offenders and defined 'accurate' responders in terms of being in the top 25 percentile of a score based on a comparison between hospital records and self-report. However, their sample did not include 36 who reported no head injury, 64 who said they had a head injury but had not attended hospital, and 44 who lived outside of the study area. On this basis, inaccurate reporters were more likely to have left school before the age of 15, to report having had more head injuries per individual and a longer time since head injury (e.g. more than five years). The accuracy of self-report for whether or not loss of consciousness had occurred was generally poor, as was information relating to the date of the head injury (within a five year band) and the number of days of hospital admission. Accuracy was over 90% for self-reports of whether or not they had attended hospital, the names of the hospital and town, and the cause of injury. Responders appeared reasonably reliable in reporting more severe head injuries and their causes. The study therefore demonstrates how research of this kind can be useful, but further consideration of definitions of accuracy and exploration of sub-groups, where multiple mild head injuries are likely to be common, is needed.

There is also evidence to indicate that hospitalised records, which have been considered by some to be the 'gold standard' for objectivity, may not accurately reflect an individual's history of head injury (Corrigan and Bogner 2007). Around 25–33% of hospitalised head injuries are not recorded (Thornhill et al. 2000), sometimes because the head injury is not life threatening and the focus of attention falls on other injuries that are more acutely serious. For others there may be no debilitating physical injuries and the person may seem recovered, especially if there has not been an assessment of post traumatic amnesia. In addition, there may be some who have multiple head injuries and do not attend hospital because of the context in which the injury took place; examples are alcohol intoxication or stupor, sports injury, gang violence, domestic assault, or other crime. There are relevant sub-groups where the frequency of repeated head injury can be especially high. Some victims of domestic violence report concussive head injuries as an almost daily event. Membership rituals in some gangs in the US can involve beating to the point that soft tissues swell to the extent that the head resembles a 'pumpkin'. In examples of this kind, hospital attendance is avoided and determination of head injury history would rely on self-report (Wald et al. 2014). One study on prisoners demonstrates a further tension in this area; Diamond et al. (2007) reported that 61% of their sample received no medical care, suggesting a large number of cases have no formal record of their head injury. However 85% of their sample also reported no post traumatic amnesia, suggesting that the head injury was very mild with expectations of a good recovery. Finally, alcohol or drug intoxication may mask or mimic post traumatic amnesia, making assessment of injury severity difficult.

Hence, although medical records are considered to be objective evidence of a head injury, they may under represent the 'true' prevalence of head injury and may not be sufficient as a gold standard. On the other hand, self-report needs to use assessment tools that are valid in the context of brain injury and offending. Overall, the assessment of a history of head injury in offenders needs to reliably indicate whether any head injuries reported are likely to be of significance in terms of antisocial behaviour in order to triage effectively to intervention and support. Although prevalence studies based on records of hospitalisation in prison populations are needed, it is clear that the ideal study will need to combine this with self-report evidence and indication of functional impact.

Brain injury, the developing brain and offending

Risk taking in healthy juveniles is greater than in adults and particularly in males. Some consider this to be due to social and maturational factors. For example, Steinberg (2007) argues that logical reasoning and the ability to rate risk associated with events is similar in juveniles and adults, but juveniles are considerably more likely to take risks when in a social situation with peers. The brain and particularly the 'social brain', continues to develop until around the age of 25 and there is evidence to suggest that early damage can negatively affect social development (Lenroot and Giedd 2006). This includes features that are important for social interaction, including mentalising and theory of mind, where neuroimaging studies show evidence of continuing development during adolescence (Blakemore 2012).

There is also neurobehavioural evidence from studies in offenders to support this. Juvenile offenders with head injury are more impulsive than those without and more often report victimisation (Vaughn et al. 2014). Furthermore violent crime is more common in those who sustain a head injury before the age of 16 (Fazel et al. 2011). Of interest here is the cohort study in Northern Finland that followed up their population from birth to 31 years. These researchers reported that those with hospital records of head injury (94% were described as having concussion) had a two-fold increase in risk of mental health problems, including alcohol abuse, and a four-fold increase in risk of mental health disorders that were co-existent with criminal involvement in males (Timonen et al. 2002). A relationship between head injury in childhood, crime and mental health was found in a further Finnish study on adolescents who had been admitted as psychiatric inpatients; there was a five-fold higher risk of criminal conviction in those with hospitalised head injury than in those without and for those with a history of violent crimes this risk was elevated to six-fold (Luukkainen et al. 2012).

Other studies report an association between self-report of head injury and an elevated risk of current depressive/anxious symptoms, antisocial behaviour, and substance abuse problems in juvenile offenders in the US (Perron and Howard 2008). More specifically, deficits in social and emotional communication have been associated with offending in children and adolescents with head injury (Tonks et al. 2008). Hux et al. (1998) compared juvenile offenders with children at a normal school and found little difference in the self-reported prevalence of head injury and that in both groups, head injury appeared to be mild in the majority with no lasting effects. However, there were important differences between groups. For example, violence was the most common cause of head injury in juvenile offenders, whilst sports accidents were associated with school children who had not offended. More symptoms at the time of injury were retrospectively reported by juvenile offenders and severe concussion was more common in the delinquent (3.5%) than in the sports (1.5%) group, but numbers were small. Finally, Hux et al. (1998) report that the parents of the juvenile offenders more often reported that the head injury had long-term negative effects on academic performance, as well as behaviour and emotional control, and social activity, especially interaction with peers and family members.

Offending, causality, head injury and comorbidity

Head injury and offending are characterised by similar demographic risk factors, both being more common in younger males from deprived backgrounds. Also associated with both, is mental illness and ADHD in children (Kreutzer et al. 1995; Schofield et al. 2006b; Williams et al. 2010; Schachar et al. 2015). Drug and alcohol abuse is also more common in people seen by forensic psychiatry services if they have a history of head injury (Colantonio et al. 2007). A study in Minnesota found that prisoners with a high probability of having sustained a significant head injury more often had a history of drug dependency and made greater use of psychological services in prison than those with a low or moderate probability of head injury (Minnesota Department of Corrections 2008).

This raises the issue of causality versus coincidence with regard to head injury and offending behaviour. In a young male from a socially deprived background there is an enhanced risk of offending behaviour that is associated with a range of factors linked to social deprivation, including those listed above, early childhood experiences, education and employment. Head injury is more prevalent in offenders but does it add to the predictive value of these other factors? For example, some historical studies point to a high prevalence of head injury in offenders sentenced to death, but on closer inspection many of these individuals seem to have sustained mild head injury (McMillan 2010). There is also a line of research that has identified 'pseudopsychopathy' (Blumer and Benson 1975) or 'acquired sociopathic personality' (Damasio 1994), characterised by problems associated with reactive aggression, poor motivation, low empathy, poor planning and organisation, impulsivity, irresponsibility, lack of insight and behavioural disinhibition (Kiehl 2006). It is posited that focal brain lesions or insults to specific brain regions may underlie key deficits, such as a lack of empathic concern being associated with abnormality in para-limbic areas, and interpersonal difficulties to orbito-frontal areas (Soderstrom et al. 2002; Kiehl 2006).

Although the seminal study that attempts to unpick how head injury may be related to 'criminogenic' personality has yet to be published, there is evidence to suggest that head injury may be a significant contributor to the risk of offending. For example, Fazel et al. (2011) controlled for genetic factors and environmental experience to a significant extent by comparing siblings with and without a head injury. They found that the risk of violent crime was two times higher in siblings who had sustained a head injury, suggesting that head injury can change the trajectory of a young person's life towards greater risk of crime across a lifetime. Raine et al. (2005) examined factors that predicted a 'life-course' rather than an 'adolescence limited' pattern of offending. They found that a higher frequency of 'knock out' head injuries were associated with persisting offending from adolescence into adulthood, although an interesting finding was that neurocognitive impairment was not explained by head injury.

If relationships between abnormalities of brain function are considered more broadly (i.e. abnormality that could result from causes other than brain injury such as tumour, genetic abnormality or drug use), there has not surprisingly been a great deal of research interest on violence. For example, Schiltz et al. (2013) found that 42% of violent prisoners had previously undetected structural abnormalities on qualitative scoring of CT or MRI brain scans when compared with non-violent prisoners (26%) and non-offending controls (8%). Significant group differences were found for all areas considered (i.e. the frontal/parietal cortex, medial temporal structures, third ventricle and in the left lateral ventricle) except for the right lateral ventricle. The highest brain pathology 'scores' were for frontal areas, which has implications for executive functions such as goal directed behaviour, impulse regulation, decision-making and the moderation of social behaviour. They were not, however, able to link these abnormalities to particular types of disease processes. Although these studies suggest structural abnormality, they are not linked to diagnosis. However, a meta-analysis by Fazel and Danesh (2002) estimated that 47% of male prisoners have antisocial personality disorder (APD) and more recently Yang et al. (2008) review the evidence for APD and brain abnormality. They report prefrontal, temporal and limbic abnormality in violent and antisocial individuals on the basis of functional (PET, fMRI and SPect) and structural (MRI) imagery studies. They are careful to note that causality is not clear, that is whether APD arises from brain abnormality or results from the lifestyle associated with APD. Longitudinal studies are required to address this issue.

Overall, there remains a limited (or absent) consideration of persistent neuro-behavioural abnormalities in offenders, including in studies that report a high prevalence of head injury, and in studies focussing more widely on APD or violent behaviour. Admittedly studies of this kind are challenging to carry out with large samples but there is scope to examine samples that are representative of the prison population with and without head injury.

The criminal justice system and offenders with brain injury

There is little evidence to suggest that there has been much awareness of the prevalence of brain injury in offenders within the Criminal Justice System or of the potential link between brain injury and neurobehavioural disorders in prisoners. This is in spite of studies being published from various jurisdictions, including

Australia, Europe, New Zealand, and North and South America (Barnfield and Leathem 1998; Slaughter et al. 2003; de Souza 2003; Leon-Carrion and Chacartegui 2003; Schofield 2006a; Colantonio et al. 2014). However, there has recently been improved awareness within the Criminal Justice System of the prevalence of head injury and its potential influence on crime in the UK and elsewhere (Colantonio et al. 2014; Ferguson et al. 2012; Becroft 2013; British Psychological Society 2015; Schofield et al. 2015; National Prisoner Healthcare Network 2016).

A Brazilian study utilising a retrospective case record review of prisoners who had a psychiatric assessment (de Souza 2003) reported that few of those identified as head injured received any intervention. There are signs that prisoners with head injury can make additional demands on prison services, even though the Criminal Justice System does not routinely attempt to identify those with significant head injury. For example, studies in the US report that offenders whose self-report suggests a 'high probability' of having sustained a disabling head injury needed more time to adapt to prison life, had more major incidents in prison, and higher rates of recidivism than those with a lower probability of having had a significant head injury (Morrell et al. 1998; Piccolino and Sohlberg 2014). In a similar vein Fishbein et al. (2009) reported a study on 224 inmates that found deficits in behavioural inhibition thought to be due to head injury, associated with early drop out from treatment and less improvement in aggressive reactions.

There have been moves to address such issues through sentencing, rehabilitation and diversion. These initiatives are at relatively early stages, but are indicative of what might be achieved in the longer term. In New Zealand there is a growing recognition by the judiciary of the need for policy and legislation within court systems to match advances in 'brain science' (Becroft 2013). Accordingly, judges may take account of brain injury and social maturity when considering the length of sentences and community orders that may best meet the rehabilitation needs of offenders. For example, in England and Wales 'lack of maturity' may be considered to be a potential mitigating factor in sentencing decisions about young adults (Sentencing Council 2011). Furthermore, in England offenders aged 15–18 years are now routinely assessed on entry into custody in order that neurodevelopmental disorders may be identified. The Comprehensive Health Assessment Tool (CHAT) screening instrument assesses attention deficit and hyperactivity disorder, traumatic brain injury, autism spectrum disorders and speech and language problems (Chitsabesan et al. 2014a). The use of the CHAT was reinforced in England through the introduction of healthcare standards for the secure estate which outline a need for measures of this kind to enhance identification of neuro-disabilities and other comorbidities (Royal College of Paediatrics and Child Health 2013). From screening, further assessment can be initiated and care plans can be adapted to take account of neuro-disabilities such as head injury. Several other screening tools have been used to assess head injury in a criminal justice context. These include the Ohio State University-TBI Identification Method in its full (Bogner and Corrigan 2009; Ferguson et al. 2012) and short forms (Ray et al. 2014) and the Brain Injury Screening Instrument (Pitman et al. 2014).

In this context, systems also need to be developed to address the need for further specialist assessment and intervention. In England these include pilot projects of a link-worker scheme with adult and more recently, young offenders. The link-worker assists with assessments of head injury and in enabling prisoners to engage with staff (within prison and in re-settlement) to take account of issues associated with head injury such as memory impairment and anger control. The link-worker also helps prisoners to engage with existing rehabilitation programmes in the prison, such as education, training and addiction programmes (Chitsabesan et al. 2014b). Such initiatives are timely and require evaluation.

Over past decades, a number of preventative measures have been introduced in Western countries that have reduced the risk of serious head injury and its consequences (for example, as a result of road traffic accidents) but there remains a need for the introduction of preventative measures for other causes (Hamill et al. 2015). In relation to antisocial behaviour this could, for example, be reflected in education about head injury and its effects, or by improving legislation around safe use of alcohol. There is also a need to recommend a service pathway that will identify those who are in contact with the Criminal Justice System and who have a history of significant head injury that is having, or has had, an impact on their social behaviour or mental health, and where there is risk of further head injury. There is a need also for equity of access to service provision for prisoners with head injury and this necessitates appropriate links to brain injury services outside the Criminal Justice System. These measures may not only reduce the incidence and impact of brain injury, but they may reduce the frequency of recidivism (Williams 2012; Piccolino and Sohlberg 2014; British Psychological Society 2015).

In conclusion, given the likely scale and scope of head injury in relation to crime, it is important for more comprehensive systems based approaches to be developed for the identification, screening, assessment and intervention for brain injury in offenders and for the development of greater awareness of associated issues within criminal justice systems, as has recently been described and recommended (National Prisoner Healthcare Network 2016).

References

Baguley, IJ, Cooper, & J, Femingham, K (2006). Aggressive behaviour after head injury. How common is common? *J Head Trauma Rehabilitation*, 21, 45–56.

Barnfield,TV & Leathem, JM (1998). Incidence and outcomes of head injury and substance abuse in a New Zealand prison population. *Brain Injury*, 12(6), 455–466.

Becroft, A (2013). *'From Little Things, Big Things Grow'. Emerging Youth Justice Themes in the South Pacific*. Australasian Youth Justice Conference: Changing Trajectories of Offending and Reoffending. National Convention Centre Canberra. Australian Governement, Canberra Australia.

Blakemore, S (2012). Development of the social brain in adolescence. *J R Soc Med*, 105: 111–116.

Blumer, D & Benson, DF (1975). Personality changes with frontal lobe lesions. In: Benson, DF and Blumer, D (eds), *Psychiatric Aspects of Neurological Disease*. New York: Grune and Stratton, pp. 151–170.

Bogner, J & Corrigan, JD (2009). Reliability and predictive validity of the Ohio State University TBI identification method with prisoners. *Head Trauma Rehabilitation*, 24(4), 279–291.

British Psychological Society (2015). *Children with Neurological Disability and the Criminal Justice System*. Leicester: BPS Publications.

Cassidy, JD, Carroll, LJ, Peloso, PM, Borg, J, von Holst, H, Holm, L & Coronado, VG (2004). Incidence, risk factors and prevention of mild head injury: Results of the WHO collaborating centre task force on mild head injury. *J Rehabilitation Medicine*, (43 Suppl), 28–60.

Chitsabesan, P, Lennox, C, Theodosiou, L, Law, H, Bailey, S & Shaw, J (2014a). The development of the comprehensive health assessment tool for young offenders within the secure estate. *J Forensic Psychiatry & Psychol.*, 25(1), 1–25.

Chitsabesan, P, Lennox, C, Williams, H, Tariq, O & Shaw, J (2014b). Traumatic brain injury in juvenile offenders: Findings from the Comprehensive Health Assessment Tool Study and the development of a specialist linkworker service. *J Head Trauma Rehabilitation*, 30, 106–115.

Colantonio, A, Stamenova, V, Abramowitz, C, Clarke, D & Christensen, N (2007). Brain injury in a forensic psychiatry population. *Brain Injury*, 21(13–14), 1353–1360.

Colantonio, A, Kim, H, Allen, S, Asbridge, M, Petgrave, J & Brochu, S (2014). Head injury and early life experiences among men and women in a prison population. *Correctional Health Care*, 20(4), 271–279.

Corrigan, JD & Bogner, J (2007). Screening and identification of TBI. *J Head Trauma Rehabilitation*, 22(6), 315–317.

Damasio, AR (1994). *Decartes' Error: Error, Reason, and the Human Brain*. New York: Grosset/Putnam.

Diamond, PM, Harske, AJ, Magletta, PR, Cummins, AG & Frankowski, R (2007). Screening for head injury in an offender sample: A first look at the reliability and validity of the head injury questionnaire. *Head Trauma Rehabilitation*, 22(6), 330–338.

De Souza, CAC (2003). Frequency of brain injury in a forensic psychiatric population. *Rev Bras Psiquiatr.*, 25(4), 206–211.

Farrer, TJ & Hedges, DW (2011). Prevalence of head injury in incarcerated groups compared to the general population: A meta-analysis. *Progress in Neuro-Psychopharmacology & Biological Psychiatry*, 35, 390–394.

Farrer, TJ, Frost, RB & Hedge, DW (2013). Prevalence of traumatic brain injury in juvenile offenders: A meta-analysis. *Child Neuropsychology*, 19, 225–234.

Fazel, S & Danesh, J (2002). Serious mental disorder in 23000 prisoners: A systematic review of 62 surveys. *Lancet*, 359, 545–550.

Fazel, S, Lichtenstein, P, Grann, M & Långström, N (2011). Risk of violent crime in individuals with epilepsy and head injury: A 35-year Swedish population study. *PLoS Med*, 8(12), e1001150.

Ferguson, PL, Pickelsimer, EE, Corrigan, JD, Bogner, JA & Wald, M (2012). Prevalence of head injury among prisoners in South Carolina. *Head Trauma Rehabilitation*, 27(3), E11–E20.

Fishbein, D, Sheppard, M, Hyde, C, Hubal, R, Newlin, D, Serin, R, Chrousos, G & Alesci, S (2009). Deficits in behavioral inhibition predict treatment engagement in prison inmates. *Law and Human Behavior*, 33(5), 419–435.

Guskiewicz, KM, Marshall, SW, Bailes, J, McCrea, M, Cantu, RC, Randolph, C & Jordan, BD (2005). Association between recurrent concussion and late life cognitive impairment in retired professional football players. *Neurosurgery*, 57, 719–726.

Hamill, V, Barry, SJE, McConnachie, A, McMillan, TM & Teasdale, GM (2015). Mortality from head injury over four decades in Scotland. *J Neurotrauma*, 32, 689–703.

Karr, JE, Areshenkoff, CN & Garcia-Barrera, MA (2014). Neuropsychological outcomes of concussion: A systematic review of meta-analyses on the cognitive sequelae of mild traumatic brain injury. *Neuropsychology*, 28, 321–336.

Hux, K, Bond, V, Skinner, S, Belau, D & Sanger, D (1998). Parental report of occurrences and consequences of head injury among delinquent and non-delinquent youth. *Brain Injury*, 12(8), 667–681.

Kiehl, KA (2006). A cognitive neuroscience perspective on psychopathy: Evidence for paralimbic system dysfunction. *Psychiatry Res*, 142(2–3), 107–128.

Kreutzer, JS, Marwitz, JH & Witol, AD (1995). Interrelationships between crime, substance abuse and aggressive behaviours among persons with traumatic brain injury. *Brain Injury*, 9(8), 757–768.

Langlois, JA, Rutland-Brown, W & Wald, MM (2006). The epidemiology and impact of traumatic brain injury: A brief overview. *J Head Trauma Rehabilitation*, 21, 375–378.

Lenroot, RK & Giedd JN (2006). Brain development in children and adolescents: Insights from anatomical magnetic resonance imaging. *Neuroscience and Biobehavioral Reviews*, 30(6), 718–729.

Leon-Carrion, J & Chacartegui, FJ (2003). Blows to the head during development can predispose to violent criminal behaviour: rehabilitation of consequences of head injury is a measure for crime prevention. *Brain Injury*, 17(3), 207–216.

Luukkainen, S, Riala, K, Laukkanen, M, Hakko, H & Rasanen, P (2012). Association of traumatic brain injury with criminality in adolescent psychiatric inpatients from Northern Finland. *Psychiatry Research*, 200(2–3), 767–772.

McKee, AC, Cantu, RC, Nowinski, CJ, MD, Gavett, BE, Budson, AE, Santini, VE, Lee, H, Kubilus, CA & Stern, RA (2009). Chronic traumatic encephalopathy in athletes: progressive tauopathy following repetitive head injury. *J Neuropathol Exp Neurol.*, Jul 68(7), 709–735.

McMillan, TM (2010). Head injury and offending. In: Brown, J & Campbell, EA (eds), *Cambridge Handbook of Forensic Psychology*, Cambridge University Press, pp. 65–70.

Minnesota Department of Corrections (2008). Initial TBI survey results: Minnesota prison system. Paper presented at the annual conference of the Minnesota Brain Injury Association, St. Cloud, MN.

Moore, E, Indig, D & Haysom, L (2014). Traumatic brain injury, mental health, substance use, and offending among incarcerated young people. *J Head Trauma Rehabilitation*, 29(3), 239–247.

Morrell, RF, Merbitz, CT, Jain, S & Jain, S (1998). Head injury in prisoners. *Offender Rehabilitation*, 27(3–4), 1–8, DOI: 10.1300/J076v27n03_01

Moynan, C & McMillan, TM (in submission). The prevalence of head injury in prisoners: A systematic review.

National Prisoner Healthcare Network (2016). *Brain Injury and Offending*. Edinburgh: Scottish Government.

Perron, B & Howard, M (2008). Prevalence and correlates of head injury among delinquent youths. *Criminal Behaviour and Mental Health*, 18(4), 243–255.

Piccolino, A & Sohlberg, KB (2014). The impact of head injury on prison health health services and offender management. *J Correctional Health Care*, 20, 203–212.

Pitman, I, Haddlesey, C, Ramos, SDS, Oddy, M & Fortescue, D (2014). The association between neuropsychological performance and self-reported head injury in a sample of adult male prisoners in the UK. *Neuropsychological Rehabilitation*, DOI:10.1080/09602011. 2014.973887.

Raine, A, Moffitt, TE, Caspi, A, Loeber, R, Stouthamer-Loeber, M & Lynam, D (2005). Neurocognitive impairments in boys on the lifecourse persistent antisocial path. *Abnormal Psychology*, 114(1), 38–49.

Ray, B, Sapp, D & Kincaid, A (2014). Head injury among Indiana state prisoners. *Forensic Science*, 59(5), DOI: 10.1111/1556-4029.12466

Royal College of Paediatrics and Child Health (2013). *Healthcare Standards for Children and Young People in Secure Settings.* London, England: Royal College of Paediatrics and Child Health.

Schachar, RJ, Park, LS & Dennis, M (2015). Mental health implications of Traumatic Brain Injury (TBI) in children and youth. *Can Acad Child Adolesc Psychiatry*, 24(2): 100–108.

Schiltz, K, Witzel, JG, Bausch-Holterhoff, J, Bog, B & Bogerts, B (2013). High prevalence of brain pathology in violent prisoners: A qualitative CT and MRI scan study. *Eur Arch Psychiatry Clin Neurosci.*, 263, 607–616.

Schofield, PW, Butler, TG, Hollis, SJ, Smith, NE, Lee, S J & Kelso, WM (2006a). Traumatic brain injury among Australian prisoners: Rates, recurrence and sequelae. *Brain Injury*, 20(5), 499–506. DOI:10.1080/02699050600664749

Schofield, PW, Butler, TG, Hollis, SJ, Smith, NE, Lee, SJ & Kelso, WM (2006b). Neuropsychiatric correlates of traumatic brain injury (TBI) among Australian prison entrants. *Brain Injury*, 20(13–14), 1409-1418. DOI:10.1080/02699050601130443

Schofield, P, Butler, T, Hollis, S & D'Este, C (2011). Are prisoners reliable survey respondents? A validation of self-reported traumatic brain injury (TBI) against hospital medical records. *Brain Injury*, 25(1), 74–82.

Schofield, PW, Malacova, E, Preen, DB, D'Este, C, Tate, R, Reekie, J, Wand, H & Butler, T (2015). Does head injury lead to criminality? A whole population retrospective cohort study using linked data. PLOS ONE: DOI:10.1371/journal.pone.0132558

Sentencing Council (2011). Assault: Definitive sentencing guideline. Sentencing Council, London; https://www.sentencingcouncil.org.uk/wp-content/uploads/Assault_definitive_guideline_-_Crown_Court.pdf

Shiroma, EJ, Ferguson, PL & Pickelsimeree, EE (2010). Prevalence of head injury in an offender population; a meta-analysis. *J Correctional Healthcare*, 16, 147–159.

Slaughter, B, Fann, J & Ehde, D (2003). Head injury in a county jail population: Prevalence, neuropsychological functioning and psychiatric disorders. *Brain Injury*, 17(3), 731–741.

Soderstrom, H, Hultin, L, Tullberg, M, Wikkelso, M, Ekholm, S & Forsman, A (2002). Reduced frontotemporal perfusion in psychopathic personality. *Psychiatry Research Neuroimaging*, 114, 81–94.

Steinberg, L (2007). Risk taking in adolescence. *Current Directions in Psychological Science*, 16, 55–59.

Tagliaferri, F, Compagnone, C, Korsic, M, Servadei, F & Kraus, J (2006). A systematic review of brain injury epidemiology in Europe. *Acta Neurochir (Wien)*, 148, 255–268.

Thornhill, S, Teasdale, GM, Murray, GD, McEwen J, Roy, CW & Penny, KI (2000). Disability in young people and adults one year after head injury: prospective cohort study. *BMJ*, 2000, 320, 1631e5.

Timonen, M, Miettunen, J, Hakko, H, Zitting, P, Veijola, J, von Wendt, L & Rasanen, P (2002). The association of preceding head injury with mental disorders, alcoholism and criminality: the Northern Finland 1966 Birth Cohort Study. *Psychiatry Research*, 113(3), 217–226.

Tonks, J, Slater, A, Frampton, I, Wall, SE, Yates, P & Williams, WH (2008). The development of emotion and empathy skills after childhood brain injury. *Developmental Medicine and Child Neurology*, 51, 8–16.

Vaughn, MG, Salas-Wright, CP, Delis, M & Perron, B (2014). Correlates of head injury among juvenile offenders: A multi-site study. *Criminal Behaviour and Mental Health*, 24, 188–203.

Wald, MM, Helgeson, SR & Langlois, JA (2008). Traumatic brain injury among prisoners. *Brain Injury Professional*, 5, 22–25.

Williams, WH, Mewse, AJ, Tonks, J, Mills, S, Burgess, CNW & Cordan, G (2010). Head injury in a prison population: Prevalence and risk for re-offending. *Brain Injury*, 24(10), 1184–1188.

Williams, W.H. (2012). *Repairing Shattered Lives. Transition to Adult Alliance*. Barrow: Cadbury Trust.

Williams, C & Wood, RLl (2010). Alexithymia and emotional empathy following traumatic brain injury. *J Clin. ExperimentaL Neuropsychology*, 32(3), 259–267.

Wood, RLl (2001). Understanding neurobehavioural disability. In: Wood, RLl & McMillan, TM (eds), *Neurobehavioural Disability and Social Handicap Following Head injury*. Hove: Psychology Press, pp. 3–28.

Wood, RLl & Williams, C (2008). Inability to empathize following head injury. *International Neuropsychological Society*, 14, 289–296.

Yang, Y, Glenn, AL & Raine, A (2008). Brain abnormalities in antisocial individuals: Implications for the law. *Behav Sci Law*, 26, 65–83.

6

NEUROBEHAVIOURAL DISORDERS AND THE FAMILY

Jeffrey S. Kreutzer, Caron Gan and Jennifer H. Marwitz

Decades ago, clinical researchers began to evaluate family members' needs. In their study of wives and mothers Mauss-Clum and Ryan (1981) noted that the most highly rated needs early on were for clear and kind explanations of the patient's condition and discussion of realistic expectations. In order of decreasing importance, emotional support, financial counselling, and resource counselling were also indicated. Subsequent research clearly suggested that caregiver and family functioning is commonly affected by patients' neurobehavioral functioning (see Table 6.1). The consistency of findings is impressive given the variability in research designs and

TABLE 6.1 Summary of literature relating neurobehavioural functioning to family members' distress and burden and family functioning

Authors, Year	Primary Focus	Findings
Mauss-Clum, Ryan, 1981	Caregiver distress	Frustration, irritability, annoyance was common among caregivers; caregivers a common target of verbal abuse
Brooks et al., 1986	Caregiver burden	Burden increased with time postinjury; a majority reported high burden levels at five years; burden associated with neurobehavioural disturbance
Kreutzer et al., 1994a,b	Caregiver distress, family functioning	Half reported elevated distress; spouses more likely to report depression and unhealthy family functioning; distress related to neurobehavioural functioning
Marsh et al., 1998	Caregiver burden and psychosocial functioning	Depression and anxiety common; neurobehavioural problems, physical disability, social isolation predicted burden

(continued)

TABLE 6.1 Summary of literature relating neurobehavioural functioning to family members' distress and burden and family functioning *(continued)*

Authors, Year	Primary Focus	Findings
Ergh et al., 2002, 2003	Caregiver psychological distress, family functioning	Neurobehavioural dysfunction predicted distress and life satisfaction; social support was strongest predictor of family functioning and powerful moderator of distress
Anderson et al., 2009	Family functioning, psychological distress	Social, communication, and behavioural problems associated with spousal distress; cognitive and behavioral problems associated with family dysfunction
Anderson et al., 2013	Family functioning	Male caregivers more sensitive to levels of family dysfunction; family functioning directly impacted by neurobehavioural dysfunction
Schonberger, et al., 2010	Family functioning, relative's emotional well-being	Anxiety and depression predicted by patients' neurobehavioural functioning, particularly behavioural and mood changes; no differences in family functioning, anxiety, depression over time.
Kelley, et al., 2014	Burden	Burden associated with patients having more severe emotional, cognitive, and social problems

measures used. Family members, typically wives and mothers, most often assume the role of long-term caregiver. High levels of emotional distress are commonly reported. Wives seem more vulnerable than mothers, perhaps because they have a partner who is less able to share responsibilities and offer emotional support.

Kreutzer and colleagues developed the Family Needs Questionnaire (FNQ) to help professionals better understand needs in both acute and post-acute settings (Kreutzer, Serio & Berquist, 1994). Their initial investigation revealed that needs for complete, accurate, and honest information about the person's TBI were rated as most important. Later, the same investigators endeavoured to predict post-discharge needs (Serio, Kreutzer & Gervasio, 1995). Multiple regression analyses identified different predictors for parents' (e.g., survivors' impairments in attention and memory) and spouses' needs (e.g., level of neurobehavioural problems). Witol, Sander & Kreutzer (1996) utilized a longitudinal design to evaluate family needs at six and 24 months postinjury. For both time periods, health information needs were generally perceived as met, while needs relating to instrumental support were largely characterized as unmet. A larger number of emotional support and involvement with care needs were reported as not met at 24 months in comparison to six months postinjury. Needs for professional support were more frequently reported as met at 24 months postinjury. Using the FNQ, Doser and Norup examined family needs in the chronic phase post severe TBI (Doser & Norup, 2014). Health information needs were most often rated as important and most often rated as met. The need most often rated as unmet reflected the need to talk with someone who has gone through the same experience.

Sinnakaruppan and Williams (2001) provide a literature synthesis relating to caregivers' needs which appears valid today. Information needs seem to predominate, particularly relating to the effects of injury and adjusting to injury-related changes. Parents tend to report more met needs than spouses. Emotional support needs are most often rated as unmet, and unmet needs are often related to neurobehavioural changes which increase over time.

Marriage and divorce

Marital stability after TBI – While a complete understanding of couplehood after TBI is not yet established, existing research raises concern. The likelihood of marital breakdown after TBI is best described as uncertain, with studies' reported rates ranging from 15–78% (Godwin, Kreutzer, Arango-Lasprilla & Lehan, 2011). When couples separate after injury, health outcomes for patients may be affected. For example, married TBI survivors report fewer challenges with self-care than single survivors (Moore, Stambrook, Gill & Lubusko, 1992). Further, single patients can be left without essential home-based support as a foundation for long-term recovery. Interestingly, more recent exploration into marital stability presents a stark contrast to early reports (Arango-Lasprilla et al., 2008; Kreutzer, Marwitz, Hsu, Williams & Riddick, 2007).

Kreutzer et al. (2007) challenged the long-held belief that marriages after TBI typically disintegrate. Across the 120 mild, moderate, and severely injured participants, there was a 25% marital breakdown rate (separation or divorce). To clarify why some marriages may be more subject to breakdown after TBI than others, Arango and colleagues examined predictors of marital stability (Arango-Lasprilla et al., 2008). Of the 977 couples examined, 15% were separated or divorced at two years postinjury. Analysis indicated that being male or older predicted greater instability. Questions remain about the relationship between neurobehavioural outcomes and marital stability.

Marital quality after TBI – Current research suggests postinjury marital quality is dangerously affected from the caregiver's point of view (Peters et al., 1992; Wood, Liossi & Wood, 2005). In recent explorations investigating both spouse and caregiver perception of marital quality, studies have found poorer outcomes as compared to controls, as well as significantly negative pre- to postinjury changes in overall marital satisfaction (Blais & Boisvert, 2007; Burridge, Williams, Yates, Harris & Ward, 2007).

Adverse impacts to marital quality are not unexpected given what we know about neurobehavioural concerns and spouses' psychological distress and burden. With regard to neurobehavioural concerns, studies have demonstrated that a majority of survivors experience major depression in the first year postinjury (Bombardier et al., 2010). Further, caregiver depression and burden levels are primary outcome determinants.

When a child is injured

Research has shown that TBI is a leading cause of neurobehavioural problems and psychiatric disorders in children (Garcia, Hungerford & Bagner, 2015; Li & Liu, 2013). These include problems with aggression and conduct disorders, depression, anxiety, personality change (Li & Liu, 2013), increased suicidality, bullying, substance use, and antisocial behaviours (Ilie et al., 2014). Prigatano and colleagues (Prigatano, Fulton & Wethe, 2010) additionally outlined problems with rage reactions, diminished empathy, emotional lability, irritability, disinhibition, impulsivity, and socially inappropriate behaviour irrespective of the child's severity of brain injury. These problems may emerge shortly or several years after injury and often persist or even worsen over time (Catroppa, Anderson, Morse, Haritou & Rosenfeld, 2008). Neurobehavioural problems have been found to be related to poor school performance, psychiatric illness, and poor peer relations, and are a major cause of parental distress (Catroppa et al., 2008; Li & Liu, 2013).

There is a considerably large body of research on family burden and psychological distress after paediatric TBI (Aitken et al., 2009; Catroppa et al., 2008). Stress and burden among families have often been identified with concerns around the child's behavioural adjustment (Prigatano & Gray, 2007); stress around the child's school performance (Lindsay et al., 2015); concerns around the child's social isolation (Prigatano & Gray, 2007); sibling stress and negativity (Sambuco, Brookes & Lah, 2008); and uncertainty about the trajectory of the injury and the child's future potential (Gan, DePompei & Lash, 2012).

The family environment has been found to be a significant moderator of neurobehavioural impairments after TBI in children (Yeates, Taylor, Walz, Stancin & Wade, 2010). Families need access to a variety of support modalities over the life course, including education about TBI, psychosocial and instrumental support, peer support, professional counselling, skills training, family therapy, school support, financial planning, and respite (Gan, Gargaro, Brandys, Gerber & Boschen, 2010a).

Family needs early on appear to be honest, realistic, clear, and regular information about the TBI. Families need concrete and practical information about the brain injury, the recovery process, strategies for coping with new roles, and information about community and professional supports (Armstrong & Kerns, 2002; Gan et al., 2010a). Psychosocial and behavioural issues often emerge with a need to address emotional adjustments, behavioural and psychosocial issues, and parenting strategies (Aitken et al., 2009).

Attending to the needs of the entire family system becomes essential so that the child's brain injury does not become the primary focus of family life (Gan et al., 2012). Just as parents struggle to cope with the emotional impact of the trauma of the child's TBI, siblings also struggle to find effective ways of coping and may be at increased risk of developing psychological difficulties (Gan et al., 2012; Sambuco et al., 2008). Siblings can experience heightened levels of distress, increased sibling conflict, role changes and increased responsibilities, or feelings of loss related to the changes in their family (Sambuco et al., 2008). Far too often, their needs are overlooked, even though studies have consistently noted how their lives are profoundly affected (Sambuco, Brookes, Catroppa & Lah, 2012). Siblings face feelings of loss and disruption in family roles and dynamics as parents' attention is focused on the needs of the injured child, often to the detriment of other family members (Gan, DePompei & Lash, 2012). Addressing the neurobehavioural sequelae of the child with TBI is essential to alleviating the stress in the family environment so that parents can refocus their energies on the needs of uninjured family members. Studies suggest that the best predictor of sibling outcome is the behavioural functioning of the injured child (Sambuco et al., 2012).

Parents of children with TBI have identified numerous *unmet* needs around health information, education about brain injury, professional support, community support networks (Armstrong & Kerns, 2002), family support, and return to school (Hermans, Winkens, Winkel-Witlox & van Iperen, 2012). As parental perception of unmet health care needs is strongly related to family burden, meeting family needs is critical to the health of the family unit (Aitken et al., 2009). Interventions that target the identified needs of families may help to diminish the burden experienced by families.

Unlike adult TBI, dealing with school issues is a source of considerable distress for parents and considered a priority for children and their families after hospital discharge (Gan et al., 2012; Lindsay et al., 2015). Few parents know what to expect when their child returns to school. As well, many schools are ill prepared to deal with the unique needs of students with brain injury.

In summary, while the adult literature highlights the impact on wives and mothers, the paediatric literature addresses the psychosocial impact on families and siblings. The developmental considerations after paediatric TBI are also unique, with an emphasis on school issues and long-term family support needs.

Interventions to support families

Overview of adult intervention strategies

Clinicians have a fundamental role in helping families understand and cope with the effects of injury and how to manage common neurobehavioural sequelae. The fields of family counselling, family therapy, and cognitive behaviour therapy offer strategies for helping families (Kreutzer et al., 2009; Kreutzer, Marwitz, Godwin & Arango-Lasprilla, 2010). The following are descriptions of intervention strategies and techniques likely to be beneficial.

Joining – The process by which the therapist is accepted by the family as a participating team member is called joining. Many family therapists believe that problems are best solved by the family as a whole with the therapist involved as a collaborating team member. The term "therapeutic alliance" is often used to describe the quality of the relationship between therapist and family (Nichols et al., 2008). Joining is facilitated by conversing with family members to appreciate their concerns, perspectives, history, and culture without judgement (White, 2007).

Asking questions, understanding how the family functions, and respecting different points of view also facilitates the joining process (Duncan, Miller & Sparks, 2004).

Listening – In their eagerness to quickly solve families' problems, therapists may reflexively offer advice and solutions, potentially hindering progress (Aragno, 2008). Active listening is a powerful therapeutic tool for a number of reasons. Family members appreciate the opportunity to share their history, feelings and ideas. Listening to family members enhances the quality of the therapeutic relationship, can assist in identifying solutions to problems, and contributes to their confidence in problem solving (Dunst, Boyd, Trivette & Hamby, 2002; Miller & Rollnick, 2002).

Normalization – The common neurobehavioural consequences of TBI can bring on a period of prolonged stress, anxiety, and confusion for family members. Through the normalization process, families are helped to understand that the behaviours they notice may be disconcerting, but are typical brain injury sequelae (Piercy, Wetchler & Sprenkle, 1996). The process provides reassurance that professionals have experience with the problems and that the challenges they face are common and not insurmountable.

Positive reframing – is a cognitive behavioural therapy technique intended to improve affect by helping family members recognize their strengths, resources, and positive aspects of their situation (Beck, 1995). The process involves helping people to appreciate the detriments of negative thinking and the benefits of positive thinking (Nichols et al., 2008).

Skills training – The purpose of skills training is to help people improve their abilities, typically through a combination of modelling, role playing, and practice. Clinical researchers have identified a variety of skills helpful to recovery (Ducharme, 2000). Skills training focused on problem solving, goal setting, communication, stress management, and self-advocacy has the potential to benefit family members as well as persons with brain injury.

Psychoeducation – The lack of information regarding outcome, prognosis, and neurobehavioural interventions is often lamented by family members. Helping families to access and understand information is an important role for professionals. This information often needs to be repeated over time as families move through different stages of acceptance and understanding.

Resource referral – Clinicians are encouraged to remain knowledgeable about brain injury related resources in their community. Survivors and family members are often uncertain about available services and professionals can help them identify and access resources relevant to their needs.

Collaborative self-examination – Asking questions, encouraging reflection, and having family members communicate their responses is a powerful process for enhancing awareness, identifying challenges, and formulating solutions to problems. As described by Kreutzer and colleagues, family members are first asked to answer a series of questions via questionnaire (Kreutzer et al., 2009). The therapist then encourages individual family members to share their responses with one another. The following is a guided discussion of reactions to each person's responses, a process enabling development of empathy, improved communication skills, and enhanced family cohesion.

The Brain Injury Family Intervention

The Brain Injury Family Intervention (BIFI), a structured approach to treatment, was developed to improve survivors' and family members' psychological well-being, life satisfaction, access to services, and enhance family functioning (Kreutzer, Marwitz, Sima & Godwin, 2015). Addressing commonly identified needs, the BIFI comprises five two-hour sessions with each session addressing two or three topics (see Table 6.2). Each session begins with an overview of topics, includes educational and problem solving components, and concludes with a summary and assignment of homework. Intervention is guided by a therapist's manual that delineates goals, materials needed, intervention procedures, and accommodations for disabilities (Kreutzer & Taylor, 2004).

The BIFI helps families to address the neurobehavioural consequences of injury in several ways. First, patients and family members are asked to identify and discuss their recognition and perception of injury-related neurobehavioural problems. Second, families are helped to understand that personality and behavioural changes are a normal consequence of injury. Third, problem solving and skills training techniques are used to help patients improve their self-control with the help of family members.

Family systems theory (FST) is a foundation of the BIFI (Bertalanffy, 1968; Nichols & Schwartz, 2004). FST views families as interconnected systems. Namely, the feelings, actions and communications of each family member typically impact those of other family members and the family unit as a whole. The BIFI relies on family therapy techniques, including reframing, empathic reflections, validation,

TABLE 6.2 Overview of BIFI sessions and topics.

Session	Topic
I. Effects of brain injury on the survivor and family	1. What is normal after brain injury? 2. Brain injury happens to the whole family
II. Understanding recovery	3. Emotional and physical recovery are two different things 4. Mastering the art of patience 5. Coping with loss and change
III. Solving problems and setting goals	6. Setting reasonable goals 7. Solving problems effectively
IV. Managing stress and intense emotions	8. Managing stress effectively 9. Managing intense emotions
V. Strategies for optimal recovery	10. Taking care of yourself 11. Focusing on gains and accomplishments 12. Most important lessons learned and where to go from here

and normalization. Interventions also include cognitive behavioural therapy and collaborative self-examination. Educational techniques are used to help participants appreciate common injury sequelae and patterns of recovery. Psychological support techniques are used to help participants appreciate and improve their well-being. Participants also receive skills training to improve their problem solving, communication, and stress management.

The BIFI is unique in several ways. First, the person with the brain injury is a participant in the intervention. Second, training is delivered via a manual, helping to standardize the fidelity of treatment. Third, the intervention has a considerable empirical foundation (Kreutzer, Stejskal, Godwin, Powell & Arango-Lasprilla, 2010; Kreutzer et al., 2009; Kreutzer et al., 2015).

Unique aspects of working with families after paediatric TBI

Life course perspective – When a child is injured, the family must adapt to a child whose needs, abilities, and personality have changed. Families face the challenge of focusing on both the present and the future as injury has an immediate and developmental impact on the child, depending on the age of onset. Compared with adults, children with TBI often "grow into" their disabilities, falling farther and farther behind their similar age peers over time (Ewing-Cobbs et al., 2006). Functional and behavioural difficulties often persist into adulthood (Ryan et al., 2015).

Children may seem to fully recover at the outset, especially if physical symptoms resolve. Because the brain continues to develop into the mid–20s, cognitive, emotional and behavioural issues may not appear for several years, often becoming apparent when the child enters adolescence. When issues emerge, they can be difficult to distinguish from the challenges that come with normal adolescence (i.e., impulsivity, poor judgement, emotional reactivity, opposition to authority) (Gan et al., 2012). Providing education to parents around the developmental impact of TBI, the developing brain, and the potential effects of TBI on social, behavioural, and academic functioning can help parents prepare for these developmental changes. Parents of adolescents with TBI also require guidance on ways to safely negotiate the transition through the adolescent stage of family life, especially as the TBI can exacerbate the normal challenges that come with adolescence. Providing support around attainment of life skills is also vital to supporting independence and healthy transition to adulthood.

Parents may experience reactivation of their losses during developmental milestones such as the anniversary date of the injury, birthdays, transition to high school, graduation, or moving out of the family home. This type of loss experienced by families often goes unrecognized and unacknowledged by friends and family, leaving parents feeling isolated and helpless. The normalcy of these episodic loss reactions should be explained to parents as a way to foster resilience and to prepare families for recurring events over the course of the child's life. Linking parents to support groups or local brain injury associations can enhance peer support and help to reduce these feelings of isolation.

Dealing with school issues – As TBI can affect learning, peer relations, and academic functioning, working collaboratively with the school is critical, especially given the fact that the child will spend a good part of their time at school. Yet, parents often struggle when dealing with school systems, as educators often do not understand the needs of students with TBI. Rehabilitation professionals can facilitate school re-integration by helping families address the following questions: (1) What information has been provided to the school about the child's TBI?; (2) How is the school working together with the student and parents in identifying educational goals and preparing the individualized educational programme (IEP)?; (3) What are the strengths and needs of the student as identified in the IEP?; (4) What modifications and accommodations are helpful for the student?; and, (5) How are students involved in learning self-advocacy and transition planning? (Gan et al., 2012). A partnership linking clinicians, educators, families, and youth with TBI is desirable.

Family-centred approach – The fundamental principle underlying family-centred service (FCS) is that families are the most important influence on the child's development, recovery, and overall adjustment. Increasingly, FCS has been widely embraced in the field of childhood chronic illness and disability, including brain injury (Gan, Gargaro, Kreutzer, Boschen & Wright, 2010b; Gan et al., 2012). FCS is about mutual respect, information sharing, participation, and collaborative partnerships that focus on client/family strengths, needs, values, and priorities. FCS has been associated with increased client and family satisfaction, adherence to treatment recommendations, and improved client outcomes (King et al., 2000; Law, Hanna & King, 2001).

There has been a growing body of research around interventions that incorporate a family-centred approach to the management of neurobehavioural difficulties after paediatric TBI (Braga, Da Paz & Ylvisaker, 2005; Woods et al., 2014). Early family intervention is necessary to optimize parents' confidence and ability to manage emerging behavioural problems, especially as paediatric TBI is associated with an elevated risk for externalizing disorders in the transition to adulthood (Ryan et al., 2015). A recent review of family interventions after paediatric TBI concluded that parent training interventions may alleviate behavioural and emotional disturbances after paediatric TBI (Brown, Whittingham, Boyd & Sofronoff, 2013). Research findings suggest benefits to parenting skill and adjustment (Brown et al., 2013).

Brain injury family intervention for adolescents

Although several TBI family interventions have been developed for paediatric populations, most focus on younger children. One exception is the Teen Online Problem Solving (TOPS), an online problem solving therapy model which shows promising outcomes (i.e., improvements in problem-solving skills and decreased parental distress) and has the advantages of a web-based intervention (Wade et al., 2012). Although the assumption exists that most adolescents prefer online therapies, this has not necessarily been supported in the literature (Bradford & Rickwood, 2014). To address this gap, an adolescent version of the adult BIFI

TABLE 6.3 Brain Injury Family Intervention for Adolescents (BIFI-A) curriculum

Session	Module Topics
1	Assessment of changes after brain injury
2	What happens after brain injury
3	Brain injury happens to the whole family
4	Being a teen and achieving independence
5	Emotional and physical recovery
6	Coping with loss and change
7	Managing intense emotions
8	Managing stress and taking care of self
9	Setting S.M.A.R.T. goals and tracking progress
10	Learning patience and solving problems
11	School, transitions, and preparing for adulthood
12	Wrap-up – celebrating successes and accomplishments

was developed – the Brain Injury Family Intervention for Adolescents (BIFI-A). BIFI-A is a manualized face-to-face intervention that targets adolescents with TBI and the family system (Gan et al., 2010b). Face-to-face intervention allows clinicians to capture the subtleties of non-verbal communication and emotional reactions that typically occurs within the family system. Face-to-face interventions provide opportunities for a variety of modalities to facilitate engagement, learning, and practice in real-life scenarios (i.e., vignettes, role plays, discussion, and interactive activities). BIFI-A is delivered in 12 one-hour sessions (Gan, Gargaro & Kreutzer, 2013) (see Table 6.3).

The specific BIFI-A goals are to:

- Provide information about common symptoms and challenges after adolescent brain injury.
- Enhance understanding of how the brain injury has affected each member of the family and the family as a whole.
- Offer strategies for more effective problem-solving and achievement of goals.
- Facilitate coping strategies supporting the emotional recovery process.
- Instil hope, build resilience by amplifying progress and personal/family strengths.
- Foster effective communication skills to develop a strong, long-term support system.
- Provide a foundation of knowledge, strategies, and resources adolescents and families can build on for successful community living.

The BIFI-A includes a detailed step-by-step manual, scripted protocol, procedures, and practical guidelines to facilitate effective implementation. The manual includes key activities, ready-to-use handouts, tools and resources for clinicians to apply and replicate (Gan et al., 2013).

The BIFI-A was derived from paediatric family needs research and the evidence-based adult BIFI. Validation of BIFI-A outcomes has yet to be completed. Still, the BIFI-A is a promising family system intervention that merits further research.

Conclusions and future directions

The neurobehavioural consequences of brain injury have been a focus of researchers and clinicians for many years. Complex and seemingly insurmountable, neurobehavioural sequelae have been identified as long-term obstacles to living independently, working, and maintaining quality relationships. Clinicians have been concerned that the neurobehavioural consequences of injury are detrimental to family functioning and caregivers' emotional well-being. Research has suggested that neurobehavioural factors have a greater adverse impact than physical disability and cognitive impairment. Concern has been expressed about the impact of neurobehavioural disorders on marital relationships. Research is needed to determine how neurobehavioural factors influence marital stability and satisfaction.

Paediatric TBI, like adult injury, is a leading cause of neurobehavioural problems that are long-lasting and have a detrimental effect on caregiver stress and family functioning, including siblings. However, childhood TBI has both an immediate and developmental impact on the child and family as the brains of children are still developing well into adulthood. Adopting a life course perspective is essential as emerging deficits and neurobehavioural changes have an impact on peer relations, family relationships, academic functioning, attainment of life skills, and transition to adulthood. As the family environment is a significant moderator of neurobehavioural impairments after paediatric TBI, adopting a family-centred approach is key to mitigation.

The expertise of rehabilitation specialists, neuropsychologists, family therapists, and counsellors has been integrated in recent efforts to develop structured interventions addressing the needs of families. Fortunately, interventions developed for adults and children are showing positive results. More research is needed to better appreciate the impacts of promising therapies and the extent to which intervention benefit is mitigated by neurobehavioural factors. Conversely, research also needs to address the extent to which effective neurobehavioural interventions benefit family members individually and the family as a whole.

References

Aitken, M. E., McCarthy, M. L., Slomine, B. S., Ding, R., Durbin, D. R., Jaffe, K. M. & Mackenzie, E. J. (2009). Family burden after traumatic brain injury in children. *Pediatrics*, *123*(1), 199–206.

Anderson, M. I., Simpson, G. K. & Morey, P. J. (2013). The impact of neurobehavioral impairment on family functioning and the psychological well-being of male versus female caregivers of relatives with severe traumatic brain injury: Multigroup analysis. *The Journal of Head Trauma Rehabilitation*, *28*(6), 453–463.

Anderson, M. I., Simpson, G. K., Morey, P. J., Mok, M. M., Gosling, T. J. & Gillett, L. E. (2009). Differential pathways of psychological distress in spouses vs. parents of people with severe traumatic brain injury (TBI): Multi-group analysis. *Brain Injury*, *23*(12), 931–943.

Aragno, A. (2008). The language of empathy: An analysis of its constitution, development, and role in psychoanalytic listening. *Journal of the American Psychoanalytic Association*, *56*(3), 713–740.

Arango-Lasprilla, J. C., Ketchum, J. M., Dezfulian, T., Kreutzer, J. S., O'Neil-Pirozzi, T. M., Hammond, F. & Jha, A. (2008). Predictors of marital stability 2 years following traumatic brain injury. *Brain Injury*, *22*(7), 565–574.

Armstrong, K. & Kerns, K. A. (2002). The assessment of parent needs following paediatric traumatic brain injury. *Pediatric Rehabilitation*, *5*(3), 149–160.

Beck, J. S. (1995). *Cognitive therapy: Basics and beyond*. New York, N.Y.: Guilford Press.

Bertalanffy, L. V. (1968). *General System Theory: Foundations Development, Applications*. New York: George Braziller.

Blais, M. C. & Boisvert, J. M. (2007). Psychological adjustment and marital satisfaction following head injury. Which critical personal characteristics should both partners develop? *Brain Injury*, *21*(4), 357–372.

Bombardier, C. H., Fann, J. R., Temkin, N. R., Esselman, P. C., Barber, J. & Dikmen, S. S. (2010). Rates of major depressive disorder and clinical outcomes following traumatic brain injury. *JAMA: The Journal of the American Medical Association*, *303*(19), 1938–1945.

Bradford, S. & Rickwood, D. (2014). Adolescent's preferred modes of delivery for mental health services. *Child and Adolescent Mental Health*, *19*(1), 39–45.

Braga, L. W., Da Paz, A. C. & Ylvisaker, M. (2005). Direct clinician-delivered versus indirect family-supported rehabilitation of children with traumatic brain injury: A randomized controlled trial. *Brain Injury*, *19*(10), 819–831.

Brooks, N., Campsie, L., Symington, C., Beattie, A. & McKinlay, W. (1986). The five year outcome of severe blunt head injury: A relative's view. *Journal of Neurology, Neurosurgery and Psychiatry*, *49*(7), 764–770.

Brown, F. L., Whittingham, K., Boyd, R. & Sofronoff, K. (2013). A systematic review of parenting interventions for traumatic brain injury: Child and parent outcomes. *The Journal of Head Trauma Rehabilitation*, *28*(5), 349–360.

Burridge, A. C., Williams, W. H., Yates, P. J., Harris, A. & Ward, C. (2007). Spousal relationship satisfaction following acquired brain injury: The role of insight and socio-emotional skill. *Neuropsychological Rehabilitation*, *17*(1), 95–105.

Catroppa, C., Anderson, V. A., Morse, S. A., Haritou, F. & Rosenfeld, J. V. (2008). Outcome and predictors of functional recovery 5 years following pediatric traumatic brain injury (TBI). *Journal of Pediatric Psychology*, *33*(7), 707–718.

Doser, K. & Norup, A. (2014). Family needs in the chronic phase after severe brain injury in Denmark. *Brain Injury*, *28*(10), 1230–1237.

Ducharme, J. M. (2000). Treatment of maladaptive behavior in acquired brain injury: Remedial approaches in postacute settings. *Clinical Psychology Review*, *20*(3), 405–426.

Duncan, B., Miller, S. & Sparks, J. (2004). *The heroic client: a revolutionary way to improve effectiveness through client-directed, outcome-informed therapy*. San Francisco, CA: Jossey-Bass.

Dunst, C., Boyd, K., Trivette, C. & Hamby, D. (2002). Family-oriented program models and professional helpgiving practices. *Family Relations*, *51*(3), 221–229.

Ergh, T. C., Rapport, L. J., Coleman, R. D. & Hanks, R. A. (2002). Predictors of caregiver and family functioning following traumatic brain injury: Social support moderates caregiver distress. *The Journal of Head Trauma Rehabilitation*, *17*(2), 155–174.

Ewing-Cobbs, L., Prasad, M. R., Kramer, L., Cox, C. S., Jr, Baumgartner, J., Fletcher, S., Mendez, D., Barnes, M., Zhang, X. & Swank, P. (2006). Late intellectual and academic outcomes following traumatic brain injury sustained during early childhood. *Journal of Neurosurgery*, *105*(4 Suppl), 287–296.

Gan, C., DePompei, R. & Lash, M. (2012). Family assessment and intervention. In: N. Zasler, D. Katz, R. Zafonte, D. Arciniegas, M. R. Bullock & J. S. Kreutzer (Eds.), *Brain injury medicine: principles and practices* (2nd ed.). New York: Demos Medical Publishing, LLC, pp. 621–634.

Gan, C., Gargaro, J., Brandys, C., Gerber, G. & Boschen, K. (2010a). Family caregivers' support needs after brain injury: A synthesis of perspectives from caregivers, programs, and researchers. *NeuroRehabilitation*, *27*(1), 5–18.

Gan, C., Gargaro, J., Kreutzer, J. S., Boschen, K. A. & Wright, F. V. (2010b). Development and preliminary evaluation of a structured family system intervention for adolescents with brain injury and their families. *Brain Injury*, *24*(4), 651–663.

Gan, C., Gargaro, J. & Kreutzer, J. (2013). *The brain injury family intervention – adolescent version – intervention manual.* Toronto: Holland Bloorview Kids Rehabilitation Hospital.

Garcia, D., Hungerford, G. M. & Bagner, D. M. (2015). Topical review: Negative behavioral and cognitive outcomes following traumatic brain injury in early childhood. *Journal of Pediatric Psychology*, *40*(4), 391–397.

Godwin, E. E., Kreutzer, J. S., Arango-Lasprilla, J. C. & Lehan, T. J. (2011). Marriage after brain injury: Review, analysis, and research recommendations. *The Journal of Head Trauma Rehabilitation*, *26*(1), 43–55.

Hermans, E., Winkens, I., Winkel-Witlox, S. T. & van Iperen, A. (2012). Caregiver reported problems of children and families 2–4 years following rehabilitation for pediatric brain injury. *NeuroRehabilitation*, *30*(3), 213–217.

Ilie, G., Mann, R. E., Boak, A., Adlaf, E. M., Hamilton, H., Asbridge, M., Rehm, J. & Cusimano, M. D. (2014). Suicidality, bullying and other conduct and mental health correlates of traumatic brain injury in adolescents. *PloS One*, *9*(4), e94936.

Kelley, E., Sullivan, C., Loughlin, J. K., Hutson, L., Dahdah, M. N., Long, M. K., Schwab K. A. & Poole, J. H. (2014). Self-awareness and neurobehavioral outcomes, 5 years or more after moderate to severe brain injury. *The Journal of Head Trauma Rehabilitation*, *29*(2), 147–152.

King, S., Kertoy, M., King, G., Rosenbaum, P., Hurley, P. & Law, M. (2000). *Perceptions about family-centered service delivery for children with disabilities.* Hamilton, ON: McMaster University, CanChild Center for Childhood Disability Research.

Kreutzer, J. S., Stejskal, T. M., Godwin, E. E., Powell, V. D. & Arango-Lasprilla, J. C. (2010). A mixed methods evaluation of the brain injury family intervention. *NeuroRehabilitation*, *27*(1), 19–29.

Kreutzer, J. S., Gervasio, A. H. & Camplair, P. S. (1994a). Patient correlates of caregivers' distress and family functioning after traumatic brain injury. *Brain Injury*, *8*(3), 211–230.

Kreutzer, J. S., Gervasio, A. H. & Camplair, P. S. (1994b). Primary caregivers' psychological status and family functioning after traumatic brain injury. *Brain Injury*, *8*(3), 197–210.

Kreutzer, J. S., Marwitz, J. H., Godwin, E. E. & Arango-Lasprilla, J. C. (2010). Practical approaches to effective family intervention after brain injury. *The Journal of Head Trauma Rehabilitation*, *25*(2), 113–120.

Kreutzer, J. S., Marwitz, J. H., Hsu, N., Williams, K. & Riddick, A. (2007). Marital stability after brain injury: An investigation and analysis. *NeuroRehabilitation*, *22*(1), 53–59.

Kreutzer, J. S., Marwitz, J. H., Sima, A. P. & Godwin, E. E. (2015). Efficacy of the brain injury family intervention: Impact on family members. *The Journal of Head Trauma Rehabilitation*, *30*(4), 249–260.

Kreutzer, J. S., Serio, C. & Berquist, S. (1994). Family needs following brain injury: A quantitative analysis. *Journal of Head Trauma Rehabilitation*, 9(3), 104–115.

Kreutzer, J. S., Stejskal, T. M., Ketchum, J. M., Marwitz, J. H., Taylor, L. A. & Menzel, J. C. (2009). A preliminary investigation of the brain injury family intervention: Impact on family members. *Brain Injury*, 23(6), 535–547.

Kreutzer, J. S. & Taylor, L. A. (2004). *Brain injury family intervention manual*. Richmond, VA: National Resource Center for Traumatic Brain Injury.

Law, M., Hanna, S. & King, G. (2001). *Factors affecting family-centered service delivery for children with disabilities*. Hamilton, ON: McMaster University, CanChild Centre for Childhood Disability Research.

Li, L. & Liu, J. (2013). The effect of pediatric traumatic brain injury on behavioral outcomes: A systematic review. *Developmental Medicine and Child Neurology*, 55(1), 37–45.

Lindsay, S., Hartman, L. R., Reed, N., Gan, C., Thomson, N. & Solomon, B. (2015). A systematic review of hospital-to-school reintegration interventions for children and youth with acquired brain injury. *PloS One*, 10(4), e0124679.

Mauss-Clum, N. & Ryan, M. (1981). Brain injury and the family. *Journal of Neurosurgical Nursing*, 13(4), 165–169.

Miller, W. R. & Rollnick, S. (2002). *Motivational Interviewing: Preparing People for Change* (2nd ed.). New York, N.Y.: Guilford Press.

Moore, A. D., Stambrook, M., Gill, D. D. & Lubusko, A. A. (1992). Differences in long-term quality of life in married and single traumatic brain injury patients. *Canadian Journal of Rehabilitation*, 6(2), 89–98.

Nichols, L. O., Chang, C., Lummus, A., Burns, R., Martindale-Adams, J., Graney, M. J., Coon D.W. & Czaja, S. (2008). The cost-effectiveness of a behavior intervention with caregivers of patients with Alzheimer's disease. *Journal of the American Geriatrics Society*, 56(3), 413–420.

Nichols, M. P. & Schwartz, R. C. (2004). *Family Therapy Concepts and Methods* (6th ed.). Boston, MA: Pearson Education, Inc.

Peters, L. C., Stambrook, M., Moore, A. D., Zubek, E., Dubo, H. & Blumenschein, S. (1992). Differential effects of spinal cord injury and head injury on marital adjustment. *Brain Injury*, 6(5), 461–467.

Piercy, F. P., Wetchler, J. L. & Sprenkle, D. H. (1996). *Family Therapy Sourcebook* (2nd ed.). New York, N.Y.: Guilford.

Prigatano, G. P., Fulton, J. & Wethe, J. (2010). Behavioral consequences of pediatric traumatic brain injury. *Pediatric Health*, 4(4), 447–455.

Prigatano, G. P. & Gray, J. A. (2007). Parental concerns and distress after paediatric traumatic brain injury: A qualitative study. *Brain Injury*, 21(7), 721–729.

Ryan, N. P., Hughes, N., Godfrey, C., Rosema, S., Catroppa, C. & Anderson, V. A. (2015). Prevalence and predictors of externalizing behavior in young adult survivors of pediatric traumatic brain injury. *The Journal of Head Trauma Rehabilitation*, 30(2), 75–85.

Sambuco, M., Brookes, N., Catroppa, C. & Lah, S. (2012). Predictors of long-term sibling behavioral outcome and self-esteem following pediatric traumatic brain injury. *The Journal of Head Trauma Rehabilitation*, 27(6), 413–423.

Sambuco, M., Brookes, N. & Lah, S. (2008). Paediatric traumatic brain injury: A review of siblings' outcome. *Brain Injury*, 22(1), 7–17.

Schonberger, M., Ponsford, J., Olver, J. & Ponsford, M. (2010). A longitudinal study of family functioning after TBI and relatives' emotional status. *Neuropsychological Rehabilitation*, 20(6), 813–829.

Serio, C., Kreutzer, J. S. & Gervasio, A. (1995). Predicting family needs after traumatic brain injury: Implications for intervention. *Journal of Head Trauma Rehabilitation*, 10(2), 32–45.

Sinnakaruppan, I. & Williams, D. M. (2001). Family carers and the adult head-injured: A critical review of carers' needs. *Brain Injury, 15*(8), 653–672.

Wade, S. L., Walz, N. C., Carey, J., McMullen, K. M., Cass, J., Mark, E. & Yeates, K. O. (2012). A randomized trial of teen online problem solving: Efficacy in improving caregiver outcomes after brain injury. *Health Psychology: Official Journal of the Division of Health Psychology, American Psychological Association, 31*(6), 767–776.

White, M. (2007). *Maps of narrative practice.* New York, N.Y.: Norton.

Witol, A., Sander, A. M. & Kreutzer, J. S. (1996). A longitudinal analysis of family needs following traumatic brain injury. *NeuroRehabilitation, 7*, 175–187.

Wood, R. L., Liossi, C. & Wood, L. (2005). The impact of head injury neurobehavioural sequelae on personal relationships: Preliminary findings. *Brain Injury, 19*(10), 845–851.

Woods, D. T., Catroppa, C., Godfrey, C., Giallo, R., Matthews, J. & Anderson, V. A. (2014). Challenging behaviours following paediatric acquired brain injury (ABI): The clinical utility for a manualised behavioural intervention programme. *Social Care and Neurodisability, 5*(3), 145–159.

Yeates, K. O., Taylor, H. G., Walz, N. C., Stancin, T. & Wade, S. L. (2010). The family environment as a moderator of psychosocial outcomes following traumatic brain injury in young children. *Neuropsychology, 24*(3), 345–356.

PART II

Assessment methodologies

7

PROBLEMS ASSESSING EXECUTIVE DYSFUNCTION IN NEUROBEHAVIOURAL DISABILITY

Rodger Ll. Wood and Erin Bigler

Executive abilities have been described as meta-cognitive activities that control and integrate other cognitive activities (Burgess et al., 2000; Stuss, Picton & Alexander, 2001). They have been linked with functions essential to community independence, such as – dealing with novelty, planning and organising activities, sequencing actions to complete a task, showing initiative, self-monitoring to adapt behaviour to changing life events, and attention control (Fuster, 2001; Stuss & Alexander, 2007). Executive abilities rely heavily on functions of the prefrontal cortex that are vulnerable to traumatic brain injury (TBI). Whilst therefore executive dysfunction is a core feature of neurobehavioural disability (NBD), it is not always an obvious feature and may appear in a subtle form, especially when the injured person has made a good physical recovery or exhibits, what appears to be, good intelligence. For example, it is not unusual for families to misinterpret loss of the ability to initiate activity as 'laziness'. Such misinterpretations can cause tension within families. Therefore, one of the challenges facing rehabilitation practitioners, particularly neuropsychologists, is how to recognise executive characteristics of NBD before they have a damaging impact on a person's inter-personal abilities, disrupting family relationships, further undermining the individual's capacity for community independence.

The early identification of executive dysfunction is often not easy, especially when a person is still in a hospital or rehabilitation setting. For example, if a person's mobility is constrained by physical injury, there is little opportunity to employ those executive abilities that underpin many aspects of purposeful, goal-directed behaviour. Deficits in executive function may also be masked or minimised by the structure implicit in a rehabilitation environment. In such settings patients are given a timetable of activities that dictates where they should be and what they should be doing at different times throughout each day. Consequently, individuals are relieved of the responsibility to make decisions. They do not have to plan and structure their own time, or initiate activities in a spontaneous, adaptive and purposeful manner. Recognition of NBD can therefore be delayed until recovery has progressed to the point where the person is expected to take more responsibility for everyday activities of daily living, usually after discharge from the rehabilitation hospital, when there may be little or no opportunity for outreach community support. Many family doctors, to whom families may initially turn to for help, are ill-equipped to understand the nature and significance of abnormalities that comprise NBD. Families therefore struggle to cope with problems they do not understand and that have no 'medical' explanation or treatment, yet still have major implications for interpersonal relationships and family cohesion. However, whilst the behavioural deficits that reflect disorders of executive functions may become obvious to family members (even though they may not construe them in terms of disability), the particular cognitive deficits responsible for disorders of behaviour may be difficult to identify especially if an assessment is restricted to a person's performance on a range of cognitive tests.

The neuropsychological assessment

It has long been known that a disturbance of executive functions can exist in the absence of any measurable impairment on standardised tests of cognitive ability. For example, Newcombe and Artioli Fortuny (1979), Lezak (1983), and Shallice and Burgess (1991b) all noted that patients with executive dysfunction can perform equally well as healthy controls on traditional neuropsychological tests. As recently as 2006, Wood and Liossi noted that tests traditionally used in neuropsychological assessment have been inconsistent in their ability to identify executive dysfunction, yet much of clinical neuropsychology has continued to use these traditional measures. The main concern has been that tests that purport to measure specific cognitive functions using composite scores do not have a predictable relationship to cognitive impairment in everyday life (Lezak, 1995). Ponsford, Sloan and Snow (1995) also noted that it is frequently difficult to predict how results on psychometric tests reflect an individual's daily life and roles in society. When placed in situations in which they should be able to function (based on measured cognitive ability), many fail to adapt skills to the task at hand; make errors they do not detect; fail to adjust behaviour as the situation changes; lack the ability to anticipate or plan ahead; respond badly to negative feedback; and fail to execute tasks properly, not because they don't know what to do but because they cannot sequence the actions necessary to achieve a goal.

More recently, Burgess and Alderman (2003) stated that – "People with executive impairment can exhibit serious difficulties performing everyday tasks when neuropsychological test performance suggests only minor cognitive changes have occurred" (p. 388). Gilbert and Burgess (2008) noted that this was particularly evident in people who had suffered damage to the rostral prefrontal cortex (RPFC), many of whom perform well on standard neuropsychological tests, such as the Wisconsin Card Sorting Test, yet had particular difficulty in real-world 'multitasking' situations.

They pointed out that the RPFC underpins high-level human abilities, such as combining two distinct cognitive operations in order to perform a single task, or trying to work out what other people are thinking ('mentalising'), or reflecting on information we retrieve from long-term memory (for example, trying to work out when we last saw a person familiar to us). They proposed that the RPFC serves as a 'gateway' between cognitive processes directed towards current incoming perceptual information, versus information that we generate ourselves and, whilst vital to everyday behaviour, is not something easily measured by conventional clinical tests.

'Normal' performance on traditional neuropsychological measures has been observed in patients with very extensive frontal pathology evident on neuroimaging (Bigler, 1988; Eslinger & Damasio, 1985). This has been particularly evident when injury involves the ventromedial prefrontal cortex (VMPF). Damage to this area is associated with a lack of insight, lack of initiative, irritability, social inappropriateness, poor judgement, lack of persistence, indecisiveness, emotional lability, blunted emotional experience, apathy, inappropriate affect, poor frustration tolerance, and inflexibility. However, many individuals with this type of injury are capable of performing normally on all manner of conventional neuropsychological tests that assess intellectual functions, working memory, or attention, as well as 'frontal lobe tests' such as the Wisconsin Card Sorting Test and the Tower of Hanoi, which place demands on abstract thinking and flexible responding (Tranel, 2002). They can also perform normally on tests that measure the application of knowledge pertaining to social conventions and moral reasoning, providing those tasks are administered in a verbal format, or in a structured laboratory or clinical setting. However, they manifest profound inability to express emotion and to experience feelings relative to complex personal and social situations, such as guilt. The lack of ecological validity in executive tests designed for neuropsychological assessment in an office setting is especially worrying in a medico-legal context when neuropsychologists are called upon to advise the Court how brain injury has compromised a person's ability to function in the real world. This chapter will therefore explore some of the reasons for poor ecological validity and offer recommendations that potentially allow an alternative method of identifying NBD based on structural observations of behaviour whilst translating observed performance within a neuroscientific frame of reference.

Problems relating to the assessment procedure

Shallice and Burgess (1991a) identified a number of problems in the way executive tests are administered, any of which could reduce their sensitivity to identify salient features of executive dysfunction that have ecological value:

a) The examiner prompts test behaviour, preventing an assessment of the patient's ability to self-initiate an action.
b) Tests are of short duration, whereas in real life people have to maintain goal-directed behaviour over long time spans.

c) Only one problem is addressed at any time, compared to real life when people have to balance several ideas or activities simultaneously.
d) The person being assessed is not required to set priorities or to deal with competing task demands, which is usually a requirement of community living.
e) There is no requirement to activate an intention after a delay, therefore, there is no need to use prospective memory.

One could add to these points the following features common to neuropsychological assessment settings:

a) Tests are usually given in a quiet environment, free of distraction, even though most people with NBD describe distractibility as a frequent and intrusive problem affecting memory and the continuity of thinking.
b) The impact of fatigue on speed and efficiency of information processing is usually not included in the assessment because test administration may be spaced over several days, even weeks, to accommodate problems of fatigue. This may have ethical value but it prevents a clear assessment of the impact of fatigue on cognition.
c) When assessments are carried out continuously over several hours there is no prescribed method regarding the order in which tests should be administered to capture most clearly the effect of fatigue on mental flexibility. This is something often left to the experience and acumen of the individual clinician.
d) The examiner prompts test behaviour, preventing an assessment of a person's ability to self-initiate an action. Unless individuals can apply knowledge spontaneously in a way that allows them to adapt to changing situations then the value of an assessment, particularly intelligence testing, is limited. A failure to identify problems of initiative, or a lack of drive and motivation, represents a fundamental flaw in the assessment process. Information about the person's ability to carry out and sustain activities needs to be elicited from observations by the neuropsychologist during the assessment of cognitive abilities if possible, but the quality and accuracy of such observations are subject to variations in experience and the ability of individual clinicians.

Problems with existing executive test structures

The role of attention

The context in which assessments are carried out and the procedural weaknesses referred to above emphasise a problem intrinsic to many existing tests – their failure to assess attention control. Stuss and Alexander (2007) argue that many features of what we refer to as NBD can be explained as impairments in attentional control processes that are highly vulnerable to TBI. In real life a person continually has to direct and re-direct attention based on changing environmental circumstances and intentions. We have to monitor several ideas or actions simultaneously and select and react to relevant stimuli. By contrast, in a clinical assessment we only ask a person to focus upon one thing at a time, reflecting serial processing whereas real life requires parallel processing (Schneider & Shiffrin, 1977; Wood & Grafman, 2003). When one examines the role of attention in everyday life we can see that the attentional loading on routine everyday activities is far greater than usually captured on clinical tests, which is why many people with frontal brain injury can succeed on tests yet fail to cope in the community. One probable exception to this is the Test of Everyday Attention (Robertson et al., 1995) which employs tests of divided attention that are comparable to real life settings and can identify different patterns of attentional deficit that are likely to have an impact on community independence.

Test–retest reliability

Rabbitt (1997) pointed out that most tests of executive functions are limited by their own test–retest reliabilities. A major feature of executive dysfunction is that people can cope with familiar tasks (the actions of which are usually over-learned) yet still experience difficulty acquiring new skills. By implication, only novel tasks can pick up deficits in executive functions. However, tasks can only be novel once! Repeated presentation of the same task, even after a six-month delay, means that it is no longer novel, which reduces the sensitivity of the task to executive dysfunction and, when test–retest reliabilities are measured, the correlation is usually low.

Task structure

Lezak et al. (2004) addressed the problem of structure that is inherent in many tests of cognitive function –

> Assessment of executive function involves the paradoxical situation in which a task is structured in such a way that it prevents an assessment of the patients ability to make structure themselves . . . Patients may perform well on time-limited, highly structured tasks but still be unable to function independently in real world activities.
>
> *(p180)*

This is essentially a re-statement of the criticism of test structure and procedure made by Shallice and Burgess (1991a). It emphasises the problems associated with the context in which assessments take place but also points out that the design of tests themselves undermines their sensitivity.

Intelligence

Duncan, Burgess and Emslie (1995) argued that many tests of executive ability measure primarily a non-specific intellectual function reminiscent of general intelligence 'g'. This theoretical proposition has received empirical support from studies on head injured patients (Stokes & Bajo, 2003; Wood & Liossi, 2007). Research findings support clinical observations of discordance between performance on tests of intelligence and everyday functional abilities (see the case of MN reported by Wood and Rutterford, 2004) suggesting that highly intelligent patients cope effectively with the executive demands of consulting room executive tests, even though they lack the mental flexibility to cope with comparable (but simultaneous) cognitive demands in real life. Clinical neuropsychology has known of these test deficiencies for some time but continues to perpetuate problems intrinsic to many tests rather than solve them.

The frontal paradox

Frontal brain injury has the effect of dislocating knowledge from the means of applying knowledge, what Walsh (1985) referred to as the *frontal paradox*. As early as 1964 Teuber (1994) commented on *"The difference between knowing and doing"* when assessing patients with frontal brain injury. He noted that some people with frontal injury are able to verbalise how to carry out a procedure but fail to translate that knowledge into action. Stuss and Benson (1986) also commented on speech having an important programming and regulating role in behaviour. They noted that frontal damage can disturb this regulatory role, also pointing out that patients may verbalise correctly but fail to use the information to direct behaviour. This dislocation between the ability to verbalise an intention and a failure or inability to act on that intention suggests that the term *Strategy Application Disorder* offered by Burgess (2000) might have been a better way of describing some features of NBD than incorporating them under the rubric of executive dysfunction.

The frontal paradox can be explained by the failure of language to mediate actions, something that is not usually addressed either by neuropsychologists or speech and language therapists. Luria (1973) proposed that human activity is evoked by intentions and formulated by speech to define a certain goal. Intentions are initially mediated by external speech, and later by internal speech. He argued that 'inner speech' directs attention to salient features of an activity then mediates the monitoring of performance by comparing the outcome with the original intention. When learning a task children (and adults) often use language overtly to focus attention and regulate their actions. As complex actions sequences become more familiar (through practice and repetition) the control over the sequence of discrete units of action changes from overt speech to covert (or inner) speech. Inner speech was considered responsible for mediating complex forms of behaviour by creating an internal plan to achieve a goal. However, after frontal injury Luria noted that many patients failed to act upon their stated intentions. Verbal commands remained in memory but no longer initiated action and therefore lost their regulating influence.

Unfortunately, the approach adopted my many neuropsychologists is to focus on what a person states they will do without taking into consideration observations from relatives or significant others about the actual behaviour of the person in real life (see Draper & Ponsford, 2009). In the UK this is usually evident in the context of medico-legal reporting. Some 'experts' to the Court will make a judgement of a claimant's mental capacity based upon how the claimant describes what they will do with money once compensation is awarded, rather than take into consideration observations from others who comment upon the erratic and impulsive actions of the claimant, both in general and with regard to fiscal irresponsibility in particular. It is unwise, even negligent, to form opinions on how test performance is likely to influence everyday behaviour without carefully interviewing those with direct experience of the person's real-world behaviour over a period of time.

The development of 'specialised' tests

Burgess (2003) described conventional executive tests used by neuropsychologists as crude and unspecified in terms of the cognitive processes that they engage. Efforts have therefore been made to develop specialised tests of executive ability that rely on the concept of *veridicality* – the degree to which performance on a test empirically relates to measures of everyday functioning, allowing clinicians to predict social and functional abilities relevant to real world settings from test performance. However, some of these tests have not proved as sensitive to NBD as originally hoped.

Behavioural Assessment Dysexecutive Syndrome [BADS]

This group of tests developed by Wilson et al. (1996) based their ecological face validity on the Dysexecutive Questionnaire [DEX], which is a supplementary subtest of the BADS. The standardisation of these tests was conducted on 78 brain injured patients but only 59 per cent had suffered closed head injury (Wilson et al., 1998). Therefore the tests did not necessarily address problems of executive ability that are mainly associated with NBD after head trauma. When measured against the DEX only moderate negative correlations were established between each of the six individual tests and the ratings made by 'significant others' of executive problems in community settings. An independent evaluation by Norris and Tate (2000) found that only one of the BADS subtests (Zoo Map) correlated with independent ratings on the DEX, but this was not in the expected direction.

Hayling and Brixton tests

These tests developed by Burgess and Shallice (1997) were standardised on 91 patients with circumscribed neoplastic and haemorrhagic lesions but did not include a head trauma sample (Burgess et al., 1998). When used with patients who have circumscribed lesions, performance on the Brixton test appears to dissociate inductive reasoning, monitoring, and working memory, all of which are mediated by the left lateral frontal cortex, from processes that monitor behaviour mediated by the right lateral cortex (Reverberi et al., 2005). A similar left hemisphere bias can be made about the Hayling test. When used in association with functional imaging techniques to identify cortical areas responsible for verbal initiation and suppression in normal subjects, left frontal activation was predominant (Nathaniel-James, Fletcher & Frith, 1997). However, use of the Hayling and Brixton tests with head trauma patients has produced less clear results. Bajo and Nathaniel-James (2001) compared Hayling and Brixton performance with the DEX. They found that Hayling – part 1 (initiation) correlated weakly (.21–.28) with all three DEX factors (response suppression, intentionality, and executive memory) and the Brixton Test correlated moderately with the executive memory factor (.40). However, Hayling – part 2 (response suppression) did not correlate significantly with scores on any of the three DEX factors. It appears therefore that whilst the Hayling and Brixton tests of executive function may be useful in cases of circumscribed cerebral lesions, their clinical utility in the assessment of executive abnormalities in patients who have suffered TBI remains uncertain.

Temporal discounting

This paradigm measures a tendency for some individuals to prefer smaller sooner rewards over larger later rewards, which research has shown to be unaffected by real versus hypothetical rewards (Johnson & Bickel, 2002). The choice of a delayed larger reward is assumed to reflect self-control, whilst opting for an immediate smaller reward is said to exemplify impulsivity and poor judgement (Klapproth, 2011). Temporal discounting methods have been applied to substance abuse, attention deficit hyperactivity disorder, and problem gambling (see Critchfield & Kollins, 2001 for a review). Recently, this paradigm was employed to examine decision-making in a group of patients following brain injury (Wood & McHugh, 2013). Participants with TBI who performed normally on conventional neuropsychological tests were compared with matched healthy controls. Each of the two groups demonstrated temporal discounting; that is, the subjective value of the reward decreased with increasing delay before gratification. However, the TBI group discounted more than the controls, suggesting that their decision-making was more impulsive. This implies that the performance of the TBI group reflected a need for immediate gratification which, anecdotally, was an observation often made by relatives of those who performed badly on the test. However, a direct comparison between discounting performance and financial decision-making in real world activities has yet to be made.

The IOWA Gambling Task (IGT)

This complex decision-making paradigm has been developed to help neuropsychologists identify abnormalities of functioning attributable to the VMPFC (Bechara et al., 1994; Bechara, Damasio & Damasio, 2000). It evaluates emotion-based decision-making when faced with ambiguous contingencies and uncertain consequences (Manes et al., 2002; Bowman and Turnbull, 2004). Cotrena et al. (2014) recorded poor decision making on the IGT in patients with TBI, regardless of lesion location and severity. The IGT proved to be equally sensitive to both frontal and non-frontal lesions.

Structured observational procedures

Lezak (1995) noted that cognitive impairments that compromise aspects of everyday behaviour are not easily elicited by the usual neuropsychiatric or neuropsychological examination yet are apparent to those who observe such individuals going about their usual activities. Many real world activities have a sequence or structure with core features of executive function, such as planning, organisation, and working memory. By observing individuals carrying out these activities one can identify cognitive deficiencies associated with neurobehavioural disability.

The multiple errands test

This procedure was developed by Shallice and Burgess (1991a) and has been described by Burgess (2003) as a test with, *"the most obvious ecological validity in current use"*, one that is *"highly sensitive both to brain damage in general and to specific executive problems"* (pp. 315–316). It involves aspects of prospective memory, problem solving, an ability to follow rules, as well as the ability to plan and organise a task.

The first step is to designate a test area, usually in a small shopping precinct. The person being assessed has to follow a list of instructions pertinent to the shops in the area, e.g. – 1 Buy a street map; 2 Buy a pound of tomatoes; 3 Buy a bottle of Vitamin C; 4 Get an appointment for an eye-test; 5 Buy a newspaper; 6 Buy 3 × 2" screws. Certain rules have to be followed: a. Spend as little money as possible; b. Take as little time as possible; c. Shops must only be entered once; d. Shops are only entered to buy something; e. When you leave a shop tell the examiner what you have bought; f. Do the tasks in any order. A prospective memory element is included by asking the person to meet at a certain place ~15 minutes after starting the task. A final element of the task involves problem solving: For example, name the shop that sells the most expensive item; name the coldest place in Britain yesterday; what is the value of the pound against the dollar?

Whilst this structured task allows the examiner to evaluate aspects of executive function in a real-world setting, employing the principle of verisimilitude, it is time consuming and not conducive to many clinicians' idea of a routine clinical examination, principally because it is not an office-based test and has to be conducted in a community setting, subject to the vagaries of weather, public reaction and occasional professional embarrassment. Recent refinements are attempting to address this limitation (Alderman et al., 2003; Knight, Alderman & Burgess, 2002).

The 'bacon and egg test'

Some research suggest that cooking tasks may be more sensitive to executive deficits than traditional neuropsychological measures (Fortin, Godbout & Braun, 2003;

Tanguay Davidson et al., 2014). Fortin et al. (2003) found no difference between a head-injured group and controls on a standardised neuropsychological assessment, yet the patient group showed diminished ability to cook a meal. They concluded that impaired planning and prospective memory functions, whilst not captured by standardised tests, still contributed to diminished ability to cook a meal in the patient group.

The act of cooking a meal requires several executive functions, including capacity to multitask, plan, sequencing, and time management. One author (RLW), when working in a post-acute rehabilitation setting, frequently asked patients who performed well on standardised tests but exhibited poor functioning in real-world tasks, to complete a task of cooking grilled bacon, fried egg, and boiled potatoes, in the training kitchen on a community rehabilitation unit. This task involves planning discrete action sequences and time perception. For example, potatoes have to be peeled and put on to boil 10–15 minutes before the bacon can be placed under the grill. Finally, a few minutes before other items are ready, the eggs should be put into the hot oil. A frequent observation was that patients would start boiling the potatoes and grilling the bacon simultaneously, with the result that the latter was burnt or the former under-cooked. In some cases, every item was cooked simultaneously, even when the patient had previously correctly explained the temporal sequence of each action, to ensure that they understood the procedure (an example of what Teuber described as the *difference between knowing and doing*). Such an activity is one of many daily activities central to community life that has a prescribed action sequence and temporal framework that can be incorporated into an assessment of neurobehavioural disability. Some allowance may need to be made for slight variations in approach to the neuropsychological elements of the task that reflect executive functions but the correctness, or otherwise, of the task is usually easy to recognise.

Computer simulations of real world activity

An interactive computerised version of the cooking task referred to above has been developed by Doherty et al. (2015) as an ecological measure of executive functioning. The task has four difficulty levels, each level having different processing demands to increase the cognitive load. Task variables were expected to tap into very specific processes intrinsic to real world cooking tasks. They found that the computerised task compared favourably with a real cooking task in the identification of executive deficits.

Other computerised tests have been constructed to provide a virtual version of the multiple errands task (Rand et al., 2009) or to simulate other types of everyday life activities, such as working in an office environment. For example, Jansari et al. (2014) created a virtual office environment that significantly differentiated between 17 individuals with TBI and 30 healthy controls. However, to date, performance on this test has not been compared to similar task performance in a comparable real life office setting.

However, the cost of developing these technologies is significant and there may still be a significant gap between the technology used in computer simulations and the scientific requirements associated with psychometric testing. It is also the case that computer simulations cannot fully replicate the uncertainties of everyday life. For example, what happens in a real kitchen is multisensorial – the kettle whistling, the smell of the toast burning, the need to inspect eggs to see if they are cooking evenly. Therefore, it is understandable that the ecological validity of a test will equate to one conducted in the natural environment. However, the rapid evolution of interactive computing, such as that used in virtual reality applications, points to the potential for exceptionally life-like testing environments, including 4-D simulations that can include a variety of sensory stimuli such as vibration, odours, and tactile components. Ultimately, the value of computerised simulations will be determined by the extent to which they can predict everyday functional performance in the real world.

Conclusions

Characteristics that comprise neurobehavioural disability (NBD) can vary considerably from person to person according to the specific structures implicated in traumatic brain injury as well as a person's age, their pre-morbid personality, intellectual capability (with potential for cognitive reserve), the nature or quality of post-injury rehabilitation, and the quality of family or social support. It is a complex yet often subtle form of disability but one that can have a pervasive adverse influence on psychosocial recovery. There is a general consensus by internationally recognised neuroscientists that many of the tests currently used in a neuropsychological assessment lack the ecological sensitivity to reflect how executive dysfunction influences the character of NBD or restricts capacity for community independence. The challenge for neuropsychological assessment will be to develop measures that are more reliable in detecting aspects of executive dysfunction that have implications for NBD and community independence. Until this is achieved more reliance may need to be placed on observations by family and friends, structured and quantified in the context of rating scales. However, the reliability and validity of many existing scales has recently been questioned (Wood, Alderman & Williams, 2008), partly because they contain statements that rely on interpretations or inferences of the disabled person's behaviour rather than reflecting observations of overt behaviour. A new scale, the SASNOS, has been proposed as a more objective method of identifying and assessing the severity of observable behaviours associated with neurobehavioural disability, which has better psychometrics than other rating procedures (Alderman, Wood & Williams, 2011). It could therefore be argued that until there is a major paradigm shift in the methods and procedures used by neuropsychologists, rating scales, such as the SASNOS, based on structured behavioural observations, by family members or close friends, as well as the person with TBI (to obtain a measure of insight) will be a more reliable method of assessing the nature and ecological impact of executive deficits associated with neurobehavioural disability.

References

Alderman, N., Wood, R.Ll. & Williams, C. (2011). The development of the St Andrew's-Swansea Neurobehavioural Outcome Scale: Validity and reliability of a new measure of neurobehavioural disability and social handicap. *Brain Injury*, 25, 83–100.

Alderman, N., Burgess, P.W., Knight, C. & Henman, C. (2003). Ecological validity of a simplified version of the multiple errand test. *J Int Neuropsychological Society*, 9, 31–44.

Bajo, A. & Nathaniel-James, D. (2001). *The Hayling and Brixton Tests of Dysexecutive Syndrome. What do they measure in everyday life?* Poster 4th World Congress on Brain Injury, Turin, Italy.

Bechara, A., Damasio, A.R., Damasio, H. & Anderson, S.W. (1994). Insensitivity to future consequences following damage to human prefrontal cortex. *Cognition*, 50, 7–15.

Bechara, A., Damasio, H., Damasio, A.R. (2000). Emotion, decision making and the orbitofrontal cortex. *Cereb Cortex*, 10, 295–307.

Bigler, E.D. (1988). Frontal lobe damage and neuropsychological assessment. *Arch Clin Neuropsychol.*, 3, 279–297.

Bowman, C.H. & Turnbull, O.H. (2004). Emotion-based learning on a simplified card game: The Iowa & Bangor gambling tasks. *Brain and Cognition*, 55(2), 277–282.

Burgess, P.W. (2000). Strategy application disorder. The role of the frontal lobes in human multitasking. *Psychol Res.*, 13, 25–42.

Burgess, P. (2003). Assessment of executive function. In: Halligan, P.W., Kishka, U., Marshall, J.C., eds. *Handbook of Clinical Neuropsychology*. Oxford: Oxford University Press, pp. 302–322.

Burgess, P.W. & Shallice, T. (1997). *The Hayling and Brixton Tests*. Bury St Edmunds, England: Thames Valley Test Company Limited.

Burgess, P.W. & Alderman, N. (2003). Assessment and rehabilitation of the dysexecutive syndrome. In: Goldstein, L. & McNeil, J.E., eds. *Clinical Neuropsychology*. Chichester, UK: Wiley, pp. 185–211.

Burgess, P.W., Alderman, N., Evans, J., Emslie, H. & Wilson, B.A. (1998). The ecological validity of tests of executive function. *J Int Neuropsychol Soc.*, 4, 547–558.

Burgess, P.W., Veitch, E., de Lacy Costello, A. & Shallice, T. (2000). The cognitive and neuroanatomical correlates of multitasking. *Neuropsychologia*, 38, 848–863.

Cotrena, C., Branco, L.D., Zimmermann, N., Cardoso, C.O., Grassi-Oliveira, R. & Fonseca, R.P. (2014). Impaired decision-making after traumatic brain injury: The Iowa Gambling Task. *Brain Inj.*, 28(8), 1070–1075.

Critchfield, T.S. & Kollins, S.H. (2001). Temporal discounting: Basic research and the analysis of socially important behavior. *J Appl Behav Anal.*, Spring 34(1), 101–122.

Doherty, T., Barker, L. A., Denniss, R., Jalil, A. & Beer, M.D. (2015). The cooking task: Making a meal of executive functions. *Frontiers in Behavioral Neuroscience*, 9, 1–23.

Draper, K. & Ponsford, J. (2009). Long-term outcome following traumatic brain injury: A comparison of subjective reports by those injured and their relatives. *Neuropsychol Rehabil.*, 19, 645–661.

Duncan, J., Burgess, P. & Emslie, H. (1995). Fluid intelligence after frontal lobe lesions. *Neuropsychologia*, 33, 261–268.

Eslinger, P.J. & Damasio, A.R. (1985). Severe disturbance of higher cognition after bilateral frontal lobe ablation: Patient EVR. *Neurology*, 35, 1731–1741.

Fortin, S., Godbout, L. & Braun, C.M. (2003). Cognitive structure of executive deficits in frontally lesioned head trauma patients performing activities of daily living. *Cortex*, 39, 273–291.

Fuster, J.M. (2001). The prefrontal cortex – an update: time is of the essence. *Neuron.*, 30, 319–333.

Gilbert, S.J. & Burgess, P.W. (2008). Executive function. *Current Biology*, 18(3), 12 February, 110–114.

Jansari, A.S., Devlin A., Agnew, R., Akesson, K., Murphy, L. & Leadbetter, T. (2014). Ecological assessment of executive functions: A new virtual reality paradigm. *Brain Impairment*, 15, 71–87.

Johnson, M.W. & Bickel, W.K. (2002). Within-subject comparison of real and hypothetical money rewards in delay discounting. *J Exp Anal Behav.*, 77, 129–146.

Klapproth, F. (2011). Temporal decision making in simultaneous timing. *Front Integr Neurosci.*, Oct 28, 5, 71. doi: 10.3389/fnint.2011.00071.

Knight, C., Alderman, N. & Burgess, P.W. (2002). Development of a simplified version of the multiple errands test for use in hospital settings. *Neuropsychol Rehab.*, 12, 231–255.

Lezak, M.D. (1983). *Neuropsychological Assessment*. New York: Oxford University Press.

Lezak, M.D. (1995). *Neuropsychological Assessment*. (2nd ed.). New York: Oxford University Press.

Lezak, M.D., Howieson, D.B. & Loring, D.W. (2004). *Neuropsychological Assessment* (4th ed.), New York: Oxford University Press.

Luria, A.R. (1973). *The Working Brain*. London: Penguin.

Manes, F., Sahakian, B., Clark, L., Rogers, R., Antoun, N., Aitken, M. & Robbins, T. (2002). Decision-making processes following damage to the prefrontal cortex. *Brain*, 125, 624–639.

Nathaniel-James, D.A., Fletcher, P. & Frith, C.D. (1997). The functional anatomy of verbal initiation and suppression using the Hayling Test. *Neuropsychologia*, Apr, 35(4), 559–566.

Newcombe, F. & Artioli I Fortuny, L.A. (1979). Problems and perspectives in the evaluation of psychological deficits after cerebral lesions. *International Journal of Rehabilitation Medicine*, 1, 182–192.

Norris, G. & Tate, R.L. (2000). The Behavioural Assessment of the Dysexecutive Syndrome (BADS): Ecological, concurrent and construct validity. *Neuropsychol Rehabil.*, 10, 33–45.

Ponsford, J., Sloan, S. & Snow, S. (1995). *Traumatic Brain Injury. Rehabilitation for Everyday Adaptive Living*. East Sussex, UK: Lawrence Erlbaum Associates.

Rabbitt, P. (1997). Do "frontal tests" measure executive function? Issues of assessment and evidence from fluency tests. In: Rabbitt, P., ed., *Methodology of Frontal and Executive Function*. Hove: Psychology Press, pp. 191–214.

Rand, D., Basha-Abu Rukan, S., Weiss, P.L. & Katz, N. (2009). Validation of the virtual MET as an assessment tool for executive functions. *Neuropsychol. Rehabil.*, 19, 583–602.

Reverberi, C., Lavaroni, A., Gigli, G.L., Skrap, M. & Tim, S. (2005). Specific impairments of rule induction in different frontal lobe subgroups. *Neuropsychologia*, 43(3), 460–472.

Robertson, I.H., Ward, T., Ridgeway, V. & Nimmo-Smith, I. (1996). The structure of normal human attention: The test of everyday attention. *J Int Neuropsychol Soc.*, Nov, 2(6), 525–534.

Schneider, E. & Shiffrin, R.M. (1977). Controlled & automatic information processing: detection, search, and attention. *Psychological Review*, 84, 1, 1–66.

Shallice, T. & Burgess, P. W. (1991a). Deficits in strategy application following frontal lobe damage in man. *Brain*, 114, 727–741.

Shallice, T. & Burgess, P.W. (1991b). Higher-order cognitive impairments and frontal lobe lesions in man. In: Levin, H.S., Eisenberg, H.M., Benton, A.L., eds., *Frontal Lobe Function and Dysfunction*. New York: Oxford University Press, pp. 125–138.

Stokes, N. & Bajo, A. (2003). The relationship between general intelligence, performance on executive functioning tests and everyday executive function difficulties. *Brain Injury.*, 17, 174.

Stuss, D.T. & Benson, D.F. (1986). *The Frontal Lobes*. New York: Raven Press.

Stuss, D.T., Picton, T.W. & Alexander, M.P. (2001). Consciousness, self-awareness and the frontal lobes. In: Salloway, S.P., Malloy, P.F. & Duffy, J.D., eds., *The Frontal Lobes and Neuropsychiatric Illness.* Washington: American Psychiatric Publishing, pp. 101–109.

Stuss, D.T. & Alexander, M.P. (2007). Is there a dysexecutive syndrome? *Philosophical Transactions B. The Royal Society,* 362, 901–905.

Tanguay, A.N., Davidson, P.S., Guerrero Nuñez, K. & Ferland, M.B. (2014). Cooking breakfast after a brain injury. *Front. Behav. Neurosci.,* 8, 272.

Teuber, H.L. (1964). The riddle of frontal lobe functions in man. In: Warren, J.M., Akert, K., eds., *The Frontal Granular Cortex and Behaviour.* New York: McGraw Hill, pp. 410–444.

Tranel, D. (2002). Emotion, decision making, and the ventromedial prefrontal cortex. In: Stuss, D.T. & Knight, R.T., *Principles of the Frontal Lobe.* New York: Oxford University Press.

Walsh, K.W. (1985). *Understanding Brain Damage: A Primer of Neuropsychological Evaluation.* London: Longman Group Ltd.

Wilson, B.A., Alderman, N., Burgess, P.W., Emslie, H. & Evans J.J. (1996). *Behavioural Assessment of the Dysexecutive Syndrome.* Bury St. Edmunds: Thames Valley Test Company.

Wilson, B.A., Evans, J.J., Emslie, H., Alderman, N. & Burgess, P. (1998). The development of an ecologically valid test for assessing patients with a dysexecutive syndrome. *Neuropsychological Rehabilitation,* 8(3), 213–228.

Wood, J.N. & Grafman, J. (2003). Human prefrontal cortex: Processing and representational perspectives. *Nat Rev Neurosci.,* 4, 139–147.

Wood, R.Ll. & Rutterford, N. (2004). Relationships between measured cognitive ability and reported psychosocial activity after bilateral frontal lobe injury: An 18 year follow-up. *Neuropsychol Rehabil.,* 14, 329–350.

Wood, R.Ll. & Liossi, C. (2006). The ecological validity of executive tests in a severely brain injured sample. *Arch Clin Neuropsychol.,* 21, 429–437.

Wood, R.Ll. & Liossi, C. (2007). The relationship between general intellectual ability and performance on ecologically valid tests in a severe brain injury sample. *J Int Neuropsychol Soc.,* 13, 90–98.

Wood, R.Ll., Alderman, N. & Williams, C. (2008). Assessment of neurobehavioural disability: A review of existing measures and recommendations for a comprehensive assessment tool. *Brain Injury,* 22, 905–918.

Wood, R.Ll. & McHugh, L. (2013). Decision making after traumatic brain injury: A temporal discounting paradigm. *J Int Neuropsychol Soc.,* 19, 1–8.

8

NEUROIMAGING IN THE EVALUATION OF NEUROBEHAVIOURAL DISABILITY AND SOCIAL HANDICAP FOLLOWING TRAUMATIC BRAIN INJURY

Erin Bigler

A basic premise for a neuroimaging chapter on the relation of brain imaging findings to neurobehavioural disability (NBD) and social handicap following traumatic brain injury (TBI) is that where damage occurs in the brain makes a difference. An additional basic premise is that neuroimaging methods can identify neural systems that underlie social-emotional functioning where damage relates to NBD and social handicap. A third premise is that neuroimaging identified pathology that involves social-emotional neural systems provides objective support that deficits in neurobehavioural functioning relate to the TBI.

It may seem overly simple to start off with such basic statements but there are two factors why this chapter begins with such fundamental declarations. First, the topic for this chapter charts new territory. If one enters the terms "neuroimaging", "neuro-behavioural disability" and "TBI" into a search of National Library of Medicine, there is not a single article identified that use all those terms in combination. There is considerable research on neuroimaging variables as predictors of outcome from TBI (Cristofori & Levin, 2015), but little of this research has focused on neurobehavioural disability and social functioning.

Second, understanding the brain's role in social-emotional functioning was mostly overlooked until the mid to late twentieth century. Not until 30 years ago did neuropsychiatric disorders become linked with neurobehavioural disability in schizophrenia, autism, anxiety and mood-based disorders. Adolphs (1999) seminal paper on "Social Cognition and the Human Brain" provided a foundation for inte-grating neuroanatomy, neuroimaging and social-emotional functioning in both the "normal" as well as injured brain. From Adolphs' writings on this topic excellent heuristic models on the social-emotional and neural bases of social functioning emerged as summarized in Figure 8.1 from Adolphs (2009). The role that neuro-imaging played in bringing this about cannot be overstated because prior to

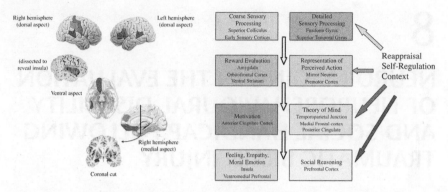

FIGURE 8.1 Key cortical and subcortical structures that form a social brain network. Used with permission from Adolphs (2009).

contemporary neuroimaging there were no methods to noninvasively examine the brain and behaviour in the living individual.

Brain regions involved in social cognition and emotional functioning as outlined in Figure 8.1 overlap with regions most likely damaged following TBI, as shown in Figure 8.2 from Yeates et al. (2007) using a technique referred to as voxel-based morphometry (VBM). There is substantial overlap in areas vulnerable to damage and those brain regions involved in social-emotional functioning. The VBM analysis based on MRI studies obtained more than a year post injury, show in red the locations where brain reductions in grey matter voxels occurred, an indication of atrophy. The results are from a mixed group of male and female TBI patients compared with age and sex-matched healthy controls with no history of TBI. The so-called social-emotional processing areas of the brain in Figure 8.1 overlap with the areas typically damaged by TBI. Furthermore, all of the subcortical areas listed by Adolphs in Figure 8.1 likewise, are vulnerable to the effects of TBI (Wilde et al., 2007).

Although presented as a model for social-emotional outcome from brain injury in children, the model proposed by Yeates et al. (2007) likewise applies to all ages with just slight modification. This model, presented in Figure 8.3, notes the inter-active effects of numerous variables shown by the bi-directional arrows between social information processing, social interaction and social adjustment, each of which may be affected by the location and type of pathology present (red arrow). Once injured, if the brain is slowed or hampered in processing and distinguishing what are important internal versus external social-emotional cues, significant dysregulation of social-emotional functioning may emerge, resulting in disability. The model was for children with TBI, so parental and family status plays a critical role. The family milieu and social support network, of course, continues to play a critical role for the individual with brain injury at any age (Holland & Schmidt, 2015; Winter, Moriarty, Robinson & Newhart, 2015). Accordingly, this model applies to adults with the substitution of "family and social support network" instead of "parenting style". Additionally, for an adult model, vocational support

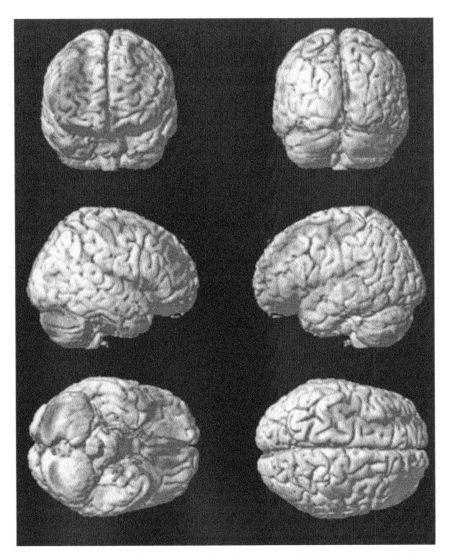

FIGURE 8.2 Red areas reflect regions of significant reduction in grey matter density, a marker of cortical atrophy compared with a control sample, adapted from Yeates et al. (2007). Used with permission from the American Psychological Association. Note the overlap of damage with the social brain network in Figure 8.1.

and functioning is another critical variable in outcome following TBI (see Wood, 2013) that is not in the model presented in Figure 8.3.

Interestingly, there is also another level of overlap involving the same brain regions outlined in Figures 8.1 and 8.2 that relates to both injury and age at the time of injury and that is the brain is constantly changing over the lifespan. In children,

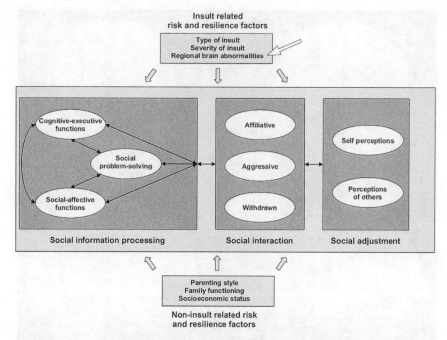

FIGURE 8.3   An integrative, heuristic model of social competence helpful in understanding the dimensions of social-emotional functioning that may be influenced by brain injury (from Yeates et al. (2007), used with permission from the American Psychological Association). The red arrow points to where in the social brain network the brain injury occurs and how it influences different attributes of social function.

a pruning process results in grey matter reductions in cortical volume that reflects healthy brain development, but by adulthood, age-mediated reductions reflect degeneration (Bigler, 2013b, 2015b; Spitz et al., 2013). Regardless of whether pruning or age-typical loss in grey matter, these changes also influence the social-emotional neural centres of the brain with the brain dynamically changing in response to environmental, genetic, and factors related to personal health and lifestyle issues. Clinically these ever-changing, age-mediated differences mean that each brain injury needs to be assessed not only in terms of where pathology may reside, but the stage of neurodevelopmental cycle at the time of injury. Furthermore, since emotional maturity and decision making abilities are intimately tied to these developmental processes (and frontotemporolimbic connectivity), TBI has often been characterized as disrupting age-appropriate emotional behaviour (Ryan et al., 2015).

In an attempt to address this complex topic from a neuroimaging perspective, discussion will first begin with the different types of magnetic resonance (MR) scans along with the types of lesions or abnormalities that can be defined by neuroimaging and their relevance to social outcome. From what has been presented in Figures 8.1 and 8.2, damage that results in identifiable pathology in frontal or temporal lobes and limbic system, or subcortically within the thalamus and/or basal ganglia, will disrupt network connectivity of these regions with other brain regions (see Hayes, Bigler & Verfaellie, 2015) and puts the patient at risk for NBD.

"Lesions" and their neuroimaging location in TBI and the social-emotional brain

The lesion term is in quotation marks because at the macroscopic level of detection afforded by neuroimaging, TBI lesions or abnormalities appear as a consequence of numerous factors, especially time post-injury where traumatic lesions may be only identifiable with certain kinds of imaging techniques and may be present at one stage post-injury and not at others (Bigler, 2001). This chapter will only cover structural imaging using CT and MR imaging (MRI) the most commonly used and universally accepted neuroimaging methods in TBI. Functional MRI (fMRI) has not yet found its way into routine clinical practice and therefore, will not be reviewed.

Acute neuroimaging findings. CT is the typical day of injury (DOI) scan because it is extremely fast (imaging can be completed within minutes) and has none of the restrictions associated with the strong magnetic fields used in performing MR studies. CT is excellent for identifying medically significant pathology that may require immediate intervention to manage skull fractures, haemorrhage, cerebral oedema or any combination of the former. Figure 8.4 is from a TBI patient where acute DOI CT showed a small haemorrhagic lesion in the frontal lobe. Figure 8.5 shows another patient who sustained skull fractures and various haemorrhagic lesions and cerebral oedema. These CT imaging studies establish DOI baseline pathology.

Some DOI abnormalities like oedema and certain aspects of haemorrhage may be transient (see Bigler, 2013a, 2015a) and sometimes the only abnormalities observed are on the acute imaging. Also important (see Figures 8.4, 8.6 and 8.7) is that what appears as an acute injury may have damaging effects far beyond where the focal lesion or abnormality occurred. Likewise, degenerative changes may occur subsequent to baseline findings so, when available, it is always important to compare acute with chronic imaging.

Chronic neuroimaging findings. Follow-up neuroimaging during the chronic phase of TBI is best done with MRI. The typical MR sequences clinically performed are shown in Figure 8.4 in a patient who sustained a severe TBI and include a) the T1-weighted image for anatomical localization (and as will be discussed later, for image quantification), b) T2-weighted imaging that is particularly sensitive in depicting cerebrospinal fluid (CSF), c) susceptibility weighted imaging (SWI) which is particularly sensitive to prior haemorrhage, and d) the fluid attenuated inversion recovery (FLAIR) sequence, which is especially sensitive in detecting white matter signal abnormalities. Additional details about clinical neuroimaging and these MR sequences in TBI can be found in Bodanapally et al. (2015).

The DOI CT scan in Figure 8.4 shows a small haemorrhage in the left frontal lobe (red arrow) but no detectable haemorrhagic lesion in the right frontal lobe.

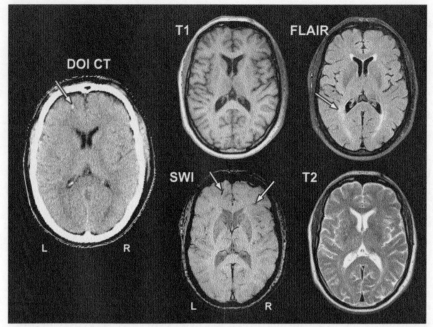

FIGURE 8.4 Day-of-injury (DOI) CT scan (on the left) compared with two years' post-injury MRI studies on the right. Fluid attenuated inversion recovery (FLAIR) shows white matter hypointense signal abormnalities (bright white) including deep white matter (red arrow) changes in the occipitotemporal white matter. Susceptibility weighted imaging (SWI) detects prior haemorrhagic lesions where the red arrows point to identifiable regions where residual haemorrhage from the TBI can be identified. T2-weighted imaging is best for differentiating cerebrospinal fluid (CSF) spaces as well as abnormal tissue changes.

However, on follow-up MRI the prior left frontal haemorrhage is not only detected but there is also indication of prior haemorrhage in the right frontal region and elsewhere (see Figure 8.6). When the SWI scan is searched, there are actually numerous haemorrhagic lesions scattered throughout the brain, especially in the frontal lobe region. In TBI, presence of SWI-defined haemorrhagic lesion is a marker for diffuse axonal injury (DAI, Beauchamp et al., 2011; Di Ieva et al., 2015), which is a subset of traumatic axonal injury (TAI) reflected as reduced white matter volume and FLAIR hyperintense signal abnormalities in conventional MRI studies (Bigler, 2015b; Hayes et al., 2015). Since TAI/DAI pathologies are associated with general disability in those with TBI, the presence of SWI abnormalities has implications for being associated with greater residual cognitive and behavioural impairment (Adams et al., 2011). Some SWI abnormalities are likely not specific to haemorrhage since the shear-strain effects on blood vessels may stretch veins which

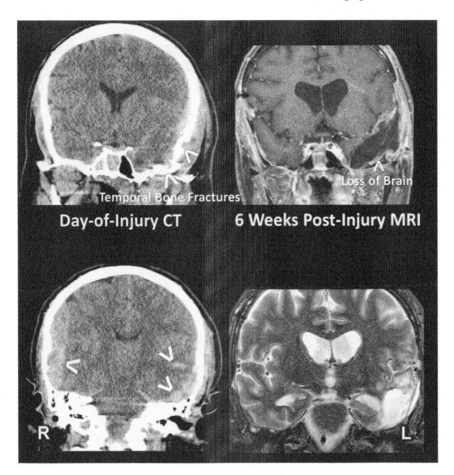

FIGURE 8.5 Images on the left are coronal CT obtained on DOI where the top (black arrows) point to depressed temporal bone fractures associated with bleeding on the surface (subdural) and within the brain. The coronal CT image on the bottom left is further back, which shows the ventricular system to be compressed, a sign of increased intracranial pressure with a large epidural haematoma on the right (black arrow) and the scattered haemorrhages on the left (as previously described). R = right. L = Left.

in turn may cause pooling of blood in the vessel, which also is detected by SWI (Di Ieva et al., 2015).

One of the advanced neuroimaging methods to explore white matter integrity is diffusion tensor imaging (DTI, Mueller, Lim, Hemmy & Camchong, 2015). DTI studies performed on the patient shown in Figures 8.4 and 8.6 show loss of white matter tracts in the anterior distribution of the corpus callosum (see Figure 8.7). Furthermore, as shown in Figure 8.6, whilst haemorrhages were scattered throughout both frontal lobes there were associated white matter changes on the FLAIR and

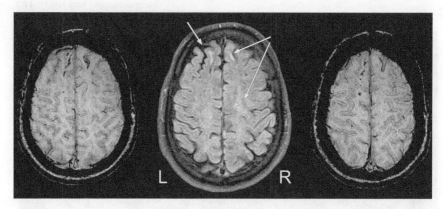

FIGURE 8.6 On the extreme left and right, these are examples of SWI findings in the same patient as in Figure 8.4 with a FLAIR image in the middle. Dark splotches reflect where prior shear-strain injury has occurred. On the FLAIR image, the left arrow points to a prominent frontal sulcus indicative of frontal atrophy with the red arrows on the right pointing to white matter hyperintensities, reflective of white matter damage. A hyperintense FLAIR abnormality is also adjacent to the red arrow on the left.

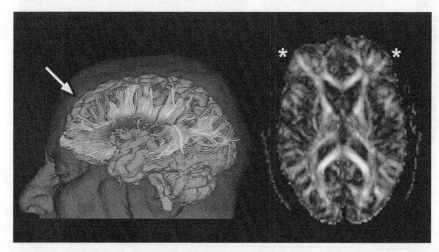

FIGURE 8.7 (Left) Diffusion tensor imaging (DTI) tractography superimposed on the 3-D lateral view of the brain. The major tracts that project across the corpus callosum typically fan out with an even array but the red arrow points to a major gap in the frontal projections that relate to the focal shearing pathology and residual haemorrhagic lesions as shown in Figures 8.4 and 8.6. (Right) Axial view of a DTI colour map in this patient where green reflects aggregate pathways oriented in an anterior-posterior direction, warm colours (orange-red) reflect side-to-side projecting tracts and blue are vertically oriented tracts. Compare the clarity and distribution of colours in the DTI map just beneath where the asterisks are located. In a non-damaged brain, the projecting directions as indicated by the colour and colour intensity should be similar and symmetric, which they are not in this patient, a reflection of damage.

frontal atrophy had evolved in association with the haemorrhagic lesions. Such findings infer loss of bi-hemispheric integration across both frontal lobes as well as probable disrupted frontal connectivity with the rest of the brain. Significant NBD was present in this patient in the form of lack of initiative, change in personality and temperament, mood dysregulation (major depression) and poor social judgement, all frequent sequelae of TBI implicating frontal pathology (Riggio & Wong, 2009). The damage from the TBI did not leave the patient with cognitive disability per se, but rather the residual deficits and disability would be best characterized as neurobehavioural.

While the case portrayed in Figure 8.4 focused on what may appear to be subtle pathology on the DOI scan, it turns out to just be the-tip-of-the-iceberg in regards to the extent of chronic lesions. In contrast, the case presented in Figure 8.5 starts off with massive pathology that includes all of the common forms of traumatic haemorrhages as observed in acute CT. The coronal DOI CT scan in Figure 8.5 shows presence of an epidural haematoma and in the opposite hemisphere, scattered subarachnoid haemorrhage, subdural and intraparenchymal as well as a very swollen (oedematous) brain (note the smallness of the lateral ventricles as an indication of increased intracranial pressure). By two months post-injury a coronal MRI scan at a somewhat similar level shows generalized ventricular dilation, an indication of brain atrophy, along with loss of temporal lobe tissue. These changes over time from the DOI to the chronic phase are often the best predictors of rehabilitation outcome and likely relate to NBD (Koponen, Taiminen, Hiekkanen & Tenovuo, 2011). From the DOI scan, if no additional imaging was available for review just that scan alone would be sufficient to conclude that frontotemporal damage occurred in key emotional-social brain areas. Not surprisingly, NBD occurred in this patient dominated by personality and affective changes.

There are some incredibly exciting advanced neuroimaging techniques on the horizon that will revolutionize how neuropsychology and medicine use neuro-imaging in assessing the TBI patient (Sullivan & Bigler, 2015). These techniques will permit more specific identifications and assessments of neural and cognitive-emotional-behavioural networks with high degrees of precision and quantification (see Bigler, 2015b). Complex network connectivity analyses are being established that likely will have important clinical utility in examining the damaged brain (Hayes et al., 2015). Where damage is located can be shown three-dimensionally, as was presented in Figure 8.7. In the future, size, shape, contour, thickness, connectivity strength and structural as well as metabolic integrity will likely be identifiable for any given structure, region or network of the brain.

Complexity of inferring disability from neuroimaging

Prior to the advent of CT and MRI, assessment of "higher cortical function" including emotional behaviour, was very much viewed from an assumed lesion-localization perspective (Margolin, 1991). The problem with that view was that outside of basic motor and sensory areas, and to a certain extent language, higher cortical functions were not organized by locale but rather by networks (Catani et al., 2012). If localization does not work as presupposed by earlier tradition in neuropsychology, it means that the size and localization of a lesion may not be that predictive of outcome. The case presented in Figure 8.8 is also from a severe TBI and demonstrates this point. The images are from the chronic stage and depict extensive temporal lobe encephalomalacia and atrophy, some generalized white matter pathology in frontotemporal regions bilaterally, pronounced right side hippocampal atrophy, and temporal lobe volume loss bilaterally. Despite this severe injury, months of inpatient and outpatient rehabilitation resulted in this patient having relatively good recovery of function, able to live in a mostly independent

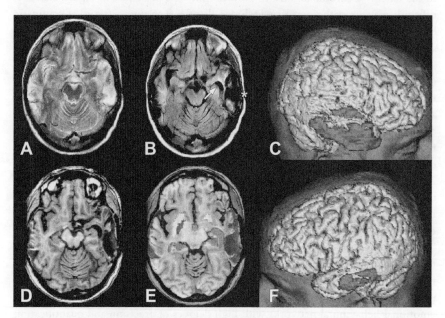

FIGURE 8.8   These MR images were obtained more than 2 years post-injury and show extensive bi-temporal lobe damage. (A) T2-weighted imaging showing excess CSF associated with encephalomalacia in both temporal lobes. (B) T1-weighted imaging showing the marked dilation of the right temporal horn associated with hippocampal atrophy. The dark area adjacent to the asterisk reflects absence of any viable brain tissue. (C) 3-D reconstruction of surface brain anatomy where the red reflects loss of right temporal lobe tissue. (D) FLAIR images that show hyperintense signal abnormalities with temporal and frontal lobe parenchyma. (E) Colour map highlighting where quantitative analyses were performed, including the cortical surface of the temporal lobes (red), ventricle (green), hippocampus (yellow), lenticular nucleus (pink and blue) with general brain tissue shown in flesh tone. (F) 3-D depiction of surface rendered view of the left hemisphere showing the location of cortical damage to the left temporal lobe.

fashion as well as return to full-time employment, although much less demanding and provided with accommodations. Mood dysregulation remained an important clinical issue treated with medication, as did impaired sleep. Reportedly, the patient was very high functioning prior to injury, which may have afforded the individual with some degree of cognitive reserve (Bigler & Stern, 2015). Compared with pre-injury levels of ability the patient was disabled, but in terms of criteria like the Glasgow Outcome Scale, this individual would not be classified as disabled. The point to make with this case is that lesions and their associated pathology as depicted in neuroimaging studies always require clinical correlation. There is not a 1:1 association with lesions and disability, except for when there is brainstem pathology, which has a high incidence level of permanent disability (Bigler et al., 2006).

Clearly the patient in Figure 8.8 had damage to the social-emotional brain network, yet not the level of neurobehavioral impairment that might be expected. TBI research is just beginning to examine resiliency factors in recovery from brain injury (McAllister, 2011; Yurgil et al., 2014). The interface between neuro-biologically based resiliency, response to neurorehabilitation, family, community and social support, as well as genetic factors relating to recovery and adaptation, and how these factors influence social-emotional brain networks, is simply unexplored territory.

As already mentioned, there is little systematic research relating neuroimaging findings specific to neurobehavioural disability that is relevant to neurobehavioral outcome after TBI. Some of this literature is based on case study findings (see Bigler et al., 2013). One exception is the study by Dennis et al. (2013), conducted in a paediatric TBI sample that examined lesion burden within social-emotional brain regions that make up what is referred to as theory of mind (ToM) networks. In the Dennis et al. study, lesions/abnormalities that involved the posterior cingulate/retrosplenial cortex, hippocampal formation, including entorhinal cortex and para-hippocampal cortex were associated with poorer ToM performance in children with TBI. Impaired ToM functioning is thought to be one of the factors associated with social disability following TBI (Bellerose et al., 2015; Spikman et al., 2012). Part of the reason for such relationships is that if the individual with brain damage is unable to detect social cues or empathize with what other individuals may be experiencing they will function awkwardly in social situations which may lead to rejection (Kelly, McDonald & Kellett, 2013). Although not specifically examined using neuroimaging, brain damage that alters social awareness and participation would probably increase the likelihood for NBD.

Theory of Mind (ToM) findings and social-emotional networks

ToM research may be very important in understanding social disability following TBI. Impaired self-awareness accompanies frontal lobe damage (Spikman & van der Naalt, 2010). The combination of impaired self-awareness with impaired ability to empathize with other humans in social situations or process the complexities of social behaviour in others can add to the complexity of neurobehavioural deficits,

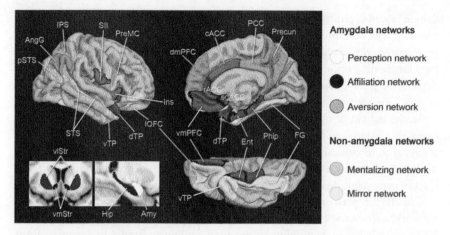

FIGURE 8.9 In this schematic, Bickart et al. (2014a) depict corticolimbic networks associated with social impairment in patients with frontotemporal dementia (see also Figure 8.10) used with permission from BMJ publishing. This is an open access publication with additional details concerning this figure at pubmed.gov and reference Bickart et al.

so understanding how TBI-related damage influences ToM functions is critical for our understanding the dimensions of NBD.

ToM studies involving individuals with TBI began about 15 years ago (see Channon & Crawford, 2000; Martin & McDonald, 2003) and have provided important insights into potential social-emotional deficits (Hynes, Stone & Kelso, 2011; McDonald, 2013). Bickart and colleagues (2014b) postulate that the amygdala acts as a major hub in brain networks that support social behaviour, as shown in Figure 8.9. Similarly, Ibañez and Manes (2012) show that the regional cortical degeneration in the behavioural variant of frontotemporal dementia specifically affects frontal polar, orbitofrontal, and anterolateral temporal regions, as depicted in Figure 8.11. Figures 8.1 and 8.2 point out that regions critical for ToM functions are the social-emotional regulatory regions of the brain, the same areas most likely damaged in TBI.

Accordingly, the behavioural variant of frontotemporal dementia provides an interesting framework to view neurobehavioural disability from TBI. The fronto-temporal degeneration in neurodegenerative disease results in frontotemporal atrophy and likely the frontotemporal atrophy from TBI results in similar disruptions of social-emotional networks that lead to neurobehavioural disability. In support of this connection, the history of TBI is associated with earlier onset dementia, including frontotemporal dementia (Deutsch, Mendez & Teng, 2015; LoBue et al., 2015; Wang et al., 2015), solidifying the importance of using the degenerative disease models as shown in Figures 8.9 and 8.10 since frontotemporal dementia results in indisputable NBD.

A   Social context network model   B   bvFTD atrophy pattern

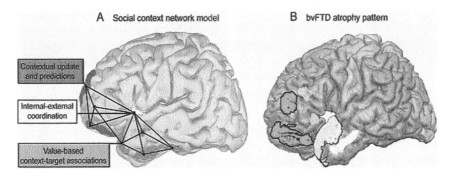

FIGURE 8.10   This network schematic from Ibañez and Manes (2012) depicts the Social Context Network Model (SCNM) in A where significant frontal and temporal lobe atrophy results in damage to these networks in the behavioural variant of frontotemporal dementia (bvFTD, B). Note the overlap of these frontotemporal regions that alter social-emotional behaviour in bvFTD and regions damaged in TBI (refer back to Figure 8.2). This is an open access publication with additional details concerning this figure at pubmed.gov and reference Ibañez and Manes (2012).

Depression, anxiety and depression following TBI

New onset or exacerbation of existing disorders of depression and anxiety are now well-established findings in patients who experience a TBI (Max, 2014; Rao et al., 2015), where presence of depression and anxiety relate to long-term disability (McMillan, Teasdale & Stewart, 2012). Unfortunately, there are no systematic neuroimaging studies that have examined the role of brain pathology in association with NBD. As reviewed by Max (2014), at least in a paediatric population, and by Rao et al. (2015) in an adult population, there is a relation between frontotemporal pathology and disorders of mood, anxiety and attention. Until a few years ago, there was a prevailing assumption that post-traumatic stress disorder (PTSD) did not coexist with TBI, but this has been roundly disproven; PTSD can be a very disabling condition, associated with TBI at all levels of injury severity (Tanev et al., 2014). Again, systematic studies involving neuroimaging, PTSD and NBD are just now being conducted (Wilde et al., 2015).

The heterogenity and diversity of the lesions in TBI

The Social Outcomes of Brain Injury in Kids (SOBIK) specifically examined social behaviour in paediatric TBI (Bigler et al., 2013; Dennis et al., 2013), although the focus was not on disability determination. Summation of this research showed that injury severity related to social impairment, but even some with mild TBI (mTBI) did not escape from having social-emotional sequelae (Yeates et al., 2013). From a neuroimaging perspective, however, the relations with pathology were generally

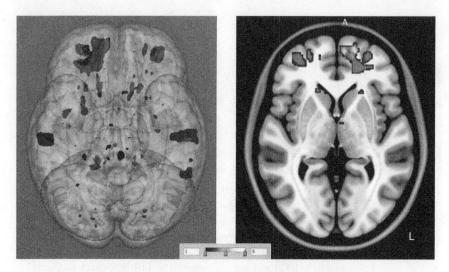

FIGURE 8.11 (Left) The scattered lesions indentified in the SOBIK investigation show the frontotemporal distribution of lesions but little overlap as shown in an axial template image of the brain on the right. (Right) Distribution of white matter lesions on the FLAIR sequence in the SOBIK investigation showing some overlap within the left (L = Left) frontal lobe, but the frequency bar shows that out of 72 children with TBI who were scanned, no more than 5 had overlapping areas of where white matter damage occurred in the frontal lobe.

weak, but as the reasons for this were explored it became apparent that a large component of this related to the diversity of lesion location in TBI.

Figure 8.11 shows the diverse distribution of MRI identified abnormalities in the SOBIK children with a frontotemporal orientation in lesion distribution but minimal overlap. What this means is that TBI does not result in any kind of uniform pathology common to all who sustain TBI. Indeed, each injury is unique to the individual. This likely means that no one lesion or abnormality will define whether NBD occurs or not.

Numerous methods are currently being developed to assess TBI in an integrated fashion, far beyond the size and location or even "lesion burden" (Bigler, 2015b; Hayes et al., 2015). A multimodality approach to image analysis will utilize numerous datapoints extracted from neuroimaging studies to identify where network pathology may reside (see Goh, Irimia, Torgerson & Horn, 2014). As network analysis techniques evolve, these hold great promise for neuroimaging methods to provide additional information about damage to the social brain network and development of NBD.

The "normal" scan and neurobehavioural disability following TBI

In terms of frequency of injury, mTBI dominates but the majority having no abnormal findings on conventional neuroimaging (Yuh, Hawryluk & Manley, 2014).

If one considers the resolution of current neuroimaging this is entirely understandable, since the typical conventional MRI is not done with sub-millimetre resolution. Since neural cells are measured in microns, pathology present at only a cellular level is below detection by conventional standards.

Clearly there are electrophysiological and advanced neuroimaging methods that show residual pathology in mTBI in the absence of conventional imaging findings (see Clark et al., 2015; Corradini & Persinger, 2014). There are currently no universally accepted clinical methods using advanced MRI techniques to consistently demonstrate relationships between disability and mTBI although very promising advances are being made (Bigler, 2013a, 2015a). The point to be made in this section is that there does not need to be neuroimaging "proof" of an abnormality for someone to have significant NBD. Someone who has experienced a clinically significant TBI NBD can occur in the absence of positive neuroimaging findings.

Uniqueness of each brain injury and the importance of "clinical correlation"

As impressive as some brain pathology may be when viewed from a neuroimaging perspective it may not be predictive of poor outcome (Bruce et al., 2015), as was shown in Figure 8.8. In this case, obvious structural damage could be shown but did not necessarily result in social and emotional changes that were profoundly disabling, at least at the time when evaluated. Each case has to be assessed on its own merits and at this point in time there is no unique structural pathology that un-equivocally relates to NBD. While the argument is made in this chapter that presence of structural damage to "social brain" areas provides some objectivity in support of evidence for damage to social-emotional regulatory centres of the brain, it nevertheless requires clinical correlation and clinician judgement to make that conclusion.

Returning to Figure 8.8, the patient did have cognitive problems and used electronic memory aids. A wonderfully supportive family helped the patient cope and provided social context and support. In other circumstances without this kind of support, given the extensiveness of damage, it would likely be that serious NBD would have resulted. Indeed, it may still be the case that because of changes over time the TBI patient in Figure 8.8 will have a lifetime of increased vulnerability for adverse neuropsychiatric outcome and onset of major NBD. Accordingly, disability determination in the TBI patient is not a one-time event as neurobehavioural status can change at any point in the patient's future.

Conclusions

At this point, there is not a definitive neuroimaging finding or image analysis technique that is specifically predictive of NBD. Nonetheless, neuroimaging has the capability of providing objective information where brain pathology may reside and whether damage involves areas in social-emotional networks of the brain related to

NBD. This still requires clinical correlation but given the complexities in making disability assessments, objectivity from neuroimaging studies represents a welcomed positive piece of information to add to the diagnostic process.

References

Adams, J. H., Jennett, B., Murray, L. S., Teasdale, G. M., Gennarelli, T. A. & Graham, D. I. (2011). Neuropathological findings in disabled survivors of a head injury. *J Neurotrauma, 28*(5), 701–709. doi: 10.1089/neu.2010.1733

Adolphs, R. (1999). Social cognition and the human brain. *Trends Cogn Sci, 3*(12), 469–479.

Adolphs, R. (2009). The social brain: Neural basis of social knowledge. *Annu Rev Psychol, 60*, 693–716. doi: 10.1146/annurev.psych.60.110707.163514

Beauchamp, M. H., Ditchfield, M., Babl, F. E., Kean, M., Catroppa, C., Yeates, K. O. & Anderson, V. (2011). Detecting traumatic brain lesions in children: CT versus MRI versus susceptibility weighted imaging (SWI). *J Neurotrauma, 28*(6), 915–927. doi: 10.1089/neu.2010.1712

Bellerose, J., Bernier, A., Beaudoin, C., Gravel, J. & Beauchamp, M. H. (2015). When injury clouds understanding of others: Theory of mind after mild TBI in preschool children. *J Int Neuropsychol Soc*, 1-11. doi: 10.1017/S1355617715000569

Bickart, K. C., Brickhouse, M., Negreira, A., Sapolsky, D., Barrett, L. F. & Dickerson, B. C. (2014a). Atrophy in distinct corticolimbic networks in frontotemporal dementia relates to social impairments measured using the Social Impairment Rating Scale. *J Neurol Neurosurg Psychiatry, 85*(4), 438–448. doi: 10.1136/jnnp-2012-304656

Bickart, K. C., Dickerson, B. C. & Barrett, L. F. (2014b). The amygdala as a hub in brain networks that support social life. *Neuropsychologia, 63*, 235–248. doi: 10.1016/j.neuropsychologia.2014.08.013

Bigler, E. D. (2001). Distinguished Neuropsychologist Award Lecture 1999. The lesion(s) in traumatic brain injury: implications for clinical neuropsychology. *Arch Clin Neuropsychol, 16*(2), 95–131.

Bigler, E. D. (2013a). Neuroimaging biomarkers in mild traumatic brain injury (mTBI). *Neuropsychol Rev, 23*(3), 169–209. doi: 10.1007/s11065-013-9237-2

Bigler, E. D. (2013b). Traumatic brain injury, neuroimaging, and neurodegeneration. *Front Hum Neurosci, 7*, 395. doi: 10.3389/fnhum.2013.00395

Bigler, E. D. (2015a). Neuropathology of mild traumatic brain injury: Correlation to neuro-cognitive and neurobehavioral findings. In F. H. P. Kobeissy (Ed.), *Brain Neurotrauma: Molecular, Neuropsychological, and Rehabilitation Aspects*. Boca Raton (FL): CRC Press/Taylor and Francis, Chapter 31.

Bigler, E. D. (2015b). Structural image analysis of the brain in neuropsychology using magnetic resonance imaging (MRI) techniques. *Neuropsychol Rev, 25*(3), 224–249. doi: 10.1007/s11065-015-9290-0

Bigler, E. D. & Stern, Y. (2015). Traumatic brain injury and reserve. *Handb Clin Neurol, 128*, 691–710. doi: 10.1016/B978-0-444-63521-1.00043-1

Bigler, E. D., Ryser, D. K., Gandhi, P., Kimball, J. & Wilde, E. A. (2006). Day-of-injury computerized tomography, rehabilitation status, and development of cerebral atrophy in persons with traumatic brain injury. *Am J Phys Med Rehabil, 85*(10), 793–806. doi: 10.1097/01.phm.0000237873.26250.e1

Bigler, E. D., Yeates, K. O., Dennis, M., Gerhardt, C. A., Rubin, K. H., Stancin, T., Taylor, G. H., Vannatta, K. (2013). Neuroimaging and social behavior in children after traumatic brain injury: findings from the Social Outcomes of Brain Injury in Kids (SOBIK) study. *NeuroRehabilitation, 32*(4), 707–720. doi: 10.3233/NRE-130896

Bodanapally, U. K., Sours, C., Zhuo, J. & Shanmuganathan, K. (2015). Imaging of traumatic brain injury. *Radiol Clin North Am, 53*(4), 695–715, viii. doi: 10.1016/j.rcl.2015.02.011

Bruce, E. D., Konda, S., Dean, D. D., Wang, E. W., Huang, J. H. & Little, D. M. (2015). Neuroimaging and traumatic brain injury: State of the field and voids in translational knowledge. *Mol Cell Neurosci, 66*(Pt B), 103–113. doi: 10.1016/j.mcn.2015.03.017

Catani, M., Dell'acqua, F., Bizzi, A., Forkel, S. J., Williams, S. C., Simmons, A., Murphy, D. G., Thiebaut de Schotten, M. (2012). Beyond cortical localization in clinico-anatomical correlation. *Cortex, 48*(10), 1262–1287. doi: 10.1016/j.cortex.2012.07.001

Channon, S. & Crawford, S. (2000). The effects of anterior lesions on performance on a story comprehension test: Left anterior impairment on a theory of mind-type task. *Neuropsychologia, 38*(7), 1006–1017.

Clark, A. L., Sorg, S. F., Schiehser, D. M., Bigler, E. D., Bondi, M. W., Jacobson, M. W., Jak, A. J. & Delano-Wood, L. (2015). White matter associations with performance validity testing in veterans with mild traumatic brain injury: The utility of biomarkers in complicated assessment. *J Head Trauma Rehabil.* doi: 10.1097/HTR.0000000000000183

Corradini, P. L. & Persinger, M. A. (2014). Spectral power, source localization and microstates to quantify chronic deficits from 'mild' closed head injury: correlation with classic neuropsychological tests. *Brain Inj, 28*(10), 1317–1327. doi: 10.3109/02699052.2014.916819

Cristofori, I. & Levin, H. S. (2015). Traumatic brain injury and cognition. *Handb Clin Neurol, 128*, 579–611. doi: 10.1016/B978-0-444-63521-1.00037-6

Dennis, M., Simic, N., Bigler, E. D., Abildskov, T., Agostino, A., Taylor, H. G., Rubin, K., Vannatta, K., Gerhardt, C. A., Stancin, T. & Yeates, K. O. (2013). Cognitive, affective, and conative theory of mind (ToM) in children with traumatic brain injury. *Dev Cogn Neurosci, 5*, 25–39. doi: 10.1016/j.dcn.2012.11.006

Deutsch, M. B., Mendez, M. F. & Teng, E. (2015). Interactions between traumatic brain injury and frontotemporal degeneration. *Dement Geriatr Cogn Disord, 39*(3–4), 143–153. doi: 10.1159/000369787

Di Ieva, A., Lam, T., Alcaide-Leon, P., Bharatha, A., Montanera, W. & Cusimano, M. D. (2015). Magnetic resonance susceptibility weighted imaging in neurosurgery: Current applications and future perspectives. *J Neurosurg*, 1–13. doi: 10.3171/2015.1.JNS142349

Goh, S. Y., Irimia, A., Torgerson, C. M. & Horn, J. D. (2014). Neuroinformatics challenges to the structural, connectomic, functional and electrophysiological multimodal imaging of human traumatic brain injury. *Front Neuroinform, 8*, 19. doi: 10.3389/fninf.2014.00019

Hayes, J. P., Bigler, E. D. & Verfaellie, M. (2015). Traumatic brain injury as a disorder of brain connectivity. *J Int Neuropsychol Soc, 22*(2), 120–37. doi: 10.1017/S13556 17715000740

Holland, J. N. & Schmidt, A. T. (2015). Static and dynamic factors promoting resilience following traumatic brain injury: A brief review. *Neural Plast, 2015*, 902802. doi: 10.1155/2015/902802

Hynes, C. A., Stone, V. E. & Kelso, L. A. (2011). Social and emotional competence in traumatic brain injury: New and established assessment tools. *Soc Neurosci, 6*(5–6), 599–614. doi: 10.1080/17470919.2011.584447

Ibañez, A. & Manes, F. (2012). Contextual social cognition and the behavioral variant of frontotemporal dementia. *Neurology, 78*(17), 1354–1362. doi: 10.1212/WNL.0b013e 3182518375

Kelly, M., McDonald, S. & Kellett, D. (2013). The psychological effects of ostracism following traumatic brain injury. *Brain Inj, 27*(13–14), 1676–1684. doi: 10.3109/ 02699052.2013.834381

Koponen, S., Taiminen, T., Hiekkanen, H. & Tenovuo, O. (2011). Axis I and II psychiatric disorders in patients with traumatic brain injury: A 12-month follow-up study. *Brain Inj, 25*(11), 1029–1034. doi: 10.3109/02699052.2011.607783

LoBue, C., Wilmoth, K., Cullum, C. M., Rossetti, H. C., Lacritz, L. H., Hynan, L. S., Hart, J. Jr. & Womack, K. B. (2015). Traumatic brain injury history is associated with earlier age of onset of frontotemporal dementia. *J Neurol Neurosurg Psychiatry*. doi: 10.1136/jnnp-2015-311438

Margolin, D. I. (1991). Cognitive neuropsychology. Resolving enigmas about Wernicke's aphasia and other higher cortical disorders. *Arch Neurol, 48*(7), 751–765.

Martin, I. & McDonald, S. (2003). Weak coherence, no theory of mind, or executive dysfunction? Solving the puzzle of pragmatic language disorders. *Brain Lang, 85*(3), 451–466.

Max, J. E. (2014). Neuropsychiatry of pediatric traumatic brain injury. *Psychiatr Clin North Am, 37*(1), 125–140. doi: 10.1016/j.psc.2013.11.003

McAllister, T. W. (2011). Neurobiological consequences of traumatic brain injury. *Dialogues Clin Neurosci, 13*(3), 287–300.

McDonald, S. (2013). Impairments in social cognition following severe traumatic brain injury. *J Int Neuropsychol Soc, 19*(3), 231–246. doi: 10.1017/S1355617712001506

McMillan, T. M., Teasdale, G. M. & Stewart, E. (2012). Disability in young people and adults after head injury: 12–14 year follow-up of a prospective cohort. *J Neurol Neurosurg Psychiatry, 83*(11), 1086–1091. doi: 10.1136/jnnp-2012-302746

Mueller, B. A., Lim, K. O., Hemmy, L. & Camchong, J. (2015). Diffusion MRI and its role in neuropsychology. *Neuropsychol Rev, 25*(3), 250–271. doi: 10.1007/s11065-015-9291-z

Rao, V., Koliatsos, V., Ahmed, F., Lyketsos, C. & Kortte, K. (2015). Neuropsychiatric disturbances associated with traumatic brain injury: A practical approach to evaluation and management. *Semin Neurol, 35*(1), 64–82. doi: 10.1055/s-0035-1544241

Riggio, S. & Wong, M. (2009). Neurobehavioral sequelae of traumatic brain injury. *Mt Sinai J Med, 76*(2), 163–172. doi: 10.1002/msj.20097

Ryan, N. P., Catroppa, C., Cooper, J. M., Beare, R., Ditchfield, M., Coleman, L., Silk, T., Crossley, L., Beauchamp, M. H. & Anderson, V. A. (2015). The emergence of age-dependent social cognitive deficits after generalized insult to the developing brain: A longitudinal prospective analysis using susceptibility-weighted imaging. *Hum Brain Mapp, 36*(5), 1677–1691. doi: 10.1002/hbm.22729

Spikman, J. M. & van der Naalt, J. (2010). Indices of impaired self-awareness in traumatic brain injury patients with focal frontal lesions and executive deficits: Implications for outcome measurement. *J Neurotrauma, 27*(7), 1195–1202. doi: 10.1089/neu.2010.1277

Spikman, J. M., Timmerman, M. E., Milders, M. V., Veenstra, W. S. & van der Naalt, J. (2012). Social cognition impairments in relation to general cognitive deficits, injury severity, and prefrontal lesions in traumatic brain injury patients. *J Neurotrauma, 29*(1), 101–111. doi: 10.1089/neu.2011.2084

Spitz, G., Bigler, E. D., Abildskov, T., Maller, J. J., O'Sullivan, R. & Ponsford, J. L. (2013). Regional cortical volume and cognitive functioning following traumatic brain injury. *Brain Cogn, 83*(1), 34–44. doi: 10.1016/j.bandc.2013.06.007

Sullivan, E. V. & Bigler, E. D. (2015). Neuroimaging's role in neuropsychology: Introduction to the special issue of neuropsychology review on neuroimaging in neuropsychology. *Neuropsychol Rev, 25*(3), 221–223. doi: 10.1007/s11065-015-9296-7

Tanev, K. S., Pentel, K. Z., Kredlow, M. A. & Charney, M. E. (2014). PTSD and TBI co-morbidity: Scope, clinical presentation and treatment options. *Brain Inj, 28*(3), 261–270. doi: 10.3109/02699052.2013.873821

Wang, H. K., Lee, Y. C., Huang, C. Y., Liliang, P. C., Lu, K., Chen, H. J., Li, Y. C. & Tsai, K. J. (2015). Traumatic brain injury causes frontotemporal dementia and TDP-43 proteolysis. *Neuroscience, 300*, 94–103. doi: 10.1016/j.neuroscience.2015.05.013

Wilde, E. A., Bigler, E. D., Hunter, J. V., Fearing, M. A., Scheibel, R. S., Newsome, M. R., Johnson, J. L., Bachevalier, J., Li, X. & Levin, H. S. (2007). Hippocampus, amygdala, and basal ganglia morphometrics in children after moderate-to-severe traumatic brain injury. *Dev Med Child Neurol, 49*(4), 294–299. doi: 10.1111/j.1469-8749.2007.00294.x

Wilde, E. A., Bouix, S., Tate, D. F., Lin, A. P., Newsome, M. R., Taylor, B. A., Stone, J. R., Montier, J., Gandy, S. E., Biekman, B., Shenton, M. E. & York, G. (2015). Advanced neuroimaging applied to veterans and service personnel with traumatic brain injury: state of the art and potential benefits. *Brain Imaging Behav.* doi: 10.1007/s11682-015-9444-y

Winter, L., Moriarty, H., Robinson, K. M. & Newhart, B. (2015). Rating competency in everyday activities in patients with TBI: Clinical insights from a close look at patient-family differences. *Disabil Rehabil,* 1–11. doi: 10.3109/09638288.2015.1077531

Wood, R. L. (2013). Recognising and assessing neurobehavioural disability after traumatic brain injury. *NeuroRehabilitation, 32*(4), 699–706. doi: 10.3233/NRE-130895

Yeates, K. O., Bigler, E. D., Dennis, M., Gerhardt, C. A., Rubin, K. H., Stancin, T., Taylor, H. G. & Vannatta, K. (2007). Social outcomes in childhood brain disorder: a heuristic integration of social neuroscience and developmental psychology. *Psychol Bull, 133*(3), 535-556. doi: 10.1037/0033-2909.133.3.535

Yeates, K. O., Gerhardt, C. A., Bigler, E. D., Abildskov, T., Dennis, M., Rubin, K. H., Stancin, T., Gerry Taylor, H. G. & Vannatta, K. (2013). Peer relationships of children with traumatic brain injury. *J Int Neuropsychol Soc, 19*(5), 518–527. doi: 10.1017/S1355617712001531

Yuh, E. L., Hawryluk, G. W. & Manley, G. T. (2014). Imaging concussion: A review. *Neurosurgery, 75 Suppl 4,* S50–63. doi: 10.1227/NEU.0000000000000491

Yurgil, K. A., Barkauskas, D. A., Vasterling, J. J., Nievergelt, C. M., Larson, G. E., Schork, N. J., Litz, B. T., Nash, W. P. & Baker, D. G., Marine Resiliency Study Team (2014). Association between traumatic brain injury and risk of posttraumatic stress disorder in active-duty Marines. *JAMA Psychiatry, 71*(2), 149–157. doi: 10.1001/jamapsychiatry.2013.3080

PART III

Treatment and rehabilitation

9

EXECUTIVE IMPAIRMENTS

Jon Evans

Introduction

The construct of executive functions is broad. Packwood, Hodgetts, and Tremblay (2011) conducted a latent semantic analysis (LSA) on the definitions of executive functions in 60 highly cited papers. LSA is a statistical technique used in the study of language to examine the semantic overlap between words and passages of text. Across the 60 papers they found 68 terms for executive functions and 98 tasks used to assess them. The LSA reduced the number of terms to 50, which clearly still reflects a very large number of different definitions. The most common terms used were planning, working memory, set-shifting, inhibition and fluency. A hierarchical cluster analysis was also used to examine which tests were used to examine which executive functions, which reduced the 50 different terms to a set of 18 constructs. But as Packwood et al. note, this is still 'too many abilities, definitions, and tasks to provide any meaningful taxonomy' (p. 461).

Historically, it is accepted that at least some executive functions are supported by the frontal lobes. One of the most influential recent models in support of this is that of Stuss (2007; 2011). In his model, Stuss proposed that the prefrontal regions of the frontal lobes have four different (but related) functions: (1) *executive cognitive functions* are high level cognitive skills (planning, monitoring, energising, switching, inhibiting) that are involved in the control of more automatic functions and are mediated by the lateral pre-frontal cortex. Stuss divides these according to hemisphere. The primary function of the left dorsolateral pre-frontal cortex is referred to as *task-setting*, broadly equating to the concept of planning. The primary function of the right dorsolateral pre-frontal cortex is *monitoring*; (2) *Behavioural-emotional self-regulatory functions* are mediated by the ventral pre-frontal cortex and involve integrating the motivational, reward/risk, emotional, and social aspects of behaviours; (3) *Energisation regulating functions* are dependent upon superior medial frontal regions and deficits here result in apathy or abulia; (4) The frontal polar regions, particularly on the right, have a role in '*metacognitive aspects of human nature*' (Stuss, 2011). This latter construct is rather loosely defined, with Stuss linking it in part to Burgess' Gateway hypothesis of Area 10 (Burgess, Gilbert, & Dumontheil, 2007). The Gateway hypothesis refers to the function of shifting attention from the external world to internal goals and intentions in order to regulate behaviour towards the effective achievement of intended goals. This system is critical for successful performance of prospective memory tasks. Stuss also refers to deficits in this region causing difficulties with theory of mind tasks, though the precise relationship between these concepts is not entirely clear.

The main components of the Stuss model map well onto the older model of Shallice and Burgess (1996), which in turn was an extension of the classic Norman and Shallice (1986) conceptualisation of the Supervisory Attention System (SAS), which Baddeley (1986) also equated with his concept of the central executive component of working memory. Shallice and Burgess (1996) describe the role of the SAS in terms of a series of processes relating to problem solving and behavioural regulation, or goal/task management. There are three broad components involving planning, initiation and monitoring/regulation.

Another highly cited model is that of Miyake et al. (2000) who conceptualised frontal lobe functions in terms of three systems including *shifting* (mental set), *inhibition* and *updating* (working memory). They derived these three constructs from a confirmatory factor analysis of data from the performance of a sample of healthy controls on a number of different tasks considered to make demands on frontal lobe executive functions, examples of which include the Wisconsin Card Sorting Test (which loaded on the shifting factor), Tower of Hanoi (which loaded on the inhibition factor) and a tone monitoring task (which loaded on the updating factor).

Whilst the concept of executive functions is clearly multifaceted and still evolving, this chapter will focus on the functions that are required for effective problem solving and goal/task management. Drawing on the models discussed above, the processes included are those necessary for planning, for initiating actions, and for monitoring actions against an intended goal.

Deficits in executive functions and their functional implications

Given that there are multiple executive functions, so there are a wide range of possible deficits and associated impacts on everyday living. In the same way that the term executive function is too broad to be helpful in understanding the cognitive processes encompassed by this term, so the terminology relating to deficits in executive functions is equally limited. The term dysexecutive syndrome was introduced by Baddeley in his 1986 book, *Working Memory*, and then used by Baddeley and Wilson (1988). Baddeley wanted to move away from the concept of a 'frontal lobe syndrome' to defining the types of problems that commonly arise from frontal lobe damage, not in terms of a shared anatomical location but in terms of common cognitive functions. Baddeley (1986) suggested this should be a stop-gap term, but it is clearly one that has stood the test of time. However, in terms of understanding the nature of deficits in specific processes, the term does not get us very far, because patients may present with widely varying forms of difficulties. We need therefore to be more specific in our formulation of specific processes that are impaired and the particular aspects of everyday functioning likely to be affected.

Impaired task setting/planning

People who do not, or cannot, plan may be perceived as impulsive, doing the first thing that comes to mind without thinking of the consequences. They are described as lacking judgement, being poor at decision making and are seen as disorganised – wasting large amounts of time because of not having planned ahead.

Evans (2008) describes the case of Steven, a 35-year-old businessman who suffered a severe head injury in a road traffic accident. His CT scan showed diffuse axonal injury and right frontal lobe contusions. His most striking problem was impulsivity. In situations where he was being given instructions he would begin a task before instructions had been fully explained, later having to stop and ask for help when he inevitably reached a point in the task that he did not know how to complete. He seemed unable to hold in mind complex instructions in order to plan actions. In social situations he tended to dominate conversations, where he tended to jump in to put over his point of view, failing to allow others their turn in the conversation.

Some people with planning difficulties are not impulsive and may cope with routine everyday tasks independently, but because they find it difficult to plan they may be limited to following everyday routines with habitual, familiar activities. They do very little spontaneously unless triggered by routine and habit, or prompted by an external source. Depending on a person's pre-morbid experience and knowledge, this may mean a person can complete complex (previously familiar) tasks, but novel situations are problematic (see Shallice & Burgess, 1991). The problem of being able to carry out routine (complex) tasks but having major difficulties with novel problems was also very nicely illustrated in von Cramon's and Matthes-von Cramon's (1994) case of a doctor who suffered a severe head injury during his medical training. Despite being able to complete his training, he found it difficult to deal with novel problems, and non-routine, or changing, situations.

Impaired initiation

People who have difficulties with initiation fail to translate intention into action. If prompted they may be able to carry out tasks, but they cannot get started – they find it very difficult to self-initiate actions. They are highly dependent on others to prompt them to carry out everyday tasks, particularly those that are not very routine or habitual (which are typically prompted by something in their environment). Behaviourally this is somewhat similar to the difficulties arising from a failure to plan ahead described in the previous section, but with these patients the inability to initiate actions is more marked and may occur even when a person clearly intends to act. Patient RP (Evans, Emslie, & Wilson, 1998; Fish et al., 2008) is an example of someone with a major difficulty with initiation. RP had a stroke affecting the medial frontal lobe bilaterally. She had a combination of severe initiation difficulties, and attentional problems, which meant that she found it difficult to initiate actions, but she was also frequently distracted by things in her environment that were irrelevant to her current task. Thus she was someone with both initiation and monitoring difficulties.

Impaired monitoring

People who fail to monitor and regulate their behaviour may drift off-task and so again may be perceived as disorganised and unable to follow through with intentions. This may arise from a failure to notice errors (a basic attentional monitoring deficit) or a failure to keep in mind the main thing they are trying to achieve and use this memory to stay on task. In everyday task situations they may be distracted by something unrelated to the main goal they are trying to achieve and so fail to complete things effectively, or may simply forget to switch from one thing to another, despite apparently remembering the overall task goal. This 'goal neglect' (Duncan, 1986), is similar to Luria's description of patients with frontal lobe damage in which he described how an intention (arising from a verbal instruction to do something) remained in their memory but failed to control their actions (Luria, 1966; 1973). This difficulty may result in reports of forgetting to do things (prospective memory difficulties) that arise not because a person has forgotten what has to be done, but because of a failure to keep the intention active so that it is implemented at the right time. This problem may result from lesions in the rostral pre-frontal cortex, or Brodmann Area 10. Burgess, Gilbert, and Dumontheil (2007) have demonstrated that Area 10 is activated in prospective memory tasks in which participants are doing one task, but have to remember to do something different later in the task (akin to the idea of remembering to buy milk on the way home from work). This leads to the development of Burgess' Gateway hypothesis, which suggests that different regions of Area 10 are responsible for allocating attention to either the external world, or to self-generated or self-maintained thoughts (e.g. intentions). The supervisory attentional gateway 'operates as a "gateway" between the internal mental life that occurs independently of environmental stimuli, and the mental life that is associated with interaction with the outside world' (Burgess, Gilbert, & Dumontheil, 2007, p. 292).

In social conversational situations, patients with monitoring difficulties may be tangential because they cannot keep in mind the main topic of a conversation. Alternatively, they may dominate conversations, failing to take turns, because they do not notice the social cues that signal the points in a conversation when it is time to stop talking and hand over the conversation to someone else.

Rehabilitation of executive impairments

The evidence base and clinical guidelines

The evidence base relating to cognitive rehabilitation interventions has grown to the point that systematic reviews have been undertaken and clinical guidelines written. This includes interventions specifically relating to the rehabilitation of executive deficits. That said, the quality of cognitive rehabilitation research studies is acknowledged to be poor and so confidence in the results, in terms of implications for clinical practice, is limited. This is perhaps best reflected in the one Cochrane review of interventions for the rehabilitation of executive dysfunction in people with stroke and other forms of acquired brain injury. Chung et al. (2013) reported that 8280 potentially relevant studies were initially identified from searches, but after application of the inclusion/exclusion criteria (e.g. limiting included studies to randomised controlled trials) only 19 studies were included (with 907 participants), of which only 13 could provide data for meta-analysis. Not surprisingly, given the broad construct of executive functions, a wide range of interventions was reflected in the included studies. Furthermore, Chung et al. set their primary outcome measure of interest to be an overall total score on two neuropsychological assessment batteries that examine executive functions – the Behavioural Assessment of the Dysexecutive Syndrome (Wilson et al., 1996) and the Hayling and Brixton (Burgess & Shallice, 1997). This choice of primary outcomes was perhaps not the best given the modest test-retest reliability of these measures. Indeed, most studies on rehabilitation outcome focus more on functional outcomes measures. However, wide variability in outcome measures across studies clearly meant that there was no obvious choice that would be reflected consistently in the literature. Perhaps inevitably then, Chung et al. concluded that there was 'insufficient high-quality evidence to reach any generalised conclusions about the effect of cognitive rehabilitation on executive function' (p. 2).

Other reviewers, however, have been more positive about the literature and have felt confident enough to draw conclusions for clinical practice. For example, Cicerone and colleagues completed a review of cognitive rehabilitation for traumatic brain injury and stroke literature, including studies of interventions for executive functioning, with the original review being updated twice, most recently in 2011 (Cicerone et al., 2011). Cicerone et al. (2011) made no recommendations in relation to stroke but concluded that there was sufficient evidence to recommend that 'meta-cognitive strategy training' focused on training self-monitoring and emotional regulation should be a practice standard for people with executive dysfunction after TBI. They said that training in formal problem-solving strategies and their application to everyday situations and functional activities is recommended during post-acute rehabilitation after TBI. Finally, they noted that group based interventions could also be considered. Several other systematic reviews have come to broadly the same conclusions (Boelen, Spikman, & Fasotti, 2011; Kennedy et al., 2008), which are also reflected in the Scottish Intercollegiate Guideline Network (SIGN) guidelines for Brain Injury Rehabilitation for Adults (SIGN 130, 2013). Recently the INCOG group (Tate et al., 2014) also reviewed the literature and produced a set of guidelines. These included:

1   Metacognitive strategy instruction should be used with adults with TBI for difficulty with problem solving, planning, and organisation. These strategies should be focused on everyday problems and functional outcomes. It was noted that metacognitive strategy instruction is optimised when the patient has awareness of the need to use a strategy, and can identify contexts in which the strategy should be used. Common elements of all metacognitive strategies are self-monitoring and incorporation of feedback into future performance.
2   Strategies to improve the capacity to analyse and synthesise information should be used with adults with TBI who have impaired reasoning skills.
3   Group-based interventions may be considered for remediation of executive and problem-solving deficits after TBI.

Tate et al. (2014) produced an algorithm to help select an intervention relevant to a person's needs. The algorithm is helpful but does not consider how severity of impairment would affect treatment selection. Figure 9.1 presents an algorithm adapted from memory rehabilitation (Evans, 2009b) to illustrate the process of selecting interventions to support executive functioning which will be used in the next section to explain choice of intervention for executive impairment.

Specific interventions

The algorithm begins by emphasising that selection of interventions should be set in the context of specific rehabilitation goals. All guidance emphasises that it is important that people are supported to apply strategies to practical, everyday situations and hence it is important to consider from the outset how interventions for executive dysfunction will relate to the specific goals of the client. Even if an assessment has identified evidence of executive impairment it is important to consider whether other cognitive or emotional difficulties are impacting on a person's functioning and may be affecting their ability to achieve the rehabilitation goals. If so, other interventions need to be identified and implemented, perhaps alongside the specific executive dysfunction interventions.

Addressing insight and awareness difficulties

Central to the recommendations of Tate et al. (2014) is consideration of insight and awareness. For clients who are not aware of deficits, interventions that rely on self-initiation are unlikely to be useful. So in this situation interventions to support the development of awareness are needed (see Chapter 11). These may include education (including in group formats), feedback (which may include being providing opportunities in a safe way for exposure to difficulties), and support to monitor for errors/problems to facilitate awareness.

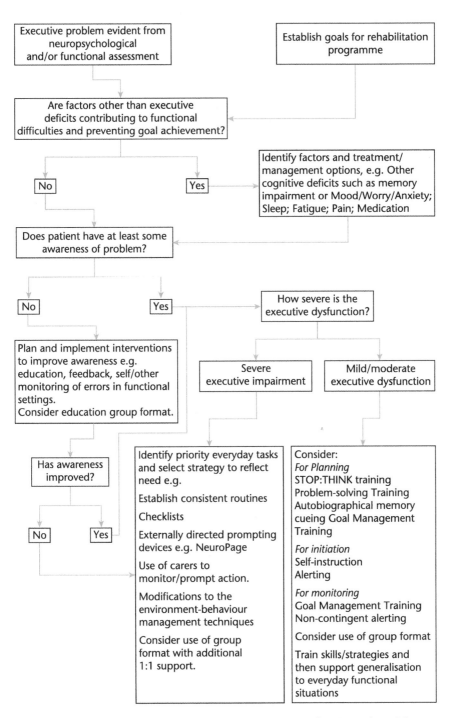

FIGURE 9.1 Algorithm for treating impairments in executive function, adapted from Evans (2009b) and Tate et al. (2014)

Use of routine, checklists, and external control

For some people interventions to improve awareness of deficits may not be feasible or successful. When this is the case, the approach should be to find ways to reduce the executive demands on the person. This may involve establishing consistent routines allowing behaviours to be cued by environmental triggers in such a way that they become habitual. Alternatively, it may be feasible to use checklists to support a person to carry out specific tasks. The dysexecutive medical doctor described by Von Cramon and Matthes von Cramon (1994) was an example of someone who made good use of a checklist. He was working in a pathology laboratory, but was impulsive in reaching diagnoses from autopsy information. He was provided with a checklist that listed each of the steps involved in the systematic process of diagnosis. Over time he was able to remember the steps, which he applied as a routine – an external support became an internal routine that enabled a relatively complex skill to be completed using established knowledge but without the need for self-organisation skills. Checklists thus scaffold behaviour – they provide the structure and the individual steps so that the person with executive dysfunction does not need to rely on organising an activity themselves. Often this form of support is provided by a carer, but assistive technology may also be helpful (see Chapter 16).

Improving planning and problem solving

In situations where a person has some awareness of difficulties it is important to consider whether the level of impairment (either in executive functioning or other cognitive functions) is such that they may be able to engage in learning meta-cognitive strategies and whether they are likely to implement them in everyday situations. For those considered sufficiently able (there are no clear metrics for how to determine this), 'meta-cognitive' strategies, to improve control of the process of problem-solving and goal management, may be useful. In relation to difficulties with planning/problem solving a number of studies have demonstrated benefit from interventions focused on training problem solving. Von Cramon et al. (1991) described and evaluated a Problem Solving Therapy (PST) group based intervention. Broadly similar approaches have been described by Rath et al. (2003), Evans (2009a), and Miotto et al. (2009) and (2010). A core common feature is teaching people to be systematic and structured in their problem solving and planning, rather than hasty and impulsive. Clients are encouraged to use a 'STOP:THINK' strategy to manage their impulsivity. The aim is to make it routine for people to consider possible solutions to a problem before rushing to act. One way to practise this is to ask people to think aloud whilst tackling a problem-solving task – during this process the tendency to jump to a conclusion can be highlighted and the STOP:THINK strategy introduced. The dysexecutive businessman Steven described earlier (Evans, 2008), was helped to manage his impulsivity by being given STOP:THINK training, then supported to implement this in everyday situations through the use of notes attached to a personal digital organiser that he looked at regularly. He was also prompted by staff at the beginning of sessions to try to remember to pause and think before starting, as well as during, activities. In addition, he was taught counselling skills as a way of encouraging him to take turns in conversations more effectively (i.e. learning to listen more effectively rather than impulsively dominating conversations). He learnt to make notes during meetings to remember points he wanted to raise (rather than interrupting for fear of not remembering what he wanted to say).

Having stopped to think, clients learn to question whether the problem they are facing has just one solution or whether there are several options. If there is not one obvious solution it is necessary to identify options and this may involve reflecting on previous experience of similar situations. We know that people with brain injury are less likely to draw on autobiographical experience to generate solutions to everyday problems (Dritschel et al., 1998). Hewitt, Evans, and Dritschel (2006) found that if people with head injury were given brief training on using autobiographical experiences to solve problems they drew more on personal experience when tackling hypothetical problem scenarios, such that the overall effectiveness of their problem solving was rated as better. This approach was incorporated in the group intervention described by Evans (2009a). This group programme focused on attention and goal management and ran over a 12-week period with one 2-hour session per week. Each session involved a combination of education, practical tasks to practise applying strategies and to illustrate an aspect of attention, problem solving or goal management, and finally setting/reviewing homework tasks.

Once a solution to a problem is identified, the individual steps involved are listed. Spikman et al. (2010) noted in their multifaceted treatment programme that patients were taught to apply the General Planning Approach (GPA), emphasising the formulation of intended activities and tasks in terms of goals and steps leading to these goals. Daily life goals were verbalised explicitly and concretely in terms of when, where, with whom, with what and how long, on a worksheet. Patients learned to formulate concrete steps leading to previously set goals and put these steps in the right order (p. 119). This approach of explicitly setting out task steps is also a core component of Goal Management Training (GMT) (Levine et al., 2011) which is discussed later in relation to improving monitoring.

Improving initiation

Having formulated a plan of action involving a series of steps the plan must be implemented and actions initiated. Difficulties with initiation may arise for several different reasons. A person may be depressed, lacking in motivation and initiative. If a formulation indicates that problems of initiation are mood-related then an intervention focused on management of mood will be the priority. If, however, the difficulty does not appear to be mood related but is a more basic deficit in the ability to initiate intended action, perhaps arising specifically from damage to the superior medial frontal lobe and associated striatal structures, then a different approach is needed. For those with mild difficulties a self-instructional strategy could be considered. Evans (2003) described the case of David, who suffered a stroke causing an internal capsule infarct. He had significant difficulties with a range of attention and executive functions, including problems with initiation of actions. He was not depressed or lacking motivation, but just found it very difficult to start tasks despite sometimes having a clear intention to do something. At other times when there was no external driver for his actions he was unable to spontaneously think of things to do, so did very little. As one part of a comprehensive rehabilitation programme, David was trained to use a self-instructional approach involving a phrase that he selected ('Just Do It') and successfully used to prompt himself. Initially this was paired with an alarm to help him start tasks, but also to stop tasks and move on to other things. In time he could use the phrase without the need for the alarm. In David's case he had sufficient cognitive ability to use a self-instructional strategy. However, this may not be feasible for many people. So, the question becomes how to use external prompts to support initiation. For many people it is the case that a carer performs this role, but this may result in tension because the client feels nagged. Alternatives such as everyday routines and checklists may provide enough of a cue to act that a person overcomes their difficulty with self-initiation. Another option is an alarm or other alerting device that provides a strong arousing stimulus that is sufficient to kick-start an action. In the case of RP (Evans et al., 1998; Fish et al., 2008), this was achieved by use of the Neuropage system. Specific behavioural tasks that could be prompted at specific times were identified and these times programmed into the paging system. At the appropriate moment the alert was sent to a pager. This successfully improved the ability to take medication and carry out a range of other everyday tasks without the need to be prompted by RP's husband (which also reduced the burden on him). This same function can now be carried out by mobile/ smart phones where reminders can be delivered by SMS text messages or via calendar functions in the phone. RP had a combination of an initiation difficulty and a problem with sustaining attention to an intended task, or in other words a goal maintenance problem. In her case she did not forget what she intended to do (she could tell you when asked) but the intention seemed to be unable to be maintained actively enough in mind, leading to 'goal neglect' (Duncan, 1986). For RP the alert delivered by the pager seemed to help her initiate actions but also maintain an intention long enough to complete an intended task. Before using the Neuropage, if she managed to initiate setting off to the kitchen to take her medication there was a strong chance that she would get distracted along the way and never make it to her medication. However, with the pager, once an action was initiated she seemed to be able to hold the intention in mind long enough to complete the task. This idea of supporting the maintenance of a goal during the period of completing a multi-step task is a central aim of Goal Management Training.

Improving monitoring

Successful goal management requires formation of a plan of action, initiation of the plan, and finally effective monitoring to ensure that actions are carried out as planned and that those actions lead to achievement of the intended outcome. A core aim of Goal Management Training is goal maintenance. Goal Management Training (GMT) (Levine et al., 2011) was developed by Ian Robertson from Duncan's (1986) concept of goal neglect, and has now been developed into a commercially available package (http://www.baycrest.org/research/rotman-research-institute/centre-for-brain-fitness/). The idea of GMT is that patients with frontal lobe damage fail to generate goal lists (the steps in a multi-step task) and/or may fail to monitor progress towards achieving sub- or main goals. The training has 5 stages, which include (1) Stop and think what I am doing, (2) Define the main task, (3) List the steps required, (4) Learn the steps, (5) Whilst implementing the steps, check that I am on track, or doing what I intended to do. The first four components overlap with elements of Problem Solving Therapy, but GMT is less focused on making decisions about how to solve a problem and more focused on completing tasks for which the series of steps is clear. The fifth step involves learning a mental checking routine. The concept of a mental blackboard is used to illustrate working memory. This is a nice analogy because, like working memory, a blackboard has limited capacity and things are easily rubbed off. So GMT participants are taught the idea of placing the steps of a task on their mental blackboard, then checking regularly to see if the steps are still on it (i.e. are still actively in mind) and so likely to be remembered at the right time. Burgess and his colleagues (Burgess et al., 2007) have demonstrated that rostral pre-frontal cortex is particularly important in the process of switching attention from the external world to mental intentions (such as things to do in the future), which is critical to maintenance of intentions over time, successful prospective remembering and goal achievement.

Spontaneously using a mental-checking routine is likely to be difficult for some people. An alternative approach is to use some form of external alert to prompt a goal-review process. The use of a non-contingent external alerting (via SMS text messaging) in combination with GMT has been shown to be beneficial in improving functional performance on an everyday prospective remembering task (Fish et al., 2007). Rather than prompting specific actions at specific times a more general alert is delivered to prompt a 'goal review' by the patient. Fish et al. sent SMS text messages that said simply STOP, the patients having been trained to use this to prompt them to: Stop; Think about what you are doing and what tasks you have to do; Organise (i.e. plan for any tasks that need to be done later); and Proceed (i.e. carry on with current activity).

Krasny-Pacini, Chevignard, and Evans (2014) reviewed the evidence for the effectiveness of GMT. They concluded that there is insufficient evidence for the effectiveness of GMT as a standalone intervention, but there was stronger support for its use in the context of a more comprehensive intervention programme, such as being combined with problem solving training as in the intervention packages of Spikman et al. (2010) and Evans (2009a).

Interventions for people with more severely impaired executive functions

For many people after brain injury, it will not be possible to rely only on interventions that involve self-initiation of mental strategies. Even if a person has some awareness of their difficulties, those with more severe cognitive impairment may not be able to utilise most of the 'meta-cognitive' interventions. So the strategies outlined earlier that focus on reducing executive demands and providing external support are the most appropriate.

A note on generalisation

It is important to reiterate the importance of ensuring that interventions are set in the context of a person's rehabilitation goals. The beginning of the algorithm notes that a key step is identifying the goals for a person's rehabilitation programme. Having identified that an impairment of executive functions is contributing to everyday difficulties and is thus blocking achievement of goals, then an intervention can be identified. However, when implementing strategies, it is necessary to ensure that they are being used in functional situations relevant to the rehabilitation goals. It is not sufficient to learn strategies that can be used within a group training session or just within the rehabilitation centre when cued by staff. To ensure that the strategies are applied in functionally relevant situations, it is important to look at how an individual may be prompted to use them. For the GMT strategies, SMS text alerts may be helpful to prompt goal review. In some of the group interventions there is a gradual transfer of practice from hypothetical tasks through to real-life problems and tasks done initially within training sessions, then as specific homework, and then, hopefully, spontaneously in everyday life but with recording/reporting of use.

Conclusions

Executive dysfunctions come in many different forms and represent a major challenge for rehabilitation services. Given theoretical inconsistencies it is perhaps not surprising that there is not a strong evidence base relating to rehabilitation interventions in this domain. However, the last few decades have seen important developments in theory, assessment and rehabilitation so that it is now possible to provide a formulation of a person's executive functioning in the context of a theoretical framework that we can then relate to interventions aimed at targeting specific deficits. Selection of interventions needs to take into account level of awareness of, and severity of, impairment. For those with milder forms of deficits meta-cognitive interventions based on teaching strategies for managing impulsivity, training problem-solving and goal management, perhaps supported by prompting technology and applied in functionally relevant situations are recommended. For those with more severe impairment, the solution is to select functionally important activities and identify how to reduce the executive demand of the tasks and provide external support in the form of checklists, prompts or contingency-management interventions.

References

Baddeley, A.D. (1986). *Working Memory*. Oxford: Oxford University Press.

Baddeley, A.D., & Wilson, B.A. (1988). Frontal amnesia and the dysexecutive syndrome. *Brain and Cognition, 7*, 212–230.

Boelen, D.H.E., Spikman, J.M., & Fasotti, L. (2011). Rehabilitation of executive disorders after brain injury: Are interventions effective? *Journal of Neuropsychology, 5*, 73–113. doi:10.1348/174866410x516434

Burgess, P.W., Gilbert, S.J., & Dumontheil, I. (2007). Function and localization within rostral prefrontal cortex (area 10). *Philosophical Transactions of the Royal Society B-Biological Sciences, 362*(1481), 887–899. doi:10.1098/rstb.2007.2095

Burgess, P.W., & Shallice, T. (1997). *The Hayling and Brixton Tests*. Bury St Edmunds, UK: Thames Valley Test Company.

Chung, C.S.Y., Pollock, A., Campbell, T., Durward, B.R., & Hagen, S. (2013). Cognitive rehabilitation for executive dysfunction in adults with stroke or other adult non-progressive acquired brain damage. *Cochrane Database of Systematic Reviews*, Issue 4. Art. No.: CD008391. doi: 10.1002/14651858.CD008391.pub2

Cicerone, K.D., Langenbahn, D.M., Braden, C., Malec, J.F., Kalmar, K., Fraas, M., Felicetti, T., Laatsch, L., Harley, J.P., Bergquist, T., Azulay, J., Cantor, J., & Ashman, T. (2011). Evidence-based cognitive rehabilitation: Updated review of the literature from 2003 through 2008. *Archives of Physical Medicine and Rehabilitation, 92*, 519–530.

von Cramon D., & Matthes-von Cramon, G. (1994). Back to work with a chronic dysexecutive syndrome. *Neuropsychological Rehabilitation, 4*, 399–417.

von Cramon, D., Matthes-von Cramon, G., & Mai, N. (1991). Problem-solving deficits in brain injured patients: A therapeutic approach. *Neuropsychological Rehabilitation, 1*, 45–64.

Dritschel, B.H., Kogan, L., Burton, A., Burton, E., & Goddard, L. (1998). Everyday planning difficulties following traumatic brain injury: a role for autobiographical memory. *Brain Injury, 12*(10), 875–886. Retrieved from <Go to ISI>://WOS:000076003100006

Duncan, J. (1986). Disorganisation of behaviour after frontal lobe damage. *Cognitive Neuropsychology, 3*, 271–290.

Evans, J.J. (2003). Rehabilitation of the dysexecutive syndrome. In Wilson, B.A. (Ed.) *Neuropsychological Rehabilitation: Theory and Practice*. Lisse: Swets and Zeitlinger. pp 53–70.

Evans, J.J. (2008). Executive and attentional problems. In: Tyerman, A. and King, N. (Eds.) *Psychological Approaches to Rehabilitation after Traumatic Brain Injury*. Blackwell: Oxford. pp. 193–223.

Evans, J.J. (2009a). The cognitive group part 1: Attention and goal management. In: Wilson, B.A., Gracey, F., Evans, J.J., & Bateman, A. (Eds.) *Neuropsychological Rehabilitation: Theory, Therapy and Outcomes*. Cambridge: Cambridge University Press. pp. 91–97.

Evans, J.J. (2009b). Remediation of memory disorders. In, Gelder, M.G., Lopez-Ibor, J.J., and Andreason, N. (Eds.) *New Oxford Textbook of Psychiatry, 2nd Ed*. Oxford: Oxford University Press. pp. 419–425.

Evans, J.J., Emslie, H. & Wilson, B.A. (1998). External cueing systems in the rehabilitation of executive impairments of action. *Journal of the International Neuropsychological Society, 4*, 399–408.

Fish, J., Evans, J. J., Nimmo, M., Martin, E., Kersel, D., Bateman, A., Wilson, B. A., & Manly, T. (2007). Rehabilitation of executive dysfunction following brain injury: 'Content-free' cueing improves everyday prospective memory performance. *Neuropsychologia, 45*(6), 1318–1330. doi:10.1016/j.neuropsychologia.2006.09.015

Fish, J., Manly, T., & Wilson, B.A. (2008) Long-term compensatory treatment of organizational deficits in a patient with bilateral frontal lobe damage. *Journal of the International Neuropsychological Society, 14*(1), 154–163.

Hewitt, J., Evans, J. J., & Dritschel, B. (2006). Theory driven rehabilitation of executive functioning: Improving planning skills in people with traumatic brain injury through the use of an autobiographical episodic memory cueing procedure. *Neuropsychologia, 44*(8), 1468–1474. doi:10.1016/j.neuropsychologia.2005.11.016

Kennedy, M.R.T., Coelho, C., Turkstra, L., Ylvisaker, M., Sohlberg, M.M., Yorkston, K., Chiou, H. H., & Kan, P.F. (2008). Intervention for executive functions after traumatic brain injury: A systematic review, meta-analysis and clinical recommendations. *Neuropsychological Rehabilitation, 18*(3), 257–299. doi:10.1080/09602010701748644

Krasny-Pacini, A., Chevignard, M., & Evans, J. (2014). Goal management training for rehabilitation of executive functions: A systematic review of effectiveness in patients with acquired brain injury. *Disability and Rehabilitation, 36*(2), 105–116. doi:10.3109/0963828 8.2013.777807

Levine, B., Schweizer, T.A., O'Connor, C., Turner, G., Gillingham, S., Stuss, D.T., Manly, T., & Robertson, I.H. (2011). Rehabilitation of executive functioning in patients with frontal lobe brain damage with goal management training. *Frontiers in Human Neuroscience, 5*. doi:10.3389/fnhum.2011.00009

Luria, A.R. (1973). *The Working Brain: An Introduction to Neuropsychology.* New York, NY: Basic Books.

Luria, A.R. (1966). *Higher Cortical Functions in Man.* New York: Basic Books.

Miotto, E.C., Evans, J.J., de Lucia, M.C.S., & Scaff, M. (2009). Rehabilitation of executive dysfunction: A controlled trial of an attention and problem solving treatment group. *Neuropsychological Rehabilitation, 19*(4), 517–540. doi:10.1080/09602010802332108

Miyake, A., Friedman, N.P., Emerson, M.J., Witzki, A.H., Howerter, A., & Wager, T.D. (2000). The unity and diversity of executive functions and their contributions to complex "frontal lobe" tasks: A latent variable analysis. *Cognitive Psychology, 41*(1), 49–100. doi:10.1006/cogp.1999.0734

Norman, D., & Shallice, T. (1986) Attention to action. In: Davidson, R.J., Schwartz, G.E., and Shapiro, D. (Eds.) *Consciousness and Self-Regulation.* New York: Plenum Press. pp. 1–18.

Packwood, S., Hodgetts, H. M., & Tremblay, S. (2011). A multiperspective approach to the conceptualization of executive functions. *Journal of Clinical and Experimental Neuropsychology, 33*(4), 456–470. doi:10.1080/13803395.2010.533157

Rath, J.F., Simon, D., Langenbahn, D.M., Sherr, R.L., & Diller, L. (2003). Group treatment of problem-solving deficits in outpatients with traumatic brain injury: A randomised outcome study. *Neuropsychological Rehabilitation, 13*(4), 461–488. doi:10.1080/09602010343000039

Scottish Intercollegiate Guideline Network (SIGN) (2013). *Brain Injury Rehabilitation for Adults.* Edinburgh: Healthcare Improvement Scotland.

Shallice, T., & Burgess, P. (1996). The domain of supervisory processes and temporal organization of behaviour. *Philosophical Transactions of the Royal Society B-Biological Sciences, 351*(1346), 1405–1411. doi:10.1098/rstb.1996.0124

Shallice, T., & Burgess, P. W. (1991). Deficits in strategy application following frontal-lobe damage in man. *Brain, 114*, 727–741. doi:10.1093/brain/114.2.727

Spikman, J.M., Boelen, D.H.E., Lamberts, K.F., Brouwer, W.H., & Fasotti, L. (2010). Effects of a multifaceted treatment program for executive dysfunction after acquired brain injury on indications of executive functioning in daily life. *Journal of the International Neuropsychological Society, 16*(1), 118–129. doi:10.1017/s1355617709991020

Stuss, D. (2007). New approaches to prefrontal lobe testing. In: Miller, B.L. and Cummings, J.L. (Eds.) *The Human Frontal Lobes: Functions and Disorders, Second Edition.* New York: Guilford. pp. 292–305.

Stuss, D. (2011). Functions of the frontal lobes: Relation to executive functions. *Journal of the International Neuropsychological Society,* 17, 759–765.

Tate, R., Kennedy, M., Ponsford, J., Douglas, J., Velikonja, D., Bayley, M., & Stergiou-Kita, M. (2014). INCOG recommendations for management of cognition following traumatic brain injury, Part III: Executive function and self-awareness. *Journal of Head Trauma Rehabilitation, 29*(4), 338–352. doi:10.1097/htr.0000000000000068

Wilson, B.A., Alderman, N., Burgess, P.W., Emslie, H., & Evans, J.J. (1996). *The Behavioural Assessment of Dysexecutive Syndrome.* Flempton: Thames Valley Test Company.

10

CHALLENGING BEHAVIOUR

Nick Alderman

When is behaviour challenging?

Any starting point for managing challenging behaviour after TBI is deciding if behaviour *is* challenging to the point that merits intervention. This may sound obvious, but in actual fact it is a process of decision making soaked in moral judgement and potentially an ethical minefield. The question must always be 'is it right to try and change this person's behaviour?' Decision making is further complicated if the person lacks capacity, perhaps because of poor insight, making it clinically necessary to impose an intervention without informed consent.

Despite the extensive literature on management of neurobehavioural disability (NBD), there is surprisingly little consideration about what constitutes challenging behaviour. There is no universal taxonomy and considerable variability exists between researchers regarding consistency in definitions of behaviour, including those acknowledged as being universally problematic, such as aggression (Wood, Alderman & Williams, 2008) and inappropriate sexual behaviour (Johnson, Knight & Alderman, 2006). Lack of critique and guidance in the literature is even more unusual considering growing acknowledgment that NBD renders the TBI population as inherently 'risky', whilst at the same time increasing regulation, external scrutiny, and attention to an individual's rights, creates a growing tension between doing nothing and intervening.

Beyond the constraining influence of regulation, the challenge in deciding what constitutes behaviour worthy of intervention is illustrated in Table 10.1. This lists 13 behaviours referred for intervention in neurobehavioural rehabilitation (NBR) services that 10 experienced practitioners ranked in order as 'challenging and requiring intervention': Table 10.1 shows the mean rank order. Not surprisingly, there was high agreement between clinicians regarding the more overt behaviours being categorised as challenging at the top of the table, including physical aggression.

TABLE 10.1 Behaviours referred for intervention by NBR services placed in mean rank order

Behaviour referred	Mean rank rating appropriateness for intervention	Standard deviation
Physical assaults on other people	9.6	0.84
Touching people	8.5	0.97
Not cooperating with therapy	8.1	1.52
Invading people's personal space	8.0	1.16
Frequent swearing and bad language	8.0	1.76
Lying on the floor	6.7	1.89
Leaving the hospital/unit (absconding)	6.7	3.56
Doing nothing	5.9	3.21
Interrupting other people talking	5.7	1.64
Poor table manners	5.7	1.89
Talking too much	4.6	2.01
Being rude	4.6	2.17
Calling women 'love'	3.6	2.40

However, variance associated with some of the lower ranked items suggests agreement is less straightforward, suggesting that perception of behaviour was subject to multiple sources of bias.

Recent research suggests families adopt a broader definition of challenging behaviour than is accepted by clinicians and researchers. Tam, McKay, Sloan and Ponsford (2015) highlighted expression of anger, overt aggression, socially inappropriate behaviour, repetitive and dangerous behaviours, and behavioural change secondary to cognitive impairment. It was not just the immediate (usually adverse) consequences of these behaviours that relatives found challenging, but also longer-term impact, including reduced social contact, increased stress through avoiding triggers, dropping out of education and work, reduced living standards, and changes in family dynamics and roles.

Given the multivariate causation of NBD it is unlikely that a taxonomy that triggers 'standardised' interventions will ever exist. Attempts to generalise definitions of TBI challenging behaviour include those cited in the first edition of this book: behaviours that increase vulnerability, limit or delay access to community resources, and decrease the likelihood of attaining full recovery potential (Alderman, 2001). Consideration of the following range of key points will help clinicians decide if the behaviour is challenging and whether it is right to intervene.

Interpretation

Often 'snap' decisions are made regarding whether behaviour is problematic. This process is partly a perception of the individual who observed it, influenced by multiple factors including beliefs, attitudes, context, local social norms, and tolerance of what is acceptable. For example, swearing in the company of friends on a night out may be conventional (even encouraged), but the same behaviour in the context of a therapy session can be interpreted as challenging behaviour.

Intent

Attributions about intent are further influenced by subjective interpretation of the observer. Observation of stressful events introduces potential bias which can result in individuals having very different views regarding causation (Buchanan, Tranel & Adolphs, 2006), especially those perceived as sexually motivated (Johnson, Knight & Alderman, 2006). It is essential that decision making regarding intent is conducted in a way that highlights objectivity and informs the formulation process (see 'Assessment').

Immediate impact

Determining the immediate physical, mental and emotional harm of the behaviour will further influence the likelihood of labelling behaviour as challenging (Bezeau, Bogod & Mateer, 2004) and is often the chief objective of formal risk assessment.

Long-term impact

What future options may be denied by the presence of challenging behaviour? This includes participation in rehabilitation programmes so individuals can attain their optimal potential and reintegration into family life and participation in community activities. Social autonomy of both the person with TBI and their family may be adversely affected due to the impact of neurobehavioural disability and changes to role status. The relationship between TBI and offending is especially noteworthy (see Chapter 5). It is increasingly evident that NBD increases likelihood of offending and contact with forensic services. Recent reviews (see Williams, 2012) highlight that TBI is over represented amongst offenders: whilst less than 10 per cent of the general population sustains TBI, rates amongst offender groups are typically 50–80 per cent. These reviews have further highlighted associations between TBI and offending with aggression. Furthermore, offenders with TBI receive their first custodial sentence at a younger age, and rates of recidivism are higher with more prison sentences (Williams, Mewse, Tonks, Mills, Burgess & Cordan, 2010; Pitman, Haddlesey & Fortescue, 2013). These findings imply current custodial and forensic approaches are ineffective in managing challenging behaviour of offenders with TBI, whilst NBR programmes with proven efficacy are not routinely available to this group. Clearly, access to NBR is a priority.

Consideration of these factors within the context of the prevailing legislative framework further influences decisions about the challenging element of behaviour and whether intervention is necessary. Deciding whether behaviour warrants attempts at change is a complex decision involving consideration of context, risk to self and others, appreciation of what will be lost and gained by not intervening, and determining if resources to instigate change are available.

Interventions for TBI challenging behaviour: a process model to manage decision making

As stated earlier, multivariate causes of challenging behaviour and variability in what this comprises, mitigate against a universal taxonomy and a prescriptive catalogue of standardised interventions: these must necessarily be individualised. Nevertheless, a framework can be applied that structures how information is collected, manages clinical decision making and evaluation of interventions, regardless of therapeutic model. Such a methodology was described in the first volume of this book (Alderman, 2001, pp. 184–185) and remains relevant for contemporary applications. The original scheme had six discrete stages but more recently an abridged version was proposed, comprising four stages (assessment, formulation, intervention, evaluation) which is easier to comprehend (Alderman, 2015, p. 165). This encourages a systematic, objective approach to challenging behaviour, with the further benefit of generating evidence-based outcomes (see Figure 10.1).

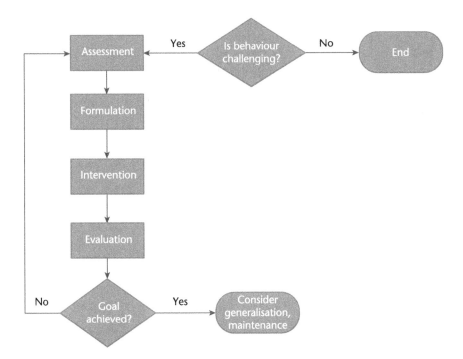

FIGURE 10.1   Flowchart describing the process of intervention for ABI challenging behaviour

Stage 1: Assessment

Collecting relevant information about behaviour

The prequel to assessment is deciding if behaviour warrants intervention. After this, the first step is to assess behaviour by collecting relevant information, including the extent of neurocognitive impairment, influence of environmental factors, insight and awareness, and historical information regarding the person's behaviour.

The goal of assessment is to identify factors that drive and maintain challenging behaviour to create a formulation regarding its function. There is an array of methods to inform this stage of the process, some of which will now be described.

Neurocognitive tests

Tests of cognitive function theoretically provide an important means of revealing areas of impairment and a window into brain–behaviour relationships. However, in group studies, convincing associations between tests and overt measures of behaviour are variable; consequently, making associations between tests and an individual's behaviour must be treated with caution (see Chapter 7). Lack of test–behaviour congruence should not be taken as evidence that deficits in attention, memory or executive function in particular do not impact on behaviour. Rather, unless stated, clinicians must recognise that neurocognitive tests are not designed or validated for this purpose (Burgess & Alderman, 2013). Variance unaccounted for by test performance further reflects that causes of behaviour disturbance are multivariate and unlikely to be attributed to cognitive impairment. In the context of challenging behaviour, results of neuropsychological assessment will help validate other sources of information and contribute to the formulation.

Interviews

Information can be collected using structured interview schedules from the person with TBI, families, clinicians and care staff. Interviews can be a useful resource for quickly harvesting a detailed history, including onset and development of challenging behaviour. However, disorders of self-awareness can result in unrealistic self-appraisal and a tendency to understate difficulties, casting doubt on the validity of self-report in reliably informing the process (Port, Willmott & Charlton, 2002). As discussed earlier, relying totally on information from families and/or clinicians is error prone and needs supplementing from other sources. For example, when events have taken place some time ago, the level of detail recalled will be degraded. Formation of new memories at the time of incidents is not a passive process and subject to bias from beliefs, knowledge, expectations and emotions, which further shape and potentially distort recall of events.

Risk assessment tools

There is evidence that formal risk assessment tools employed in forensic and secure psychiatric services have proved effective in managing risk. The current generation comprises actuarial and structured professional judgement (SPJ) tools, such as the Short-Term Assessment of Risk and Treatability (START) (Webster, Martin, Brink, Nicholls & Middleton, 2004), a structured clinical guide for short-term assessment and management of multiple risks, including aggression.

Presence of NBD renders the TBI population inherently 'risky'. At one extreme, disorders of drive and motivation result in self-neglect; at the other, very challenging behaviour, especially violence, results in multiple risks. Safely managing this risk is a key priority. On the face of it, risk management tools have much to offer people with TBI. However, there is a compelling lack of evidence in the literature to confirm this. One study conducted by the author and colleagues suggests use of the START does not make any unique contribution to prediction of risk of violence in TBI than that already obtained from routinely completing a basket of outcome measures in rehabilitation. It was argued SPJ tools are not conceptualised for TBI and therefore do not adequately capture the wide range of potential drivers underpinning challenging behaviour. Nevertheless, it was felt tools designed for TBI would very likely make a meaningful contribution and a worthy object of future research (Alderman, Major and Brooks, 2016).

Rating scales

Rating scales provide useful proxy measures of behaviour and symptoms of NBD, especially when collecting information through other sources is restricted. Two are especially worthy of note. The 'Overt Behaviour Scale' (OBS: Kelly, Todd, Simpson, Kremer & Martin, 2006) was developed to record challenging behaviours displayed by people with TBI in community settings. More recently, the 'St Andrew's-Swansea Neurobehavioural Scale' (SASNOS: Alderman, Wood & Williams, 2011) has been introduced, consisting of 49 items measuring five principal domains of NBD. Both the OBS and SASNOS were conceptualised for TBI. They are straight-forward to administer and score, provide a profile of strengths and weaknesses, and have known psychometric properties, enabling them to make valuable contributions to assessment, formulation and measuring outcome.

Rating scales designed to inform assessment regarding possible functions of challenging behaviour are especially relevant when an operant conceptual frame-work is used to understand behaviour. Indirect assessment methods, such as the Functional Assessment Interview (O'Neill, Horner, Albin, Sprague et al., 1997) are quick to administer and provide a wide range of information, but are open to bias and error for the reasons cited regarding interviews.

Observational recording measures

An advantage of observational recording measures is that they provide data that are less susceptible to the sorts of observer error discussed earlier. They prompt documentation of standardised variables as soon as possible after incidents, provid-ing objective information to test assumptions about behaviour in the formulation stage. They also have known psychometric qualities underpinned by operational definitions of what constitutes the behaviours being assessed.

The 'Overt Aggression Scale – Modified for Neurorehabilitation' (OAS-MNR) (Alderman, Knight & Morgan, 1997) generates a set of codes employed as a short-hand means of capturing complex sequences of behaviour. The routine deployment of observational recording measures provides a prospective system for collecting information about challenging behaviour. In services where all staff are trained in their use there is a clear expectation that they capture relevant behaviour, providing an indirect form of functional analysis that makes a significant contribution to assessment.

The OAS-MNR was developed using an operant conceptual framework to create a standardised method of reporting aggression in NBR programmes. It has operational definitions based on observable criteria of four categories of aggressive behaviour: verbal aggression, aggression against objects, self and other people. Each is rated regarding four levels of severity defined using objective criteria (mild, moderate, severe and very severe). It comprises a valid, means of capturing information regarding type and severity of aggression, along with associated settings and events, antecedents and interventions. It has good inter-rater reliability with weighted Kappa values in excess of 0.90 (Alderman, Knight & Morgan, 1997) and good convergent validity (Alderman, 2007; Giles & Mohr, 2007). Whilst there are many measures of aggression, only the OAS-MNR and an extended version of this (Giles & Mohr, 2007) have been validated for TBI.

Direct functional assessment

Observational recording measures represent one means of conducting a functional analysis to determine how challenging behaviour serves some purpose to an individual. Indirect functional assessment methods involve gathering data from which function can be inferred using informants, questionnaires and rating scales. In contrast, direct functional assessment utilises formalised observation as the means of establishing environmental determinants of behaviour, and provides the most error-free assessment methodology. Direct approaches fall under one of two broad methodological categories; descriptive assessments and experimental functional analysis. Both have strengths and weaknesses: a third variant, structured descriptive assessment was derived by combining their positive attributes into a single hybrid assessment.

Advanced primarily by Freeman, Anderson and Scotti (2000), the structured descriptive assessment has two defining features. First, systematic presentation of different classes of antecedent events relating to behaviour functions. This feature partly resembles the rationale of an experimental functional analysis. However, consequences are not manipulated but instead, naturally occurring responses transpire. Second, it is conducted in the natural environment by typical care providers. This feature resembles a descriptive assessment and contrasts with an experimental functional analysis, which involves artificial settings and unknown experimenters.

There are only a few accounts describing direct descriptive assessment in the TBI literature but these provide evidence of its benefits. Rahman, Oliver and Alderman (2010) used descriptive assessments to demonstrate 88 per cent of challenging behaviours shown by nine people were functional, most serving a demand-escape purpose. Although indirect functional assessment is widely used in TBI challenging behaviour interventions, the authors proposed that adopting direct assessment methods leads to better outcomes. The same investigators published an account that utilised structured descriptive assessment in investigations of four people in which systematic manipulation of antecedent variables (only) were conducted by typical caregivers in the normal environment (Rahman, Alderman & Oliver, 2013). A principal advantage was that assessment was conducted for an average of only 2.25 hours with each person, but was sufficient to reliably demonstrate functional relationships regarding behaviour.

Applications of technology

Reports regarding use of technology in managing cognitive impairment are prolific, with electronic aids such as SenseCam (Hodges, Berry & Wood, 2011) are achieving public recognition. Application of technology in assessment of TBI challenging behaviour is gathering some momentum. For example, in studies by Rahman and colleagues cited above, handheld computers and observational software were utilised to increase reliability of data collection and provide a high degree of analytical detail. O'Neill and Findlay (2014) described how novel biofeedback was used in interventions for challenging behaviour for two inpatients with TBI. Clinically significant improvement was noted in both cases and the authors advocated future potential applications of biofeedback technology in management of challenging behaviour driven by emotional dysregulation.

Stage 2: Formulation

Formulation is the creation of a hypothesis about causes, precipitants, and maintaining influences of a person's psychological, interpersonal, and behavioural problems and is used to inform and drive treatment.

Once relevant information has been collected, it is used with reference to an appropriate therapeutic conceptual framework to generate a hypothesis about what is driving and maintaining challenging behaviour. The formulation process draws together information from multiple sources and is integrated with knowledge from the literature regarding TBI and behaviour. Interpreting information gleaned from assessment within this wider context further enriches understanding of behaviour and ensures formulations are valid, reliable and consequently likely to result in effective treatment. For detailed information regarding formulation see Sturmey (2009).

The origins of NBD are complex. Information collected in assessment will necessarily need to reflect the complete range of underlying causes, especially those concerning the principal sources of behaviour change, damaged neural systems and neurocognitive impairment, and a range of additional influencing variables that are known from the literature to further impact on how NBD translates into social handicap. These include: the environment; post-injury learning; pre-morbid personality; mental health needs including neuropsychiatric disorders; disorders of awareness and poor insight; and adjustment issues. Challenging behaviour as an expression of NBD may be primarily attributable to one of these drivers, or a combination of several, or even all of them. In addition, challenging behaviour may be one of many adverse outcomes from TBI which rarely results in one identifiable problem. Instead, people routinely acquire a range of cognitive, behavioural, emotional, psychosocial, physical and functional impairments that interact to produce unique symptom-led profiles of bewildering complexity. Consequently, people with TBI comprise a non-homogeneous population with a wide range of needs. Formulation will necessarily need to consider a comprehensive set of variables to optimise validity of hypotheses about challenging behaviour. This further reinforces the point made throughout this chapter regarding shortfalls in attempting to create a taxonomy of challenging behaviour and a corresponding list of standardised interventions. In the opinion of the author, prescribing set interventions in the absence of a formulation will only work by chance. Effective interventions are individualised, being the product of highly detailed assessment and formulation.

To illustrate this Alderman (2015) described some potential variables underlying aggression which included: different neurological causes; executive function disorders; environmental factors; post-injury learning, especially reinforcement of behaviours that lead to avoidance-escape. A good formulation will be based on the literature regarding TBI and behaviour change, along with information relevant to the individual and the outputs of the various tools described above. These are used to create a hypothesis regarding what is driving and maintaining behaviour.

A clear example of how information from assessment is integrated into the therapeutic framework underpinning treatment comes from operant learning theory. Under this model, the probability of behaviour operating on the environment and reoccurring is partly dependent on its contingencies, such as whether it is rewarded (positive and negative reinforcement), not rewarded, or an expected reward is withheld (extinction), or whether the action results in aversive consequences (positive punishment) or loss of something of value (negative punishment). The functional analytical approach described above provides a methodology that highlights relationships between behaviour and the environment; tools like the OAS-MNR are especially useful in determining these. Identifying what purpose behaviour serves through functional analysis directly informs the formulation. For example, aggressive behaviour is frequently found to fulfil an escape/avoidance function, for example in response to therapy demands, and is consequently maintained through positive reinforcement (Alderman, 2007). Having a clear understanding of the function of behaviour and how it is being maintained will signpost intervention approaches most likely to be effective.

Stage 3: Intervention

Although a range of therapeutic approaches are employed in the management of challenging behaviour, recent reviews continue to testify to the effectiveness of behavioural approaches above others across a range of rehabilitation, residential and community settings (Alderman & Wood, 2013; Alderman, Knight & Brooks, 2013; Wood & Alderman, 2011). Reasons are multifarious but chief among them is that learning theory, especially operant conditioning, has special relevance to TBI as it provides a conceptual structure that facilitates understanding of the relationship between behaviour and environmental contingencies, whilst also acknowledging the role of neurocognitive impairment in the development and maintenance of disorders, and constraints upon adaptive learning.

Contingency management vs. positive behaviour supports

The range of possible interventions is best illustrated by categorising them into two discrete sets: those based on modifying consequences of behaviour; and those concerned with fulfilling the function or need in a different (acceptable) way.

The earlier literature regarding application of behavioural approaches in TBI interventions emphasised contingency management, that is, deliberate manipulation of consequences to encourage or discourage behaviour. There exists a wide range of methods with a good evidence base for use in TBI including differential reinforcement, token economies, extinction procedures (such as situational time-out) and response cost (see Alderman & Wood, 2013).

However, more recently, methods that successfully manage antecedents that trigger behaviour have been advocated attracting various descriptors, although the term 'positive behaviour supports' (PBS) appears to be most widely cited (Johnston, Foxx, Jacobson, Green & Mulick, 2006). PBS approaches endeavour to increase the likelihood that individuals will engage in behaviours that enable them to succeed. The chief component is antecedent control, including avoidance of known triggers. However, a range of other methods apply including: promotion of choice and control; daily routine; setting expectations to ensure success; errorless learning to avoid frustration and optimise skill acquisition; alternative strategies to challenging behaviour which serve an escape-avoidance function; increasing opportunities for positive interaction; and increasing cue saliency and anticipation. Examples of the application of PBS are numerous, including reduction of absconding from hospital (Manchester, Hodgkinson, Pfaff & Nguyen, 1997).

In practice, PBS and contingency management procedures are used simultaneously. For example, Rothwell, LaVigna and Willis (1999) described a multi-component intervention to reduce aggressive behaviour driven by anxiety, low self-esteem and cognitive impairment. PBS techniques included ecological change (maximising choice in planning activities, use of a timetable) and 'positive programming' (anxiety management training, automated cues to regularly enable this, daily feedback to emphasise strengths and achievements, education about TBI).

Contingency management approaches included not responding to aggression, delivery of social reinforcement at other times, and provision of a 15-minute fixed interval differential reinforcement programme. This combination of approaches successfully reduced verbal and physical aggression over 17 weeks, illustrating how a combination of methods is ideally suited when intervening in TBI challenging behaviour.

Such methods are especially effective when delivered in an NBR service structured as a *therapeutic milieu,* one which generates a social climate that increases awareness, improves motivation, encourages success and routinely reinforces appropriate behaviour and skills, promoting alternative means to challenging behaviour of meeting needs. Well managed operant methods are instrumental in creating enriched environments because they work to change the behaviour of other people in the first instance, promoting constructive engagement and mediating expectations about what can realistically be achieved. This encourages development of a positive social climate that promotes therapeutic relationships and good outcomes, and provides an excellent basis for intervening when behaviour serves an avoidance–escape function.

Other challenging behaviours may be chiefly mediated by neurocognitive impairment, especially those impacting on working memory and executive functions. These can create difficulties with self-monitoring where reduction in the ability to utilise and respond to naturally occurring feedback in the environment leads to cues being missed and 'behavioural perseveration' occurring as a result. These types of impairment explain difficulties in social interaction that often characterise TBI, described by relatives as lack of tact, selfishness or ignorance. In these cases, operant approaches that consistently present explicit feedback to increase a person's awareness can be helpful. Interventions using differential reinforcement techniques can prove beneficial in improving awareness over short time periods. More severe impairment may require intense applications, such as response–cost, an operant procedure based on the principle of negative punishment. An alternative that may be more acceptable is 'Self-Monitoring Training'. Although there are differences, a characteristic of both response cost and self-monitoring training is the provision of immediate feedback to circumvent barriers to new learning secondary to working memory deficits, a motor response that facilitates procedural learning, and availability of reward contingent on either inhibition of challenging behaviour or acquisition of new skills (see Alderman & Wood, 2013).

Stage 4: Evaluation

A characteristic feature of behavioural interventions, further reinforced by the model described here, is that efficacy is readily demonstrable and innate to the process used. Individual clinical work effectively constitutes an individual case study, but in contrast to the uncontrolled or descriptive approach, reliance on objective assessment, especially collection of data regarding behaviour (either through direct observation or use of proxy measures), enables outcome to be measured using single-case experimental design methodologies.

The definitive account of these remains that of Barlow and Hersen (1984), with subsequent descriptions made of how these can be utilised in interventions for people with TBI becoming available (Alderman, 2002). By comparing repeated measures of behaviour during the assessment stage with those made during the intervention allows judgements to be made regarding efficacy. As well as these reversal design methodologies, multiple baseline designs are available, especially in the case where two or more concurrent interventions are employed and learning is anticipated.

Regular assessment using questionnaires and rating scales validated for TBI also enables response to the therapeutic milieu in rehabilitation to be tracked; these measures may also be pooled to enable construction of service level indicators of performance, although vigilance must be maintained regarding extreme variance and outliers in the data which can markedly skew results (Alderman, Knight, Stewart & Gayton, 2011).

Conclusions

There is no doubt that behavioural interventions are effective in the management of challenging behaviour after TBI, especially when delivered in the context of NBR. Other therapeutic approaches have beneficial impact, but these require further work to determine outcomes, including pharmacological interventions (Fleminger, Greenwood & Oliver, 2006). Multicomponent behavioural interventions, utilising both PBS and contingency management methods, provide the best approach in practice as these are well suited to the complexities underpinning challenging behaviour.

This chapter has focused on issues that define challenging behaviour and describe a framework to guide the process of intervention. This stance was taken as there is considerable variability between researchers regarding what constitutes challenging behaviour, and some indication that thresholds are different for families. Drivers of challenging behaviour after TBI are also complex and multivariate, whilst prevailing legislation and fluctuating ideas about how individual rights are best preserved, prevent both a taxonomy of behaviour and a prescriptive catalogue of standardised interventions being described. Interventions must be designed to meet individual needs. It is hoped the advice presented here will give practical assistance to clinicians.

References

Alderman, N. (2015). Acquired brain injury, trauma and aggression. In: G. Dickens, M. Picchioni and P. Sugarman (Eds.), *Handbook of Specialist Secure Inpatient Mental Healthcare*. London: The Royal College of Psychiatrists, pp. 163–178.

Alderman, N. (2007). Prevalence, characteristics and causes of aggressive behaviour observed within a neurobehavioural rehabilitation service: predictors and implications for management. *Brain Injury*, 21, 891–911.

Alderman, N. (2002). Individual case studies. In: S. Priebe and M. Slade (Eds.), *Evidence in Mental Health Care*. Hove: Brunner-Routledge, pp. 142–157.

Alderman, N. (2001). Management of challenging behaviour. In: R.Ll. Wood and T. McMillan (Eds.), *Neurobehavioural Disability and Social Handicap Following Traumatic Brain Injury*. Hove: Psychology Press.

Alderman, N. and Wood, R.Ll. (2013). Neurobehavioural approaches to the rehabilitation of challenging behaviour. *NeuroRehabilitation, 32*, 761–770.

Alderman, N., Knight, C. and Morgan, C. (1997). Use of a modified version of the Overt Aggression Scale in the measurement and assessment of aggressive behaviours following brain injury. *Brain Injury, 11*, 503–523.

Alderman, N., Knight, C. and Brooks, J. (2013). Rehabilitation approaches to the management of aggressive behaviour disorders after acquired brain injury. *Brain Impairment (Special Issue: state of the art reviews on mental health in traumatic brain injury), 14*, 5–20.

Alderman, N., Knight, C., Stewart, I. and Gayton, A. (2011). Measuring behavioural outcome in neurodisability. *British Journal of Neuroscience Nursing, 7*, 691–695.

Alderman, N., Wood, R.Ll. and Williams, C. (2011). The development of the St Andrew's–Swansea Neurobehavioural Outcome Scale: Validity and reliability of a new measure of neurobehavioural disability and social handicap. *Brain Injury, 25*, 83–100.

Alderman, N., Major, G. and Brooks, J. (2016). What can structured professional judgement tools contribute to management of neurobehavioural disability? Predictive validity of the Short-Term Assessment of Risk and Treatability (START) in acquired brain injury. *Neuropsychological Rehabilitation*. DOI: 10.1080/09602011.2016.1158115.

Barlow, P.H. and Hersen, M. (1984). *Single Case Experimental Designs: Strategies for Studying Behaviour Change* (2nd edition). New York: Pergamon.

Bezeau, S.C., Bogod, N.M. and Mateer, C.A. (2004). Sexually intrusive behaviour following brain injury: Approaches to assessment and rehabilitation. *Brain Injury, 18*, 299–313.

Buchanan, T.W., Tranel, D. and Adolphs, R. (2006). Impaired memory retrieval correlates with individual differences in cortisol response but not autonomic response. *Learning and Memory, 13*, 382–387.

Burgess, P.W. and Alderman, N. (2013). Executive dysfunction. In: L.H. Goldstein and J.E. McNeil (Eds.), *Clinical Neuropsychology: a Practical Guide to Assessment and Management for Clinicians* (2nd edition). Chichester, West Sussex: John Wiley & Sons, Ltd. Wiley-Blackwell, pp. 185–210.

Fleminger, S., Greenwood, R.J. and Oliver, D.L. (2006). Pharmacological management for agitation and aggression in people with acquired brain injury. *Cochrane Database Systematic Review*. Issue 4. Art. No.: CD003299. DOI: 10.1002/14651858.CD003299.pub2.

Freeman, K.A., Anderson, C.M. and Scotti, J.R. (2000). A structured descriptive methodology: Increasing agreement between descriptive and experimental analyses. *Education and Training in Mental Retardation and Developmental Disabilities, 35*, 55–66.

Giles, G.M. and Mohr, J.D. (2007). Overview and inter-rater reliability of an incident-based rating scale for aggressive behaviour following traumatic brain injury: the Overt Aggression Scale-Modified for Neurorehabiltation-Extended (OAS-MNR-E). *Brain Injury, 21*, 505–511.

Hodges, S., Berry, E. and Wood, K. (2011). SenseCam: a wearable camera that stimulates and rehabilitates autobiographical memory. *Memory, 19*, 685–956.

Johnson, C., Knight, C. and Alderman, N. (2006). Challenges associated with the definition and assessment of inappropriate sexual behaviour amongst individuals with a neurological impairment. *Brain Injury, 20*, 687–693.

Johnston, J.M., Foxx, R.M., Jacobson, J.W., Green, G. and Mulick, J.A. (2006). Positive behavior support and applied behavior analysis. *The Behavior Analyst, 29*, 51–74.

Kelly, G., Todd, J., Simpson, G., Kremer, P. and Martin, C. (2006). The Overt Behaviour Scale (OBS): A tool for measuring challenging behaviours following ABI in community settings. *Brain Injury, 20,* 307–319.

Manchester, D., Hodgkinson, A., Pfaff, A. and Nguyen, F. (1997). A non-aversive approach to reducing hospital absconding in a head-injured adolescent boy. *Brain Injury, 11,* 271–277.

O'Neill, B. and Findlay, G. (2014). Single case methodology in neurobehavioural rehabilitation: Preliminary findings on biofeedback in the treatment of challenging behaviour. *Neuropsychological Rehabilitation, 24,* 365–381.

O'Neill, R.E., Horner, R.H., Albin, R.W., Sprague, J.R., Storey, K. and Newton, J.S. (1997). *Functional Assessment and Program Development for Problem Behavior: A Practical Handbook* (2nd edition). Pacific Grove, CA: Brooks/Cole Publishing Company.

Pitman, I., Haddlesey, C. and Fortescue, D. (2013). *The Prevalence of Traumatic Brain Injury Among Adult Male Offenders in the UK. Briefing Paper by the Disabilities Trust.* http://www.thedtgroup.org/media/338403/Prison%20Research%20Briefing.pdf

Port, A., Willmott, C. and Charlton, J. (2002). Self-awareness following traumatic brain injury and implications for rehabilitation. *Brain Injury, 16,* 277–89.

Rahman, B., Alderman, N. and Oliver, C. (2013). The application of a structured descriptive assessment methodology with traumatic brain injury survivors to identify the function of challenging behaviour. *Neuropsychological Rehabilitation: An International Journal, 23,* 501–527.

Rahman, B., Oliver, C. and Alderman, N. (2010). Descriptive analysis of challenging behaviours shown by adults with acquired brain injury. *Neuropsychological Rehabilitation, 20,* 212–238.

Rothwell, N.A., LaVigna, G.W. and Willis, T.J. (1999). A non-aversive rehabilitation approach for people with severe behavior problems resulting from brain injury. *Brain Injury, 13,* 521–533.

Sturmey, P. (Ed.) (2009). *Clinical case formulation: varieties of approaches.* Chichester: John Wiley & Sons.

Tam, S., McKay, A., Sloan, S. and Ponsford, J. (2015). The experience of challenging behaviours following severe TBI: a family perspective. *Brain Injury, 29,* 813–821.

Webster, C.D., Martin, M., Brink, J., Nicholls, T.L. and Middleton, C. (2004). *Short-term Assessment of Risk and Treatability (START).* St Josephs Healthcare, Hamilton and British Columbia Mental Health and Addiction Services.

Williams, H. (2012). *Repairing shattered lives: brain injury and its implications for criminal justice.* Report published by the Barrow Cadbury Trust on behalf of the Transition to Adulthood Alliance. http://yss.org.uk/wp-content/uploads/2012/10/Repairing-Shattered-Lives_Report.pdf

Williams, W.H., Mewse, A.J., Tonks, J., Mills, S., Burgess, C.N.W. and Cordan, G. (2010). Traumatic brain injury in a prison population: prevalence, and risk for reoffending. *Brain Injury, 24,* 1184–1188.

Wood, R.Ll. and Alderman, N. (2011). Applications of operant learning theory to the management of challenging behaviour after traumatic brain injury. *Journal of Head Trauma Rehabilitation, 26,* 202–211.

Wood, R.Ll., Alderman, N. and Williams, C. (2008). Assessment of neurobehavioural disability: a review of existing measures and recommendations for a comprehensive assessment tool. *Brain Injury, 22,* 905–918.

11

INTERVENTIONS FOR ADJUSTMENT, IMPAIRED SELF-AWARENESS AND EMPATHY

Hamish McLeod, Fiona Ashworth and Tom M. McMillan

Psychological therapy can have an important role in successful neurobehavioural rehabilitation, but there is a need for improved understanding of mechanisms of change, combined with a substantial increase in the quality of the primary outcome evidence base (McMillan, 2013). The need for improved treatments is exemplified by the long shadow cast by poor emotional adjustment and impaired interpersonal relationship skills commonly experienced after traumatic brain injury (TBI). This chapter provides an analysis of the issues that require attention with respect to adjustment, self-awareness and empathy, and the evidence for psychological interventions. We finish by presenting potentially fruitful areas for future development.

An unmet treatment need

Psychological problems following TBI can continue long after acute medical issues and physical disability has resolved. A key issue in psychological recovery is adjustment to life changes, including social roles. Indeed, it is common, late after injury, for relatives to comment that whilst there has been little change in impairment severity, the person with TBI, as well as the family, have adapted to a change in lifestyle and learned to avoid situations that provoke socially challenging behaviour. This process might take years (Wood & Rutterford, 2006) during which there may be the breakdown of social relationships and employment (see Kreutzer et al. this volume). Following the injury, poor adjustment can limit engagement in, and hence the effectiveness of, neurorehabilitation (Ownsworth & Clare, 2006). Limited adjustment can be associated with denial ('I am not impaired as a result of the brain injury') or expressed as poor judgement ('I am impaired as a result of the brain injury, but I can return to work next week'). Together with impaired empathy, denial can often place a substantial strain on relationships via fundamental changes in the way in which the person regulates their own behaviour and relates to others. Previously warm and engaging people may suddenly seem uncaring, disengaged, abrupt, self-absorbed and lacking remorse. They may become a source of stress and worry because of their poor judgement and erratic regulation of previously manageable social and behavioural roles (Vaishnavi, Rao & Fann, 2009).

The loss of social roles following brain injury can be associated with fundamental changes in self-concept that in turn can be associated with severe anxiety and depression. This picture is further complicated by the high incidence of pre-injury psychiatric disorders in those with TBI (Bombardier et al., 2010; Jorge & Robinson, 2003). Psychological factors such as mood and self-esteem have also been found to predict changes in disability late after injury (SIGN, 2013). These aspects highlight the complexity of psychological difficulties that can arise when individuals struggle to adjust to their new circumstances following brain injury.

The central importance of adjustment and self-awareness to a good recovery and the successful outcome of neurobehavioural interventions have long been recognised. Restoration of impaired identity of self, via compensatory strategies and adjustment, was seen as key to successful rehabilitation in early work by Goldstein (see McMillan, 2013). Sadly, these problems with psychological functioning have not stimulated the development of a coherent array of evidence-based treatment options. This makes it hard to specify effective treatment strategies and to develop new, more efficient, effective, and scalable complex interventions (Craig et al., 2008; Moore et al., 2015b). As an example, the data to guide psychological treatment of depression following TBI is so limited that treatment guidelines have not been able to stipulate an empirically supported approach (SIGN, 2013). The evidence for managing anxiety disorders after brain injury is not much better except for limited evidence that CBT is indicated for acute stress disorder and the recommendation that CBT should be part of a holistic rehabilitation programme (SIGN, 2013; Soo & Tate, 2007). These are substantial limitations as lower levels of emotional distress are a particularly strong predictor of favourable post-injury outcome (Schonberger et al., 2014). If this association between adjustment, awareness, emotional disturbance and recovery is modifiable by psychological therapy, then there is great potential for improving outcomes for a currently neglected group.

The need for targeted treatments

Among the many possible reasons for low penetration of psychological interventions in post-TBI recovery is the fact that a substantial proportion of patients display awareness and motivational problems that directly impede help seeking and treatment engagement (Flashman & McAllister, 2002; Pagulayan, Temkin, Machamer & Dikman, 2007). Some may exhibit general problems in thinking about the mental states of others (i.e. their capacity for theory of mind is degraded (Bibby & McDonald, 2005)); or they may experience specific impairments in understanding the emotional needs of others (Hooker, Verosky, Germine, Knight & D'Esposito, 2008). These problems with self-awareness and insight are well recognised following TBI (Ownsworth et al., 2007) but treatment guidelines are largely silent about the best way to respond therapeutically to these needs because of a lack of evidence (SIGN, 2013). This may in part arise from the fact that impaired awareness can take different forms. To complicate matters, being more aware of difficulties can induce depression in some cases (Malec, Testa, Rush, Brown & Moessner, 2007), whereas denial can reflect the use of unproductive avoidant coping strategies that may super-ficially appear to be protective but actually elevates the risk of depression (Kortte, Wegener & Chwalisz, 2003).

The need to adapt standard psychological therapies to take account of cognitive impairments is already an acknowledged need (Block & West, 2013; Bornhofen & McDonald, 2008) but we also have to learn more about the specific therapeutic mechanisms and techniques that yield the greatest benefits for problems of psychological adjustment, empathy, or self-awareness after TBI.

The following is a selective review of the treatment outcome literature where psychological therapies have been applied to psychological adjustment, awareness, or empathy, either alone or in combination. Each study is described in terms of design and type of treatment, patient characteristics, treatment parameters, main outcome and further findings.

An overview of treatment studies

The three summary tables below bring together key studies addressing problems of awareness (Table 11.1); studies targeting post-injury emotional and psychological adjustment (Table 11.2); and trials that address deficits in empathy and problems representing the mental and emotional state of others (Table 11.3). Studies on acquired brain injury of various aetiologies are included given the paucity of studies on TBI and together they represent data on 252 people. The studies range from single cases to large samples (N= 71), with most reporting data on small groups of 10 to 20 participants. These small sample sizes are likely to be a major contributor to the lack of clear cut effects across trials. Broadly, there are six distinguishable therapeutic approaches in the 12 studies:

- compassion focused therapy
- supportive psychotherapy
- cognitive behaviour therapy
- metacognitive skills and awareness training
- facial emotion discrimination training
- emotion and mental state discrimination training using written vignettes

The modes of treatment delivery included groups, conventional individual therapy, computer-based approaches with therapist support, and augmented rehabilitation approaches where scaffolding and problem-solving coaching were provided to help with the completion of practical tasks. The delivery settings varied between inpatient and outpatient care in a mixture of public health service and university research centres across high income countries. Of the target domains, the biggest range of data and largest number of studies addressed empathic awareness and the decoding

TABLE 11.1 Awareness focused intervention studies

Study	Design and type of treatment	Patient characteristics	Main outcomes	Treatment parameters	Findings and observations
Cheng & Man (2006)	Pre-post comparison design with random allocation in referral sequence. Awareness Intervention Training versus 'Conventional Rehabilitation'.	21 adults receiving inpatient TBI rehabilitation (index injury severity not stated) 11:10 experimental vs. control conditions	Self awareness of deficits Functional independence Activities of daily living	Individual sessions delivered at two 20–30 minute sessions per day, up to five days per week for four weeks. Interventions targeted self-knowledge of deficits, awareness of changed abilities, goal setting and task regulation practice. Modalities of training :involved psychoeducation and copious task related feedback.	Awareness scores improved for the experimental group but no difference was observed for functioning scores. Total potential dose amounts to 40 sessions of treatment, about 20 hours of contact.
Goverover et al. (2007)	RCT Awareness training added to ADL skills training using structured tasks (e.g. packing a lunchbox; paying a bill).	20 community patients with mild-moderate ABI of various aetiologies. 10:10 treatment vs. control	General and task specific awareness ADL performance Self regulation skills	6 sessions of <45 minutes delivered over 3 weeks. Awareness training recipients got task relevant feedback, prompting, scaffolding, and help with problem solving.	Active condition patients showed superior functional performance and self-regulation skills compared to controls. Between group changes in task specific self-awareness did not reach significance.

TABLE 11.2 Emotional adjustment studies (depression and anxiety)

Study	Design and type of treatment	Patient characteristics	Main outcomes	Treatment parameters	Findings and observations
Ashworth et al. (2011)	Single *n* case report with calculation of RCI. Patient received CFT embedded within a holistic neuropsychological rehabilitation centre.	23-year-old woman who suffered a severe TBI in a RTA.	Self-reported depression, anxiety, anger, and self concept.	The initial 6 sessions used CBT formulation and techniques but following a reformulation to address self-criticism the remaining 18 sessions focused on CFT techniques.	RCI was observed for pre-post improvement in anxiety, depression, and self-concept.
Ashworth (2014)	Single *n* case report with calculation of RCI. Patient received individual CFT.	29-year-old man who suffered a severe TBI in a RTA.	Self-reported depression, anxiety, self-criticism/attacking, and self-reassurance.	Individual CFT (16 sessions) delivered over 3 months. Session content based on CFT principles aimed at addressing underlying self-criticism/attacking.	RCI was observed for pre-post improvement in anxiety, depression. Pre-post treatment reduction in self-criticism/attacking and increase in self-reassurance.
Ashworth et al. (2014)	Mixed methods naturalistic uncontrolled design. Compassion Focused Therapy (CFT).	12 patients with ABIs from various aetiologies enrolled in an 18-week outpatient neuropsychological rehabilitation programme.	Pre-post treatment change in anxiety, depression, self-criticism/attacking, and self-reassurance plus 3 month follow-up.	Individual CFT (mean = 16 sessions) and 'mood group' run on CFT principles (4 sessions) embedded within a comprehensive holistic rehabilitation programme.	Pre-post treatment reductions were observed in anxiety, depression, self-criticism, and self hatred and these were sustained at 3 month follow-up for retained patients (n=9).

Study	Design	Participants	Outcome measures	Treatment	Results
Hofer et al. (2010)	Uncontrolled within subjects pre-post evaluation of change. Treatment was described as general psychotherapy with an emphasis on improving coping with the emotional consequences of acquired brain injury.	11 patients with moderate to severe ABI of traumatic or vascular aetiologies who met DSM criteria for Adjustment Disorder.	Self rated depression and coping skills.	Treatment followed a period of intensive inpatient and/or outpatient neuropsychological rehabilitation. Phases of treatment included promoting acceptance, reconstructing self-image, finding new meaning, and setting goals. Participants received an average of 23 sessions ,range 9–30) over a period of 12 to 18 months.	6 patients returned a significant RCI for improvement in depression scores. Significant group level improvements were seen for depression and self-reported coping.
Ashman et al. (2014)	RCT of CBT (n = 22) versus Supportive Psychotherapy (SPT) (n = 21).	43 patients with head injury ranging from mild-moderate to severe completed treatment who met DSM criteria for depressive mood disorder and/or had a baseline BDI score over 20.	Remission of depression and pre-post treatment reduction in BDI score.	16 individual sessions delivered over 3 months. Treatment session content was guided by written manuals for each arm of the trial.	Both treatment groups displayed pre-post reductions in depression symptoms. 35% of the CBT group and 17% of the SPT group achieved full remission at the end of treatment (no statistically significant difference).

Notes: RCI – Reliable Change Index; RCT – Randomised Controlled Trial; BDI – Beck Depression Inventory; ABI – Acquired Brain Injury; DSM – American Psychiatric Association Diagnostic and Statistical Manual

TABLE 11.3 Empathy focused intervention studies

Study	Design and type of treatment	Patient characteristics	Main outcomes	Treatment parameters	Findings and observations
Radice-Neumann et al. (2009)	RCT Comparison of Facial Affect Recognition (FAR) training versus Emotional Processing from written context training.	19 patients with ABI from traumatic causes.	Affect recognition from visual and written stimuli, adaptive functioning.	Affect recognition involved training sensitivity to affect displays in others and awareness of one's own emotions. Social emotional training involved guided processing of written stories. Training was provided 3 times per week for up to 3 weeks for both conditions (average 6.5 days for both conditions).	Facial affect recognition training was associated with broader improvements in social emotional information processing.
Bornhofen et al. (2008)	RCT (active treatment vs. waitlist control) with multiple baseline measurement and one month follow-up. Treatment involved teaching emotion processing and discrimination skills.	11 outpatients with severe TBI and clinical evidence of social awkwardness or interpersonal difficulties. 5:6 Active treatment vs. waitlist control.	Accurately labelling emotions in static photos and video clips. Social functioning.	25 hours of training across 8 weeks. Hierarchically structured tasks beginning with simple discrimination of emotion states and working up to more complex dynamic judgements and shaping of self-instructional training. Errorless learning procedures were employed.	Treated patients showed greater ability to detect emotional deviations from neutral expressions and to accurately discriminate between emotional states in each other. No effect for psychosocial functioning. Improvements were durable over one month follow-up.

Study	Design	Sample	Outcomes	Intervention	Results
Bornhofen et al. (2008)	RCT with two treatment arms (self instructional training vs. errorless learning) and waitlist control with one month and 6 month follow-ups. Initial allocation was 6 participants to each arm.	18 outpatients who had suffered a severe TBI more than 6 months previously and were reported to have social functioning difficulties (e.g. apparent difficulty processing social cues).	Static (photos) and dynamic (videos) facial affect processing plus assessment of ability to make accurate social inferences. Self reported psychosocial functioning, depression, and anxiety.	Weekly 2.5 hour treatment sessions for 10 weeks. Therapy procedures were manualised to promote consistency.	Both intervention arms showed improvements in discrimination of facial emotions and inferring emotional cues from context. Self instructional training was showed signs of being superior.
O'Neill & McMillan (2012)	Between groups repeated measures comparison of compassionate imagery training versus relaxation training on empathy as the main outcome. Allocation to condition was randomised.	24 inpatients with severe head injury and problems with social-emotional information processing.	Empathy quotient, fear of compassion, self-compassion, and self-rated relaxation scores.	Compassionate Imagery training or Relaxation Training was delivered individually in a single 30-minute session according to a scripted protocol that ensured uniformity for both groups.	No significant effects were observed for empathy, subjective relaxation or fear of compassion. A trend toward improved self-compassion was observed for both groups ($p = .07$).
Neumann et al. (2015)	Multisite RCT with two experimental treatment arms (face processing training or social story processing training) or a comparison treatment (non-social cognitive brain training online games). Outcomes were assessed at post-treatment, 3 and 6 month follow-up.	71 patients with moderate to severe TBI incurred more than one year previously who had significant problems with facial information processing.	Pre-specified primary outcomes were facial affect recognition and emotional inference from written stories. Empathy was assessed as a secondary outcome.	Therapist supported computer delivered training in 9 one hour sessions three times per week for three weeks.	Facial emotional information processing was significantly better for patients who received the face processing intervention and this effect was durable over 6 month follow up. These effects did not generalise to processing social stories.

of emotional and mental states in others. This appears to be an area of substantial activity in recent times.

Main findings and outcomes

These studies provide some indications of the positive outcomes that can be achieved for problems with empathy, adjustment, or awareness following TBI or acquired brain injury more generally. But, further work is required to refine and validate treatment options given the conflicting findings and methodological weaknesses of the studies.

There are contradictory findings across the two trials that primarily focused on improving awareness. Both used strategies that could be considered to be metacognitive, in that the participants were helped to take an observer perspective on their actions and use this awareness to adopt more effective behavioural choices. Despite these similarities in general approach, one study reported enhanced awareness and no functional behavioural change (Cheng & Man, 2006), while the other showed improvement in functioning with no awareness changes (Goverover, Johnston, Toglia & DeLuca, 2007).

The five studies that addressed post-injury psychological adjustment (Table 11.2) used CBT, compassion focused therapy (CFT), or supportive psychotherapy to target self-understanding and processing of emotions after TBI. Interestingly, the description of the treatment techniques and the rationale across the studies suggests a unifying theme of promoting self-understanding and self-acceptance. In the case of CFT, these outcomes are shaped via compassionate mind training as an antidote to self-criticism, self-attack, and coldness towards the post-injury self. Although the CFT studies outlined here addressed anxiety and depression, the therapy also aims to develop the different elements of compassion within oneself, including empathy. The results of these five studies suggest that the therapy techniques had some beneficial effect on emotional adjustment as found in depressive symptom scores. There are also hints that these approaches are associated with durable effects on other emotional outcomes such as reduced anxiety, as well as secondary appraisal processes, such as reduced self-attack and improved coping. The main problem when interpreting these studies is the use of uncontrolled designs, which means that change might be attributable to non-specific therapeutic factors such as therapist attention and support (Mansell, 2011). Also, the relatively weak experimental designs allow little scope for inferring mechanisms of change.

The final set of studies includes examples of programmatic research that attempts to replicate and build on findings across a series of studies. These five studies share a 'dismantling' approach where elements of an intervention are identified and then systematically tested relative to other elements. As these elements are likely to be germane to the content of holistic rehabilitation, this approach begins to address a major limitation in the psychotherapy literature – that psychotherapeutically active ingredients of holistic rehabilitation are rarely empirically assessed (see Chapter 14). The main finding in four of the five studies addressing empathic awareness is that the ability of people with TBI to discriminate emotional states from visual-facial cues can be improved and these effects can be durable over time. What is less clear is whether training in one modality (e.g. using written vignettes describing socio-emotional information) can generalise to fluent processing in another stimulus category (e.g. face cue discrimination) and whether those skills generalise to produce improvements in social relations (see Chapter 3).

Analysis of intervention techniques and strategies

The foregoing description of intervention studies highlights a few key patterns that characterise the wider TBI treatment literature. First, there is considerable variation in the general approach to selecting therapeutic strategies. Three studies imported protocols that were based on a broad psychological therapy model (e.g. CBT or CFT) and investigated whether the treatment works for people with TBI. This 'package' driven approach is common in the history of psychological interventions such as CBT, whereby protocols were tested for efficacy across an increasing array of diagnoses and clinical populations (Butler, Chapman, Forman & Beck, 2006). The other main approach has been to apply a technique or strategy that focuses on a proposed mediator of a clinical problem. This kind of study attempts to tie the therapeutic intervention very clearly to a putative mechanism that could explain the cause and/or maintenance of a problem (e.g. improving facial affect recognition skills to reduce insensitive behaviour arising from low empathy). However, the mixed findings suggest a remaining need for a more fundamental re-consideration of the techniques and strategies used to help people with TBI overcome problems arising from poor empathy, unawareness, or difficulties of adjustment. The problem is not a fundamental lack of viable techniques and strategies, but rather an insufficient momentum and coordination of research effort. This presents an opportunity to specify parameters that should support the development of more effective TBI interventions. Fortunately, recent efforts aimed at improving an understanding of the development and implementation of complex interventions have led to approaches that can be useful in producing more effective interventions for problems with adjustment, empathy, and/or awareness after TBI.

Building more effective complex interventions

The past two decades have seen a more systematic approach to understanding how complex interventions work in mental health and why they are sometimes difficult to implement at scale across a variety of contexts. This work was stimulated by the frequently observed problem that efficacious treatments may be endorsed in clinical standards and guidelines but are then used rarely in 'routine' clinical services (Haddock et al., 2014). Recognition of this problem stimulated the development of guidance frameworks for treatment developers to enable them to plan to determine not only whether a complex intervention is efficacious, but also how it can be transferred into routine care (Murray et al., 2010). The need for this kind of systematic approach for TBI is evident given the lack of data on effective psychosocial treatments (SIGN, 2013); Davidson et al., 2015; Cicerone et al., 2011) and presents an opportunity to focus on the development of therapy protocols that can be delivered at scale and taught to 'real world' clinicians (Hogue, Ozechowski &

Robbins, 2013; Sholomskas et al., 2005; Singla et al., 2014). An initial step will be to analyse promising interventions in a way that promotes a better understanding of mechanisms of change and a more targeted approach that maps interventions to needs (e.g. Michie & van Stralen, 2011). A strong theory-informed approach to psychological treatment development that targets specific symptoms and underlying processes can reduce the interpretative problems that arise by continuing to add elements into already complicated protocols. The following quote captures the problem: 'Multi-element packages are often loosely bound . . . having the quality of collections of elements. As new manuals are written they combine elements of older packages, mixed together into a kind of technological stew' (Hayes, Long, Levin & Follette, 2013, p. 873). To ensure that psychological therapies remain an important contributor to neurobehavioural rehabilitation, there is a need to focus the evaluation of treatment trials, not just on broad outcomes, but also on mechanisms of change.

Capability, opportunity, and motivation as key factors in psychosocial treatments following TBI

A major element of psychological therapy focuses on behaviour change that promotes adaptive functioning and improved wellbeing. However, achieving durable change that persists across contexts, and continues after active treatment has been withdrawn, can be challenging. One response to this challenge is to develop explicit models of how these various change elements fit together. As an example, Susan Michie and colleagues developed the COM-B model. This proposes that behaviour change is influenced by three key factors: 1. Physical and psychological capabilities (e.g. skills and knowledge that need to be learned, consolidated, or amplified); 2. Motivational factors (both automatic and consciously represented); and 3. The repeated creation of opportunities to engage in, and rehearse, the target behaviour (see Michie & van Stralen, 2011 for a full description and rationale for this approach). The intervention studies reviewed above typically address some, but not all of these elements (e.g. skills may be taught but not linked to salient motivational factors). This tendency for TBI treatment packages to incompletely address all key areas of behaviour change might explain some of the observed problems with treatment generalisation and durability.

Problems with generalisation of treatment-effects is a major issue for many focused psychological interventions, especially for people experiencing cognitive impairments (Cella, Reeder & Wykes, 2015). This highlights a complicated but important need in the development of interventions for recovery from TBI; the creation of motivational salience that can sustain behaviour change once active intervention is withdrawn or phased out. Some interventions target motivational salience implicitly (e.g. via conditioning processes) while others attempt to increase conscious awareness of the rewarding feelings associated with achieving desired goal outcomes (e.g. Cheng & Man, 2006; Hofer, Holtforth, Frischknecht & Znoj, 2010). Some third wave CBT strategies such as Acceptance and Commitment Therapy (ACT) augment goal setting by adding a deliberate focus on the clarification and pursuit of personal values that can be used to organise behavioural choices and persistence in the face of challenges (Whiting, Simpson, McLeod, Deane & Ciarrochi, 2012). The benefits of this approach to generalisation of outcomes is yet to be demonstrated under trial conditions, but there are theoretical arguments that support the use of ACT as an intervention to address psychological adjustment after TBI (Kangas & McDonald, 2011; Soo, Tate & Lane-Brown, 2011). However, the evidence that many interventions show inconsistent outcomes, erratic generalisation, and mixed acceptability to patients suggests that a substantial amount of work on tapping the salient motivational processes is needed to provide the momentum for lasting behavioural change (see Kring & Barch, 2014) for a discussion of parallel issues relevant to improving motivation in people with schizophrenia).

Known unknowns and the future development of psychological therapy for awareness, empathy and adjustment

Given the costs associated with persistent disability and the expense of multimodal holistic treatment approaches, there are economic and quality of life benefits from improving design, evaluation, dissemination, and delivery of focused psychological interventions for TBI. But, there are many unknowns. For example, the impact of acquired neurocognitive deficits on the capacity to utilise psychological interventions is an area of substantial challenge (e.g. Doering & Exner, 2011). One common assumption is that there is a need to adapt psychological interventions in order to accommodate problems with memory, attention and concentration but the evidence base to guide such adaptations is very limited (Block & West, 2013). None of the studies reviewed above shed light on whether the capacity to benefit from therapy for low awareness, empathy and emotional adjustment is strongly affected by neurocognitive deficits. A planned approach to describing and measuring adjustments to the therapy process should help identify which adaptations give the most benefit for the greatest number of patients (e.g. improving the description and analysis of what happens in sessions will help to distil and describe key mechanisms of change; see Forman, Chapman, Herbert & Goetter, 2012, for an example).

Conclusion

Psychological intervention studies highlight innovative work aimed at improving outcomes for people experiencing problems with adjustment, empathy, or awareness following TBI. But, the evidence for treatment effectiveness is very limited and generalisation of treatment effects is generally poor. There has been insufficient attention to the motivational factors that can have an impact on the durability of behavioural change over time. These issues have been confronted in the psychological treatment of other complex problems (e.g. psychosis) and there is hope that beneficial outcomes can be achieved for TBI despite the challenges of severe symptoms, concomitant cognitive impairment, and significant loss of social functioning. But, like the lessons learned from other applied areas of psychological intervention, there is a need to take a systematic approach to understanding mechanisms of change and to view the treatments for TBI in terms of complex intervention development (Hayes et al., 2013; Moore et al., 2015a; Moore et al., 2015b).

References

Ashman, T., Cantor, J. B., Tsaousides, T., Spielman, L. & Gordon, W. (2014). Comparison of cognitive behavioral therapy and supportive psychotherapy for the treatment of depression following traumatic brain injury: a randomized controlled trial. *J Head Trauma Rehabil, 29*(6), 467– 478.

Ashworth, F., Gracey, F., & Gilbert, P. (2011). Compassion focused therapy after traumatic brain injury: Theoretical foundations and a case illustration. *Brain Impairment, 12*(2), 128–139.

Ashworth, F. (2014). Soothing the injured brain with a compassionate mind: building the case for compassion focused therapy following acquired brain injury. *Neuro-Disability and Psychotherapy, 39*, 41–79.

Bibby, H., & McDonald, S. (2005). Theory of mind after traumatic brain injury. *Neuropsychologia, 43*(1), 99–114. http://doi.org/10.1016/j.neuropsychologia.2004.04.027

Block, C. K., & West, S. E. (2013). Psychotherapeutic treatment of survivors of traumatic brain injury: Review of the literature and special considerations. *Brain Injury, 27*(7–8), 775–788. http://doi.org/10.3109/02699052.2013.775487

Bombardier, C. H., Fann, J. R., Temkin, N. R., Esselman, P. C., Barber, J., & Dikmen, S. S. (2010). Rates of major depressive disorder and clinical outcomes following traumatic brain injury. *JAMA: the Journal of the American Medical Association, 303*(19), 1938–1945.

Bornhofen, C., & McDonald, S. (2008). Comparing strategies for treating emotion perception deficits in traumatic brain injury. *The Journal of Head Trauma Rehabilitation, 23*(2), 1–13.

Butler, A., Chapman, J., Forman, E., & Beck, A. (2006). The empirical status of cognitive-behavioral therapy: A review of meta-analyses. *Clinical Psychology Review, 26*(1), 17–31. http://doi.org/10.1016/j.cpr.2005.07.003

Cella, M., Reeder, C., & Wykes, T. (2015). Cognitive remediation in schizophrenia—now it is really getting personal. *Current Opinion in Behavioral Sciences, 4*, 147–151. http://doi.org/10.1016/j.cobeha.2015.05.005

Cheng, S. K. W., & Man, D. W. K. (2006). Management of impaired self-awareness in persons with traumatic brain injury. *Brain Injury, 20*(6), 621–628. http://doi.org/10.1080/02699050600677196

Cicerone K. D., Langenbahn D. M., Braden C., Malec J. F., Kalmar K., Fraas M., et al (2011). Evidence-based cognitive rehabilitation: updated review of the literature from 2003 through 2008. Arch Phys Med Rehabilitation, *92*(4), 519–530.

Craig, P., Dieppe, P., Macintyre, S., Michie, S., Nazareth, I., & Petticrew, M. (2008). Developing and evaluating complex interventions: The new Medical Research Council guidance. *Bmj, 337*(sep29 1), a1655–a1655. http://doi.org/10.1136/bmj.a1655

Davidson, K., McMillan, T. M., Chung, K. (2015). Neurological Disorders. In: *The Matrix A Guide to Delivering Evidence-Based Psychological Therapies in Scotland.* NHS Education Scotland, Edinburgh.

Doering, B., & Exner, C. (2011). Combining neuropsychological and cognitive–behavioral approaches for treating psychological sequelae of acquired brain injury. *Current Opinion in Psychiatry, 24*(2), 156–161. http://doi.org/10.1097/YCO.0b013e328343804e

Flashman, L. A., & McAllister, T. W. (2002). Lack of awareness and its impact in traumatic brain injury. *NeuroRehabilitation – an Interdisciplinary Journal, 17*(4), 285–296.

Forman, E. M., Chapman, J. E., Herbert, J. D., & Goetter, E. M. (2012). Using session-by-session measurement to compare mechanisms of action for acceptance and commitment therapy and cognitive therapy. *Behavior Therapy, 43*(2), 341–354.

Goverover, Y., Johnston, M. V., Toglia, J., & DeLuca, J. (2007). Treatment to improve self-awareness in persons with acquired brain injury. *Brain Injury*, *21*(9), 913–923. http://doi.org/10.1080/02699050701553205

Haddock, G., Eisner, E., Boone, C., Davies, G., Coogan, C., & Barrowclough, C. (2014). An investigation of the implementation of NICE-recommended CBT interventions for people with schizophrenia. *Journal of Mental Health*, 1–4. http://doi.org/10.3109/09638237.2013.869571

Hayes, S. C., Long, D. M., Levin, M. E., & Follette, W. C. (2013). Treatment development: Can we find a better way? *Clinical Psychology Review*, *33*(7), 870–882. http://doi.org/10.1016/j.cpr.2012.09.009

Hofer, H., Holtforth, M. G., Frischknecht, E., & Znoj, H.-J. (2010). Fostering adjustment to acquired brain injury by psychotherapeutic interventions: A preliminary study. *Applied Neuropsychology*, *17*(1), 18–26. http://doi.org/10.1080/09084280903297842

Hogue, A., Ozechowski, T. J., & Robbins, M. S. (2013). Making fidelity an intramural game: Localizing quality assurance procedures to promote sustainability of evidence-based practices in usual care. *Clinical Psychology: Science and Practice*, *20*(1), 60–77.

Hooker, C. I., Verosky, S. C., Germine, L. T., Knight, R. T., & D'Esposito, M. (2008). Mentalizing about emotion and its relationship to empathy. *Social Cognitive and Affective Neuroscience*, *3*(3), 204–217. http://doi.org/10.1093/scan/nsn019

Jorge, R., & Robinson, R. G. (2003). Mood disorders following traumatic brain injury. *International Review of Psychiatry*, *15*(4), 317–327. http://doi.org/10.1080/0954026031000 01606700

Kangas, M., & McDonald, S. (2011). Is it time to act? The potential of acceptance and commitment therapy for psychological problems following acquired brain injury. *Neuropsychological Rehabilitation*, *21*(2), 250–276. http://doi.org/10.1080/09602011.2010.540920

Kortte, K. B., Wegener, S. T., & Chwalisz, K. (2003). Anosognosia and denial: Their relationship to coping and depression in acquired brain injury. *Rehabilitation Psychology*, *48*(3), 131–136. http://doi.org/10.1037/0090-5550.48.3.131

Kring, A. M., & Barch, D. M. (2014). The motivation and pleasure dimension of negative symptoms: Neural substrates and behavioral outputs. *European Neuropsychopharmacology*, *24*(5), 725–736. http://doi.org/10.1016/j.euroneuro.2013.06.007

Malec, J. F., Testa, J. A., Rush, B. K., Brown, A. W., & Moessner, A. M. (2007). Self-assessment of impairment, impaired self-awareness, and depression after traumatic brain injury. *Journal of Head Trauma Rehabilitation*, *22*(3), 156.

Mansell, W. (2011). Core processes of psychopathology and recovery: 'Does the Dodo bird effect have wings?'. *Clinical Psychology Review*, *31*(2), 189–192. http://doi.org/10.1016/j.cpr.2010.06.009

McMillan, T. M. (2013). Outcome of rehabilitation for neurobehavioural disorders. *NeuroRehabilitation – an Interdisciplinary Journal*, *32*(4), 791–801. http://doi.org/10.3233/NRE-130903

Michie, S., & van Stralen, M. M. (2011). The behaviour change wheel: A new method for characterising and designing behaviour change interventions. *Implementation Science*, *6*, 42. DOI: 10.1186/1748-5908-6-42

Moore, G. F., Audrey, S., Barker, M., Bond, L., Bonell, C., Hardeman, W., Moore, L., O'Cathain, A., Tinati, T., Wight, D., Baird, J. (2015a). Process evaluation of complex interventions: Medical Research Council guidance. *Bmj*, *350*(mar19 6), h1258–h1258. http://doi.org/10.1136/bmj.h1258

Moore, G., Audrey, S., Barker, M., Bond, L., Bonnell, C., Hardeman, W., Moore, L., O'Cathain, A., Tinati, T., Wight, D., Baird, J. (2015b). *Process evaluation of complex interventions* (pp. 1–134). Medical Research Council.

Murray, E., Treweek, S., Pope, C., MacFarlane, A., Ballini, L., Dowrick, C., Finch, T., Kennedy, A., Mair, F., O'Donnell, C., Ong, B. N., Rapley, T., Rogers, A., & May, C. (2010). Normalisation process theory: a framework for developing, evaluating and implementing complex interventions. *BMC Medicine*, *8*(1), 63.

Neumann, D., Babbage, D. R., Zupan, B. & Willer, B. (2015). A Randomized controlled trial of emotion recognition training after traumatic brain injury. *J Head Trauma Rehabil*, *30*(3), E12–E23.

O'Neill, M. & McMillan, T. M. (2012). Can deficits in empathy after head injury be improved by compassionate imagery? *Neuropsychological Rehabilitation*, *22*(6), 836–851.

Ownsworth, T., Clare, L. (2006). The association between awareness deficits and rehabilitation outcome following acquired brain injury. *Clinical Psychology Review*, *26*(6), 783–795.

Ownsworth, T., Fleming, J., Strong, J., Radel, M., Chan, W., & Clare, L. (2007). Awareness typologies, long-term emotional adjustment and psychosocial outcomes following acquired brain injury. *Neuropsychological Rehabilitation*, *17*(2), 129–150.

Pagulayan, K., Temkin, N., Machamer, J., & Dikman, S. (2007). The measurement and magnitude of awareness difficulties after traumatic brain injury: A longitudinal study. *Journal of the International Neuropsychological Society*, *13*, 561–570.

Radice-Neumann, D., Zupan, B., Tomita, M., & Willer, B. (2009). Training emotion processing in persons with traumatic brain injury. *Journal of Head Trauma Rehabilitation*, *24*(5), 31–323.

Schonberger, M., Ponsford, J., McKay, A., Wong, D., Spitz, G., Harrington, H., & Mealings, M. (2014). Development and predictors of psychological adjustment during the course of community-based rehabilitation of traumatic brain injury: A preliminary study. *Neuropsychological Rehabilitation*, *24*(2), 202–219. http://doi.org/10.1080/09602011.2013.878252

Scottish Intercollegiate Guidelines Network (2013). *Brain Injury Rehabilitation in Adults*. Edinburgh: Healthcare Improvement Scotland.

Sholomskas, D. E., Syracuse-Siewert, G., Rounsaville, B. J., Ball, S. A., Nuro, K. F., & Carroll, K. M. (2005). We don't train in vain: A dissemination trial of three strategies of training clinicians in cognitive-behavioral therapy. *Journal of Consulting and Clinical Psychology*, *73*(1), 106–115. http://doi.org/10.1037/0022-006X.73.1.106

Singla, D. R., Weobong, B., Nadkarni, A., Chowdhary, N., Shinde, S., Anand, A., Fairburn, C. G., Dimijdan, S., Velleman, R., Weiss, H., Patel, V. (2014). Improving the scalability of psychological treatments in developing countries: An evaluation of peer-led therapy quality assessment in Goa, India. *Behaviour Research and Therapy*, *60*, 53–59. http://doi.org/10.1016/j.brat.2014.06.006

Soo, C., & Tate, R. L. (2007). Psychological treatment for anxiety in people with traumatic brain injury. *Cochrane Database of Systematic Reviews*, 2007, Issue 3. Art. No.: CD005239. DOI: 10.1002/14651858.CD005239.pub2

Soo, C., Tate, R. L., & Lane-Brown, A. (2011). A systematic review of Acceptance and Commitment Therapy (ACT) for managing anxiety: Applicability for people with acquired brain injury? *Brain Impairment*, *12*(1), 54–70.

Vaishnavi, S., Rao, V., & Fann, J. R. (2009). Neuropsychiatric problems after traumatic brain injury: Unraveling the silent epidemic. *Psychosomatics*, *50*(3), 198–205. http://doi.org/10.1176/appi.psy.50.3.198

Whiting, D. L., Simpson, G. K., McLeod, H. J., Deane, F. P., & Ciarrochi, J. (2012). Acceptance and Commitment Therapy (ACT) for psychological adjustment after traumatic brain injury: Reporting the protocol for a randomised controlled trial. *Brain Impairment*, *13*(03), 360–376. http://doi.org/10.1017/BrImp.2012.28

Wood, R. L., & Rutterford, N. A. (2006). Psychosocial adjustment 17 years after severe brain injury. *Journal of Neurology, Neurosurgery & Psychiatry*, *77*, 71–73.

12

ANXIETY AND DEPRESSION FOLLOWING TBI

Jennie Ponsford

The many changes in cognition, behaviour and personality that comprise NBD after TBI can have a major impact on independence, vocational and recreational pursuits and social and personal relationships which, in turn, can have serious psychological consequences. The way a person responds to these impacts will be influenced by the injury circumstances and severity, the person's developmental stage and pre-injury psychosocial adjustment, as well as post-injury supports. Having a history of psychiatric disorder places the individual at greater risk of negative psychiatric consequences following a TBI (Gould, Ponsford, Johnston & Schönberger, 2011a).

Studies of psychological disorders following TBI suggest that around 50 per cent have had mental health problems at some time before the injury. Substance use disorders are the most common pre-injury diagnosis, followed by depression, and anxiety disorders (Goodinson, Ponsford, Johnston & Grant, 2009; Gould, Ponsford, Johnston & Schönberger, 2011b). Gould et al. (2011b) found that 61 per cent of a group of individuals with moderate to severe TBI, were diagnosed with a psychiatric disorder in the first year after injury. There was a significant post-injury decline in substance use disorders, most likely due to hospital recommendations for abstinence for one year post-injury. However, the rates of major depressive disorder (42 per cent) and anxiety disorders (44 per cent) were substantially higher post-injury and far exceeded one year rates in the general population. These disorders were comorbid in approximately 75 per cent of cases. The most common form of anxiety was classed as anxiety disorder not otherwise specified (NOS), which generally included subthreshold symptoms of generalised anxiety or post-traumatic stress disorder (PTSD), specific phobia, panic disorder (PD) and social phobia, with relatively low rates of obsessive compulsive disorder and agoraphobia (Gould et al., 2011b).

The reported frequency of psychiatric disorders is higher in cohorts with moderate to severe TBI than in groups with predominantly mild injuries, such as those studied by Deb et al. (1999), Jorge et al. (2004) and Bombardier et al. (2010).

Cross-sectional studies show a steady increase in onset of disorders up until 2–3 years post-injury, when the rate tends to plateau (Ashman et al., 2004; Goodinson et al., 2009). However, elevated rates of depression have been reported as long as 10 and 30 years post-injury (Hibbard, Uysal & Kelpler, 1998; Koponen et al., 2002). Although rates of substance use are high prior to injury these decline substantially in the first year after injury, although studies have found that they may climb in the second year after injury (Ponsford, Whelan-Goodinson & Bahar-Fuchs, 2007). Thus depression and anxiety disorders are the most common psychological issues arising following TBI, often occurring comorbidly.

Managing anxiety and depression after TBI

While pharmacological interventions are relevant and useful in many cases, people with TBI are at risk of side effects with psychotropic medications, and no pharmacological intervention has been shown to consistently alleviate anxiety or depression without significant side-effects in individuals with TBI (Warden et al., 2006). More importantly, pharmacological treatments cannot address the psychosocial factors that contribute to psychological distress following brain injury. Psychological treatments potentially equip individuals with TBI with strategies to manage problems independently in the longer term, thus offering potentially more lasting effects (Fann, Hart & Schome, 2009).

There is, however, very limited evidence regarding the efficacy of any psychological therapies following brain injury. Cognitive difficulties with attention, memory and executive function may limit the person's capacity to understand therapeutic concepts and implement strategies in their daily lives. Some individuals with TBI will therefore not be able to benefit from psychological therapy. For them, pharmacological treatment or environmental modifications may represent the only options. However, therapy may be adapted to reduce the impact of these problems.

Cognitive behaviour therapy

Notwithstanding the limited evidence regarding efficacy of psychological interventions, cognitive behavioural therapy (CBT) is arguably the most commonly used psychotherapeutic approach in individuals with TBI (Judd & Wilson, 2005). In the general clinical population, CBT is the recommended psychological treatment for depression and anxiety disorders (Butler, Chapman, Forman & Beck, 2006). CBT applies adaptive thinking and behavioural strategies to manage emotional problems (Beck, Rush, Shaw & Emery, 1979). Client and therapist work together collaboratively to identify current problems and develop a case formulation of factors underpinning their development and maintenance. The client is engaged in active problem solving using practical strategies and homework exercises, with the aim of enabling the client to manage their own problems (Persons, 2008).

CBT is based on two foundations: 1) learning theory, which uses conditioning model and associational learning to explain the development of maladaptive behaviour patterns, and 2) a cognitive model which postulates that individuals develop psychological disorders as a consequence of (often inaccurate) "core beliefs" or perceptions, based on early experience and the influence of significant others. These powerful mediational forces influence how they interpret the world and plan and evaluate behaviour. Belief systems lead to conditional assumptions, such as, "To be worthwhile I must be successful at work/have many friends /have a stable relationship." Following a brain injury, the individual may no longer be able to meet these standards, resulting in development of "Negative Automatic Thoughts" (NATs). These thoughts may lead to unpleasant emotional responses, behaviours and physiological responses and these responses, themselves, may contribute to and maintain depression or anxiety. Such thoughts and responses have a two-way relationship with environmental occurrences. CBT aims to disrupt the negative cycle maintaining depression or anxiety (Beck et al., 1979), teaching behavioural skills such as graded exposure, activity scheduling, relaxation and social skills, and cognitive skills such as challenging unhelpful thoughts.

All psychological therapies, including CBT are reliant on the client attending to and remembering the content of therapy, being able to communicate verbally, and having self-awareness and self-monitoring skills. TBI commonly causes impairment of these skills. Due to executive difficulties they may fail to generalise and implement strategies in everyday life. A survey of psychologists treating clients with TBI by Judd and Wilson (2005) identified impaired memory as the most common impediment to the establishment of a therapeutic alliance and progress in therapy, followed by inflexible thinking and lack of insight. It is usually necessary to adapt psychological therapy methods to minimise the impact of these problems on potential benefit from therapy. The structured nature of CBT enables adaptations to allow for cognitive impairments. Written aids, cues and repetition are components of CBT that can be extended for people with TBI. CBT can also be adapted to reduce the emphasis on abstract concepts, and increase focus on concrete behavioural strategies and goals. The therapist needs to assess or be aware of the cognitive limitations of the client prior to commencing therapy and to adapt the prescribed techniques as necessary. Sessions may need to be kept short, focusing on just one or two rather than several issues or goals. Repetition may be built into therapy, and important points recorded in a therapy notebook. This notebook would also include a summary of the assessment, agreed therapy goals, homework and any other relevant information. Additional handouts and pictorial aids may be used to illustrate concepts and, along with lists of positives and negatives, included in the notebook. If writing in a notebook is not feasible due to physical, visual or language problems or poor literacy, video- or audio recording of sessions for subsequent review may be possible.

There is generally a need to focus on concrete, personally meaningful examples and behaviours. Behavioural experiments in reality testing may be used to enhance self-awareness and build a collaborative understanding. Setting of concrete goals and frequent review of these can assist the processes of self-reflection and sense of achievement. Use of catchy phrases or personally meaningful metaphors as prompts for adaptive behaviour may be written on cue cards or strategically placed on noteboards. Mobile phones or handheld computers can be used as prompting devices. Due to the clients' executive and memory problems, booster sessions are likely to be needed to maintain therapy gains.

Involving a family member or close friend as a 'co-therapist' may facilitate the therapy processes, provided this is acceptable to, and in the interests of, the client. Family members may provide exemplars of the individual's responses in certain situations, their precipitating circumstance and consequences, support homework exercises, including monitoring of thoughts and behavioural responses, provide feedback to encourage adaptive responses and otherwise prompt adherence to strategies discussed in therapy. This will maximise potential to carry over and maintain gains after completion of therapy. When engaging with family members the therapist needs to be sensitive to issues of control or overprotectiveness, which may render their input unhelpful.

CBT has been the most frequently reported approach used to address psychological problems following TBI. It has been applied with some success to address depression (Ashman, Cantor, Tasaosides, Spielman & Gordon, 2014; Fann et al., 2014; Montgomery, 1995), anxiety (Bryant, Moulds, Guthrie & Nixon, 2003; Hodgson, McDonald, Tate & Gertler, 2005; Hsieh et al., 2012a; Hsieh et al., 2012c; Tiersky et al., 2005) and emotional distress (Bradbury et al., 2008), to manage anger (Medd & Tate, 2000) and to enhance self-esteem and problem-solving (Rath et al., 2003) and adaptive coping (Anson & Ponsford, 2006; Backhaus, Ibarra, Klyce, Trexler & Malec, 2010), the last two studies being group interventions. Some of these studies have had methodological weaknesses including a lack of controls and small samples, with a number including only mild or moderate TBI cases (Soo & Tate, 2007; Waldron, Casserly & O'Sullivan, 2013). Nevertheless, several randomised controlled trials (RCTs) have shown significant benefits of CBT in reducing anxiety disorders following TBI. Bryant et al. (2003) reported success of 5 CBT sessions in treating Acute Stress Disorder in 24 mild TBI cases, with treated cases less likely to show PTSD at the end of therapy and 6 months later. Hodgson and colleagues (2005) evaluated CBT for social anxiety in 12 cases (9 with TBI) and found significantly reduced depression and anxiety, but not social phobia at post-treatment and 1-month follow-up. CBT delivered in combination with cognitive rehabilitation to 20 people with mild–moderate TBI resulted in reduced anxiety symptoms (Tiersky et al., 2005).

RCTs of CBT for depression have not had such positive findings, however. When comparing the effects of CBT with that of supportive counselling Ashman et al. (2014) reported no greater reduction in depression on the Beck Depression Inventory II (BDI-II) immediately following 16 sessions of CBT, with both groups making similar gains. Fann et al. (2014) treated individuals with complicated mild to severe TBI and Major Depressive Disorder with 12 CBT sessions emphasising behavioural activation or usual care. CBT was administered either in-person (n = 18) or via telephone (n = 40). On the primary outcome measure, the clinician-rated 17-item Hamilton Depression Rating Scale (HAMD-17), there were no significant effects relative to usual care. However, there were gains on the patient-reported Symptom Checklist-20 (SCL-20) at follow-up and in participants completing 8 sessions or more. The group differences in these studies may have been weakened by the fact that controls had received some active treatment. However, it is also arguable that the relative lack of success of these studies treating depression may, in part, be attributable to their failure to address anxiety. As anxiety is comorbid with depression in a significant proportion of cases (Gould et al., 2011b) it would seem important to trial interventions that address *both* anxiety and depression.

Our research group has recently conducted a RCT evaluating the efficacy of Adapted CBT preceded by three sessions of Motivational Interviewing (MI+CBT) or three sessions of non-directive counselling (NDC+CBT) in alleviating anxiety and depression symptoms in 95 individuals with mild, but predominantly moderate to very severe TBI (mean age 42 years, mean PTA 22 days), in comparison with a waitlist control group (Ponsford et al., in press). The manualised 3-week MI and 9-week CBT interventions were adapted for people with TBI by incorporating concrete examples, pictorial cues, modelling and role plays, handouts and repetition, as well as 3 CBT booster sessions 9 weeks after the end of CBT. Compared with wait list controls, both Adapted CBT groups showed a greater reduction in anxiety symptoms on the Hospital Anxiety and Depression Scale and in depression symptoms on the Depression Anxiety and Stress Depression Scale (primary outcomes) and greater gains in psychosocial functioning on the Sydney Psychosocial Reintegration Scale (secondary outcome) at follow-up 30 weeks after commencing the trial (18 weeks post-intervention). The group receiving Motivational Interviewing did not show greater gains than the group receiving Non-Directive Counselling prior to CBT, however. The findings of this study suggest that modified CBT with booster sessions over extended periods may alleviate anxiety and depression following TBI.

Motivational interviewing

To be beneficial, psychological therapy necessitates active client engagement. In recent years Motivational Interviewing (MI) has emerged as a method of increasing engagement in therapy and motivation to change. MI is a client-centred form of therapy that is designed to explore and resolve ambivalence to change (Miller & Rollnick, 2002). Whereas CBT teaches clients how to change their thoughts and behaviour, MI focuses on why they might want to change (Arkowitz, Westra, Miller & Rollnick, 2008). The pros and cons of change are reviewed with the client, but the decision as to whether to engage in therapy is left up to them. MI adheres to the principles of *collaboration* (respecting clients' views), *evocation* (building on client values and goals to elicit intrinsic motivation) and *autonomy* (empowering clients to make informed decisions), using open-ended questions, affirmation, reflective listening and summarising. The therapist selectively reinforces and highlights the discrepancy between the client's current functioning and their aspirations, thereby facilitating the client's arguments for and commitment to change, whilst also making it clear that it is the client's responsibility to follow through with plans.

MI was originally developed to address substance use problems (Miller & Rollnick, 2002). However, it has since been used in a variety of contexts. MI has been shown to be effective as a stand-alone treatment, and to enhance motivation and engagement prior to formal treatment (Lundahl, Kunz, Brownell, Tollefson & Burke, 2010). MI has been used to increase engagement in CBT for anxiety disorders, with better completion rates, more active involvement and homework compliance (Westra & Dozois, 2006).

As with CBT, cognitive impairments may limit the injured individuals' ability to benefit from MI. However, it has been most frequently used in groups likely to have such impairments, including those with substance abuse or psychiatric disorders (Lundahl et al., 2010). Using concrete summaries and worksheets to explore the pros and cons of change and provide take home reminders may be helpful. In TBI populations, MI has been used to reduce alcohol and other substance use, with mixed success (Bombardier & Rimmele, 1999; Cox et al., 2003; Tweedly, Ponsford & Lee, 2012). Whilst pilot studies have suggested MI may be used successfully as a prelude to CBT for anxiety and depression (Hsieh et al., 2012b; Hsieh et al., 2012c), the recently completed study by our research group, discussed in the previous section (Ponsford et al., in press) did not find that MI conferred a significant advantage over that delivered by non-directive counselling and CBT.

Bombardier and colleagues (2009) developed a telephone intervention program consisting of MI, problem solving and behavioural activation to reduce symptoms and improve adjustment for individuals with mild – severe TBI. Emotional outcome assessed in the group as a whole on the Brief Symptom Inventory was not significantly better in the intervention group. Of the participants who were depressed at the time of recruitment, those receiving the telephone intervention reported fewer depression symptoms at one year post-injury. However, it was not clear which were the effective elements of this multifactorial intervention. The researchers suggested MI may have addressed depression and injury-related behavioural and executive deficits and recommended that future studies should incorporate standardised diagnostic interviews and explore active ingredients in treatment.

Mindfulness-based therapies: acceptance and commitment therapy

Mindfulness-based psychotherapies have also been used in the treatment of anxiety and depression following TBI. Mindfulness-based interventions focus on altering the individual's relationship with their psychological experiences rather than reducing symptoms. These include Mindfulness-Based Cognitive Therapy, Dialectical Behavioural Therapy and Acceptance and Commitment Therapy (ACT)

(Hayes, Luoma, Bond, Masuda & Lillis, 2006). In contrast to CBT, ACT focuses more on values than on changing thoughts, beliefs or perceptions. The individual is encouraged to accept their psychological and emotional experiences rather than trying to change them, and to focus on the values that they want to guide their life, making a commitment to act in a way that is consistent with or fulfils those values. ACT has been shown to be efficacious in treating anxiety and depression in otherwise healthy individuals (Hayes et al., 2006; Ruiz, 2010).

In the context of brain injury, ACT encourages the individual to engage in a purposeful and meaningful life, in spite of their injury-related difficulties. It avoids the need to apply strategies to address symptoms that may be challenging in the face of cognitive impairments (Kangas & McDonald, 2011; Soo, Tate & Lane-Brown, 2011; Wong, 2008). Wong (2008) reported a case study employing ACT to treat depression in a man with TBI. Post-treatment he showed improved mood, reduced hopelessness and worthlessness and increased goal attainment. However, although a RCT is underway in America there have been no published trials evaluating ACT in individuals with TBI.

In the only RCT of mindfulness therapy, Bedard et al. (2014) enrolled 38 participants with TBI and depression in a 10-week mindfulness-based cognitive therapy group intervention. This included meditation, breathing exercises, yoga, awareness of thoughts and feelings, acceptance and staying in the present, customised to address TBI issues such as poor attention, memory and fatigue, encouraging daily mediation practice, and incorporating repetition and handouts to compensate for cognitive difficulties. The intervention group showed a greater reduction in Beck Depression Inventory-II scores on completion of therapy than a waitlist control group, with gains maintained at 3-month follow-up. Mindfulness-based therapies, including ACT do, however, require the individual to exert considerable control over their thought processes, as does CBT. Therefore adaptation of therapy to compensate for cognitive limitations is likely to be necessary. As Soo et al. (2011) concluded from a systematic review, the choice of CBT or ACT may depend on the personal preferences of the client. Alternatively elements of both therapies may be combined (Orsillo, Roemer & Barlow, 2003).

Compassion focused therapy

Compassion focused therapy (CFT) is based on the assumption that attachment and affiliative behaviours, such as kindness, care, support, encouragement and validation serve to regulate threat-based emotions (Gilbert, 2005). It thereby draws on attachment theory and the neurophysiology of affective regulation. Therapy focuses on developing these behaviours/emotions in order to cope with or eliminate negative thoughts. Ashworth, Gracey and Gilbert (2011) reported the use of CFT in a girl, with an abusive father, who experienced low self-esteem and symptoms of anxiety, depression and anger following a TBI. Applying CBT strategies did not alleviate her low mood. She was very self-critical. Using CFT techniques she learned to apply self-soothing imagery to counter her over-active threat system, identifying a 'perfect nurturer', developing the image with associated soothing emotions and practising self-soothing by bringing this image to mind repeatedly. The therapy resulted in reduced anxiety and depression symptoms and increased self-esteem. The application of positive psychology principles such as those used in these therapies to address mental health issues after brain injury represents a growing focus of psychological interventions. However, a great deal more evaluation of such interventions is required (Evans, 2011).

Conclusions

Anxiety and depression occur in a significant proportion of individuals with TBI and are associated with poorer functional outcomes. Evidence in support of pharmacological treatments for these problems is limited. Psychological interventions have potential to produce more lasting gains but their effectiveness may be reduced by cognitive impairments. There is some emerging evidence that therapy adapted to include a focus on more concrete goals, written and pictorial aids and including repetition and booster sessions may result in gains over extended periods of time. While CBT aims to eliminate thoughts and behaviours that contribute to anxiety and depression and facilitates behavioural strategies to manage symptoms, mindfulness therapies, including acceptance and commitment therapy, focus more on accepting their psychological experiences and focusing on behaving in a way that is consistent with the values that they want to guide their life than on managing symptoms. Compassion focused therapy encourages use of kindness, care, support, encouragement and validation serve to regulate threat-based emotions. All of these interventions do require active control over thought processes, which is challenging for individuals with brain injury. There is a significant need for more research identifying what works and for whom in addressing these key impediments to quality of life following brain injury.

References

Anson, K., & Ponsford, J. (2006). Evaluation of a coping skills group following traumatic brain injury. *Brain Injury, 20*(2), 167–178.

Arkowitz, H., Westra, H. A., Miller, W. R., & Rollnick, S. (Eds.) (2008). *Motivational Interviewing in the Treatment of Psychological Problems.* New York: Guilford Press.

Ashman, T. A., Spielman, L. A., Hibbard, M. R., Silver, J. M., Chandna, T., & Gordon, W. A. (2004). Psychiatric challenges in the first 6 years after traumatic brain injury: Cross-sequential analyses of Axis I disorders. *Archives of Physical Medicine and Rehabilitation, 85*, 36–42.

Ashman, T. A., Cantor, J. B., Tasaosides, T., Spielman, L., & Gordon, W. (2014). Comparison of cognitive behavior therapy and supportive psychotherapy for treatment of depression following traumtic brain injury: A randomized controlled trial. *Journal of Head Trauma Rehabilitation, 29*(6), 467–478. doi: 10.1097/HTR.0000000000000098

Ashworth, F., Gracey, F., & Gilbert, P. (2011). Compassion focused therapy after traumatic brain injury: Theoretical foundations and a case illustration. *Brain Impairment, 12*(2), 128–139.

Backhaus, S. L., Ibarra, S. L., Klyce, D., Trexler, L. E., & Malec, J. F. (2010). Brain injury coping skills group: A preventative intervention for patients with brain injury and their caregivers. *Archives of Physical Medicine & Rehabilitation, 91*(6), 840–848.

Beck, A. T., Rush, A. J., Shaw, B. F., & Emery, G. (1979). *Cognitive Therapy of Depression.* New York: The Guilford Press.

Bedard, M., Felteau, M., Marshall, S., Cullen, N., Gibbons, C., Dubois, S., Maxwell, H., Mazmanian, D., Weaver, B., Rees, L., Gainer, R., Klein, R., & Moustgaard, A. (2014). Mindfulness-based cognitive therapy reduces symptoms of depression in people with a traumatic brain injury: results from a randomized controlled trial. *Journal of Head Trauma Rehabilitation, 29,* E13–22.

Bombardier, C. H., Bell, K. R., Temkin, N. R., Fann, J. R., Hoffman, J., & Dikmen, S. (2009). The efficacy of a scheduled telephone intervention for ameliorating depressive symptoms during the first year after traumatic brain injury. *Journal of Head Trauma Rehabilitation, 24*(4, July–Aug), 230–238.

Bombardier, C. H., Fann, J. R., Temkin, N. R., Esselman, P. C., Barber, J., & Dikmen, S. S. (2010). Rates of major depressive disorder and clinical outcomes following traumatic brain injury. *JAMA, 303,* 1938–1945.

Bombardier, C. H., & Rimmele, C. T. (1999). Motivational interviewing to prevent alcohol abuse after traumatic brain injury: A case series. *Rehabilitation Psychology, 44*(1), 52–67.

Bradbury, C. L., Christensen, B. K., Lau, M. A., Ruttan, L. A., Arundine, A. L., & Green, R. E. (2008). The efficacy of cognitive behaviour therapy in the treatment of emotional distress after acquired brain injury. *Archives of Physical Medicine and Rehabilitation, 89*(12 Suppl), S61–68.

Bryant, R. A., Moulds, M., Guthrie, R., & Nixon, R. D. (2003). Treating acute stress disorder following mild traumatic brain injury. *American Journal of Psychiatry, 160*(3), 585–587. doi: 10.1176/appi.ajp.160.3.585

Butler, A. C., Chapman, J. E., Forman, E. M., & Beck, A. T. (2006). The empirical status of cognitive-behavioral therapy: A review of meta-analyses. *Clinical Psychology Review, 26*(1), 17–31.

Cox, W. M., Heinemann, A. W., Miranti, S V., Schmidt, M., Klinger, E., & Blount, J. (2003). Outcomes of systematic motivational counseling for substance use following traumatic brain injury. *Journal of Addictive Diseases, 22*(1), 93–110. doi: 10. 1 300/J069v 22nO 1_07

Deb, S., Lyons, I., Koutzoukis, C., Ali, I., & McCarthy, G. (1999). Rate of psychiatric illness 1 year after traumatic brain injury. *American Journal of Psychiatry, 156,* 374–378.

Evans, J. (2011). Positive psychology and brain injury rehabilitation. *Brain Impairment, 12*(2), 117–127.

Fann, J. R., Hart, T., & Schome, K. G. (2009). Treatment for depression after traumatic brain injury: A systematic review. *Journal of Neurotrauma, 26*(12), 2383–2402. doi: 10.1089/neu.2009.1091

Fann, J. R., Bombardier, C. H., Vannoy, S., Dyer, J., Ludman, E., Dikmen, S., Marshall, K., Barber, J., & Temkin, N. (2014). Telephone and in-person cognitive behavioral therapy for major depression after traumatic brain injury: A randomized controlled trial. *Journal of Neurotrauma, 35,* 45–57. doi: 10.1089/neu.2014.3423

Gilbert, P. (2005). *Compassion: Conceptualisation, Research and Use in Psychotherapy.* Hove, UK: Routledge.

Goodinson, R., Ponsford, J., Johnston, L., & Grant, F. (2009). Psychiatric disorders following traumatic brain injury: Their nature and frequency. *Journal of Head Trauma Rehabilitation, 24*(5), 324–332.

Gould, K. R., Ponsford, J. L., Johnston, J., & Schönberger, M. (2011a). Predictive and associated factors of psychiatric disorders after traumatic brain injury: A prospective study. *Journal of Neurotrauma, 28*(7), 1149–1154.

Gould, K. R., Ponsford, J. L., Johnston, L., & Schönberger, M. (2011b). The nature, frequency and course of psychiatric disorders in the first year after traumatic brain injury, a prospective study. *Psychological Medicine, 41*(10), 2099–2109.

Hayes, S. C., Luoma, J. B., Bond, F. W., Masuda, A., & Lillis, J. (2006). Acceptance and Commitment Therapy: Model, processes and outcomes. *Behaviour Research and Therapy, 44*, 1–25.

Hibbard, M. R., Uysal, S., Kelpler, K., Bogdany, J., & Silver, J. (1998). Axis I psychopathology in individuals with traumatic brain injury. *Journal of Head Trauma Rehabilitation, 13*, 24–39.

Hodgson, J., McDonald, S., Tate, R., & Gertler, P. (2005). A randomised controlled trial of a cognitive behavioural therapy program for managing social anxiety after acquired brain injury. *Brain Impairment, 6*, 169–180.

Hsieh, M., Ponsford, J., Wong, D., Schönberger, M., McKay, A., & Haines, K. (2012a). A cognitive behaviour therapy (CBT) programme for anxiety following moderate to severe traumatic brain injury (TBI): two case studies. *Brain Injury, 26*(2), 126–138.

Hsieh, M., Ponsford, J., Wong, D., Schönberger, M., McKay, A., & Haines, K. (2012b). Development of a motivational interviewing programme as a prelude to CBT for anxiety and depression following traumatic brain injury. *Neuropsychological Rehabilitation, 22*(4), 563–584. doi: 10.1080/09602011.2012.676284.

Hsieh, M., Ponsford, J., Wong, D., Schönberger, M., Taffe, J., & McKay, A. (2012c). Motivational interviewing and cognitive behavior therapy for anxiety following traumatic brain injury: A pilot randomized controlled trial. *Neuropsychological Rehabilitation, 22*(4), 585–608. doi: doi:10.1080/09602011.2012.67886

Jorge, R. E., Robinson, R. G., Moser, D., Tateno, A., Crespo-Facorro, B., & Arndt, S. V. (2004). Major depression following traumatic brain injury. *Archives of General Psychiatry, 61*, 42–50.

Judd, D., & Wilson, S. L. (2005). Psychotherapy with brain injury survivors: An investigation of the challenges encountered by clinicians and their modifications to therapeutic practice. *Brain Injury, 19*(6), 437–449.

Kangas, M., & McDonald, S. (2011). Is it time to act? The potential of acceptance and commitment therapy for psychologicla problems following acquired brain injury. *Neuropsychological Rehabilitation, 21*, 250–276. doi: 10.1080/09602011.2010.540920

Koponen, S., Taiminen, T., Portin, R., Himanen, L., Isoniemi, H., Heinonen, H., Hinkka, S., & Tenovuo, O. (2002). Axis I and II psychiatric disorders after traumatic brain injury: A 30-year follow-up study. *The American Journal of Psychiatry, 159*, 1315.

Lundahl, B. W., Kunz, C., Brownell, C., Tollefson, D., & Burke, B. L. (2010). A meta-analysis of motivational interviewing: Twenty-five years of empirical studies. *Research on Social Work Practice, 20*(2), 137–160. doi: 10.1177/1049731509347850

Medd, J., & Tate, R. (2000). Evaluation of an anger management therapy programme following acquired brain injury: A preliminary study. *Neuropsychological Rehabilitation, 10*, 185–201.

Miller, W. R., & Rollnick, S. (2002). *Motivational Interviewing: Preparing People for Change* (2nd ed.). New York: The Guilford Press.

Montgomery, G. K. (1995). A multi-factor account of disability after brain injury: implications for neuropsychological counselling. *Brain Injury, 9*(5), 453–469.

Orsillo, S. M., Roemer, L., & Barlow, D. H. (2003). Integrating acceptance and mindfulness into existing cognitive-behavioural treatment for GAD: A case study. *Cognitive and Behavioral Practice, 10*, 222–230.

Persons, J. B. (2008). *The Case Formulation Approach to Cognitive-behavior Therapy (Guides to Individualized Evidence-based Treatment)*. New York: The Guilford Press.

Ponsford, J., Whelan-Goodinson, R., & Bahar-Fuchs, A. (2007). Alcohol and drug use following traumatic brain injury: A prospective study. *Brain Injury, 21*, 1385–1392.

Ponsford, J., Lee, N., McKay, A., Wong, D., Haines, K., Alway, Y., Downing, M., Furtado, C., & O'Donnell, M. (2015). Efficacy of motivational interviewing and cognitive behavioral therapy for anxiety and depression symptoms following traumatic brain injury. *Psychological Medicine*. Published online Dec 2015; *1*, 1–12. doi:10.1017/S0033291715002640

Rath, J. F., Simon, D., Langenbahn, D. M., Sherr, R. L., & Diller, L. (2003). Group treatment of problem solving deficits in outpatients with traumatic brain injury: A randomised outcome study. *Neuropsychological Rehabilitation, 13*, 461–488.

Ruiz, F. J. (2010). A review of Acceptance and Commitment Therapy (ACT) empirical evidence: Correlational, experimental psychopathology, component and outcome studies. *International Journal of Psychology and Psychological Therapy, 10*, 125–162.

Soo, C., & Tate, R. (2007). Psychological treatment for anxiety in people with traumatic brain injury. *Cochrane Database of Systematic Reviews, 3*, Art. No.: CD005239. Retrieved from doi:10.1002/14651858.CD005239.pub2.

Soo, C., Tate, R. L., & Lane-Brown, A. (2011). A systematic review of acceptance and commitment therapy (ACT) for managing anxiety: Applicability for people with acquired brain injury? *Brain Impairment, 12*(1), 54–70.

Tiersky, L. A., Anselmi, V., Johnston, M. V., Kurtyka, J., Roosen, E., Schwartz, T., & DeLuca, J. (2005). A trial of neuropsychologic rehabilitation in mild-spectrum traumatic brain injury. *Archives of Physical Medicine & Rehabilitation, 86*, 1565–1574.

Tweedly, L., Ponsford, J., & Lee, N. J. (2012). Investigation of the effectiveness of brief interventions to reduce alcohol consumption following traumatic brain injury. *Journal of Head Trauma Rehabilitation, 27*(5), 333–341.

Waldron, B., Casserly, L. M., & O'Sullivan, C. (2013). Cognitive behavioural therapy for depression and anxiety in adults with acquired brain injury: What works for whom? *Neuropsychological Rehabilitation, 23*, 64–101. doi: 10.1080 /09602011.2012.724196

Warden, D. L., Gordon, B., McAllister, T. W., Silver, J. M., Barth, J. T., Bruns, J., Drake, A., Gentry, T., Jagoda, A., Katz, D. I., Kraus, J., Labbate, L. A., Ryan, L. M., Sparling, M. B., Walters, B., Whyte, J., Zapata, A., & Zitnay, G. (2006). Guidelines for the pharmacologic treatment of neurobehavioral sequelae of traumatic brain injury. *Journal of Neurotrauma, 23*(10), 1468–1501.

Westra, H. A., & Dozois, D. J. (2006). Preparing clients for cognitive behavioral therapy: A randomized pilot study of motivational interviewing for anxiety. *Cognitive Therapy and Research, 30*(4), 481–498.

Wong, D. (2008). Acceptance and commitment therapy following acquired brain injury: A useful alternative? *Brain Impairment, 9*(1), 70.

13

FATIGUE AND SLEEP DISTURBANCE FOLLOWING TBI

Jennie Ponsford

In recent years there has been an increasing awareness that fatigue and sleep disturbance are amongst the most common complaints of individuals with TBI across the spectrum of injury severity. Fatigue has been reported by up to 32–73 per cent of individuals with mild, moderate and severe TBI (Baumann, Werth, Stocker, Ludwig & Bassetti, 2007; Borgaro, Baker, Wethe, Prigatano & Kwasnica, 2005; Ponsford, Cameron, Fitzgerald, Grant & Mikocka-Walus, 2011). Outcome studies suggest that fatigue levels may decline somewhat in the first 6–12 months post-injury but may remain steady or rise slightly thereafter (Bushnik, Englander & Wright, 2008; Ponsford et al., 2012). However, there is considerable individual variability across individuals in terms of patterns of fatigue over time. Sleep disturbances are also frequently reported following TBI, and may contribute to fatigue (Baumann et al., 2007; Ouellet, Beaulieu-Bonneau & Morin, 2006).

Persistent fatigue affects the individual's capacity to engage in a broad range of activities. There may be reduced stamina for work, resulting in a need to work part-time and rest after work, with reduced energy for domestic or family activities. Students may need to expend greater effort to learn, with fatigue limiting concentration, so that less time can be devoted to homework. Fatigue may also limit energy for social interactions and/or recreational pursuits, resulting in withdrawal, greater time spent at home and consequent social isolation (Stulemeijer, van der Werf, Blieijenberg, Biert, Brauer & Vos, 2006). Depression may develop as a result of the experience of chronic fatigue and its consequences over extended periods and this may in turn exacerbate fatigue. In spite of its pervasive effects, the manifestations and causes of fatigue following brain injury are not well understood and there are no well-established treatments.

What is fatigue?

Fatigue is a symptom that everyone experiences. It is also a subjective phenomenon with variable terminology, which makes it difficult to measure. Aaronson et al. (1999) define fatigue as "The awareness of a decreased capacity for physical and/or mental activity due to an imbalance in the availability, utilization, and/or restoration of resources needed to perform activity" (p. 46). Resources may be physiological or psychological. Thus physiological fatigue may be caused by depletion of energy, hormones, neurotransmitters or a reduced number of neural connections, due to brain injury. This type of fatigue is a direct result of brain injury or dysfunction. Alternatively, fatigue may be associated with muscle weakness or other changes or injuries in the peripheral nervous system. DeLuca (2005) distinguished between primary and secondary fatigue. Primary fatigue is caused by disease processes, such as Multiple Sclerosis (MS), whereas secondary fatigue reflects the compounding effects of factors such as emotional distress, sleep disturbance and pain. Causes of primary fatigue following TBI would include mechanical brain changes such as diffuse axonal injury, impaired excitability of the motor cortex and hypopituitarism, whereas causes for secondary fatigue include sleep disorders, pain and depression (Bushnik et al., 2008). Fatigue may be a symptom of depression and depression in turn may cause sleep disruption and fatigue. Anxiety may also disturb sleep. Thus there is a bidirectional relationship between emotional distress and fatigue and sleep disturbance; emotional distress may contribute to sleep disturbances and exacerbate fatigue. The experience of fatigue thus likely reflects a combination of various influential factors.

What factors are associated with fatigue?

Cantor et al. (2008) found that secondary factors accounted for more variance in fatigue in healthy controls than in individuals with brain injury, suggesting that the injury itself may make a unique contribution to fatigue. However, identifying the injury-related factors underpinning fatigue has proven challenging. Self-reported fatigue has not been significantly associated with injury severity per se (Borgaro et al., 2005; Ponsford et al., 2012; Ziino & Ponsford, 2005). However, there is some evidence of its association with cognitive impairment. Brain injury frequently results in reduced speed of information processing speed and impaired attention, memory and/or executive function. As a consequence of these difficulties many individuals with TBI find cognitively demanding tasks more effortful. Several studies have shown an association between impairments of attention and processing speed and levels of fatigue (Ashman et al., 2008; Ziino & Ponsford, 2006a). There is also some evidence suggesting that performing a cognitively demanding task has a greater psychophysiological impact, measured by rise in blood pressure, on individuals with TBI, than it does in healthy individuals, and that this rise in blood pressure is in turn associated with subjective fatigue (Ziino & Ponsford, 2006b). There is no clear association between fatigue and engagement with everyday activities, but this has not been systematically studied. The subjective experience of fatigue is likely to be determined by the complex interaction of functional disability with lifestyle demands, which is difficult to quantify and idiosyncratic.

The theory that fatigue may be associated with injury-related neuroendocrine abnormalities, specifically, Growth Hormone Deficiency (GHD) which is commonly documented in people with TBI, has not been supported in studies to date (Englander, Bushnik, Oggins & Katznelson, 2010). Baumann and colleagues (2009) suggest that loss of hypocretin neurons caused by hypothalamic injury results in reduced CSF Hypocretin-1, which is a wake-promoting neurotransmitter. This is said to cause increased daytime sleepiness in individuals with TBI. Excessive Daytime Sleepiness (EDS) is tiredness, drowsiness or feeling the need to nap when one wants to be awake, after insufficient sleep or sleep disruption/disorder (e.g., sleep apnoea, circadian rhythm disorder). Whilst this construct is theoretically distinct from fatigue, many individuals may experience daytime sleepiness as fatigue.

Of the possible causes of secondary fatigue, pain has emerged as a factor in several studies (Bushnik et al., 2008; Cantor et al., 2008; Ponsford et al., 2012). Whilst there has been no established relationship between fatigue and presence of orthopaedic injuries, taking analgesic medication is modestly related to fatigue levels (Ponsford et al., 2012). Depression and anxiety are also strongly associated with self-reported fatigue in individuals with brain injury (Cantor et al., 2008; Englander et al., 2010; Ponsford et al., 2012).This relationship is likely to be bi-directional. Fatigue may be a symptom of depression. However, we have found that the experience of fatigue over an extended period of time was associated with the development of depression and anxiety six months later, whereas presence of depression did not lead to subsequent reporting of fatigue (Schönberger, Herrberg & Ponsford, 2014). A subsequent study using path analysis showed that fatigue predicted anxiety, depression and daytime sleepiness, and that depression, in turn, contributed further to daytime sleepiness as well as poor vigilance performance, while anxiety tended to predict reduced daytime sleepiness, thereby demonstrating the complex interrelationships of these various factors with fatigue (Ponsford, Schönberger & Rajaratnam, 2014).

Sleep disturbance

Greater fatigue has also been associated with poor sleep quality or sleep disturbances in several studies (Bushnik et al., 2008; Cantor et al., 2008; Ponsford et al., 2012). Sleep disturbances are reported by 30 to 80 per cent of individuals with TBI and likely contribute to fatigue (Mathias & Alvaro, 2012). These changes have been documented, both in the acute recovery stages in patients in inpatient rehabilitation (Makley, English, Drubach, Kreuz, Celnik & Tarwater, 2008; Rao et al., 2008) and over many years after injury (Ouellet et al., 2006; Ponsford, Parcell, Sinclair, Roper & Rajaratnam, 2013). They are reported across the spectrum of injury severity, from mild to severe and, like fatigue, impact negatively on participation in daily activities (Cantor et al., 2008). Sleep complaints following TBI include insomnia, hypersomnia and excessive daytime sleepiness and sleep apnoea (Mathias & Alvaro, 2012). Ponsford et al. (2013) found that a cohort with TBI reported significantly poorer sleep quality and greater daytime sleepiness than healthy controls. Sleep diaries revealed longer sleep onset latency, poorer sleep efficiency, longer sleep duration and more frequent daytime napping in the TBI group, as well as earlier bedtimes and greater total sleep duration. Anxiety, depression and pain, were associated with poorer sleep quality. Greater injury severity was also associated with a need for longer sleep time. Subjective reports of a decline in sleep quality, longer time taken to get to sleep and increased nighttime awakenings have been confirmed in objective polysomnographic sleep studies. Some of these studies have also revealed changes in sleep-wake cycles, specifically an increase in slow wave or deep sleep (Orff, Ayalon & Drummond, 2009) and changes in Rapid Eye Movement (REM) sleep (Shekleton, Parcell, Redman, Phipps-Nelson, Ponsford & Rajaratnam, 2010).

Causes of sleep disturbance following TBI

Similar to fatigue, the aetiology of sleep disturbances following TBI has not been established and is likely multi-factorial. Injury to brain regions, pathways, and neuro-transmitter systems associated with sleep regulation, including the suprachiasmatic nucleus, hypothalamus, midbrain and ascending reticular activating system may occur (Baumann et al., 2009). Circadian Rhythm Sleep Disorders and delayed circadian timing have been reported in patients with mild TBI and insomnia (Ayalon, Borodkin, Dishon, Kanety & Dagan, 2007). The timing of sleep is regulated by the circadian (~24-h) pacemaker in the hypothalamic suprachiasmatic nuclei, which generate and maintain circadian rhythms, including pineal melatonin synthesis. Melatonin plays a role in the circadian regulation of sleep-wakefulness. Shekleton et al. (2010) found lower levels of evening melatonin production in individuals with TBI, associated with REM sleep, but not sleep efficiency or night-time awakenings. This finding suggests the circadian regulation of melatonin synthesis may be disrupted following TBI.

Like fatigue, sleep disturbances have also been associated with pain, depression and anxiety (Ouellet et al., 2006; Ponsford et al., 2013). However although depression exacerbates sleep disturbances following TBI, it does not entirely account for them (Shekleton et al., 2010). Fatigue may contribute to sleep problems by increasing the frequency of daytime napping, in turn disrupting night-time sleep quality (Ouellet & Morin, 2006). Thus, as with fatigue, sleep disturbances appear to be associated multiple factors, including organic brain changes affecting sleep cycles and circadian regulation of melatonin synthesis, as well as secondary factors including depression and pain.

Treatment of fatigue and sleep disturbance

Research findings from studies such as those discussed in this chapter can be used to inform treatments for fatigue and sleep disturbance following TBI. There is currently very limited evidence of successful application of interventions to alleviate fatigue in people with TBI. Given the numerous factors shown to contribute to fatigue a comprehensive assessment process is needed. Potential contributing factors that need to be assessed would include various aspects of attention and processing speed, medications, pain levels, anxiety and depression and changes in sleep patterns. Each problem would then need to be addressed accordingly.

Behavioural and psychological interventions

Adaptations can be made to the individual's lifestyle to minimise the impact of cognitive and physical limitations. This may involve making adjustments to work or study loads and time spent engaging in various activities. The individual may require considerable assistance and support in finding the right balance in activity levels. It is likely to be necessary at the same time to address psychological issues related to making such changes in lifestyle, using cognitive behaviour therapy techniques. If there are problems with attention and speed of thinking, adjustments may be made to the pace or demands of activities, including removal of distractions or multi-tasking demands, scheduling regular rest breaks and performing the most demanding activities at the time of day when the individual is most alert. Where there is sufficient self-awareness, strategies recommended in the Time Pressure Management (TPM) approach developed by Fasotti, Kovacs, Eling and Brouwer (2000) to manage information overload may be useful. This involves building awareness of ways in which mental slowness may affect task performance, and using self-instruction to take "managing steps" before or during a task to reduce time pressure (e.g., asking for repetition or asking another person to slow down their delivery of information). The application of the steps is first demonstrated overtly, followed by overt self-instruction with written prompts that are gradually withdrawn. The strategies are then applied under more distracting conditions (e.g., with a radio playing in the background) and in a range of situations. Fasotti et al. (2000) found that individuals receiving TPM instruction took more steps to manage time pressure, and this resulted in greater and more lasting gains than were seen in a control group. The authors highlight the importance of self-awareness of the need for use of the strategies in their successful application. The approach has also been shown to be beneficial in stroke patients (Winkens, Van Heugten, Wade, Habets & Fasotti, 2009).

Changes may be needed in terms of activity levels including work or study loads. The individual may benefit from support in finding the right balance between rest and activity levels in order to minimise fatigue. For many individuals, having to reduce time spent in productive activity may cause considerable distress and necessitate a reframing of the value and importance of various aspects of their life and shifting of focus from the negative impacts of the injury. This can be achieved through cognitive behavioural therapy (CBT), a structured form of psychological therapy aimed at altering patterns of thoughts and behaviours to change how emotion is experienced (Beck, 1995). Problems with memory, concentration and executive control over behaviour commonly associated with TBI may limit engagement in and benefit from such psychological intervention. However, CBT can be successfully adapted for people with TBI (Ponsford & Hsieh, 2012).

People with TBI have reduced activity levels and cardiovascular fitness relative to the healthy population. Fatigue, as well as physical limitations, likely contributes to this. Therefore it has been argued that physical fitness training may alleviate fatigue following TBI. However, studies of physical conditioning programs have shown mixed findings. A Cochrane review (Hassett, Moseley, Tate & Harmer, 2009) reported that only one of four identified randomised controlled trials of fitness training improved cardiovascular fitness in individuals with TBI. Only one of the trials, namely that of Bateman, Culpan, Pickering, Powell, Scott and Greenwood (2001), evaluated the impact of the training on subjective fatigue, and found no significant effect. One of the two studies evaluating the effects of regular exercise on mood, by McMillan, Robertson, Brock and Chorlton (2002), found a reduction in depression. One further study has since reported the positive effects of exercise in reducing depression symptoms following TBI (Wise, Hoffman, Powell, Bombardier & Bell, 2012). Thus, there is at this point in time no clear evidence that fitness training alleviates fatigue following TBI. However, a more recent trial by Zedlitz, Rietveld, Geurts and Fasotti (2012), in stroke patients, found enhanced reduction in fatigue by augmenting cognitive therapy with graded activity training.

For individuals reporting sleep disturbance it is important to refer for assessment by a sleep physician who can assess for the presence of obstructive sleep apnoea, periodic limb movement and other sleep disorders that may be contributing to sleep disturbances and prescribe appropriate treatment. Objective assessment of sleep using polysomnography is also desirable because subjective reports of sleep patterns are not always accurate. Where it is identified that pain, anxiety or depression are contributing to sleep disturbance, these will need to assessed and treated as appropriate. Instruction in sleep hygiene techniques, including avoidance of naps if this interferes with night-time sleep, adhering to a regular schedule of time spent in bed, and avoiding time spent in bed awake may be provided. Training in progressive muscle relaxation techniques and methods of minimising worrying thoughts are also important components of therapy for sleep disturbance. Ouellet and Morin (2007) reported the success of eight weekly sessions of CBT involving stimulus control, sleep restriction, cognitive restructuring, sleep hygiene education and fatigue management in alleviating insomnia in a case series of 11 individuals with TBI, with declines in time spent awake and increased sleep efficiency, and reduced general and physical fatigue, maintained one and three months later. However, no controlled trials of such interventions have been reported.

Pharmacological treatment

In the domain of pharmacological treatments, hypnotic and benzodiazepine-like compounds (Zolpidem and Zopiclone) are not indicated for long-term use in the treatment of sleep disturbance. They are associated with adverse effects, which include impaired cognitive function and reduced daytime alertness, hallucinatory behaviour, sleepwalking and altered sleep architecture (Grunstein, 2002).

Modafinil is a wake-promoting drug approved in the USA for the treatment of excessive sleepiness associated with narcolepsy, obstructive sleep apnoea and shift work disorder. It has been used in the treatment of fatigue in individuals with multiple sclerosis and TBI. A randomised controlled trial by Jha and colleagues (2008), investigating the use of Modafinil in a general TBI sample, found no significant reduction in subjective fatigue, with a trend towards reduced daytime sleepiness in the fourth week, but not the 10th week of treatment. Another trial of Modafinil in 20 people experiencing fatigue/sleepiness problems (Kaiser et al., 2010) showed a reduction in daytime sleepiness but no effect on fatigue.

The finding that evening melatonin production may be reduced following TBI (Shekleton et al., 2010) suggests that melatonin supplementation may improve sleep quality in these individuals. Only one randomised controlled trial has evaluated the efficacy of melatonin as compared with Amitriptyline in treating sleep disturbances in seven people with TBI and chronic sleep difficulties (Kemp, Biswas, Neumann & Coughlan, 2004). No significant improvement was observed in subjective sleep parameters for either Melatonin or Amitriptyline, although findings were limited by the small sample size. A larger trial of Melatonin for treatment of sleep disturbance following TBI is currently being conducted by our research group.

Light therapy

Bright Light Therapy represents another potential treatment for fatigue and daytime sleepiness. Light exerts non-visual effects on several biological functions. In healthy and patient populations exposure to light reduces sleepiness, has arousing effects on various biological parameters, increases vigilance performance and improves mood. Greatest improvements in alertness and depressed mood have been obtained with exposure to blue light (Lockley, Evans, Scheer, Brainard, Czeisler & Aeschbach, 2006). Daily home-based blue light therapy has been shown to reduce depressive symptoms in seasonal affective disorder (Glickman, Byrne, Pineda, Hauch & Brainard, 2006).

We conducted a pilot randomised controlled trial involving 30 individuals with TBI who self-reported fatigue and/or sleep disturbance (Sinclair, Ponsford, Taffe, Lockley & Rajaratnam, 2014). Treatment with high-intensity blue light therapy resulted in reduced fatigue and daytime sleepiness during the treatment phase, not observed with yellow light therapy or no treatment control conditions, with evidence of return to almost baseline levels four weeks after treatment cessation. Whilst this finding needs to be confirmed in a larger sample, it suggests that blue light therapy may be effective in alleviating fatigue and daytime sleepiness following TBI and may offer a non-invasive, safe, and non-pharmacological alternative to current treatments.

Conclusions

Fatigue and sleep disturbance are key factors that limit return to various life roles after a TBI. These are underpinned by injury-related factors, including cognitive impairment, changes in sleep rhythms and circadian regulation of Melatonin as well as a range of secondary factors, including pain, depression and anxiety. Assessment of each of these potential contributing factors is important as a basis for most effective treatment. Management strategies may include activity pacing and sleep hygiene techniques delivered in the context of cognitive behavioural therapy, with contributing pain and mood problems addressed as needed. Light therapy holds promise as a means of reducing subjective fatigue and daytime sleepiness. Trials of Melatonin to improve sleep quality are warranted.

References

Aaronson, L.S., Teel, C.S., Cassmeyer, V., Neuberger, G.C., Pallikkathayil, L., Pierce J., Williams, P.D. & Winegate, A. (1999). Defining and measuring fatigue. *Image – The Journal of Nursing Scholarship*, *31*, 45–50.

Ashman, T.A., Cantor, J.B., Gordon, W.A., Spielman, L., Egan, M., Ginsberg, A., Engmann, G., Dijkers, M. & Flanagan, S. (2008). Objective measurement of fatigue following traumatic brain injury. *Journal of Head Trauma Rehabilitation*, *23*(1), 33–40.

Ayalon, L., Borodkin, K., Dishon, L., Kanety, H. & Dagan, Y. (2007). Circadian rhythm sleep disorders following mild traumatic brain injury. *Neurology*, *68*, 1136–40.

Bateman, A., Culpan, F.J., Pickering, A.D., Powell, J.H., Scott, O.M. & Greenwood, R.J. (2001). The effect of aerobic training on rehabilitation outcomes after recent severe brain injury: a randomized controlled evaluation. *Archives of Physical Medicine and Rehabilitation*, *82*(2), 174–82.

Baumann, C.R., Werth, E., Stocker, R., Ludwig, S. & Bassetti, C.L. (2007). Sleep-wake disturbances 6 months after traumatic brain injury: A prospective study. *Brain*, *130*(7), 1873–83.

Baumann, C.R., Bassetti, C.L., Valko, P.O., Haybaek, J., Keller, M., Clark, E., Stocker, R., Tolnay, M. & Scammell, T.E. (2009). Loss of hypocretin (orexin) neurons with traumatic brain injury. *Annals of Neurology*, *66*(4), 555–9.

Beck, J. (1995). *Cognitive Therapy: Basics and Beyond*. New York: Guilford Press.

Borgaro, S.R., Baker, J., Wethe, J.V., Prigatano, G.P. & Kwasnica, C. (2005). Subjective reports of fatigue during early recovery from traumatic brain injury. *Journal of Head Trauma Rehabilitation*, *20*(5), 416–25.

Bushnik, T., Englander, J. & Wright J. (2008). Patterns of fatigue and its correlates over the first 2 years after traumatic brain injury. *Journal of Head Trauma Rehabilitation*, *23*(1), 25–32.

Cantor, J.B., Ashman, T., Gordon, W., Ginsberg, A., Engmann, C., Egan, M., Spielman, L., Dijkers, M. & Flanagan, S. (2008). Fatigue after traumatic brain injury and its impact on participation and quality of life. *Journal of Head Trauma Rehabilitation*, *23*(1), 41–51.

DeLuca, J. (2005). Fatigue: Its definition, its study, and its future. In: DeLuca, J. (Ed.), *Fatigue as a Window to the Brain*. Cambridge, MA: MIT Press, pp. 319–25.

Englander, J., Bushnik, T., Oggins, J. & Katznelson, L. (2010). Fatigue after traumatic brain injury: Association with neuroendocrine, sleep, depression and other factors. *Brain Injury*, *24*(12), 1379–88.

Fasotti, L., Kovacs, F., Eling, P.A.T.M. & Brouwer, W.H. (2000). Time pressure management as a compensatory strategy training after closed head injury. *Neuropsychological Rehabilitation*, *10*, 47–65.

Glickman, G., Byrne, B., Pineda, C., Hauch, W.W. & Brainard, G.C. (2006). Light therapy for seasonal affective disorder with blue narrow-band light-emitting diodes (LEDs). *Biological Psychiatry*, *59*, 502–7.

Grunstein, R. (2002). Insomnia. Diagnosis and management. *Australian Family Physician*, *31*(11), 995–1000.

Hassett, L., Moseley, A.M., Tate, R. & Harmer, A.R. (2009). Fitness training for cardiorespiratory conditioning after traumatic brain injury (Review). *The Cochrane Library*, Issue 3.

Jha, A., Weintraub, A., Allshouse, A., Morey, C., Cusick, C., Kittelson, J., Harrison-Felix, C., Whiteneck, G. & Gerber, D. (2008). A randomized trial of modafinil for the treatment of fatigue and excessive daytime sleepiness in individuals with chronic traumatic brain injury. *Journal of Head Trauma Rehabilitation*, *23*(1), 52–63.

Kaiser, P.R., Valko, P.O., Werth, E., Thomann, J., Meier, J., Stocker, R., Basetti, C.L. & Baumann, C.R. (2010). Modafinil ameliorates excessive daytime sleepiness after traumatic brain injury. *Neurology*, *75*(20), 1780–5.

Kemp, S., Biswas, R., Neumann, V. & Coughlan, A. (2004). The value of melatonin for sleep disorders occurring post-head injury: A pilot RCT. *Brain Injury*, *18*(9), 911–19.

Lockley, S.W., Evans, E.E., Scheer, F.A., Brainard, G.C., Czeisler, C.A. & Aeschbach, D. (2006). Short-wavelength sensitivity for the direct effects of light on alertness, vigilance, and the waking electroencephalogram in humans. *Sleep*, *29*(2), 161–8.

McMillan, T., Robertson, I.H., Brock, D. & Chorlton, L. (2002). Brief mindfulness training for attentional problems after traumatic brain injury: a randomised control treatment trial. *Neuropsychological Rehabilitation*, *12*(2), 117–25.

Makley, M.J., English, J., Drubach, D.A., Kreuz, A.J., Celnik, P.A. & Tarwater, P.M. (2008). Prevalence of sleep disturbance in closed head injury patients in a rehabilitation unit. *Neurorehabilitation and Neural Repair*, *22*, 341–7.

Mathias, J.L. & Alvaro, P.K. (2012). Prevalence of sleep disturbances, disorders, and problems following traumatic brain injury: A meta-analysis. *Sleep Medicine*, *13*, 898–905.

Orff, H.J., Ayalon, L. & Drummond, S.P. (2009). Traumatic brain injury and sleep disturbance: a review of current research. *Journal of Head Trauma Rehabilitation*, *24*, 155–65.

Ouellet, M.C., Beaulieu-Bonneau, S. & Morin, C.M. (2006). Insomnia in patients with traumatic brain injury: Frequency, characteristics, and risk factors. *Journal of Head Trauma Rehabilitation*, *21*(3), 99–212.

Ouellet, M.C. & Morin, C.M. (2006). Subjective and objective measures of insomnia in the context of TBI. *Sleep Medicine*, *7*(6), 486–97.

Ouellet, M.C. & Morin C.M. (2007). Efficacy of cognitive-behavioural therapy for insomnia associated with traumatic brain injury: a single case experimental design. *Archives of Physical Medicine and Rehabilitation*, *88*(12), 1581–92.

Ponsford, J. & Hsieh, M.Y. (2012). Psychological interventions for emotional and behavioural problems following brain injury. In N.D. Zasler, D.I. Katz & R.D. Zafonte (Eds.), *Brain Injury Medicine: Principles and Practice* (2nd edition). New York: Demos Medical, pp. 1067–85.

Ponsford, J., Cameron, P., Fitzgerald, M., Grant, M. & Mikocka-Walus, A. (2011). Long term outcomes after uncomplicated mild traumatic brain injury: A comparison with trauma controls. *Journal of Neurotrauma*, *28*(6), 937–48.

Ponsford, J.L., Ziino, C., Parcell, D.L., Shekleton, J.A., Redman, J.R., Phipps-Nelson, J. & Rararatnam, S.M.W. (2012). Fatigue and sleep disturbance following traumatic brain injury – Their nature, causes and potential treatments. *Journal of Head Trauma Rehabilitation*, 27(3), 224–33.

Ponsford, J.L., Parcell, D.L., Sinclair, K., Roper, M. & Rajaratnam, S.W. (2013). Changes in sleep patterns following traumatic brain injury: A controlled study. *Neurorehabilitaiton and Neural Repair*, 27(7), 613–21.

Ponsford, J., Schönberger, M. & Rajaratnam, S. (2014). A model of fatigue following traumatic brain injury. *Journal of Head Trauma Rehabilitation*, Published online 9 April 2014. doi: 10.1097/HTR.0000000000000049.

Rao, V., Spiro, J., Vaishnavi, S., Rastogi, P., Mielke, M., Noll, K., Cornwell, E., Schretlen, D. & Makley, M. (2008). Prevalence and types of sleep disturbances acutely after traumatic brain injury. *Brain Injury*, 22(5), 381–6.

Schönberger, M., Herrberg, M. & Ponsford, J. (2014). Fatigue as a cause, not a consequence of depression and daytime sleepiness: A cross-lagged analysis. *Journal of Head Trauma Rehabilitation*, 29(5), 427–31.

Shekleton, J.A., Parcell, D.L., Redman, J.R., Phipps-Nelson, J., Ponsford, J.L. & Rajaratnam S.M.W. (2010). Sleep disturbance and melatonin levels following traumatic brain injury. *Neurology*, 74(21), 1732–8.

Sinclair, K., Ponsford, J., Taffe, J., Lockley, S.W. & Rajaratnam, S.W. (2014). Randomised controlled trial of blue light therapy for fatigue following traumatic brain injury. *NeuroRehabilitation and Neural Repair*, 28(4), 303–13.

Stulemeijer, M., van der Werf, S., Blieijenberg, G., Biert, J., Brauer, J. & Vos, P.E. (2006). Recovery from mild traumatic brain injury: a focus on fatigue. *Journal of Neurology*, 253(8), 1041–7.

Winkens, I., Van Heugten, C.M., Wade, D.T., Habets, E. & Fasotti, L. (2009). Efficacy of time pressure management in stroke patients with slowed information processing: A randomized controlled trial. *Archives of Physical Medicine & Rehabilitation*, 90(10), 1672–9.

Wise, E.K., Hoffman, J.M., Powell, J.M., Bombardier, C.H. & Bell, K.R. (2012). Benefits of exercise maintenance after traumatic brain injury. *Archives of Physical Medicine & Rehabilitation*, 93, 1319–23.

Zedlitz, A.M.E.E., Rietveld, T.C.M., Geurts, A.C. & Fasotti, L. (2012). Cognitive and graded activity training can alleviate persistent fatigue after stroke. A randomized, controlled trial. *Stroke*, 43, 1046–51.

Ziino, C. & Ponsford, J. (2005). Measurement and prediction of subjective fatigue following traumatic brain injury. *Journal of the International Neuropsychological Society*, 11, 416–25.

Ziino, C. & Ponsford, J. (2006a). Selective attention deficits and subjective fatigue following traumatic brain injury. *Neuropsychology*, 20(3), 383–90.

Ziino, C. & Ponsford, J. (2006b). Vigilance and fatigue following traumatic brain injury. *Journal of the International Neuropsychological Society*, 12, 100–10.

14

PSYCHODYNAMIC PSYCHOTHERAPY AFTER SEVERE TRAUMATIC BRAIN INJURY

George P. Prigatano and Christian E. Salas

Introduction

Holistic approaches to neuropsychological rehabilitation of persons who suffer severe traumatic brain injury (TBI) have considered psychotherapy, or broadly defined psychotherapeutic interventions, as a core component of treatment programs. It has been noted by many authors that psychotherapy is necessary to help patients engage in the rehabilitation process, realistically cope with the permanent cognitive and behavioral effects of severe TBI, improve interpersonal relationships with others, return to a productive life style and re-establish a personal sense of meaning to their life "in the face of," "not despite" the effects of their brain injury (Ben-Yishay and Diller, 2011; Klonoff, 2010; Prigatano, 1991, 1999, 2012; Prigatano et al., 1986; Prigatano and Ben-Yishay, 1999; Wilson, 1997). Goldstein (1954), the founder of holistic approaches to neuropsychological rehabilitation, clearly stated the importance of psychotherapy as the following quote demonstrates:

> The treatment of patients suffering from brain damage must aim at two goals. Firstly, eliminating the damage, retraining the lost functions and reducing the mechanisms which have been built to protect the individual against catastrophe and anxiety. Secondly, helping the patient to bear without resentment the restrictions which are necessary. From this latter aspect it becomes evident that psychotherapy is essential in the treatment of all patients with organic defects.
>
> *(Goldstein, 1954, p. 143)*

It is the central premise of this chapter that psychodynamic insights into a patient's psychological development prior to their brain injury – methods of coping with anxiety, attitudes toward parental figures, and personal motivational goals – are of great influence in how patients adjust to the effects of a brain injury during and after rehabilitation, this, despite the fact that they may not be aware of them. Understanding these characteristics of the patient allows for the therapist and rehabilitation teams to work with them more effectively and substantially aid their adjustment process.

Shedler (2010) has eloquently described the biases of academicians in dismissing the evidence in favor of psychodynamic psychotherapy for non-brain dysfunctional individuals. These biases equally apply to clinicians in brain injury rehabilitation, who sometimes misunderstand the nature of psychodynamic insights, and how they can contribute to the treatment of persons with and without a brain disorder (Salas, 2014; Wilson, 2014). Within the context of this brief chapter, an attempt will be made to illustrate how psychodynamic insights can help guide psychotherapeutic interventions with persons who have severe TBI, which results in a meaningful reduction of their disability and social handicap.

A generic definition of psychotherapy relevant to a psychodynamic approach

Coetzer (2007) has noted that the Generic Model of Psychotherapy proposed by Orlinsky and Howard (1995) may be of relevance to the psychotherapy of persons following a severe TBI. This model has been described as "a research-based metatheory of psychotherapy" (Orlinsky, 2009, p. 320), which identifies six core dimensions that are common across various forms of psychotherapy. Three of the six dimensions have particular significance to the present discussion of psychodynamic approaches to psychotherapy, within the context of holistic approaches to neuropsychological rehabilitation. They are: the therapeutic bond, self-relatedness, and the "in-session impacts."

While psychodynamic psychotherapy encompasses many other features (Shedler, 2010), it does stress the importance of the therapeutic alliance or bond. The therapeutic alliance is important in at least two ways. First, patient and therapist must want to work together and feel the commitment of both to deal effectively with the problems the patient experiences. Second, the therapist's observations of how the patient is relating to them can provide useful insights as to conscious and non-conscious attitudes/beliefs of the patient that also influences interpersonal relationships and their manner of coping with conflicts and anxiety.

Psychodynamic approaches to psychotherapy have always emphasized the therapeutic value of self-reflection—that is, the person observing their own personal reactions, thought processes, and ways of behaving. Self-reflection can be therapeutic when the person is able to verbalize how distressing thoughts and feelings are affecting them in the present as well as in the past. Individuals with severe TBI often have difficulties putting thoughts into words and observing a connection between their emotional reactions and impaired cognitive capacity. Recent studies have re-affirmed the self-regulatory power of labeling feelings (e.g. Hariri, Bookheimer & Mazziotta, 2000; Lieberman et al., 2011). Teaching persons with severe TBI "to make sense" of their cognitive and behavioral problems can be extremely helpful in the process of adapting to a brain disorder (Salas et al., 2013; Salas & Coetzer, 2015).

Self-reflection also implies developing self-awareness, which is an active process where individuals are often surprised by what they observe about themselves. Some patients can recognize how present ways of feeling and thinking are heavily influenced by early life experiences. This is perhaps one of the most important observations of early psychoanalytic theorists (Adler, 1927) and is easily appreciated (if one is looking for it) in day treatment neuropsychological rehabilitation programs that are holistic in nature.

A third feature of psychodynamic psychotherapies is the importance of the patient's emotional reactions during a psychotherapy session or during activities that occur in a therapeutic milieu (i.e. in-session impacts). What does the patient actually experience when he is talking to the psychotherapist about his personal life, or what he may experience while working in a cognitive rehabilitation task or any other rehabilitation activity? Which emotions are expressed or kept secret? How do these emotions affect the person at other times during the day? How do they help or hinder the patient's adjustment to a brain disorder? Having a sense of the "roots" of these emotional reactions helps patients to grasp how past experiences/beliefs/conflicts are influencing them *now*. This is a major contribution of psychodynamic psychotherapy.

Types of psychotherapy and the level of care they provide

Salas and Prigatano (in preparation) have described four levels of psychological care that different forms of psychotherapy address. To place psychodynamic psychotherapy in context of other approaches, it is useful to summarize them, even though they will be described in more detail in other chapters of this book. Cognitive oriented behavioral therapies primarily focus on the first level of care—namely, symptom reduction. Here, the goal is often to reduce the level of depression, anxiety, anger or irritability (e.g. Kinney, 2001). Cognitive behavioral therapies also attempt to reduce addictive behaviors that reflect pre-injury adjustment difficulties or problems in copying exacerbated by a brain disorder (e.g. Cox et al., 2003). This represents a second level of care. Newer approaches to CBT include mindfulness training and acceptance and commitment therapy.

Psychodynamic psychotherapy focuses on individuals' personalities and how their reactions to the brain disorder impact relationships with others and attitudes about work. Here the goal is not just re-framing their thoughts about themselves, but to help the person experience relationships (including the psychotherapeutic relationship) in a manner that brings about a more integrated, adaptive individual. The focus of the psychodynamic approach is, therefore, on "the sense of self" and its relationship to others, a third level of care (Freed, 2002; Salas, 2012).

There is a fourth level of care that is of importance for neuropsychological rehabilitation. This level focuses on the conscious and unconscious strivings of the individual to deal with adversity and loss. When addressing these existential needs, psychotherapy's main goal becomes helping individuals establish a new or renewed sense of purpose or meaning in life. If successful, it helps with Goldstein's (1954) expressed goal of accepting restrictions without resentment. Jungian approaches to psychotherapy have been especially helpful in this regard (Prigatano, 2012).

Applying psychodynamic approaches to psychotherapy with patients with severe cognitive and behavioral disorders

A reasonable question for rehabilitationists to ask is how do you apply psychodynamic insights to a young adult with severe cognitive and behavioral disorders secondary to severe TBI? Traditional methods of just "talking to them" may get nowhere in helping them. However, psychodynamic insights can help therapists talk to a person in a manner that captures what the person is struggling with at different levels of his/her existence. The words can relate to both the conscious and unconscious strivings of the individual. If done properly, the patient feels understood by the therapist as a person, not just as someone who has a TBI, and this dialogue helps the patient "make sense" of his/her clinical condition (Salas & Coetzer, 2015; Salas et al., 2013).

Despite caricatures that portray psychodynamic psychotherapies as obscure and complicated, psychodynamic oriented interventions used with brain-injured population are quite straightforward. Through a collaborative dialogue, a narrative is built around quite simple, but existentially relevant questions. What is the patient experiencing now in their rehabilitation? How do they see themselves now versus before the injury? How do they relate now, and in the past, to parental figures and significant others? How does the patient feel about having limitations and needing help from others? What did they want from life before the brain injury? Have those aspirations changed since the TBI? These questions are perhaps similar to the questions that any good clinician would formulate. However, the psychodynamic oriented psychotherapist pays attention not only to the literal responses offered by the patient, but also to what is implied or avoided in their answers.

The old Chinese proverb that "fore warned is fore armed" clearly applies to the psychological and rehabilitation work with a given patient. Knowing whom this person was in the past and now helps determine how you can talk to them and also how you can engage them in collaborative work. If you can relate to the patient's phenomenological experience and reduce his/her confusion (Prigatano, 1999), then they will begin to trust you and follow your guidance because they sense you know what you are talking about as it relates to them. It is the combination of neuropsychological knowledge of the patient, with a psychodynamic understanding of them, which is vital for effective psychotherapy. The patient now senses you want to help them as a person, not simply behaviorally adjust to a brain disorder.

Presently, the major way to demonstrate the value of a psychodynamic perspective is via clinical examples—because each patient is different in terms of his/her underlying brain disorder and psychodynamic make-up. Likewise clinical examples also provide reasonable insights into why we may have failed to help a person with severe TBI using this approach. Multiple experiences of "success" and "failures" when providing psychodynamic psychotherapy with a person with severe TBI are unfortunately necessary to effectively provide this service. Getting supervision or feedback from colleagues trained in psychodynamic theory and practice can also be helpful.

Clinical examples of the efficacy of psychodynamic psychotherapy in reducing social handicap after severe TBI

Two major social handicapping conditions after severe TBI are the inability to return to work and difficulties in social re-integration. Holistic neuropsychological rehabilitation programs address these problems (Prigatano et al., 1986; Prigatano, 1999). For some, the goal is a return to gainful employment; for others it is voluntary work that is rewarding to them. Patients with very severe cognitive and behavioral impairments may not be able to achieve either goal. Angry and aggressive patients often fall within this category. These patients can become quite socially isolated without adequate help.

A middle-age married businessman suffered a severe TBI affecting multiple regions of his brain, but with perhaps the greatest involvement in the temporal lobes. This was assumed in light of neuroimaging findings and his performance on various neuropsychological tests. He had severe memory impairment, difficulties in controlling aggressive or angry responses during group meetings, and a tendency to misperceive the actions and intentions of others.

One day, during a group exercise that was part of a holistic program, he angrily jumped up and threatened another patient who had mildly provoked him. He was about to hit the other patient, when the psychotherapist intervened. The therapist knew how confused the patient was in his thinking as well as how badly he missed his wife, who was living in another state since his brain injury. The therapist also knew that this patient's sense of authority and need for control and power (something Adler (1927) insightfully wrote about) was a crucial theme in his psychological development and was now eroded. He also knew that the patient was very controlling of his wife before the brain injury. He knew all of this after lengthy discussions with him, his wife and his parents. Thus, when the patient was about to strike another patient, the psychotherapist calmly addressed him by his first name and acknowledged that he was very upset and offended. Saying those words out loud actually helped calm the patient down for a few seconds. The therapist then asked the patient to simply walk with him (away from the confrontational setting), and he accepted since he viewed the therapist as caring and helpful.

As the therapist and patient walked around the building several times, the patient yelled and screamed about how mad he was with his fellow patient; how mad he was with his wife; how mad he was with life; how mad he was that he lost his job, position, power and status. He was profoundly humiliated by it all. The therapist acknowledged these feelings and commented that all human beings want to have a sense of power and respect from others. All human beings want a partner who loves them and wants to be with them. The sad fact was that this was not possible for the patient, at this particular time. However, his desires and reactions were understandable. The question was how to help him now. The patient, on his own, stated that being around people was often "too much" for him. It was agreed that he would do better in a rehabilitation program that reduced his contact (and conflict) with people. With the active intervention of his psychotherapist, he was transferred to a rural community and rehabilitation program that focuses on long walks on the prairie, working with animals, and enjoying their (the animals) non-critical acceptance of him as he is now. With time, the patient was able to improve his behavioral outbursts, but remained severely cognitively impaired. He ultimately made a good adjustment working in a farming community with appropriate medications and an active support of outpatient rehabilitation therapists. He missed his wife, but the affection of the animals he cared for helped him.

What is the contribution of a psychodynamic perspective in this case? Understanding the patient's psychological history was very relevant to how he was approached. From a non-psychoanalytic perspective, the patient's reaction would simply reflect a behavioral problem, a mix of disinhibition, inadequate social skills and paranoid ideation. However, that approach misses an important point. The patient was not simply angry; he was offended. A valuable aspect of his premorbid self was threatened by the social interaction with the other patient. Understanding this underlying and somewhat hidden motivation of the patient's behavior allowed the therapist's intervention to be effective. It temporarily soothed him and opened up options in his rehabilitation that he could accept. This was with "less resentment" than might be expected. Long-term psychiatric hospitalization was avoided.

Another example, which highlights Jungian contributions to neuropsychological rehabilitant and psychotherapy, has been discussed in some detail elsewhere (Prigatano, 2012). A summary of the case will be provided to demonstrate the important role of establishing meaning after severe TBI, and how symbols can be used to generate, and elaborate, meaning despite marked cognitive deficits. A young man suffered a severe TBI secondary to a motor vehicle accident. It rendered him aphasic and hemiplegic. The patient and his mother wanted nothing to do with talking about feelings, addressing the psychological reactions to the injury or their relationship. They simply wanted "bigger and better" speech and language therapy to overcome his aphasia. Treated in the context of a holistic rehabilitation program, this patient met with other patients struggling with the various consequences of their brain disorders. He observed their struggles and made comments during group psychotherapy about his personal struggles. By the end of 6 months of intensive work with him, the patient spontaneously brought in a drawing reflecting what he was experiencing. The drawing reflected his cognitive confusion and unawareness. The drawing also reflected a sense of renewed direction to his life (see Figure 14.1). Discussing the drawing, the patient reported that even with his permanent aphasia he could work with children with severe physical and mental handicap. Such therapeutic realization, as well as his mother's blessing (which was very important to him), motivated him to choose this line of work that facilitated the process of accepting

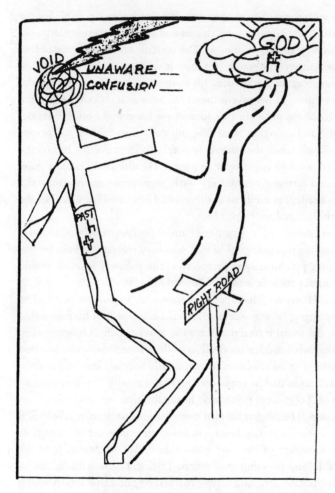

FIGURE 14.1 Spontaneous drawing by a traumatic head-injury patient at the
completion of a rehabilitation program

the restrictions in his life with minimal resentment and improving his social
re-integration.

Psychodynamic oriented group psychotherapy: the role of music, stories and fairytales

Many patients with severe TBI have a difficult time consciously introspecting about
their life and personal feelings. Talking in groups about their emotional experiences
at times appears ineffective and can be disturbing to some patients. Years ago, we
discovered the potential role of using symbols in music, movies and fairytales as
therapeutic tools to build personal meaning (Prigatano, 1999). For example, in the

context of group psychotherapy (a common activity of holistic programs), all members (including the psychologists) were asked to play their favorite song in the group. No one would interpret the choice of a particular song. Rather, all group members would simply talk about how a particular song affected them. What feelings, emotions, thoughts were experienced as they listen to the music of another.

One patient, a woman with severe cognitive and behavioral problems, chose Michael Jackson's song "Man in the Mirror." While she was angry most of the time because of her physical and cognitive limitations, after working in the holistic program, she began to realize the need to take a good look at herself and start to change her attitudes in order to make the world (and her world) a better place. Even though this therapeutic realization was heavily influenced by her past history, what is more interesting here is that such elaboration was not possible without the use of this therapeutic "artifact." In the song, aspects of herself could be projected and then observed and reflected upon.

Similarly, the use of movies and fairytales appears to have a similar effect, helping patients to compensate for their cognitive difficulties when manipulating inform-ation. The use of visual and graphic information to address the process of identity re-construction has been also employed by non-psychodynamic therapists with impressive results (Ylvisaker & Feeney, 2000; Ylvisaker et al., 2008). From a psy-chodynamic perspective, these concrete "therapeutic artifacts" offer a golden path to access conscious and unconscious strivings of patients. They also facilitate the understanding of personal reactions to the brain injury and the rehabilitation process. The hero's journey (for a discussion on the relevance of this symbol in neuropsychological rehabilitation see Prigatano, 2012), depicted in many favorite movies, is often a topic of discussion that brings out moving expressions of feelings the patient could not simply initiate without the aid of some art form.

Clinical examples of when psychodynamic psychotherapy failed after severe TBI: what happens when restrictions cannot be accepted because psychodynamic conflicts are not adequately treated

Case examples, of course, are considered to be anecdotes, not scientific evidence. Yet, they can provide important insights as to when psychodynamic psychotherapy, or other psychological therapies, may not have been helpful. Two brief examples will be described. The first patient had "a drinking problem" before she suffered a severe TBI in a motor vehicle accident. The drinking problem was down played when she was first evaluated. As an athletic young woman, she wanted to regain her physical skills and return to a previous life style. However, that life style focused on childhood pursuits, something that was reflected in her favorite fairytale: "Peter Pan." After one year of intensive holistic neuropsychological rehabilitation, she seemed willing to accept living in a new geographical location she did not really like. She also, at first, agreed to engage in a voluntary job she did not really like either. At the end of her rehabilitation program, she mentioned for the first time her intense fear of her mother. She did not want to talk about it, but wanted her psychotherapist to know about it. This important attachment issue, which was a part of her psychological make-up, was never addressed. She eventually returned to her old life style, which included heavy drinking and self-destructive relationships. She eventually died of complications related to alcoholism.

The second patient also had significant physical and cognitive limitations secondary to a "moderate to severe" TBI. Her physical limitations greatly affected her sense of female beauty, which she always strived to maintain. In the course of psychotherapy, she stated that her father never respected her for her intellect, and that she only received attention from him in the form of comments about her physical attractiveness. Not surprisingly, after her TBI, she felt more estranged from him. Eventually he died and she began a series of problematic relationships with men. When she returned for post rehabilitation psychotherapy, she initially agreed to do voluntary work. Nevertheless, her motivation to work was not authentic, but a response to her relationship with the therapist. In her mind, her therapist was like a father, who controlled her and forced her to do something she did not want. Unfortunately, these psycho-historical issues were never successfully dealt with during the treatment. As a consequence, feelings of resentment towards the therapist, for controlling her and forcing her to do something she did not want, emerged. This resulted in her terminating psychotherapy and a continued destructive pattern of relationships with men after the injury.

It is useful to compare this latter patient's reactions with another female patient who also struggled with issues of physical beauty, but in a different fashion. This illustrates the highly idiosyncratic nature of the psychological conflicts triggered by brain injury. The patient was a young woman who never felt "pretty," but took pride in her intellect. Since her brain injury reduced her cognitive capacity, she became withdrawn and depressed. She was not referred for neuropsychological rehabilitation per se, but for the treatment of her depression. Unlike the former patient, this patient had a number of dreams that she discussed with her therapist. The dream content reflected her sadness and anger over how she changed, but not anger toward the psychotherapist. As the therapeutic relationship unfolded, sexual feelings toward the therapist emerged and were openly discussed. This patient began to realize these erotic feelings really meant she wanted love and a sense of personal recognition from a parental figure. She then was able to connect these feelings with childhood memories as well as to the importance that helping others had for her. With time, anti-depressive medication and psychological work, she accepted a major change in her work status since it still gave her a personal sense of meaning. She also maintained her relationship with her husband and had no depressive relapses.

A brief note about the importance of dreams

Historically, a key feature of psychodynamic psychotherapy has been the consideration of dreams as a tool to understand not only unconscious motivations, but also whether the patient's psychological attitudes and approach to personal problems have actually changed as a result of psychotherapy. Patients with severe TBI often do not report dreaming after their injuries. However, as they recover some do begin to report having dreams. Unfortunately, no one has yet systematically studied the dreams of persons with severe TBI and how they relate to their rehabilitation process and outcome. However, working with this population, the value of dreams in understanding the patient's experience has become obvious, particularly as a tool to access aspects of the patient's experience that are not verbalized during psycho-therapy. Consider this example. A young man, who was also aphasic after a severe TBI, was struggling to alter his job expectations for the future. He had a difficult time putting into words what he was feeling. However, one day he spontaneously told his psychotherapist about a dream he had. The dream content was very simple. In the dream he was crying, but only out of the left eye. When asked about what he thought the dream may signify, he stated that he was told he had a left-sided brain injury and that is why he had so much difficulty talking and was unable to pursue his career choice. The therapist simply made the comment that the dream may also reflect his unexpressed sadness over his losses. He knotted his head, showed sadness in his face and said very little. Nevertheless, this simple thera-peutic realization appeared to strengthen greatly the bond between patient and therapist.

Factors that limit the therapeutic alliance when working with persons who have severe TBI

A major goal of psychodynamic psychotherapy, within the context of holistic neuropsychological rehabilitation programs, is to facilitate the engagement in rehabilitation activities the patient may resist. This is a challenging task, since a good portion of TBI patients present with cognitive impairments and reduced self-awareness (Prigatano, 1999). They don't "see the need," for example, to use memory compensation techniques in everyday life.

What are the mechanisms that facilitate or hinder engagement? The literature on therapeutic alliance offers important insights. Bordin (1979) suggests that the therapeutic alliance is composed of three elements. First is the interpersonal bond, which has both conscious and unconscious influences. Second is agreement on goals (i.e. therapist and patient agree on what they want to achieve). Third is agreement on tasks (i.e. means used to accomplish treatment goals). Different components of the working alliance can be compromised when treating individuals with TBI. For example, anosognosia can challenge the establishment of common goals, cognitive impairments can impede the use of specific tasks and pre-existing psychological conflicts can undermine the generation of an emotional bond. Research on the effectiveness of holistic approaches to neuropsychological rehabilitation has consistently found that the quality of the working alliance relates to treatment outcome (e.g., Prigatano et al., 1994; Klonoff, Lamb & Henderson, 2001). A meta-analysis conducted by Martin, Garske and Davis (2000) has also demonstrated the importance of the working alliance in psychotherapy outcome with persons who do not have brain disorders.

Critics of psychodynamic psychotherapy after severe TBI: a response with suggestions for future research

A common criticism of psychodynamic ideas in neuropsychological rehabilitation is that they are not suitable for cognitively impaired patients. The argument is that patients with severe cognitive impairments are too rigid in their thought process and/or have no emotional awareness of their behavioral difficulties to benefit from insight oriented psychotherapies. This issue has not been neglected by psychodynamic psychotherapists working in the field. A variety of "technical modifications" have been used to facilitate a psychodynamic dialogue at the cognitive level of the patient. The use of drawings, songs, movies and fairytales are examples of how psychodynamic issues can be expressed in a meaningful way. The expressed goal is to understand how premorbid characteristics of the patient influence their symptom picture and may be used to aid their rehabilitation process even with severely impaired individuals (e.g. the first patient discussed in this chapter).

In fact, this approach is extremely similar to the one used by non–psychodynamic clinicians who have employed also "therapeutic artifacts" [identity maps] to optimize patients' cognition and address existential and identity issues (Ylvisaker & Feeney, 2000). More recently, other theoretical and technical modifications have been suggested to address the problem on concreteness after TBI in the context of psychodynamic interventions (Salas & Coetzer, 2015; Salas et al., 2013). Future studies are needed to understand how patients use these technical modifications and explore what mechanisms explain their clinical effectiveness.

The potential value of psychodynamic ideas for neuropsychological rehabilitation should also be consider in light of Wilson and Gracey's (2010) suggestion that rehabilitation programs require integrative theoretical models that can guide clinicians' efforts in both understanding and modifying behavior. Overarching models offer a set of principles in which rehabilitation professionals can rely in order to guide the logic of their decision making process. This is extremely relevant for person-centered rehabilitation models, which adapt interventions to patients and not patients to interventions. In this context, psychodynamic ideas are of great value, and can contribute to this set of principles, specifically in relation to the understanding and management of emotional reactions of the patient and the rehabilitation team. Such an idea is not new, and has been implemented in emblematic rehabilitation programs (Prigatano, 1999; Klonoff, 2010).

Another common criticism of psychodynamic psychotherapies is the lack of scientific evidence to support its effectiveness (i.e., the lack of randomized control trials [RCT]). An important response to this criticism is that psychodynamic psycho-therapies cannot be directly compared to cognitive therapies since they target different levels of care (Salas and Prigatano, in preparation). Cognitive therapies target symptom reduction, a variable that can be easily quantified and translated to experimental paradigms where "objective" changes can be measured and RCT employed. In contrast, psychodynamic therapies operate at the third and fourth level of care, thus targeting psychological processes that are most complex and profoundly personal. There is no simple way of measuring these outcomes. However, the long-term outcome of holistic neuropsychological rehabilitation, which incorporates psychodynamic psychotherapy, might be compared to day treatment programs that do not incorporate psychodynamic insights and interventions. This approach could provide indirect scientific evidence of its effectiveness.

It is also important to recognize that presently there is a lack of "critical mass" of clinicians and researchers to develop effectiveness studies of psychodynamic interventions. This is partly due to the absence of psychodynamic teaching in programs that train clinical psychologists and neuropsychologists, which are heavily biased towards short and manualized cognitive-behavioural interventions. Such emphasis is also influenced by Health Services policies, which favour "cost-effective" interventions that are extremely limited in time and predominantly focused on symptom removal during the acute and sub-acute stages of rehabilitation. Any clinician working with TBI knows, however, that brain injury is a lifelong problem, and that a reduction in symptoms does not necessarily means successful emotional adjustment to the changes brought by the injury.

Cognitive models of the mind and behavioural approaches often do not adequately address the patient's personality before a brain injury, and how patient's previous psychohistory can influence the way patients think and behave after the injury. We propose that psychodynamic insights aids the rehabilitation process for many patients by attempting to understand and treat emotional disturbances which may not be obvious, but are extremely important in the patient's long term adjustment. Such an approach often leads to a more integrated and "holistic" understanding of the individual. Perhaps the best evidence for the effectiveness of psychodynamic psychotherapy will be the demonstration that the degree of "resentment" patients experience over the restrictions in their life, several years post treatment, will be substantially lower than patients not receiving this form of care.

Acknowledgments

Funding to George P. Prigatano was obtained from the Newsome Chair and economic support from the Lou and Evelyn Grubb's Philanthropic Gift, Department of Clinical Neuropsychology allowed time to prepare portions of this manuscript. The Chilean government and the Neuropsychoanalysis Foundation provided funding support to Dr. Christian E. Salas.

References

Adler, A. (1927). *Understanding Human Nature.* New York: Garden City Publishing Company.
Ben-Yishay, Y. & Diller, L. (2011). *Handbook of Holistic Neuropsychological Rehabilitation.* New York, NY: Oxford University Press.

Bordin, E. S. (1979). The generalizability of the psychoanalytic concept of the working alliance. *Psychotherapy: Theory, Research & Practice, 16*(3), 252.

Coetzer, B. R. (2007). Psychotherapy following traumatic brain injury: Integrating theory and practice. *Journal of Head Trauma Research, 22*(1), 39–47.

Cox, W.M., Heineman, A.W., Miranti, S.V., Schmidt, M., Klinger, E. & Blount, J. (2003). Outcomes of systematic motivational counselling for substance use following traumatic brain injury. *Journal of Addictive Diseases, 22*(1), 93–110.

Freed, P. (2002). Meeting of the minds: Ego reintegration after traumatic brain injury. *Bulletin of the Menninger Clinic, 66*(1), 61–78.

Goldstein, K. (1954). The concept of transference in functional and organic disease. *Acta Psychother Psychosom Orthopaedagog, 2*(3–4), 334–353.

Hariri, A. R., Bookheimer, S. Y. & Mazziotta, J. C. (2000). Modulating emotional responses: effects of a neocortical network on the limbic system. *Neuroreport, 11*(1), 43–8.

Kinney, A. (2001). Cognitive therapy and brain-injury: Theoretical and clinical issues. *Memory, 31*(2), 89–102.

Klonoff, P. S. (2010). *Psychotherapy after Brain Injury: Principles and Techniques.* New York, NY: The Guilford Press.

Klonoff, P. S., Lamb, D. G. & Henderson, S. W. (2001). Outcomes from milieu-based neurorehabilitation at up to 11 years post-discharge. *Brain Injury, 15*(5), 413–428.

Lieberman, M. D., Inagaki, T. K., Tabibnia, G. & Crockett, M. J. (2011). Subjective responses to emotional stimuli during labeling, reappraisal, and distraction. *Emotion Washington DC, 11*(3), 468–480.

Martin, D. J., Garske, J. P. & Davis, M. K. (2000). Relation of the therapeutic alliance with outcome and other variables: a meta-analytic review. *Journal of consulting and clinical psychology, 68*(3), 438.

Orlinsky, D. E. (2009). The "generic model of psychotherapy" after 25 years: Evolution of a research-based metatheory. *Journal of Psychotherapy Integration, 19*(4), 319–339.

Orlinsky, D. E. and Howard, K. I. (1995). Unity and diversity among psychotherapies: A comparative perspective. In: Bongar, B., Beutler, L.E. (Eds.), *Comprehensive Textbook of Psychotherapy, Theory and Practice.* New York: Oxford University Press, pp. 3–23.

Prigatano, G. P. (1991). Disordered mind, wounded soul: The emerging role of psychotherapy in rehabilitation after brain injury. *Journal of Head Trauma Rehabilitation, 6*(4), 1–10.

Prigatano, G. P. (1999). *Principles of Neuropsychological Rehabilitation.* New York: Oxford University Press, pp. 332–346.

Prigatano, G. P. (2012). Jungian contributions to successful neuropsychological rehabilitation. *Neuropsychoanalysis, 14*(2), 175–185.

Prigatano, G. P. & Ben-Yishay, Y. (1999). Psychotherapy and psychotherapeutic interventions in brain injury rehabilitation. *Rehabilitation of the Adult and Child with Traumatic Brain Injury, 3*, 271–283.

Prigatano, G. P., Fordyce, D. J., Zeiner, H. K., Roueche, J. R., Pepping, M. & Wood, B. C. (1986). *Neuropsychological Rehabilitation after Brain Injury.* Baltimore, MD: The Johns Hopkins University Press.

Prigatano, G. P., Klonoff, P. S., O'Brien, K. P., Altman, I., Amin, K., Chiapello, D., Shepherd, J., Cunningham, M. & Mora, M. (1994). Productivity after neuropsychological oriented, milieu rehabilitation. *Journal of Head Trauma Rehabilitation, 9*(1), 91–102.

Salas, C. E. (2012). Surviving catastrophic reaction after brain injury: The use of self-regulation and self-other regulation. *Neuropsychoanalysis, 14*(1), 77–92.

Salas, C. E (2014). Research digest: Identity issues in neuropsychoanalysis. *Neuropsychoanalysis, 16*(2), 153–158.

Salas, C. E. & Coetzer, R. (2015). Is concreteness the invisible link between altered emotional processing, impaired awareness and mourning difficulties after traumatic brain injury? *Neuropsychoanalysis*, (April 2015), 1–16.

Salas, C. E. & Prigatano, G. P. (in preparation). *From Meaning to Symptom Reduction: Contemporary Approaches to Psychotherapy after Traumatic Brain Injury.*

Salas, C. E., Vaughan, F. L., Shanker, S. & Turnbull, O. H. (2013). Stuck in a moment: Concreteness and psychotherapy after acquired brain injury. *Neuro-Disability and Psychotherapy*, *1*(1), 1–38.

Shedler, J. (2010). The efficacy of psychodynamic psychotherapy. *American Psychologist*, *65*(2), 98–109.

Wilson, B. (1997). Cognitive rehabilitation: How it is and how it might be. *Journal of the International Neuropsychological Society, JINS*, *3*, 487–496.

Wilson, B. A. (2014). Are psychoanalysis and neuropsychology compatible? In *Psychology Serving Humanity: Proceedings of the 30th International Congress of Psychology: Volume 2: Western Psychology* (Vol. 2, p. 84). New York: Psychology Press.

Wilson, B. & Gracey, F. (2010). Towards a comprehensive model of neuropsychological rehabilitation. In: B. Wilson, F. Gracey, J. Evans & A. Bateman (Eds.), *Neuropsychological Rehabilitation*. New York: Cambridge University Press, pp. 1–21.

Ylvisaker, M. & Feeney, T. (2000). Reconstruction of identity after brain injury. *Brain Impairment*, *12*(1), 12–28.

Ylvisaker, M., McPherson, K., Kayes, N. & Pellett, E. (2008). Metaphoric identity mapping: Facilitating goal setting and engagement in rehabilitation after traumatic brain injury. *Neuropsychological Rehabilitation*, *18*(5–6), 713–741.

15

PHARMACOLOGICAL THERAPY FOR NEUROBEHAVIOURAL DISABILITY

Richard Greenwood and Simon Fleminger

Introduction

In this chapter we discuss current pharmacological management of neurobehavioural disability (NBD), both in respect of its positive and negative characteristics, as well as related conditions. We will briefly address problems that arise in the early stage of recovery, during the period of Post Traumatic Amnesia (PTA), but focus on the pattern of disability that presents at a later stage of recovery. The drugs we consider, aim either to facilitate or inhibit the disordered neurotransmission thought to be associated with NBD, to reduce impulsive, aggressive and antisocial behaviours, or social withdrawal and isolation. Those that target neural protection, repair and regeneration, (for example progesterone, statins and erythropoietin), which may, at least in pre-clinical models, reduce many of the residual effects of TBI, are not considered.

Over the last 10 years the results of Phase III trials of drugs to facilitate brain function and reduce cognitive problems and NBD after TBI reveal a good safety record. But most do not demonstrate functional effectiveness (Diaz-Arrastia et al., 2014; Dougall et al., 2015), with the possible exception of Amantadine (Hammond et al., 2014, 2015) and Methylphenidate (Kim et al., 2012). Currently therefore, at least in the UK, drugs are often prescribed empirically to reduce risk by inhibiting, rather than normalising, the brain activity that results in NBD. However, before addressing these matters, it is important to consider the basic generic issues that underpin any psychotropic management of the brain injured patient.

Clinical assessment

Background assessment of patients with NBD must include details of pre-injury factors, which may not only have increased the risk of the original injury but also influence the nature of NBD and thus its drug treatment. For example, patients with pre-existing mental illness, particularly mood disorders and psychoses, are particularly likely to present with NBD, and these need to be treated specifically before any further treatment of the NBD is considered.

Epilepsy deserves special consideration. Tonic–clonic seizures will usually be self-evident but frontal lobe seizures or complex partial seizures may be less obviously epileptic and may be mistaken for NBD. Epileptic seizures, or their treatment, may exacerbate NBD; this is particularly likely if there are several seizures in a short space of time, either serially or continuously, and diagnostic difficulties may arise if awareness is retained during non-convulsive status epilepticus. In some patients NBD is confined to the post-ictal period, during post-ictal confusion or as a psychotic state.

Problems due to alcohol are well recognised. Alcohol intoxication is very likely to exacerbate NBD. Alcohol withdrawal can also be problematic, all the more so if withdrawal epileptic seizures are present. And finally, particularly in the in-patient or residential setting, craving for alcohol will very likely worsen NBD. Much the same can be said for all drugs of addiction. And the prescribing physician needs to be particularly alert to the patient who is addicted to benzodiazepines or other anxiolytic/sedative medication and has learned that if they present with NBD then they get immediate relief of their craving with the prescription of anxiolytic/sedative medication to manage their NBD.

Other prescribed medication needs to be reviewed. First to ensure that nothing is being prescribed that might exacerbate NBD. Drugs that have the potential to cause confusion, for example dopamine agonists or anti-cholinergics, are likely to be particularly relevant here. Levetiracetam, though an excellent anticonvulsant, which may improve NBD if it is the result of non-convulsive status epilepticus, may produce anger, aggression, nervousness, agitation, depression and insomnia as side effects (Kowski et al., 2016), and thus worsen NBD. In addition, it is important to consider any drug interactions when prescribing medication to manage the NBD.

It is important that all members of a multidisciplinary team have some understanding of how NBD is susceptible to deterioration as a result of any local or generalised systemic medical condition, especially as complications of this sort are often avoidable. Common causes include infection, pain or discomfort due to other injuries, central pain, a painful shoulder or constipation. Lack of sleep or exercise, and problems with nutritional status, anaemia, hypothyroidism and other endocrine dysfunction, occasionally as a result of post-traumatic hypothalamic-pituitary dysfunction (Ulfarsson et al., 2013), or obstructive sleep apnoea and other sleep disorders that occur following brain injury (Ouellet et al., 2015), are all likely to exacerbate fatigue and thereby increase NBD. Patients with poor diabetic control may be vulnerable to hypoglycaemia or hyperglycaemia that may result in or exacerbate behavioural problems. Secondary neurological complications need also to be ruled out, particularly due to hydrocephalus, a chronic subdural haematoma, or intracranial hypotension.

Principles of prescribing of psychotropics to the brain injured patient

By and large psychotropic medication should only be used to manage NBD when all other reasonable avenues of treatment have been tried. When prescribing psychotropic medication to the brain injured patient it is worth bearing in mind:

1   For the treatment of many cognitive and behavioural symptoms there is relatively little evidence on which to make prescribing decisions.
2   Thus the psychotropic will usually be prescribed "off label", and the condition that the psychotropic is being used to treat is not one of the conditions for which the drug is licensed.
3   Almost all psychotropics have the potential to increase confusion and impair learning, but small doses can reduce hypervigilance and make other interventions more effective.

The prescribing doctor therefore has a particular duty to ensure that they can justify the prescription. They will need to ensure that systems are in place to monitor the apparent effectiveness of the drug, and to review the prescription regularly, always with a view to reducing and stopping the medication as soon as appropriate. This issue is particularly relevant when a patient is discharged from in-patient care; often the general practitioner is left to continue the prescription with no advice as to why the patient is on the drug or how to plan for its withdrawal.

To enable these duties to be met, consultation with other members of the multidisciplinary team should take place before prescription. If a NBD has just come to light it has a good chance of rapid spontaneous resolution; a drug prescribed in the meantime will give a false impression of efficacy. It is also better not to start a medication at the same time as some other intervention or change that might also affect the NBD. For example, it is probably best to avoid starting a new psychotropic just after admission; any improvement might be due to the change in environment rather than the medication. Avoid starting two psychotropics at the same time or closely one after another; it will not be clear which has worked. A useful way to address some of these issues is to observe during a baseline period before medication is prescribed.

The prescribing doctor has a duty to ensure that the patient, and/or their family or advocates, are well informed about the potential benefits and side effects of the medication, and the conditions under which it is being prescribed. With these principles of prescribing in mind, "start low and go slow" should be the underlying principle, as the brain injured patient is particularly likely to be vulnerable to sedative side effects of psychotropic medication. Be aware of the potential for "chasing one's tail"; for example, akathisia as a side effect of antipsychotic medication will make agitation much worse. Avoid cocktails of medication; these have the potential to increase confusion, will complicate drug interactions, and make it difficult to know which drug has helped. Avoid using *as required* (PRN) anxiolytic medication to treat agitated aggressive behaviour. Pleasant anxiolytic effects of medication may reinforce the behaviour.

Early NBD: post traumatic amnesia and confusion

During the early stages of Post-Traumatic Amnesia/Confusion (PTA/C) there is often an initial period of confused, anxious, agitated and combative behaviour (Figure 15.1), that subsides when the ability to form continuous memory is restored, despite longer-term background cognitive deficits (Stuss et al.,1999; Marshman et al., 2013).

These behaviours put patients, and sometimes their carers, at risk of injury as a result of falls and absconsion, and prevent participation in rehabilitation. Hitherto, patients have often been heavily sedated, but drug side effects and the prolongation of PTA as a result of the protracted use of sedative doses of neuroleptics, especially Haloperidol, has meant that intervention now focuses on environmental adjustments and behavioural techniques, rather than the administration of drugs (see Ponsford et al., 2014). Early institution of these measures probably minimises the use of medication, and possibly shortens the duration of PTA and time for which high dependency and hospital care is required (Mysiw et al., 2006).

Extreme acute agitation may leave little choice about the use of an intramuscular or intravenous sedative, either a shorter acting benzodiazepine or a neuroleptic, often as Lorazepam or Haloperidol respectively. These drugs are often used alone, but Bieniek et al. (1998), in a small (n = 20) but admirably constructed study of psychiatric patients, showed that their combined use, as intramuscular Lorazepam (2mg) and Haloperidol (5mg), was more effective when compared with 2mg of intramuscular Lorazepam alone. In less extreme circumstances, the use of medication to reduce hypervigilance and over-arousal, until the agitation and confusion of PTA

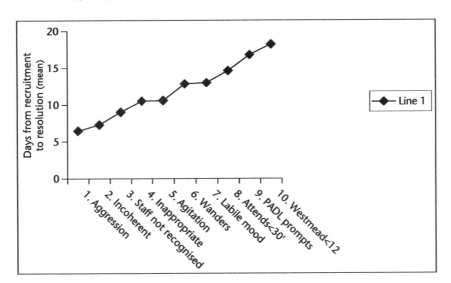

FIGURE 15.1   Resolution of behaviours over time during PTA. Resolution of aggression and agitation is followed by anxiety and confusion before PTA ends. Behaviours derived from Rancho Los Amigos levels IV (1–5) and V (6–10). (After Weir et al., 2006.)

resolves spontaneously, remains unexplored by controlled trials, and relies largely on expert consensus. Most authors recommend small doses of sedative medication if initial environmental modification fails to reduce hypervigilance and over-arousal, once pain, for example from other injuries, pressure areas and spastic spasms, infection and other co-morbidities have been treated, and the sleep-wake cycle optimised.

Practice often parallels the use of neuroleptics during hyperactive delirium in medical patients (Grover et al., 2011), using low-dose (0.25–2.0mg) Haloperidol, or, preferably, second generation neuroleptics including Olanzapine (1.25–10mg), Risperidone (0.5–2.0mg), or Quetiapine (25–100mg), which minimise extrapyramidal side effects, compared with Haloperidol. Recently Quetiapine has been shown to shorten the duration of hypoactive delirium in ITU patients (Michaud et al., 2015), which may at least be economically, if not clinically, of benefit. Its use during the agitated and confused phases of PTA might produce a similar result and is worthy of further investigation. Whether other drugs, for example beta-blockers, mood stabilising anticonvulsants or antidepressants also have a part to play remains virtually unexplored. One small (N = 21) double-blind placebo controlled trial of Propranolol over 7 weeks (initially increasing from 60mg/day by 120 mg/day increments a week to 420mg/day), found some benefit in the treatment group (Brooke et al., 1992).

Recently Bogner et al. (2015) studied medication use in 557 patients hospitalised acutely after TBI, and found that prescription of second generation neuroleptics for agitation, most often Quetiapine, Gamma-aminobutyric acid-A receptor agonists (GABA-A) and sodium channel blocking anticonvulsants, appeared to increase subsequent agitation. In contrast, Methylphenidate, an agent usually used later post-injury to promote speed of processing and attentional skills, was followed by a reduction in agitation. The explanation for this novel finding remains elusive, as does the reason that of 167 different preparations prescribed in total, Methylphenidate was prescribed 5001 times, a frequency exceeded only by the prescription of Docusate and Trazodone. That Methylphenidate would virtually never be prescribed in these clinical circumstances in the UK speaks to the complete absence of an international expert consensus, let alone evidence based guidelines, on medication use for agitated patients in PTA/C and the urgent need for collaborative study.

Later neurobehavioural disability

Over the last 25 years pre-clinical studies have demonstrated that TBI results in catecholamine (epinephrine, norepinephrine and dopamine) and cholinergic depletion, and disordered serotoninergic, GABAergic or glutamatergic transmission, and have begun to define the structure and function of the large scale brain networks and the neurotransmitters that underpin arousal, speed of processing, rewardability, apathy and motivation, mood, working memory and attentional skills, executive function, self-regulation, and learning and plasticity (Sharp et al., 2014; Yan et al., 2015; Shin & Dixon, 2015). Specific drug treatments, and latterly invasive and non-invasive brain stimulation, have at times been shown to result in improvement of both impairment and function (Kim et al., 2012; Fridman & Schiff, 2014).

A small number of Phase III clinical trials for late residual cognitive problems and NBD in the last decade have investigated whether catecholamine or cholinergic agonists facilitate brain function, usually as methylphenidate or Amantadine, or Rivastigmine or Donepezil. Single studies have used Modafinil and Atomoxetine; other studies report small series or anecdotal results (Diaz-Arrastia et al., 2014; Dougall et al., 2015). Despite clear changes in neurotransmitter function after TBI, no clear functional benefit was demonstrated in any of these trials, with the possible exception of Amantadine. Currently therefore if drugs are prescribed they are usually intended to reduce brain function and thus maladaptive symptoms or behaviours, particularly to reduce risk.

Irritability and aggression

Irritability and aggressive behaviour are frequent legacies of TBI, typically as out-bursts of anger and aggression triggered by minor arguments or frustrations, often followed by remorse. When aggression is out of control and hugely out of propor-tion to the circumstances, then it may be labelled episodic dyscontrol. Some suggest that episodic dyscontrol is likely to respond to anticonvulsant mood stabilisers, particularly Carbamazepine (Eames & Wood, 2003), but there is no evidence that episodic dyscontrol is epileptic in origin. Patients who present with aggression after TBI have often had problems with aggression before their injury, and many clinicians are less optimistic about a positive response to medication post-injury if aggression was present for many years pre-injury.

The setting and severity of the behaviour may have a bearing on which medica-tion is tried first. By and large antipsychotics are the agents that most reliably and quickly settle the violent patient, but probably have greatest potential for harm. Antipsychotics increase the risk of sudden cardiac death and possibly stroke (Glenn, 2010) and, given the evidence from animal models, repeated doses of at least the first generation antipsychotic Haloperidol are likely to impair longer term recovery from TBI, because of persisting blockade of dopaminergic, noradrenergic and serotoninergic transmission (Wilson et al., 2013; Phelps et al., 2015). Therefore, if there is significant immediate risk to the patient or others, antipsychotic medica-tion, if possible as Quetiapine, Olanzapine or Risperidone rather than Haloperidol, may be a reasonable first line. In less acute circumstances antipsychotic medication is not appropriate as a first line treatment for irritability or aggression.

Evidence specifying drugs that reduce aggression after TBI is largely weak. Early RCTs suggested that beta-blockers were helpful, but in practice they are rarely used as first line treatment (see below). There is a striking lack of RCT evidence for any other class of medication. Exceptions include two drugs that can facilitate dopamine and other catecholamine neurotransmitters, Methylphenidate and Amantadine (amantadine is also an *N*-methyl-D-aspartate (NMDA) channel antagonist). These effects are hypothesised to reflect enhanced neurotransmission in the dopamine dependent nigrostriatal, mesolimbic and frontostriatal circuits that mediate arousal, drive and focussed attention. Mooney and Haas (1993) studied 38 men during the acute stage of recovery from TBI in a single blind RCT, and found that Methylphenidate (30 mg a day over 6 weeks) reduced anger; patients were not selected on the basis of presenting with anger management problems. More recently, two randomised placebo controlled studies of Amantadine 100mg bd for irritability and aggression more than 6 months post-TBI by Hammond et al. (2014, 2015) have been published. In the initial single site study of 76 patients there was a significant reduction in irritability in the treatment group after 28 days, but not, when corrected for multiple comparisons, after either 28 or 60 days in the larger multi-site second study of 168 patients.

Given that dopamine agonists may facilitate recovery from TBI (Wagner et al., 2005) then Methylphenidate or Amantadine appear reasonable as first line treatments for irritability or aggression. However, Methylphenidate can be addictive and, because it is a stimulant, has the potential in some to increase aggressive behaviour. Based on these considerations, Amantadine may be a reasonable first line drug to use in a patient after TBI who is irritable or aggressive, though many physicians and psychiatrists will not be very familiar with its use. There are concerns that in some patients Amantadine may cause psychotic symptoms or exacerbate epilepsy (see below), and renal function should be checked before and during treatment. Whether any improvement is maintained after several months of treatment with Amantadine is uncertain; in our experience many drugs seem to improve aggression in the short term, but the aggression gradually returns despite continuation of the medication.

Another class of drugs that is reasonable as a first line treatment are the anticonvulsant mood stabilisers Carbamazepine (Azouvie et al., 1999) and Valproate (Connolly et al., 2013). There is much anecdotal or case series evidence that these drugs work, though RCTs are lacking. They are generally well tolerated and though it has been suggested that Carbamazepine but not Valproate may impair cognition, the cognitive effects of these two drugs have not been compared directly (Chew & Zafonte, 2009). Carbamazepine has the disadvantage of being more likely to produce dangerous idiosyncratic drug reactions, whereas Valproate may produce an encephalopathy, due to raised blood ammonia levels, that is easily missed. Lamotrogine may be an alternative (Pachet et al., 2003).

Antidepressants have the great advantage of being well tolerated, widely used and safe. Given that irritability is a common symptom of depression, and that depression can be difficult to identify following TBI, antidepressants are worth trying when irritability or aggression has been resistant to other classes of drug, even in the absence of typical symptoms of depression (Kant et al., 1998). SSRIs are the treatment of choice given the evidence that serotonin may be involved in impulsive and aggressive behaviour. There is some clinical evidence, particularly for Sertraline, to support their use (Warden et al., 2006). Of the classes of antidepressants, tricyclics are most likely to aggravate epilepsy and sedation and should be avoided.

Alternative agents to consider include beta-blockers, Buspirone and Lithium. The research literature on these agents is largely over 20 years old. Despite RCT evidence supporting their use (Fleminger et al., 2006), beta-blockers are not generally regarded as a first line treatment for aggression after TBI. This may be because large doses, which often result in significant side effects, may be required to achieve an effect. Lithium, though showing promising effects in an early case series of ten patients (Glenn et al., 1989), is rarely used; its neurotoxic effects are troubling and easily missed.

Despite the evidence that they may be unhelpful to recovery, antipsychotics are commonly used to control severe aggressive behaviour. Whilst atypical antipsychotic drugs have some mood stabilising effects we have experienced patients with chronic labile mood, associated with temper outbursts, who appear to benefit from a long-term low dose of Risperidone; Quetiapine may also be an agent of choice (Kim & Bijlani, 2006). There is a surprising lack of evidence about the use of Risperidone in patients with TBI, but it has been shown to be useful for the management of challenging behaviour in patients with learning disability (Gagiano et al., 2005). Olanzapine may be useful if sedation is also needed, but has the disadvantage of probably having a greater propensity to cause diabetes and epilepsy. Given that Aripiprazole has both dopamine agonist and antagonist actions it may be worth trying (Umene-Nakano et al., 2013). In our experience some patients with very severe and difficult to treat aggression appear to respond to regular Haloperidol. If Haloperidol is tried, then dosing should start low (e.g. 0.5 mg twice a day) and be increased with careful monitoring, given its potential for worse outcomes in animal models of TBI (Phelps et al., 2015), and worse extrapyramidal and cardiac side effects compared with atypical antipsychotics.

Monitoring for any patient on antipsychotic medication needs to assess the risk of postural hypotension and falling. In the longer term it is important to look for signs of the metabolic syndrome (hypertension, raised lipids, increased weight and diabetes mellitus) and extrapyramidal side effects. All patients need an ECG with particular regard to the Q-T interval. Most antipsychotic drugs, many other psychotropics (including citalopram) and many other drugs prolong the Q-T interval. Risk is increased when the patient is on multiple drugs, each with the potential to prolong the Q-T interval. Websites that list such agents, for example www.torsades.org, are useful resources for the prescribing doctor.

If the drugs described above have no significant effect on aggressive behaviour it is worth considering regular benzodiazepines, particularly if aggressive behaviour is driven by high anxiety, despite the risk of side effects. These include increasing confusion, sedation and risk of falling; tolerance requires increasingly bigger doses to achieve the same therapeutic effect, with the subsequent risk of addiction and risk of epilepsy on sudden withdrawal; and in some patients an increase in disinhibited behaviour, or paradoxical agitation. Benzodiazepines should therefore only be considered as something of a last resort.

Aggression in patients with post-traumatic epilepsy can be particularly challenging to treat and special care needs to be taken with potential drug interactions. If possible the patient should be transferred to antiepileptic medication with mood stabilising properties (e.g. Carbamazepine, Valproate or Lamotrogine). Further mood stabilising antiepileptic medication may then be added to try to control the NBD. In the absence of sufficient response it is reasonable to consider SSRI antidepressants because they are generally regarded as safe in those with epilepsy. By and large some first generation antipsychotics seem safer than atypical antipsychotics in studies on patients with epilepsy (not specifically post-traumatic epilepsy) (Lertxundi et al., 2013); Risperidone and Haloperidol seem less likely to cause seizures than Olanzapine, and to a lesser extent Quetiapine.

Whether epilepsy contraindicates the use of Amantadine to treat irritability and aggression in those with post-traumatic epilepsy is less certain. Epilepsy is listed as a contraindication for amantadine treatment (BNF, 2015), in part based on studies of amantadine for the prophylactic treatment of influenza (e.g. Atkinson et al., 1986). In two RCTs of Amantadine early after TBI at doses up to 400 mg a day, the rate of epileptic seizures was not increased (Meythaler et al., 2002; Giacino et al., 2012), but the larger of these two studies excluded those with more than one seizure in the preceding month. The studies of Hammond et al. (2014, 2015) described above excluded patients with a seizure in the preceding month. In the first study, lasting 28 days, the only seizure to occur amongst the 76 participants, half of whom received 200 mg a day of Amantadine, was in the Amantadine treated group, whilst in the second study one seizure occurred in each group. Thus Amantadine should be used with caution in those with post-traumatic epilepsy, particularly if seizures are difficult to control.

Mood disorders

Fortunately one of the commonest mood disorders after severe TBI, emotional lability, is the easiest to treat; antidepressants have a good effect (Arciniegas & Wortzel, 2014). The situation for depression, which is also common after TBI (Bombardier et al., 2010) is less optimistic. There are hints that those who are depressed and have suffered a TBI are less likely to respond to an antidepressant than those who are depressed and have no brain injury (Dinan & Mobayed, 1992). In some patients this may be because the TBI causes symptoms and signs that only mimic depression but are in fact apathy or abulia resulting from structural damage (see Siegel et al., 2014), which may respond to treatment with a dopaminergic agent. Alternatively, the patient may be depressed because of the disheartening effects of their disability, and this "reactive depression" may be less treatment responsive. On the other hand, those who are depressed after a TBI may not manifest typical symptoms of depression, so the clinician needs to be reasonably ready to try antidepressant treatment. This may particularly be the case in those who fail to improve as expected, or in fact regress; secondary depression has been shown to be associated with deterioration over time since injury (Whitnall et al., 2006).

There are surprisingly few well controlled studies of antidepressants for the treatment of depression after TBI. Indeed, in the review by Wheaton et al. (2011) the only agent to improve depression was Methylphenidate, and then only for clinician-rated rather than self-rated depression scores. We do not recommend

Methylphenidate as a first line treatment for depression given the potential for tolerance to develop, and for some patients to abuse Methylphenidate.

Despite a lack of well controlled trials, most clinicians will often use an SSRI as the first line of treatment for depression after TBI. SSRIs are by and large safe and well tolerated. But there is not much evidence to guide which one to choose. One advantage of Citalopram is that it is least likely to interfere with the metabolising enzyme cytochrome P450, and therefore tends not to affect the levels of other drugs, particularly anti-epileptics (Taylor et al., 2015). However, because of recent concerns that Citalopram prolongs the Q-T interval, the maximum recommended daily dose in the UK has been reduced; in those over 65 no more than 20mg a day is recommended. There is weak evidence that sertraline is effective (Fann et al., 2000). Fluoxetine has the advantage of producing little sedation, but is the most likely to interact with other drugs, so needs to be used with care in those on antiepileptics. Mirtazapine may be used particularly if there is sleep disturbance, because of its hypnotic effects.

If depression does not respond to first line treatment with an antidepressant then the protocols for treatment resistant depression in the absence of brain injury (e.g. Taylor et al., 2015) should be followed, taking care to tailor the treatment to the brain injured patient's vulnerability to developing side effects, and to the medication they are otherwise being prescribed.

Psychosis

Confabulation, delusional misidentification and delusional disorientation during the course of PTA should, where possible, be left to resolve spontaneously. Such phenomena, pathognomonic of organic psychosis, usually only last a few days, or weeks at most, and resolve as the PTA clears.

Later onset psychotic disorders should be treated as in any psychotic patient with no brain injury, but taking particular care of the circumstances peculiar to the patient with TBI. Though Olanzapine gets a cautious recommendation for use in psychosis after TBI (Warden et al., 2006) this is only based on two case reports. We do not feel that this is sufficient to outweigh concerns that Olanzapine may result in more side effects than, for example, Risperidone or Quetiapine.

Conclusion

Hitherto, the use of drug treatments in the context of NBD has usually focussed on secondary psychological and behavioural consequences, to treat depression and reduce risk that results from agitated and impulsive behaviours, or on persisting difficulties resulting from pre-injury health problems, which are themselves often risk factors for TBI. But they should also be regarded as interventions that may facilitate (or hamper) the behavioural and cognitive techniques used during the rehabilitation of NBD, just as improvement in functional outcome in patients with prolonged disorders of consciousness (PDoC) has been well documented (see Fridman & Schiff, 2014) using either Amantadine or Zolpidem, a GABA agonist, in patients with PDoC and one patient with akinetic mutism. Whether the use of biomarkers to characterise the results of an individual's injury and produce more effective drug treatments is only beginning to be defined (e.g. Sharp et al., 2014; Arnemann et al., 2015).

Whether gains in rehabilitation for NBD are restorative or compensatory, they are likely to be plasticity based. There is thus a long-term need to explore, and eventually routinely consider, the combined use of plasticity promoting interventions for the positive and negative features of NBD. These involve the combined use of training paradigms as well as adjunctive medication and non-invasive brain stimulation (Demirtas-Tatlidede et al., 2012), as is being investigated in the context of stroke and ageing (Chollet et al., 2014; Wessel et al., 2015). This will only happen if the nature of the impairments that lead to the NBD itself, rather than only their secondary behavioural consequences, are recognised more widely as treatment targets, not only by clinical neuroscientists, but also health professionals more generally, to accelerate both the acquisition and implementation of new knowledge.

Bibliography

Arciniegas, DB & Wortzel, HS. Emotional and behavioural dyscontrol after traumatic brain injury. *Psychiatr Clin N Am.* 2014; 37: 31–53.

Arnemann, KL, Chen, AJ, Novakovic-Agopian, T, Gratton, C, Nomura, EM & D'Esposito, M. Functional brain network modularity predicts response to cognitive training after brain injury. *Neurology* 2015; 84: 1568–74.

Atkinson, WL, Arden, NH, Patriarca, PA, Leslie, N, Lui, K-J & Gohd, R. Amantadine prophylaxis during an institutional outbreak of Type A (H1N1) Influenza. *Archives of Internal Medicine* 1986; 146: 1751–56.

Azouvi, P, Jokic, C, Attal, N, Pierre, D, Sabria, M & Bussel, B. Carbamazepine in agitation and aggressive behaviour following severe closed-head injury: Results of an open trial. *Brain Inj.* 1999; 13: 797–804.

Bieniek, SA, Ownby, RL, Penalver, A & Dominguez, RD. A double-blind study of Lorazepam versus the combination of Haloperidol and Lorazepam in managing agitation. *Pharmacotherapy* 1998; 18: 57–62.

Bogner, J, Barrett, RS, Hammond, FM, Horn, SD, Corrigan, JD, Rosenthal, J, Beaulieu, CL, Waszkiewicz, M, Shea, T, Reddin, CJ, Cullen, N, Giuffrida, CG, Young, J & Garmoe, W. Predictors of agitated behavior during inpatient rehabilitation for traumatic brain injury. *Arch Phys Med Rehabil.* 2015; 96: S274–81.

Bombardier, CH, Fann, JR, Temkin, NR, Esselman, PC, Barber, J & Dikmen, SS. Rates of major depressive disorder and clinical outcomes following traumatic brain injury. *JAMA* 2010; 303: 1938–45.

British National Formularly (BNF) 70 Eds Joint Formulary Committee, September 2015 BMJ Publishing Group Ltd and Royal Pharmaceutical Society.

Brooke, MM, Paterson, DR, Questad, KA, Cardenas, D & Farrel-Roberts, L. The treatment of agitation during initial hospitalisation after traumatic brain injury. *Arch Phys Med Rehabil.* 1992; 73: 917–21.

Chew, E & Zafonte, ZD. Pharmacological management of neurobehavioural disorders following traumatic brain injury – A state of the art review. *Journal of Rehabilitation Research and Development* 2009; 46(6): 851–78.

Chollet, F, Cramer, SC, Stinear, C, Kappelle, LJ, Baron, JC, Weiller, C, Azouvi, P, Hommel, M, Sabatini, U, Moulin, T, Tardy, J, Valenti, M, Montgomery, S & Adams, H Jr. Pharmacological therapies in post stroke recovery: Recommendations for future clinical trials. *J Neurol.* 2014; 261: 1461–8.

Connolly S, Caldwell, SB & Wilson FC. Maintaining community living with post brain injury agitation: A role for sodium valproate. *Brain Inj.* 2013; 27: 754–7.

Demirtas-Tatlidede, A, Vahabzadeh-Hagh, AM, Bernabeu, M, Tormos, JM & Pascual-Leone, A. Noninvasive brain stimulation in traumatic brain injury. *J Head Trauma Rehabil.* 2012; 27: 274–92.

Diaz-Arrastia, R, Kochanek, PM, Bergold, P, Kenney, K, Marx, CE, Grimes, CJ, Loh, LT, Adam, LT, Oskvig, D, Curley, KC & Salzer, W. Pharmacotherapy of traumatic brain injury: State of the science and the road forward: report of the Department of Defense Neurotrauma Pharmacology Workgroup. *J Neurotrauma* 2014; 31: 135–58.

Dinan, TG & Mobayed, M. Treatment resistance of depression after head injury: A preliminary study of amitriptyline response. *Acta Psychiatrica Scandinavica* 1992; 85: 292–4.

Dougall, D, Poole, N & Agrawal, N. Pharmacotherapy for chronic cognitive impairment in traumatic brain injury. *Cochrane Database Syst Rev.* 2015; 12: CD009221.

Eames, P & Wood RLl. Episodic disorders of behaviour and affect after acquired brain injury. *Neuropsychological Rehabilitation* 2003; 13: 241–58.

Fann, JR, Uomoto, JM & Katon, WJ. Sertraline in the treatment of major depression following mild traumatic brain injury. *J Neuropsychiatry Clin Neurosci.* 2000; 12: 226–32.

Fleminger, S, Greenwood, RJ & Oliver, DL. Pharmacological management for agitation and aggression in people with acquired brain injury. *Cochrane Database Syst Rev.* 2006 Oct 18; (4): CD003299.

Fridman, EA & Schiff, ND. Neuromodulation of the conscious state following severe brain injuries. *Curr Opin Neurobiol.* 2014; 29: 172–7.

Gagiano, C, Read, S, Thorpe, L, Eerdekens, M & Van Hove, E. Short- and long-term efficacy and safety of risperidone in adults with disruptive behavior disorders. *Psychopharmacology* 2005; 179: 629–36.

Giacino, JT, Whyte, J, Bagiella, E, Kalmar, K, Childs, N, Khademi, A, Eifert, B, Long, D, Katz, DI, Cho, S, Yablon, SA, Luther, M, Hammond, FM, Nordenbo, A, Novak, P, Mercer, W, Maurer-Karattup, P & Shere, M. Placebo-controlled trial of amantadine for severe traumatic brain injury. *N. Engl. J. Med.* 2012; 366: 819–26.

Glenn, MB, Wroblewski, B, Parziale, J, Levine, L, Whyte, J & Rosenthal, M. Lithium carbonate for aggressive behavior or affective instability in ten brain-injured patients. *Am J Phys Med Rehabil.* 1989; 68(5): 221–6.

Glenn, MB. Sudden cardiac death and stroke with the use of antipsychotic medications: Implications for clinicians treating individuals with traumatic brain injury. *J Head Trauma Rehabil.* 2010; 25(1): 68–70.

Grover, S, Kumar, V & Chakrabarti, S. Comparative efficacy study of haloperidol, olanzapine and risperidone in delirium. *J Psychosom Res.* 2011; 71: 277–81.

Hammond, FM, Bickett, AK, Norton, JH & Pershad, R. Effectiveness of amantadine hydrochloride in the reduction of chronic traumatic brain injury irritability and aggression. *J Head Trauma Rehabil.* 2014; 29: 391–9.

Hammond, FM, Sherer, M, Malec, JF, Zafonte, RD, Whitney, M, Bell, K, Dikmen, S, Bogner, J, Mysiw, J & Pershad, R. Amantadine irritability multisite study group.

Amantadine effect on perceptions of irritability after traumatic brain injury: Results of the amantadine Irritability multisite study. *J Neurotrauma* 2015; 32: 1230–8.

Jha, A, Weintraub, A, Allshouse, A, Morey, C, Cusick, C, Kittelson, J, Harrison-Felix, C, Whiteneck, G, Gerber, D. A randomized trial of modafinil for the treatment of fatigue and excessive daytime sleepiness in individuals with chronic traumatic brain injury. *J Head Trauma Rehabil.* 2008; 23: 52–63.

Johansson, B, Wentzel, A-P, Andréll, P, Mannheimer, C & Rönnbäck, L. Methylphenidate reduces mental fatigue and improves processing speed in persons suffered a traumatic brain injury. *Brain Inj.* 2015; 29: 758–65.

Kant, R, Smith-Seemiller, L, Zeiler, D. Treatment of aggression and irritability after head injury. *Brain Inj.* 1998; 12: 661–6.

Kim, E & Bijlani, M. A pilot study of quetiapine treatment of aggression due to traumatic brain injury. *J Neuropsych Clin Neurosci.* 2006; 18: 547–9.

Kim, J, Whyte, J, Patel, S, Europa, E, Wang, J, Coslett, HB & Detre, JA. Methylphenidate modulates sustained attention and cortical activation in survivors of traumatic brain injury: A perfusion fMRI study. *Psychopharmacology* 2012; 222: 47–57.

Kowski, AB, Weissinger, F, Gaus, V, Fidzinski, P, Losch, F & Holtkamp M. Specific adverse effects of antiepileptic drugs – A true-to-life monotherapy study. *Epilepsy Behav.* 2016; 54: 150–7.

Labiner, DM, Ettinger, AB, Fakhoury, TA, Chung, SS, Shneker, B, Tatum, Iv, WO, Mitchell Miller, J, Vuong, A, Hammer, AE & Messenheimer, JA. Effects of lamotrigine compared with levetiracetam on anger, hostility, and total mood in patients with partial epilepsy. *Epilepsia* 2009; 50: 434–42.

Laurence, AGM, Jakabek, D, Hennessy, M, Quirk, F & Guazzo, EP. Post-traumatic amnesia. *J Clin Neurosci.* 2013; 20: 1475–81.

Lertxundi, U, Hernandez, R, Medrano, J, Domingo-Echaburu, S, García, C. Antipsychotics and seizures: Higher risk with atypicals? *Seizure* 2013; 22: 141–3.

Marshman, LA, Jakabeck, D, Hennessey, M, Quirk, F, Guazzo, EP. Post-traumatic amnesia. *J Clin Neurosci.* 2013; 20: 1475–81.

Meythaler, JM, Brunner, RC, Johnson, A & Novack, TA. Amantadine to improve neurorecovery in traumatic brain injury-associated diffuse axonal injury: A pilot double-blind randomized trial. *J Head Trauma Rehabil.* 2002; 17: 300–13.

Michaud, CJ, Bullard, HM, Harris, SA & Thomas, WL. Impact of quetiapine treatment on duration of hypoactive delirium in critically ill adults: A retrospective analysis. *Pharmacotherapy* 2015; 35: 731– 9.

Mooney, GF & Haas, LJ. Effect of methylphenidate on brain injury-related anger. *Archives of Physical Medicine and Rehabilitation* 1993; 74: 153–60.

Mysiw, WJ, Bogner, J, Corrigan, J, Fugate, L, Clinchot, D & Kadyan, V. The impact of acute care medications on rehabilitation outcome after traumatic brain injury. *Brain Inj.* 2006; 20: 905–11.

Ouellet, M-C, Beaulieu-Bonneau, S & Morin, CM. Sleep-wake disturbances after traumatic brain injury. *Lancet Neurol* 2015; 14: 746–57.

Pachet, A, Friesen, S, Winkelaar, D., & Gray, S. Beneficial behavioural effects of lamotrigine in traumatic brain injury. *Brain Inj.* 2003; 17(8): 715–22.

Phelps, TI, Bondi, CO, Ahmed, RH, Olugbade, YT & Kline, AE. Divergent long-term consequences of chronic treatment with haloperidol, risperidone, and bromocriptine on traumatic brain injury-induced cognitive deficits. *J Neurotrauma* 2015; 32: 590–7.

Ponsford, J, Janzen, S, McIntyre, A, Bayley, M, Velikonja, D & Tate, R. INCOG recommendations for management of cognition following traumatic brain injury, part I: Posttraumatic Amnesia/Delirium. *J Head Trauma Rehabil.* 2014; 29: 307–20.

Ripley, DL, Morey, CE, Gerber, D, Harrison-Felix, C, Brenner, LA, Pretz, CR, Cusick, C & Wesnes, K. Atomoxetine for attention deficits following traumatic brain injury: Results from a randomized controlled trial. *Brain Inj.* 2014; 28(12): 1514–22.

Sharp, DJ, Scott, G & Leech, R. Network dysfunction after traumatic brain injury. *Nat Rev Neurol.* 2014; 10: 156–66.

Shin, SS & Dixon, CE. Alterations in cholinergic pathways and therapeutic strategies targeting cholinergic system after traumatic brain injury. *J Neurotrauma* 2015; 32: 1429–40.

Siegel, JS, Snyder, AZ, Metcalf, NV, Fucetola, RP, Hacker, CD, Shimony, JS, Shulman, GL & Corbetta, M. The circuitry of abulia: insights from functional connectivity MRI. *Neuroimage Clin.* 2014; 6: 320–6.

Silver, JM, Koumaras, B, Chen, M, Mirski, D, Potkin, SG, Reyes, P, Warden, D, Harvey, PD, Arciniegas, D, Katz, DI & Gunay, I. Effects of rivastigmine on cognitive function in patients with traumatic brain injury. *Neurology* 2006; 67: 748–55.

Stephen, LJ, Kelly, K, Parker, P & Brodie, MJ. Levetiracetam monotherapy – outcome from an epilepsy clinic. *Seizure* 2011; 20: 554–7.

Stuss, DT, Binns, MA, Carruth, FG, Levine, B, Brandys, CE, Moulton, RJ, Snow, WG & Schwartz, ML. The acute period of recovery from traumatic brain injury: posttraumatic amnesia or posttraumatic confusional state? *J Neurosurg.* 1999; 90: 635–43.

Taylor, D, Paton, C & Kapur, S. *The Maudsley Prescribing Guidelines in Psychiatry*, 12th edition. Oxford: Wiley-Blackwell; 2015.

Thomas, P, Zifkin, B, Migneco, O, Lebrun, C, Darcourt, J & Andermann, F. Nonconvulsive status epilepticus of frontal origin. *Neurology* 1999; 52: 1174–83.

Ulfarsson, T, Gudnason, GA, Rosén, T, Blomstrand, C, Sunnerhagen, KS, Lundgren-Nilsson, Å & Nilsson, M. Pituitary function and functional outcome in adults after severe traumatic brain injury: the long term perspective. *J Neurotrauma* 2013; 30: 271–80.

Umene-Nakano, W, Yoshimura, R, Okamoto, T, Hori, H & Nakamura, J. Aripiprazole improves various cognitive and behavioral impairments after traumatic brain injury: A case report. *Gen Hosp Psychiatry* 2013; 35: 103.e7–9.

Wagner, AK, Sokoloski, JE, Ren, D, Chen, X, Khan, AS, Zafonte, RD, Michael, AC & Dixon, CE. Controlled cortical impact injury affects dopaminergic transmission in the rat striatum. *J Neurochem.* 2005; 95: 457–65.

Warden, DL, Gordon, B, McAllister, TW, Silver, JM, Barth, JT, Bruns, J, Drake, A, Gentry, T, Jagoda, A, Katz, DI, Kraus, J, Labbate, LA, Ryan, LM, Sparling, MB, Walters, B, Whyte, J, Zapata, A & Zitnay, G. Guidelines for the pharmacologic treatment of neurobehavioral sequelae of traumatic brain injury. *J Neurotrauma* 2006 Oct; 23(10): 1468–501.

Weir, N, Doig, EJ, Fleming JM, Wiemers, A & Zemljic, C. Objective and behavioural assessment of the emergence from post-traumatic amnesia (PTA). *Brain Inj.* 2006; 20: 927–35.

Wessel, MJ, Zimerman, M & Hummel, FC. Non-invasive brain stimulation: An interventional tool for enhancing behavioral training after stroke. *Front Hum Neurosci.* 2015; 9: 265.

Wheaton, P, Mathias, JL & Vink, R. Impact of pharmacological treatments on cognitive and behavioral outcome in the postacute stages of adult traumatic brain injury: A meta-analysis. *J Clin Psychopharmacol.* 2011; 31: 745–57.

Whitnall, L, McMillan, TM, Murray, GD & Teasdale, GM. Disability in young people and adults after head injury: 5–7 year follow up of a prospective cohort study. *J Neurol Neurosurg Psychiatry*. 2006; 77: 640–5.

Wilson, MS, Gibson, CJ & Hamm, RJ. Haloperidol, but not olanzapine, impairs cognitive performance after traumatic brain injury in rats. *Am J Phys Med Rehabil*. 2003; 82: 871–9.

Yamamuro, K, Yoshino, H, Tamura, K, Ota, T & Kishimoto, T. Levetiracetam improves disinhibitory behavior in nonconvulsive status epilepticus. *Annals of General Psychiatry* 2014; 13: 32.

Yan, HQ, Osier, ND, Korpon, J, Bales, JW, Kline, AE, Wagner, AK & Dixon, CE. Persistent cognitive deficits: Implications of altered dopamine in traumatic brain injury. In: Kobeissy, FH (Ed.). *Brain Neurotrauma: Molecular, Neuropsychological, and Rehabilitation Aspects*. Boca Raton (FL): CRC Press/Taylor & Francis; 2015. Chapter 33.

16

ASSISTIVE TECHNOLOGY, DISABILITY AND REHABILITATION

Brian O'Neill and Alex Gillespie

Introduction

Rehabilitation aims to remediate the life-changing social handicap that results from neurobehavioural disability, allowing people to return to meaningful social lives. The changes, after brain injury, to (a) drive, (b) inhibitory and regulatory control and (c) personality contribute to the difficulties in daily life activities, life choices and social functioning that warrant specialist intervention (Wood & McMillan, 2001). Assistive technologies for cognition offer innovative and viable possibilities for ameliorating the psychosocial impact of neurobehavioural disability, which this chapter aims to demonstrate.

Assistive technology and assistive technology for cognition

The history of human civilization can be written as a history of technology (Mumford, 1934; Clark, 2003; Aunger, 2010; MacGregor, 2012). While all technology extends our abilities, *assistive technology* refers to those devices that extend abilities lost through illness or injury, defined as 'any product or service that maintains or improves the ability of individuals with disabilities or impairments to communicate, learn and live independent, fulfilling and productive lives' (BATA, 2012). According to this view, technology is a means to help people overcome a given impairment to improve functional activity, and thereby, participation in daily life.

Assistive technology for cognition (ATC) is a further refinement of technology, aimed at overcoming impairments in mental functions (LoPresti, Mihailidis & Kirsch, 2004). The field consists of technologies that enable, enhance or extend cognitive function, such as, using digital reminders to support prospective memory, navigation systems to augment spatial navigation, and prompting devices to help sequence complex behaviours (O'Neill & Gillespie, 2015). By using such tools to enhance cognition, possibilities for maximising independent activity can be realised, leading to increased social participation (O'Neill & Gillespie, 2015).

Using ATC, also called *cognitive prosthetics* (Cole, 1999), to replace damaged cognitive functions in those with brain injury is analogous to the provision of artificial limbs to persons with amputation. In cases where the cognitive impairment is limited and lesion sizes are small to medium, restoration of cognition function is possible through focused neuropsychological rehabilitation (Cicerone *et al.*, 2011). However, in cases where the lesion is large, the impairment is significant, the window for rehabilitation has been missed, or there is a degenerative process, an alternative approach is required that focuses on compensating, rather than replacing, lost function and adapting, rather than restoring, behaviour and lifestyle (Robertson & Murre, 1999).

The concept of augmenting cognitive functions through technology is not new, or even unfamiliar. Advances in information and communications technology have already revolutionised the augmentation and compensation of cognitive functions in daily social life. Smartphones, which have become ubiquitous in daily life, began as assistive tools for communication, but are now arguably primarily assistive tools for cognition. Digital photography, and the ability to search and sort images, assists autobiographical memory. Memos and note-taking tools, combined with search, are digital diaries that aid semantic memory. Alarms and reminders support organisation, planning and prospective memory. GPS maps facilitate orientation and navigation. Accelerometers enable mapping of past and current physical movement. Calculators greatly enhance calculation or estimation. These assistive tools for cognition are being used by lay people on a daily basis. Thus, careful selection, development and tailoring of these devices can provide people with cognitive impairment with a wide range of options for augmenting or compensating lost cognitive function.

The possibilities for developing cognitive supports through technology are ever-increasing. In 2016 the number of smartphone users is predicted to surpass two billion. Smart-watches and wearables (shoes, belts, bands, clothes and earbuds that gather data that is fed back to the user) are rapidly increasing technologies that will likely drive future uptake. 'Wearables' are proving popular because they are examples of well-designed 'zero-effort technologies', incorporated into every day practices and identities, and used daily (Mihailidis et al., 2011). The intuitive and reliable interface of 'wearables', stands to revolutionise the application of computing to the service of persons with cognitive impairments (O'Neill & Gillespie, 2015). The power of wearables, if they are charged and worn, is that they gather data, then process it (often remotely), presenting the user with accessible and actionable analysis as it is required. They offer an *alert* function, drawing attention to an external stimulus or internal representation that is relevant to on-going behaviour. They can *monitor* physiological indicators, contextual information, location and activities. They can *remind*, providing a time-dependent cue to engage in an activity lacking immediate environmental stimuli. They can sequence, providing step by step *micro-prompting* through tasks. They can *store and display*, presenting episodic or semantic information. They can also distract or entertain, to draw attention away from distressing sensations.

In order to conceptualise assistive technologies for cognition, Gillespie, Best and O'Neill (2012) reviewed available ATC by mapping them onto functional cognitive impairments. In contrast to previous reviews that had conceptualised ATC in terms of the technologies used, this review, provided a clear way to move from neuropsychological assessment of cognitive function to the prescription of a specific ATC. It is well established that neuropsychological assessment of cognitive function enables clinicians to understand how specific cognitive deficits impact on activities and social participation (Crepeau & Scherzer, 1993; Cullen, O'Neill & Evans, 2008; Lezak, Howieson & Loring, 2004; Strauss, Sherman & Spreen, 2006). Accordingly, using such assessments to prescribe an ATC that augments or ameliorates the specific cognitive deficit should have a positive impact on affected activities and participation (Gillespie et al., 2012). Building on this approach, we will use the existing reviews of ATC (De Joode et al., 2010; Gillespie et al., 2012; Jamieson et al., 2014; Pollack, 2005; O'Neill & Gillespie, 2015) in order to suggest technologies that might augment compensatory abilities, or ameliorate the cognitive impairments, associated with neurobehavioural disability.

Technologies that can ameliorate neurobehavioural disability

The neurobehavioural paradigm of rehabilitation arose to meet the needs of persons with disability due to: (i) Disorders of drive, including changes to initiative or motivation which prevent adequate self-care; (ii) Disorders of inhibitory and regulatory control that impair judgement in the management of one's affairs; and (iii) Disorders of personality that lead to anti-social forms of behaviour that put the person or others at risk (Wood & Worthington, 2001; Wood & McMillan, 2001). These categories are used to structure our review of how ATC can be used in neurobehavioural rehabilitation.

Disorders of drive

Brain injury related changes to drive include apathy, abulia or depression of mood which can reduce motivation to engage in activities of daily living. In severe cases, self-neglect presents as a risk to be managed (Eames, 2001). Psychostimulants, antidepressants, and other psychotropic agents, demonstrate some effectiveness in disorders of drive, although this is currently insufficient to establish guidelines for optimal pharmacotherapy (Talsky et al., 2010).

Psychological approaches on the other hand have been shown to be of value in addressing behaviour patterns reflecting low levels of drive (Wood, 1987; Wood & Worthington, 2001). In this section, interventions to support depressed mood, increase arousal, and increase awareness of body state are addressed.

Behavioural scheduling is a mainstay of psychological treatment for depression, and involves working with a person to create a list of meaningful activities which may be inherently rewarding or contribute to feelings of pleasure or self-efficacy (Fennell, 1989). In brain injury rehabilitation, scheduling often requires supportive antecedent prompts and consequential rewards, with the aim of increasing the frequency and duration of this purposeful behaviour (Wood, 1987). Time dependent reminders to engage in the activity can be effectively outsourced to a prompting technology (see 'Disorders of inhibitory and regulatory control' section below). The efficacy of these timely cues to change behaviour might be improved if the delivery system was aware of the user's behavioural or affective context. For example, mobile phone (cell phone)-based systems that use onboard sensors can issue prompts dependent on current activity or recently rated mood, to motivate users to perform a target behaviour. This approach (deployed in a system called *Mobilyze!*) has been successful in a small sample clinical trial in people with major depression, although it has yet to be trialled on people with brain injury (Burns et al., 2011). In a prospective assessment of treatment preferences for depression of mood after brain injury, supports to engage in physical exercise and counselling, either in person or over the phone were rated the highest (Fann, Hart & Schomer, 2009). Thus approaches where the phone prompts activity, can monitor activity and mood, and provide a means of communication with the treating clinician, are deemed worthy of further exploration.

Observing the motivational strategies of rehabilitation support workers during morning routines, O'Neill et al. (2013) found that drive or energising issues were prominent and needed to be skilfully addressed. Support workers often have to coax clients out of bed with suggestions of breakfast, and remind clients that having a shower allows them to feel 'fresh' and have more social appeal. These motivational prompts are then extended into personal hygiene and into getting appropriately dressed. *Micro-prompting* technology (*Guide*, www.guide-research.com) can emulate the motivational prompts and guidance provided by support workers; it augments clients' motivation and talks users through the steps of the morning routine. This technology can significantly reduce carer interventions, while maintaining personal care outcomes. It has, thus, contributed to the evidence that reduced drive may be supported by an external prompting technology (O'Neill et al., in press).

It is possible that the drive to participate in neurorehabilitation itself may be assisted by technology that makes the goals of rehabilitation more salient. Although often involved in goal setting exercises, those with impaired memory often have a scant recollection of why they are in neurorehabilitation, and it is likely that this reduces motivation to participate. Culley and Evans (2010) recruited 11 participants with acquired brain injury who had poor recall of their neurorehabilitation goals. They then used automated text-to-phone messages to remind the participants of half of their goals, with significant improvements in their recall of those prompted. Although such improved recall is likely to lead to increased motivation to pursue rehabilitation goals, further research is required to establish this link.

Finally, difficulties with drive or energisation can lead to difficulties recognising bladder or bowel sensations during sleep. Resulting incontinence can undermine independence and increase the need for personal care and, by extension, the interpersonal risk of the carer inadvertently acting as a trigger for aggression, especially if the client misperceives the intervention as an assault. Enuresis alarms are a well-evidenced approach to increasing the awareness of bladder sensation in children with primary and secondary enuresis (Glazener, Evans & Peto, 2005). The repeated pairing of loss of bladder sphincter control with the urine triggered alarm, leads to the preceding sensation of a full bladder rousing the sleeper before incontinence occurs. Secondary enuresis can often follow from acquired brain injury, and this difficulty often seems related to difficulties with drive or arousal leading to bladder signals being missed. In both childhood enuresis and incontinence following brain injury, there is similar failure to respond to bladder sensations, as such, controlled trials of the enuresis alarms by persons with brain injury appear warranted (Safaza et al., 2008).

The use of technology therefore holds some promise in supporting reduced drive. The interventions discussed above have explored the use of cues to augment understanding about physiological and mental states of the user. These cues can help to increase engagement in rewarding activities through providing timely inform-ation to make both immediate and distant goals more salient, and using external sensors to increase awareness of body sensation.

Disorders of inhibitory and regulatory control

The ability to inhibit an ongoing activity and to initiate a new activity is important for social relations, because it enables people to be timely for meetings and keep commitments. Clients with disorders that impair this ability are likely to be perceived as unreliable and rude by those they inconvenience (Yeates, Gracey & Mcgrath, 2008). Technology can augment the ability to inhibit and regulate control. For example, prompts to switch or initiate behaviours have shown evidence for effective-ness (Wilson et al., 2001; Fish et al., 2007). Basic calendar reminders and prospective memory aids are therefore likely to be effective in improving social relations with friends, family or employers through organising and structuring daily activities.

In addition to affecting the opportunities for managing social relations, time management difficulties can also lead to dependency on others. This is particularly the case for behaviours that must occur at a specified time in order to maintain health, such as taking medication or checking blood glucose levels or respiratory peak flow. If a client is unable to coordinate these activities, then the onus can fall upon other people to provide support. Importantly this repeated prompting can be perceived as 'nagging' by the client, placing a strain on care relationships. The use of devices that store schedules and prospectively remind (prompting technologies) are therefore beneficial because they can reduce the need for another person to support the activity. Examples include text prompters such as *Neuropage* (Wilson et al., 2001); and audio prompters such as *Voice Organizer* or *Memex* (Van den Broek et al., 2000).

Difficulty carrying out socially valued sequences and skilled actions are among the more debilitating aspects of neurobehavioural disability. Requiring support for basic activities of daily living also challenges identity by repositioning the person from autonomous to 'cared-for'. Microprompting technologies refer to systems that store a map of the problem space, and by acquiring context awareness, prompt users through the steps of a task. Microprompters have a growing evidence base for use across many disorders with sequencing difficulties as features (Jamieson et al., 2014). O'Neill, Best, O'Neill, Ramos and Gillespie (submitted) trialled an interactive microprompting technology (*Guide*) that emulates the verbal self-instruction that healthy adults use to prompt themselves step-by-step through everyday tasks. In a sample of 32 people with severe cognitive impairment following brain injury, this ATC reduced the need for carer support when performing the tasks of the morning routine.

Difficulties maintaining a social role can contribute to a lack of meaningful participation in people with brain injury. Inability to carry out basic hospitality sequences, such as making a cup of tea for a visitor, can lead to feelings of disempowerment, uselessness, and reduced self-esteem. The use of microprompting technologies to support such activity sequences, especially those that facilitate social interaction (such as making a cup of tea), has significant potential and deserves further research.

Disorders of personality

Changes in the way emotions are expressed can be perceived as disturbing changes to personality (Bond, Brooks & McKinlay, 1979; Gosling & Oddy, 1999) and more frequent anger expression is distressing for the individual, for staff, for loved ones, and the wider community (Bogner et al., 2001). Technologies offer the ability to signal behavioural crises more rapidly and improve their recording. AT is also providing an avenue for ameliorating negative moods, providing a safe space for training, and augmenting cognitive deficits that can cause challenging behaviour (Gillespie et al., 2012).

A general tenet of AT for cognition is that the digital devices direct information, gathered about the user, to the user to enable awareness and self-regulation (O'Neill & Gillespie, 2015). At times, safety concerns necessitate that information is routed to the care team to recruit increased support for the client. During an acute episode of aggression, the primary aim of a clinical team is the management of risk of harm by limiting the harmful behaviours, using physical restraint if required. Thus, if de-escalation strategies fail, personal attack alarms to call for staff members are essential, and are optimally based on a within-building communications loop which can display the location of the incident to colleagues using alphanumeric pagers or wall mounted screens. Epilepsy poses a risk to the individual but also, when related to episodic behavioural dyscontrol, others. Seizure alarms that sense the early stages of a seizure via electrodermal changes, might also be routed through these systems to quickly address epilepsy related risks (Poh et al., 2012).

Once behavioural incidents have occurred, accurate recording underpins the formulation of the behaviour, as well as establishing whether the intervention has reduced the frequency or intensity of the behaviour over time. The time-efficiency of long hand recording of the behaviour, antecedents and consequences can be improved if behaviours are selected from a list (for example, see the Overt Aggression Scale Modified for Neurorehabilitation; Alderman, Knight & Morgan, 1997). Spreadsheets on computers allow graphing of the collected data. But new solutions using portals on handheld devices, such as phones and tablets to secure web servers, may allow observations to be made in a few screen touches, while automatic entry of location, day, date and time and automatic graphing, would improve the efficiency of data collection, analysis and presentation.

Environmental stimulation has been associated with the likelihood of challenging behaviour, such that reducing noise or brightness of lighting can reduce the frequency of episodes (Lombard & Zafonte, 2005). Assistive technology can be used to further regulate levels of stimulation to alleviate negative mood states. For example, media players offer a widely available technical solution to facilitate the management of exogenous stimulation by providing preferred music. Park (2010) examined this effect in a group of 14 patients with acute agitation using a randomised multiple baseline design. Compared to baseline, preferred music reduced agitated behaviour more than classical or relaxing music (Park, 2010). The effect was interpreted in terms of evocation of positive memories and emotions by the familiar music (Gerdner, 1997). The study highlights the need for distractions to be tailored to the needs and interests of the clients. It also raises questions as to the potential of media players equipped with awareness of either behavioural or physiological state (as already developed for the exercise market) to deliver preferred music when timely to do so.

Assistive technology can also be used to train clients with brain injury in how to deal with situations that can trigger challenging behaviour. For example, virtual environments are being investigated as a controlled means of providing those with anger issues a safe opportunity for practising social skills in scenarios with incremental levels of difficulty (Lyons et al., 2015). Naturalistic environments and daily tasks, such as taking a bus, can be scripted within the virtual environment to offer incremental challenges to help develop and support emotional regulation.

Most frequently, however, assistive technology is used to augment a cognitive deficit that is posited to underlie the challenging behaviour. Specifically, disorientation, anosognosia, prospective memory deficits, episodic memory deficits, problems recognising emotions in others and in oneself can result in a range of behavioural outcomes that are associated with disordered personality. Assistive technologies can be used to ameliorate such cognitive domains and therefore reduce challenging behaviour in a number of ways.

First, disorientation due to primary memory impairment may present as challenging behaviour. Brown and colleagues (2012) reported a single case of a man who was frequently verbally aggressive following an intracerebral haemorrhage. His disorientation to place and time led to nocturnal wandering and aggression when redirected by care staff. To reduce interpersonal triggers to aggression, orientation information was provided using a location triggered auditory prompter known as a

Wander Reminder (Designability, 2015). The system uses a passive infrared sensor and incorporates the timed playback of recorded messages. If triggered between midnight and 7a.m., the system plays a recording which addressed the man by name, reminded him that it was the middle of the night and suggested that he return to bed. The frequency of nocturnal wanderings and, thereby of challenging behaviour, was significantly reduced and was maintained after the movement-triggered prompter was withdrawn (Brown et al., 2012). Further investigations using such technology to reduce distress and challenge are indicated.

A second cognitive impairment that can lead to challenging behaviour is anosognosia, or the lack of awareness that one has a neurological condition or disorientation to being in a rehabilitation setting. Frightening confabulations that one has been abducted, imprisoned, or that people in the environment have malign intent, can precede defensive aggression (Prigatano, 2010). These fearful thoughts can be reduced, using storing and retrieving technologies to deliver orienting messages that can reassure and improve memory formation. Brown et al. (2013) reported five people who were in a state of post traumatic amnesia three to five months post injury after traumatic brain injury. They watched tablet computer delivered video recordings of loved-ones giving scripted orientation information, concerning location, sequelae of injury, goals that they and the team were pursuing, and reassurance about the patient's safety and identity within the family group. After baseline monitoring of orientation and insight scores, the videos were then replayed to the client daily. In this series of single-case A-B designs, significant improvements in orientation awareness, and insight into assessed deficits were reported in four of the five cases. Moreover, viewing the family videos was associated with positive emotional expressions and appeared to be inherently rewarding. Though the study has limitations in design, it supports the need for further research on the use of digital media to repeatedly deliver messages from trusted sources, as a means of increasing awareness of deficit and, thereby, engagement in neurorehabilitation.

Memory supports represent a third technological means of addressing challenging behaviour. Reminding technologies have been used to help people with traumatic brain injury to manage anger. In one case study, automated text to pager reminders (via *Neuropage*) were used to support recall of interpretations elicited in Cognitive Analytic Therapy. Reminders of beliefs active during aggressive responses helped to make salient the goal of avoiding offensive and tit-for-tat behaviours after a misperceived slight, thus reducing their frequency (Yeates, Gracey & Mcgath, 2008).

Similarly, storage and retrieval devices to support episodic memory also have the potential to reduce challenging behaviour. Brindley, Bateman and Gracey (2011), used a wearable camera (Microsoft SenseCam; marketed versions include Autographer and Narrative Clip) to support memory in a man with a specific anxiety disorder, memory impairment and executive difficulties following ABI. In the SenseCam condition the man retrieved more anxiety trigger events (factual detail and internal state information such as thoughts and feelings) than when using automatic thought records or no strategy. The authors concluded that SenseCam may be useful in psychotherapies relying on retrieval of emotionally salient trigger events. These might include being able to re-live challenging behaviour episodes, in order to identify triggers. Therapeutic review of interactions resulting in anger expression might also enable the rehearsal of alternative responses, but this approach remains to be trialled.

A difficulty in recognising the emotional states of others can lead to insensitive and ineffective emotional responses (Williams & Wood, 2009). Reliable machine recognition of facial emotion is now possible (Al Zoubi, Hussain & Calvo, 2015). Prototype wearable versions of emotion recognition systems, which use visual information and identify the emotional state of others, have been trialled as an *'emotional hearing aid'* for people with autism (El-Kaliouby & Robinson, 2005). The amplification of social cues to prompt appropriate responses in people with brain injury holds potential, but remains to be tested.

Finally, alexithymia, the inability to recognise and describe one's own emotions, (Taylor, Ryan & Bagby, 1986; Taylor, Bagby and Parker, 1999; Williams & Wood, 2009), has been linked to a tendency to escalate to disruptive behaviour (Teten et al., 2008; Manninen et al., 2011; Fossati et al., 2009). Wearable biofeedback technologies can acquire awareness of affective state, and, by feeding this back to the user, thus increase awareness of their emotional state. In turn, these affect aware technologies might serve as AT by underpinning better emotional regulation. O'Neill and Findlay (2014) reported two cases of chronic emotional dysregulation and challenging behaviours after brain injury. The frequency of externalised aggression and self-injury, decreased following daily 20-minute sessions of biofeedback on heart rate variability. Effectiveness and acceptability to the users indicated that randomised control crossover study was justified and positive preliminary results from this trial have been reported (Habib, O'Neill & Evans, 2014).

Conclusions

The assistive technologies outlined here represent an early phase of a growing approach in neurorehabilitation (see also O'Neill & Gillespie, 2015). Clinical trials of technology to support cognition lag behind the continuing rapid development of technology (Gillespie, Best & O'Neill, 2012). For trials to even begin to keep pace, a conceptual and cultural shift is needed. The 'information age' arguably began with the advent of portable electronic calculators. Yet, despite their ubiquity, only one case study has been published on the efficacy of using a calculator to treat acquired dyscalculia (Martins, Ferreira & Borges, 1999). The challenge is that we have many treatments involving assistive technology that are of plausible effectiveness, but few clinical trials to evaluate their use, and this makes it difficult for clinicians to be confident in prescribing specific assistive technologies.

Randomised control trials are expensive, but the societal and commercial benefits of effective treatments to reduce disability are potentially large (see Chapter 17). At the time of writing, consumer electronics companies represent some of the wealthiest in industry. They are increasingly directing research and development activity towards the cognitive impairment market, and as the size of the population affected by impairment through injury and neurological deterioration increases, they will increasingly invest in this domain. They need to be convinced, however, that investment in this domain should include the funding of research on the efficacy of the technologies they provide – in much the same way as pharmaceutical companies fund research on efficacy of psychotropic medicines.

Neurobehavioural disability presents significant challenges to overcome, and the interventions described in the present chapter can increase the treatment options available. The use of assistive technologies can be recommended for individuals, where other options have been ruled out or where the intervention is logically indicated and is conducted under careful supervision. If carefully controlled and measured, interventions of this kind may contribute to the evidence base (Tate et al., 2014). Assistive technologies offer potentially powerful solutions for aspects of neurobehavioural disability that have, to date, proved intractable and concerted systematic investigations of interventions across cognitive domains are required to fully exploit this potential (O'Neill & Gillespie, 2015). The loop envisaged would be informed by ideas from people with brain injury and their clinicians, that are fed forwards to designers, engineers and computer scientists, who can then create tools that are scalable solutions for brain injury survivors and their neurorehabilitation teams.

References

Alderman, N., Knight, C., & Morgan, C. (1997). Use of a modified version of the Overt Aggression Scale in the measurement and assessment of aggressive behaviours following brain injury. *Brain Injury*, 11, 503–523.

Al Zoubi, O., Hussain, S., & Calvo, R. (2015). Affect-aware assistive technologies. In: O'Neill, B., & Gillespie, A. (Eds.) *Assistive Technology for Cognition*. Hove, UK: Psychology Press, pp. 47–64.

Aunger, R. (2010). Types of technology. *Technological Forecasting and Social Change*, 77(5), 762–782.

Bogner, J.A., Corrigan, J.D., Fugate, L., Mysiw, W.J., & Clinchot, D. (2001). Role of agitation in prediction of outcomes after traumatic brain injury. *American Journal of Physical Medicine and Rehabilitation*, 80(9), 636–644.

Bond, M.R., Brooks, D.N., & McKinlay, W. (1979). Burdens imposed on the relatives of those with severe brain damage due to injury. *Acta Neurochirurgia* Supplement, 28, 124–125.

Brindley, R., Bateman, A., & Gracey, F. (2011). Exploration of use of SenseCam to support autobiographical memory retrieval within a cognitive-behavioural therapeutic intervention following acquired brain injury. *Memory*, 19(7), 745–757.

British Assistive Technology Association (2012). Further Information on what assistive technology is. http://www.bataonline.org/further-assistive-technology-definition Retrieved 3.9.2015.

Brown, P., Findlay, G., Goodfellow, R., & O'Neill, B. (July, 2012). The use of movement sensors and automated voice prompts to address orientation and nocturnal wandering in an individual with acquired brain injury. *Poster at the 9th Conference of the Neuropsychological Rehabilitation Special Interest Group of the World Federation for NeuroRehabilitation (WFNR)*, Bergen, Norway.

Brown, P., Clark, A. Seddon, E., & O'Neill, B. (July, 2013). Scripted orientation videos and awareness of deficit. *Poster at the 10th Conference of the Neuropsychological Rehabilitation Special Interest Group of the World Federation for NeuroRehabilitation (WFNR)*, Maastricht, Netherlands.

Burns, M.N., Begale, M., Duffecy, J., Gergle, D., Karr, C.J., Giangrande, E., & Mohr, D.C. (2011). Harnessing context sensing to develop a mobile intervention for depression. *Journal of Medical Internet Research*, 13(3), e55.

Cicerone, K.D., Langenbahn, D.M., Braden, C., Malec, J.F., Kalmar, K., Fraas, M., Felicetti, T., Laatsch, L., Harley, J.P., Bergquist, T., Azulay, J., Cantor, J., & Ashman, T. (2011). Evidence-based cognitive rehabilitation: Updated review of the literature from 2003 through 2008. *Archives of Physical Medicine and Rehabilitation*, 92(4), 519–530.

Clark, A. (2003). *Natural-born Cyborgs: Minds, Technologies, and the Future of Human Intelligence*. New York: Oxford University Press.

Cole, E. (1999). Cognitive prosthetics: An overview to a method of treatment. *NeuroRehabilitation*, 12, 39–51.

Crepeau, F., & Scherzer, P. (1993). Predictors and indicators of work status after traumatic brain injury: A meta-analysis. *Neuropsychological Rehabilitation*, 3(1), 5–35.

Cullen, B., O'Neill, B., & Evans, J.J. (2008). Neuropsychological predictors of powered wheelchair use: A prospective follow-up study. *Clinical Rehabilitation*, 22(9), 836–846.

Culley, C. & Evans, J.J. (2010). SMS text messaging as a means of increasing recall of therapy goals in brain injury rehabilitation: a single-blind within-subjects trial. *Neuropsychological Rehabilitation*, 20(1), 103–119.

De Joode, E., van Heugten, C., Verhey, F., & van Boxtel, M. (2010). Efficacy and usability of assistive technology for patients with cognitive deficits: A systematic review. *Clinical Rehabilitation*, 24, 701–714.

Designability (2015). *Wander Reminder*. http://www.designability.org.uk/product/wander-reminder/ Retrieved 24.11.15.

Eames, P. (2001). Distinguishing consequences of ABI. In: Wood, R.L. & McMillan, T. (Eds.) *Neurobehavioural Disability and Social Handicap Following Traumatic Brain Injury*. Hove, UK: Psychology Press, pp. 29–46.

El-Kaliouby, R., & Robinson, P. (2005). The emotional hearing aid: an assistive tool for children with Asperger syndrome. *Universal Access in the Information Society*, 4(2), 121–134.

Fann, J.R., Hart, T., & Schomer, K.G. (2009). Treatment for depression after traumatic brain injury: A systematic review. *Journal of Neurotrauma*, 26(2), 2383–2402.

Fennell, M. (1989). Depression. In: Hawton, K., Salkovskis, P., Kirk, J., & Clark, D. (Eds.) *Cognitive Behavioural Therapy for Psychiatric Disorders*. Oxford, UK: Oxford University Press, pp. 169–235.

Fish, J., Evans, J.J., Nimmo, M., Martin, E., Kersel, D., Bateman, A., Wilson, B.A., & Manly, T. (2007). Rehabilitation of executive dysfunction following brain injury: "Content-free" cueing improves everyday prospective memory performance. *Neuropsychologia*, 45(6), 1318–1330.

Fossati, A., Acquarini, E., Feeney, J.A., Borroni, S., Grazioli, F., Giarolli, L.E., Franciosi, G. & Maffei, C. (2009). Alexithymia and attachment insecurities in impulsive aggression. *Attachment and Human Development*, 11(2), 165–182.

Gerdner, L.A. (1997). An individualized music intervention for agitation. *Journal of the American Psychiatric Nurses Association*, 3(6), 177–184.

Gillespie, A., Best, C., & O'Neill, B. (2012). Cognitive function and assistive technology for cognition: A systematic review. *Journal of the International Neuropsychological Society*, 18, 1–19.

Glazener, C.M., Evans, J.H., & Peto, R.E. (2005). Alarm interventions for nocturnal enuresis in children. Cochrane Library: http://onlinelibrary.wiley.com/doi/10.1002/14651858. CD002911.pub2/full Retrieved 10.12.15.

Gosling, J., & Oddy, M. (1999). Rearranged marriages: Marital relationships after head injury. *Brain Injury*, 13(10), 785–796.

Habib, F., O'Neill, B., & Evans, J.J. (2014). Biofeedback in treatment of challenging behaviour after brain injury. *Poster at the 11th Conference of the Neuropsychological Rehabilitation Special Interest Group of the World Federation for NeuroRehabilitation (WFNR)*, Limassol, Cyprus.

Jamieson, M., Cullen, B., McGee-Lennon, M., Brewster, S., & Evans, J.J. (2014). The efficacy of cognitive prosthetic technology for people with memory impairments: A systematic review and meta-analysis. *Neuropsychological Rehabilitation*, 24(3–4), 419–444.

Lezak, M.D., Howieson, D.B., & Loring, D.W. (2004). *Neuropsychological Assessment* (4th Edn). Oxford, UK: Oxford University Press.

Lombard, L.A., & Zafonte, R.D. (2005). Agitation after traumatic brain injury: Considerations and treatment options. *Archives of Physical Medicine and Rehabilitation*, 84(10), 797–812.

LoPresti, E.F., Mihailidis, A., & Kirsch, N. (2004). Assistive technology for cognitive rehabilitation: State of the art. *Neuropsychological Rehabilitation*, 14, 5–39.

Lyons, Z., Barak, O., Caleb-Solly, P., Harris, N., O'Neill, B., Ramos, S.D.S., & Watts, L. (August, 2015). Establishing design requirements for a virtual therapy aid for executive dysfunction. Paper presented at *BrainInformatics*, London, UK.

MacGregor, N. (2012). *A History of the World in 100 Objects*, London: Allen Lane.

Manninen, M., Therman, S., Suvisaari, J., Ebeling, H., Moilanen, I., & Joukamaa, M. (2011). Alexithymia is common among adolescents with severe disruptive behaviour. *The Journal of Nervous and Mental Disease*, 199(7), 506–509.

Martins, I.P., Ferreira, J., & Borges, L. (1999). Acquired procedural dyscalculia associated to a left parietal lesion in a child. *Child Neuropsychology*, 5, 265.

Mihailidis, A., Boger, J., Hoey, J., & Jiancaro, T. (2011). *Zero Effort Technologies: Considerations, Challenges, and Use in Health, Wellness and Rehabilitation*. Toronto: Morgan & Claypool Publishers.

Mumford, L. (1934). *Technics and Civilization*. New York: Harcourt, Brace and Company.

O'Neill, B., & Findlay, G. (2014). Single case methodology in neurobehavioural rehabilitation: Preliminary findings on biofeedback in the treatment of challenging behaviour. *Neuropsychological Rehabilitation*, 24(3–4), 365–381.

O'Neill, B., Gillespie, A. (2015). *Assistive Technology for Cognition*. Hove: Psychology Press.

O'Neill, B., Best, C., O'Neill, L., & Gillespie, A. (2013). Automated prompting technologies in rehabilitation and at home. *Social Care and Neurodisability*, 4(1), 17–28.

O'Neill, B., Best, C., O'Neill, L., Ramos, S.D.S., & Gillespie, A. (submitted). Step by step: Efficacy of a micro-prompting technology in reducing support needed by people with severe acquired brain injury in activities of daily living.

Park, S. (2010). Effect of preferred music on agitation after traumatic brain injury. http://deepblue.lib.umich.edu/handle/2027.42/77884 Retrieved 8.12.15.

Poh, M., Loddenkemper, T., Reinsberger, C., Swenson, N., Goyal, S., Sabtala, M., Madsen, J., & Picard, R. (2012). Convulsive seizure detection using a wrist-worn electrodermal activity and accelerometer biosensor. *Epilepsia*, 53(5), e93–e97. doi: 10.1111/j.1528-1167. 2012.03444.x

Pollack, M.E. (2005). Intelligent technology for an aging population. *AI magazine*, 26(2), 9–24.

Prigatano, G. (2010). Anosognosia after traumatic brain injury. In: Prigatano, G. (Ed.) *The Study of Anosognosia*. Oxford, UK: Oxford University Press, pp. 229–254.

Robertson, I.M., & Murre, J.M. (1999). Rehabilitation of brain damage: Brain plasticity and principles of guided recovery. *Psychological Bulletin*, 125(5), 544–575.

Safaza, I., Alacaa, R., Yasara, E., Toka, F., & Yilmaza, B., (2008). Medical complications, physical function and communication skills in patients with traumatic brain injury: A single centre 5-year experience. *Brain Injury*, 22(10), 733–739.

Strauss, E., Sherman, E., & Spreen, O. (2006). *A Compendium of Neuropsychological Tests* (3rd edn). Oxford, UK: Oxford University Press.

Talsky, A., Pacione, L.R., Shaw, T., Wasserman, L., Lenny, A., Verma, A., Hurwitz, G., Waxman, R. Morgan, A., & Bhalerao, S. (2010). Pharmacological interventions for traumatic brain injury. *British Columbia Medical Journal*, 53(1), 26–31.

Tate, R., Perdices, M., McDonald, S., Togher, L., & Rosenkoetter, U., (2014). The design, conduct and report of single-case research: Resources to improve the quality of the neurorehabilitation literature. *Neuropsychological Rehabilitation*, 24(3–4), 315–331.

Taylor, G.J., Bagby, M.R., & Parker, J.D.A. (1999). *Disorders of Affect Regulation: Alexithymia in Medical and Psychiatric Illness*. Cambridge, UK: Cambridge University Press.

Taylor, G.J., Ryan, D., & Bagby, M.R. (1986). Toward the development of a new self-report alexithymia scale. *Psychotherapy and Psychosomatics*, 44, 191–199.

Teten, A.L., Miller, L.A., Bailey, S.D., Dunn, N.J., & Kent, T.A. (2008). Empathic deficits and alexithymia in trauma-related impulsive aggression. *Behavioral Sciences & the Law*, 26(6), 823–832.

Van den Broek, M.D., Downes, J., Johnson, Z., Dayus, B., & Hilton, N. (2000). Evaluation of an electronic memory aid in the neuropsychological rehabilitation of prospective memory deficits. *Brain Injury*, 14(5), 455–462.

Williams, C., & Wood, R.L. (2009). Alexithymia and emotional empathy following traumatic brain injury. *Journal of Clinical and Experimental Neuropsychology*, 32(3), 1–11.

Wilson, B.A., Emslie, H.C., Quirk, K., & Evans, J.J. (2001). Reducing everyday memory and planning problems by means of a paging system: A randomised control crossover study. *Journal of Neurology, Neurosurgery, and Psychiatry*, 70, 477–482.

Wood, R.L. (1987). *Brain Injury Rehabilitation: A Neurobehavioural Approach*. London, UK: Croom Helm.

Wood, R.L., & McMillan, T. (2001). *Neurobehavioural Disability and Social Handicap Following Traumatic Brain Injury*. Hove, UK: Psychology Press.

Wood, R.L., & Worthington, A. (2001). Neurobehavioural rehabilitation: A conceptual paradigm. In: Wood, R.L., & McMillan, T. (Eds.) *Neurobehavioural Disability and Social Handicap*. Hove, UK: Psychology Press, pp. 107–131.

Yeates, G.N., Gracey, F., & Mcgrath, J.C. (2008). A biopsychosocial deconstruction of 'personality change' following acquired brain injury. *Neuropsychological Rehabilitation*, 18(5–6), 566–589.

Yeates, G., Hamill, M., Sutton, L., Psaila, K., Gracey, F., Mohamed, S., & O'Dell, J. (2008). Dysexecutive problems and interpersonal relating following frontal brain injury: Reformulation and compensation in Cognitive Analytic Therapy (CAT). *Neuropsychoanalysis*, 10, 43–58.

PART IV

Service delivery and development

17

SERVICE PROVISION FOR NEUROBEHAVIOURAL REHABILITATION: EFFECTIVENESS AND COST-EFFECTIVENESS

Sara Ramos, Michael Oddy and Tom M. McMillan

Introduction

This chapter considers service provision, and the evidence for the clinical and cost-effectiveness of neurorehabilitation programmes that aim to minimise the social handicap associated with neurobehavioural disability.

Following interventions from the acute intensive care services to manage often life-threatening, conditions, neurorehabilitation services may be divided into three components; acute rehabilitation, where medical considerations and 'safe management' remain foremost, post-acute rehabilitation for the chronic difficulties associated with a brain injury, and community services to provide rehabilitation and long-term care that are geared to support lifestyle and living conditions (Greenwood & McMillan, 2003).

Service provision

The trend in acute management of TBI in the UK and elsewhere has been towards developing centralised trauma services that deal with major and complex trauma that cover large geographical areas (Celso et al., 2006). The argument for such centres is that specialist expertise is best achieved when the volume of patients with particular conditions (such as complicated traumatic brain injury) is higher and where specialist medical and surgical services are readily available on one site. A side effect of this has been a move towards ward-based medical rehabilitation that follows a model for physical disability or stroke in older adults. As a result, there is real danger that the complex and heterogeneous outcome after TBI will not be served in an appropriate or effective way and neurobehavioral disorders are a clear example of this. For example, following acute medical intervention, patients in a ward-based setting who present with challenging behaviours often receive expensive one-to-one nursing and sedative medication, which may impede recovery and is not inherently therapeutic (Goldstein, 1995). A positive aspect of the introduction of major trauma centres was the development of a 'rehabilitation prescription' (Wade, 2012), designed to accompany the patient throughout the care pathway. Although good in principle, this is only likely to succeed if each 'prescription' is client-centred and can meet individual neurorehabilitation needs.

In the past 15 years or so, there has been a growth in understanding the post-acute neurorehabilitation and care needs of people after a brain injury (Cattelani et al., 2010; Cicerone et al., 2011; Geurtsen, van Heugten, Martina, & Geurts, 2010). This, coupled with financial pressures, has led to significant changes in the form that such neurorehabilitation services take.

It is difficult to generalise, but it can be argued that during this period the provision of post-acute services in the UK has become more focussed on very severe TBI and those with moderate to severe injuries are now less likely to receive inpatient neurorehabilitation. For example, Oddy and Ramos (2013a) found that a large cohort of individuals admitted to neurobehavioural rehabilitation in 2011–2012 were referred significantly earlier after injury, were more likely to be referred from hospital rather than from community settings, and required more supervision on admission, than cohorts admitted to the same rehabilitation service five to 12 years before (Wood, McCrea, Wood, & Merriman, 1999; Worthington, Matthews, Melia, & Oddy, 2006).

Community brain injury rehabilitation services seem to have been 'squeezed' by financial constraints and, as in the acute phase, there has been a trend towards more generic community rehabilitation (McMillan & Ledder, 2001) that provides for a range of neurological conditions, where referrals of people with TBI are relatively uncommon (Buckman et al., 2013) and hence where the specialist skills needed to deal with complex cognitive and emotional problems may be lacking.

The introduction of major trauma centres, rehabilitation 'prescriptions' and neurorehabilitation community teams have been important steps towards achieving the well-coordinated 'seamless service' that Wood and McMillan advocated in the first edition of this book (2001, p. 258). However, because in the UK funding for different parts of the service pathway is usually provided by different sources (health vs. social care), this often results in delays, and interruptions to service delivery (Worthington & Oldham, 2006).

In spite of these changes and limitations, provision of services for those with long-term disability and dependency as a result of TBI has increased in the last 15 years, and with the growth of the evidence base to support the effectiveness of such services, there has been an increasing recognition of the need to include specialist neurorehabilitation in costing strategies of national health services (e.g. Turner-Stokes, Sutch, & Dredge, 2012).

Clinical effectiveness and cost-effectiveness

Clinical effectiveness

The reduction of safety risks, increase in independence, the improvement in health related quality of life and ability to participate in meaningful social roles, are typically the main goals of neurobehavioural rehabilitation, and hence instruments that operationalise and measure these outcomes are appropriate indices of effectiveness.

There are several recent systematic reviews that specifically focus on post-acute neurorehabilitation (Cattelani et al., 2010; Cicerone et al., 2005, 2011; Geurtsen, van Heugten, Martina, & Geurts, 2010), and this evidence has been increasingly recognised in clinical guidelines for brain injury rehabilitation internationally (Minister for Health, 2011; National Academy of Neuropsychology, 2002; National Institute for Health and Care Excellence, 2014; Scottish Intercollegiate Guidelines Network & Health Care Improvement Scotland, 2013; The Scottish Government, 2015, The Matrix of Psychological Therapies).

All of these reviews attest to the progress that has been made in gathering evidence for the effectiveness of post-acute rehabilitation programmes, but they differ in their specific recommendations (see McMillan, 2013). Cattelani and colleagues (2010) consider that the single Class I randomised controlled trial (RCT) and the two Class II studies reporting significant treatment effects provide sufficient evidence for holistic rehabilitation programmes to be recommended as a practice standard for the treatment of people with acquired neurobehavioral impairments and psychosocial problems' (p. 61). However, they acknowledge a study by Salazar and colleagues (2000), which failed to find enhanced treatment effects for this approach when compared with a limited home-based rehabilitation programme.

Cicerone and colleagues (2011) updated their previous literature reviews (Cicerone et al., 2000, 2005) and found a total of 14 studies of post-acute, holistic rehabilitation (HR) after TBI or stroke. Of these, only two were RCTs. Both studies (Cicerone et al., 2008; Vanderploeg et al., 2008) found greater benefits for HR, compared with a control condition, immediately after the study, but only one study showed greater improvements in community functioning and productivity at follow-up in the group that received the HR intervention (Cicerone et al., 2008).

In their systematic review of 13 studies assessing the effectiveness of three different types of post-acute rehabilitation programmes, Geurtsen and colleagues (2010) were more cautious in their recommendations. Of the 13 studies reviewed, only two were RCTs evaluating 'comprehensive holistic day-treatment' programmes (Cicerone et al., 2008; Ruff & Niemann, 1990), one of which (Ruff & Niemann, 1990) had been included in Cattelani and colleagues' (2010) review as a Class II study, and in an earlier systematic review by Cicerone and colleagues (2000) as a Class Ia study. There were four studies that evaluated 'residential community reintegration' and 'neurobehavioural treatment' programmes. One group comparison study (Willer, Button, & Rempel, 1999) and two cohort studies (Geurtsen, Martina, Van Heugten, & Geurts, 2008; Gray & Burnham, 2000) evaluated the effectiveness of 'residential community reintegration' and only one study evaluated 'neurobehavioural treatment' (Wood et al., 1999). Eight of 13 studies that included a follow-up showed that post-treatment improvements were maintained. The authors recommended that 'more qualitatively high-level research needs to be performed' to clarify aspects of these programmes. More information is required about the indications for and against successful participation in these programmes in order to establish practice standards (French & Gronseth, 2008) that highlight the key therapeutic elements and optimal treatment duration (Geurtsen et al., 2010, p. 42).

There are many reasons for the differences in recommendations across the systematic reviews. Even if the search terms are the same, different inclusion and exclusion criteria or different tools to rate the quality of studies may be used. Using criteria that allow inclusion of studies of lower methodological quality (e.g. Cicerone et al., 2011) arguably gives researchers and practitioners a better overview of the breadth of evidence. On the other hand, using more stringent criteria will ensure that any recommendations are grounded only upon strong evidence, and describing programmes more closely will facilitate a more detailed assessment of the existing evidence and disentangling of key aspects of the interventions under consideration. For example, Geurtsen and colleagues (2010) looked at different 'types' of post-acute rehabilitation programmes: 'neurobehavioural interventions', 'residential community reintegration' and 'day-treatment programmes'. They concluded that there is a need to build the evidence base for some interventions (e.g. 'neuro-behavioural interventions') more than others (e.g. 'day-treatment programmes;'), and in order to obtain a greater understanding of the characteristics of patients who benefit from different types of programme. Nevertheless, all of the reviews report a growing number of studies, with increasing methodological quality, and which demonstrate positive effects of post-acute brain injury rehabilitation that appear to be maintained over time.

One issue to consider when evaluating existing evidence is the quality of study designs. RCTs are considered to be the most rigorous methodology. However, this design is not as easily implemented when evaluating complex programmes of holistic rehabilitation, as it is when evaluating the effects of drug treatments, for which it was originally developed (McMillan, 2013).

A second difficulty is the potential for considerable variation in the contents and procedures of programmes labelled as 'post-acute rehabilitation'. This gives rise to complexity in evaluating the clinical effectiveness of such programmes but, more importantly, highlights the need to provide increasingly objective and detailed descrip-tions of the constituents of each programme. Such objective and detailed descriptions are also required for the control or comparison conditions used (van Heugten et al., 2012). This would help to identify important differences between post-acute rehabilitation programmes and is an essential step in identifying the key therapeutic components of various approaches to brain injury rehabilitation. From an evidence-based evaluation perspective, service distinctions would be more usefully drawn on the basis of the goals; content of the treatment; composition of the team required to deliver it and patient profile (which should not necessarily be dictated purely on the basis of diagnosis or injury severity), than on the basis of generic definitions that do not allow clear distinctions between programmes.

Although there has been an expansion of the evidence base for post-acute neurorehabilitation, the specific components that lead to change or improvement have not been identified. Although the intensity of the intervention, incorporation of the environmental 'milieu' as part of the rehabilitation process and the involvement of the family are all thought to be key components of 'holistic' rehabilitation, which may not be found in more traditional rehabilitation approaches, there is not good evidence for the therapeutic utility of these components. From a practical perspective, it is difficult to evaluate effectiveness at different points along the pathway of recovery and rehabilitation, and it is still unclear whether provision of specialist services, even in the long-term, makes a difference, as most of the existing studies focus on rehabilitation early after injury with relatively short follow-ups of six months to one year. In some cases, patients are referred to neurobehavioural rehabilitation early in their recovery where there is a focus on improving orientation and self-awareness, and social handicap which later becomes a more significant issue, may not be adequately addressed (Johnson & Balleny, 1996). Despite these challenges, evidence for the clinical effectiveness of neurorehabilitation for neurobehavioural disability has been mounting, as has demonstration of the cost-effectiveness of rehabilitation programmes.

Cost effectiveness

Cost effectiveness analysis is a method that relates the costs of an intervention to its key outcomes or benefits. Cost-benefit analysis compares such costs with the financial value of all (or most) of an intervention's benefits (Cellini & Kee, 2010). The continuing increase in demand and competition from health services for scarce financial resources, alongside an increase in the prevalence of long-term health conditions, has led to greater emphasis upon assessment of cost-effectiveness rather than the effectiveness of treatment or rehabilitation alone.

The most common approach to cost-benefit analyses in brain injury rehabilitation has been to compare the costs of care and support before (B) and after rehabilitation (A) and subtract from that the costs of rehabilitation (R), using multipliers (m) to estimate the life-time costs. Hence, cost savings are calculated as:

$$Cost\ Savings = (B \star m) - [(A \star m) + R]$$

This approach has been exemplified by two streams of studies, one relating to early medical rehabilitation and the other to neurobehavioural rehabilitation. In terms of the former, Turner-Stokes, Paul and Williams (2006) investigated reductions in dependency and costs of care following rehabilitation in a specialist in-patient medical rehabilitation unit, which were greatest in a high dependency group. Overall, the costs of rehabilitation were estimated to be recovered through reductions in costs of care within 16 months and in the lower dependency group within

39 months. Turner-Stokes (2007) also examined the cost-efficiency of longer stay rehabilitation patients with complex neurological disabilities. The mean length of stay for 410 of these patients was 184 days. These patients showed significant reductions in dependency and costs of care. The authors argued that the additional costs of rehabilitation beyond four months (£16,766 / $25,149) were offset by the savings in costs of care within 36 months.

O'Connor, Beden, Pilling and Chamberlain (2011) investigated reductions in dependency costs for stroke patients treated in an in-patient neurological rehabilitation unit. They calculated median reductions in costs of care from £1,900 ($2,850) to £1,100 ($1,640) per week, following a median stay of 59 days. The median time to repay rehabilitation costs was 21 weeks.

A series of studies investigating savings in the costs of care following post-acute neurobehavioural rehabilitation has been conducted over the last 15 years. Whilst originating from the same rehabilitation provider, different cohorts were studied on each occasion and each cohort included participants from multiple centres. Wood et al. (1999) demonstrated significant changes in accommodation and occupation following rehabilitation in a cohort of 76. Reductions in care costs were reported for patients admitted several years post-injury. Savings were greatest for those admitted within two years of injury (notional lifetime savings of £1.1 / $1.7 million at 1999 figures), but were still significant for those admitted more than two years post-injury (notional lifetime savings of £0.4 / $0.6 million) implying that savings were attributable to neurobehavioural rehabilitation and not to natural recovery. Worthington et al. (2006) reported a cost-benefit evaluation, based on a prospective study of a different cohort of 133 adults with severe acquired brain injury (ABI). Once again, patients admitted early (within one year of injury) made the most progress, but significant gains were also evident in those admitted well after natural recovery is a likely explanation for their improvement. Sensitivity analyses, using different rates of inflation yielded projected lifetime savings of between £1.1 ($1.7) million and £0.8 ($1.2) million for those admitted within one year of injury and savings of £0.4 ($0.6) million to £0.5 ($0.8) million for those admitted more than two years post injury. Oddy and Ramos (2013a) studied a cohort of 274 adults with ABI and found projected lifetime savings of up to £1.1 ($1.7) million for individuals admitted to rehabilitation within a year of sustaining a brain injury, and of up to £0.9 ($1.4) million for those admitted more than a year after injury. McMillan, Teasdale, Weir and Stewart (2011) reported higher mortality rates for TBI survivors than case matched controls for up to 13 years after injury. The significant lifetime savings following neurobehavioural rehabilitation found in the Wood et al. (1999) and Worthington et al. (2006) studies remained when taking account of life expectancy adjustments based on these mortality rates (Oddy and Ramos, 2013a).

Taken together, these results suggest that post-acute neurobehavioural rehabilitation can have a positive impact on the lives of individuals with brain injury, and that the costs of neurobehavioural rehabilitation can be more than recouped by savings in the longer-term. For those admitted within one year post-injury, the costs of rehabilitation are typically recovered within one to two years, and time required to off-set rehabilitation costs for those admitted for neurobehavioural rehabilitation more than one year post-injury is approximately four to five years.

The basic model of evaluating cost-effectiveness can be further developed by the addition of informal care costs and productivity losses to the above model. Van Heugten and colleagues (2011) calculated the costs of a residential community reintegration programme for 33 patients with ABI and investigated the extent to which this service led to a reduction in societal costs, defined as care consumption, caregiver support, and productivity losses. The costs of the rehabilitation programme were £49,559 ($75,189) per patient. The informal care and productivity losses were reduced significantly by £9,682 ($14,689) in the year after receiving this service, and while the costs associated with number of hours of outpatient medical services increased significantly by £6,800 ($10,315) in the same period, other forms of healthcare consumption, including general practice, specialist consultations, medication and inpatient care tended to decrease. The initial societal costs per patient were £35,103 ($5,100). After rehabilitation these costs reduced to £28,817 ($43,720). Assuming a stable situation, the break-even point was eight years after completion of the rehabilitation programme.

A variation on the design of the above studies was employed by Griesbach, Kreber, Harrington and Ashley (2015). Rather than looking at actual costs before and after post-acute rehabilitation the authors asked 'certified life care planners' to create separate cost projections from patient files on admission and at discharge, thus allowing cost projections with and without rehabilitation to be compared. Rehabilitation was found to be associated with significant reductions in projected costs. As in the studies cited above, savings were greater when rehabilitation was initiated less than one year after the injury. Savings were greatest in younger patients, but improvements were found in all age groups and were similar for stroke and TBI.

Andelic and colleagues (2014) compared those who received a 'continuous chain' of rehabilitation with those who received a 'broken chain'. This referred to the fact that some patients ($n = 30$) received a seamless service, moving to the specialised rehabilitation units as soon as their medical condition stabilised, while those in the 'broken chain' group ($n = 29$) were not offered early rehabilitation at the Intensive Care Unit and there was no direct transfer from acute hospital to rehabilitation units. The authors stated that the trajectory of the patient was determined by bed availability alone. The two groups were matched on demographic variables, causes of injury, and severity of injury. The researchers found that over a five-year period, the continuous chain group had lower average costs and better health outcomes. Calculations of the Incremental Cost Effectiveness Ratio for one-year and five-year time perspectives showed that between £1,291 ($1,960) and £2,800 ($4,200) per capita could be saved by employing a continuous approach and up to four points gained on the Disability Rating Scale, demonstrating a degree of functional improvement. This study involved a modest number of patients, however, and since the reason given for the study not adopting a randomised allocation to the two trajectories was an ethical one, it is hard to accept that the allocation was solely determined by bed availability.

Enhancing rehabilitation effectiveness

The studies reviewed above give indications of how clinical and cost-effectiveness can be improved. Clinically it has been found that client-centred approaches that focus not only on reducing impairments, but also on increasing the psychological adjustment of the individual to the effects of their brain injury, seem to result in a greater participation in society and a better quality of life (Cicerone et al., 2008). There is also consistent evidence that outcome and cost-effectiveness are greater if neurorehabilitation is initiated within the first year after injury. There may be greater savings when the brain injury is more severe. Longer durations of rehabilitation may be more cost-effective than shorter episodes.

In neurorehabilitation, the main cost component is staff. Hence, means of reducing staffing costs holds the promise of increased cost-effectiveness. A number of studies proposed the use of technology to reduce the costs of brain injury rehabilitation. Kapur, Glisky and Wilson (2004) reviewed the application of external memory aids and computer-based procedures for enhancing memory function in those with non-progressive brain injury. For example, Solana and colleagues (2015) proposed the use of 'personalised' computerised cognitive exercises that are grounded in principles from neuroscience, including plasticity, and claim that this can improve the efficiency of the rehabilitation process. The use of technology also holds the promise of clinical benefits. Prompting technologies allow delivery of cognitive support in the same manner on every occasion, which in turn promotes learning. Technologies also offer discrete support to the individual, thereby reducing disability while promoting self-efficacy, and potentially reducing the risk of irritability and aggression (Gillespie & O'Neill, 2015; Oddy & Ramos, 2013b), which is often triggered by receiving support or feedback from another person (Alderman, Knight, & Henman, 2002).

Overview

The last 15 years has undoubtedly seen an increase in the evidence for both the clinical effectiveness and cost-effectiveness of brain injury rehabilitation. This evidence has been evaluated in several systematic reviews and, although the methodological quality of the studies has generally fallen short of RCTs, the accumulation of evidence has led to the recommendation that optimal outcomes can be achieved with intensive, holistic programmes, which address cognitive, emotional and behavioural difficulties, which are interdisciplinary, person-centred and focussed on goals and on the improvement of everyday function. A major difficulty in evaluating this research is that the extent and nature of the similarities and differences between programmes is difficult to ascertain.

There are a number of caveats that need to be considered when interpreting the studies discussed in this chapter. One of these is the common bias against submitting or publishing negative findings. It is feasible that some studies that show little evidence for clinical or cost-effectiveness, have not been pursued to publication by the researchers or accepted by the editors of journals.

The most common method of evaluating clinical and cost-effectiveness has been to assess the status of each individual on admission, take into account the costs of rehabilitation and contrast these with reductions in disability and care and support needs at discharge. This approach assumes that the gains made following rehabilitation will remain constant, but this is not likely to be the case. Studies that look at disability outcome in the same individuals over longer time periods report both improvement and deterioration in up to half of those with TBI, with these changes evident more than ten years post-injury (Hammond et al., 2004; McMillan, Teasdale, & Stewart, 2012; Whitnall, 2006). Earlier long-term outcome studies (Thomsen, 1984) report a general trend towards reduced dependency very late after injury that was thought to reflect improved adjustment to the effects of injury. Furthermore, the costs of care are not themselves absolute and depend on the quality and extent of the care and support offered. The assumption of constancy of clinical and economic outcomes involves an assumption of the constancy of need, but this is yet to be determined by studies on cost-effectiveness with long follow-ups. There is a common view that neurorehabilitation instigated in the first year following injury is more cost-effective than that conducted later (e.g., Turner-Stokes, 2004; Wood et al., 1999). However, there may be systematic differences in those admitted early and those admitted later. Further investigation of such differences is needed; of relevance here, though, are findings that clinical improvements and cost savings can occur even when rehabilitation is introduced several years post-injury (Oddy & Ramos, 2013a; Parish & Oddy, 2007; Wood et al., 1999; Worthington et al., 2006). These findings are important because, whereas the process of natural recovery might underlie gains in the case of early rehabilitation, this is unlikely to be the case in rehabilitation that is instigated later.

A further important point is that the two major forms of brain injury rehabilitation we have delineated are not mutually exclusive. Many patients require both acute, medically based rehabilitation, followed by post-acute (neurobehavioural) rehabilitation. The studies of acute rehabilitation have evaluated benefits on the basis that no other form of residential rehabilitation will be given, and the studies of neurobehavioural rehabilitation have not identified whether their participants have previously received acute rehabilitation. This is an important topic for further research.

As Symonds (1937) noted eight decades ago, the differences between those sustaining a brain injury can be as great as can the range of injuries. A 'one-size-fits-all' approach to neurobehavioural rehabilitation is clearly unlikely to work. The different types of service referred to in this chapter reflect this understanding to a certain extent, but the criteria for allocating individuals to the most appropriate rehabilitation service are not always implemented in practice, and the means by which allocation is achieved vary widely across geographical areas.

Whilst the evidence for the clinical and cost-effectiveness of neurobehavioural rehabilitation requires further evaluation, there is also a suggestion that there may be an under-estimation of the benefits that rehabilitation may provide. With the exception of van Heugten and colleagues' (2011) study, the measurement of outcomes and savings has largely ignored the indirect benefits of rehabilitation, such as reduction in carer strain and savings arising from reduction in the loss of productivity of family members.

Alongside the consideration of the impact of neurorehabilitation on individual needs and improvements, and on the direct and indirect care costs, the provision of neurorehabilitation needs to be informed by the epidemiology of brain injury. Looking back over the last 15 years, there has been an increase in the median age at which people sustain a traumatic brain injury, with higher incidences among women and older people (Lecky, 2015; Roozenbeek, Maas, & Menon, 2013). Looking forward to the next 15 years, this trend appears likely to continue. This clearly has implications for service design, goals and outcomes. For example, services designed primarily for younger adults may need to be modified to better meet the needs of the frail elderly with brain injury.

References

Alderman, N., Knight, C., & Henman, C. (2002). Aggressive behaviour observed within a neurobehavioural rehabilitation service: utility of the OAS-MNR in clinical audit and applied research. *Brain Injury*, *16*(6), 469–89. doi:10.1080/02699050110118458

Andelic, N., Ye, J., Tornas, S., Roe, C., Lu, J., Bautz-Holter, E., Moger, T., Sigurdardottir, S., Schanke, A. K., & Aas, E. (2014). Cost-effectiveness analysis of an early-initiated, continuous chain of rehabilitation after severe traumatic brain injury. *Journal of Neurotrauma*, *31*(14), 1313–20. doi:10.1089/neu.2013.3292

Buckman, J. E. J., Astley, J. M., Sollom, A. C., Anderson, C. A., Dendy, A., & Clinicians, N. (2013). The neurorehabilitation pathways team (NRPT): a model of good practice? *International Journal of Therapy and Rehabilitation*, *20*(1), 25–32.

Cattelani, R., Zettin, M., & Zoccolotti, P. (2010). Rehabilitation treatments for adults with behavioral and psychosocial disorders following acquired brain injury: a systematic review. *Neuropsychology Review*, *20*(1), 52–85. doi:10.1007/s11065-009-9125-y

Cellini, S. R., & Kee, J. E. (2010). Cost-effectiveness and cost-benefit analysis. In J. Wholey, H. P. Hatry, & K. E. Newcomer (Eds.), *Handbook of Practical Program Evaluation (Third Edition)* (pp. 493–530). San Francisco: Jossey-Bass.

Celso, B., Tepas, J., Langland-Orban, B., Pracht, E., Papa, L., Lottenberg, L., & Flint, L. (2006). A systematic review and meta-analysis comparing outcome of severely injured patients treated in trauma centers following the establishment of trauma systems. *The Journal of Trauma*, *60*(2), 371–8; discussion 378. doi:10.1097/01.ta.0000197916.99629.eb

Cicerone, K. D., Dahlberg, C., Kalmar, K., Langenbahn, D. M., Malec, J. F., Bergquist, T. F., Felicetti, T., Giacino, J. T., Harley, J. P., Harrington, D. E., Herzog, J., Kneipp, S., Laatsch, L., & Morse, P. A. (2000). Evidence-based cognitive rehabilitation: recommendations for clinical practice. *Archives of Physical Medicine and Rehabilitation*, *81*(12), 1596–1615. doi:10.1053/apmr.2000.19240

Cicerone, K. D., Dahlberg, C., Malec, J. F., Langenbahn, D. M., Felicetti, T., Kneipp, S., Ellmo, W., Kalmar, K., Giacino, J. T., Harley, J. P., Laatsch, L., Morse, P. A., & Catanese, J. (2005). Evidence-based cognitive rehabilitation: Updated review of the literature from 1998 through 2002. *Archives of Physical Medicine and Rehabilitation*, *86*(8), 1681–92. doi:10.1016/j.apmr.2005.03.024

Cicerone, K. D., Langenbahn, D. M., Braden, C., Malec, J. F., Kalmar, K., Fraas, M., Felicetti, T., Laatsch, L., Harley, J. P., Bergquist, T., Azulay, J., Cantor, J., & Ashman,

T. (2011). Evidence-Based Cognitive Rehabilitation: Updated Review of the Literature From 2003 Through 2008. *Archives of Physical Medicine and Rehabilitation*, *92*(4), 519–30. doi:10.1016/j.apmr.2010.11.015

Cicerone, K. D., Mott, T., Azulay, J., Sharlow-Galella, M. A., Ellmo, W. J., Paradise, S., & Friel, J. C. (2008). A randomized controlled trial of holistic neuropsychologic rehabilitation after traumatic brain injury. *Archives of Physical Medicine and Rehabilitation*, *89*(12), 2239–49. doi:10.1016/j.apmr.2008.06.017

French, J., & Gronseth, G. (2008). Lost in a jungle of evidence: We need a compass. *Neurology*, *71*, 1634–38. doi:10.1212/01.wnl.0000336533.19610.1b

Geurtsen, G. J., Martina, J. D., Van Heugten, C. M., & Geurts, A. C. H. (2008). A prospective study to evaluate a new residential community reintegration programme for severe chronic brain injury: the Brain Integration Programme. *Brain Injury*, *22*(7–8), 545–54. doi:10.1080/02699050802132479

Geurtsen, G., van Heugten, C., Martina, J., & Geurts, A. (2010). Comprehensive rehabilitation programmes in the chronic phase after severe brain injury: a systematic review. *Journal of Rehabilitation Medicine*, *42*(2), 97–110. doi:10.2340/16501977-0508

Gillespie, A., & O'Neill, B. (2015). The future of assistive technology for cognition. In B. O'Neill & A. Gillespie (Eds.), *Assistive Technology for Cognition: A Handbook for Clinicians and Developers*. Hove: Psychology Press.

Goldstein, L. B. (1995). Prescribing of potentially harmful drugs to patients admitted to hospital after head injury. *Journal of Neurology, Neurosurgery, and Psychiatry*, *58*, 753–5.

Gray, D. S., & Burnham, R. S. (2000). Preliminary outcome analysis of a long-term rehabilitation program for severe acquired brain injury. *Archives of Physical Medicine and Rehabilitation*, *81*(11), 1447–56. doi:10.1053/apmr.2000.16343

Greenwood, R. J., & McMillan, T. M. (2003). Head injury. In: R. J. Greenwood, M. P. Barnes, T. M. McMillan, & C. D. Ward (Eds.), *Handbook of Neurological Rehabilitation* (2nd ed.). Hove.

Griesbach, G. S., Kreber, L. A., Harrington, D., & Ashley, M. J. (2015). Post-acute traumatic brain injury rehabilitation: effects on outcome measures and life care costs. *Journal of Neurotrauma*, *32*(10), 704–11. doi:10.1089/neu.2014.3754

Hammond, F. M., Grattan, K. D., Sasser, H., Corrigan, J. D., Rosenthal, M., Bushnik, T., & Shull, W. (2004). Five years after traumatic brain injury: a study of individual outcomes and predictors of change in function. *NeuroRehabilitation*, *19*(1), 25–35. Retrieved from http://www.ncbi.nlm.nih.gov/pubmed/14988585

Johnson, R., & Balleny, H. (1996). Behaviour problems after brain injury: incidence and need for treatment. *Clinical Rehabilitation*, *10*(2), 173–80. doi:10.1177/026921559601000215

Kapur, N., Glisky, E. L., & Wilson, B. A. (2004). Technological memory aids for people with memory deficits. *Neuropsychological Rehabilitation*, *14*(1–2), 41–60. doi:10.1080/09602010343000138

Lecky, F. (2015). Epidemiology of traumatic brain injury: Implications for rehabilitation and long-term disability. In *Paper presented at the Brain Injury Rehabilitation Trust Conference 2015*. Manchester, UK.

McMillan, T. M. (2013). Outcome of rehabilitation for neurobehavioural disorders. *NeuroRehabilitation*, *32*(4), 791–801. doi:10.3233/NRE-130903

McMillan, T. M., & Ledder, H. (2001). A survey of services provided by community neurorehabilitation teams in South East England. *Clinical Rehabilitation*, *15*(6), 582–8. doi:10.1191/0269215501cr541oa

McMillan, T. M., Teasdale, G. M., Weir, C. J., & Stewart, E. (2011). Death after head injury: the 13 year outcome of a case control study. *Journal of Neurology, Neurosurgery & Psychiatry*, *82*, 931–5.

McMillan, T. M., Teasdale, G., & Stewart, E. (2012). Disability in young people and adults after head injury: 12-14 year follow up of a prospective cohort, (May), 12–14. doi:10.1136/jnnp-2012-302746

Minister for Health. (2011). *National Policy and Strategy for the Provision of Neuro-rehabilitation Services in Ireland 2011–2015.* Dublin.

National Academy of Neuropsychology. Cognitive rehabilitation: official statement of the National Academy of Neuropsychology (2002). Retrieved from https://www.nanonline.org/docs/PAIC/PDFs/NANPositionCogRehab.pdf

National Institute for Health and Care Excellence. (2014). NICE quality standard [QS74]. Retrieved from https://www.nice.org.uk/guidance/qs74/chapter/quality-statement-6-inpatient-rehabilitation-for-people-with-traumatic-brain-injury

O'Connor, R. J., Beden, R., Pilling, A., & Chamberlain, M. A. (2011). What reductions in dependency costs result from treatment in an inpatient neurological rehabilitation unit for people with stroke? *Clinical Medicine (London, England),* 11(1), 40–3. Retrieved from http://www.ncbi.nlm.nih.gov/pubmed/21404783

Oddy, M., & Ramos, S. D. S. (2013a). The clinical and cost-benefits of investing in neurobehavioural rehabilitation: A multi-centre study. *Brain Injury, 9052,* 1–8. doi:10.3109/02699052.2013.830332

Oddy, M., & Ramos, S. D. S. (2013b). Cost effective ways of facilitating home based rehabilitation and support. *NeuroRehabilitation, 32*(4), 781–90. doi:10.3233/NRE-130902

Parish, L., & Oddy, M. (2007). Efficacy of rehabilitation for functional skills more than 10 years after extremely severe brain injury. *Neuropsychological Rehabilitation, 17*(2), 230–43. doi:10.1080/09602010600750675

Roozenbeek, B., Maas, A. I. R., & Menon, D. K. (2013). Changing patterns in the epidemiology of traumatic brain injury. *Nature Reviews: Neurology, 9*(4), 231–6. doi:10.1038/nrneurol.2013.22

Ruff, R. M., & Niemann, H. (1990). Cognitive rehabilitation versus day treatment in head-injured adults: Is there an impact on emotional and psychosocial adjustment? *Brain Injury, 4*(4), 339–47. Retrieved from http://www.ncbi.nlm.nih.gov/pubmed/2252966

Salazar, A. M., Warden, D. L., Schwab, K., Spector, J., Braverman, S., Walter, J., Cole, R., Rosner, M. M., Martin, E. M., Ecklund, J., & Ellenbogen, R. G. (2000). Cognitive rehabilitation for traumatic brain injury: A randomized trial. *JAMA, 283*(23), 3075. doi:10.1001/jama.283.23.3075

Scottish Government. (2015). *The Matrix (2015) A Guide to Delivering Evidence-Based Psychological Therapies in Scotland.* Retrieved from: http://www.nes.scot.nhs.uk/education-and-training/by-discipline/psychology/the-matrix-(2015)-a-guide-to-delivering-evidence-based-psychological-therapies-in-scotland.aspx

Scottish Intercollegiate Guidelines Network, & Health Care Improvement Scotland. (2013). *SIGN 130: Brain injury rehabilitation in adults.*

Solana, J., Cáceres, C., García-Molina, A., Opisso, E., Roig, T., Tormos, J. M., & Gómez, E. J. (2015). Improving brain injury cognitive rehabilitation by personalized telerehabilitation services: Guttmann neuropersonal trainer. *IEEE Journal of Biomedical and Health Informatics, 19*(1), 124–31. doi:10.1109/JBHI.2014.2354537

Symonds, C. P. (1937). Mental disorder following head injury. *Proceedings of the Royal Society of Medicine, 30*(9), 1081–94. doi:10.1177/003591573703000926

Thomsen, I. V. (1984). Late outcome of very severe blunt head trauma: a 10-15 year second follow-up. *Journal of Neurology, Neurosurgery, and Psychiatry, 47*(3), 260–8. Retrieved from http://www.ncbi.nlm.nih.gov/pubmed/6707671

Turner-Stokes, L. (2004). The evidence for the cost-effectiveness of rehabilitation following acquired brain injury. *Clinical Medicine, 4*(1), 10–12. Retrieved from http://www.ncbi.nlm.nih.gov/pubmed/14998259

Turner-Stokes, L. (2007). Cost-efficiency of longer-stay rehabilitation programmes: can they provide value for money? *Brain Injury, 21*(10), 1015–21. doi:10.1080/02699050701591445

Turner-Stokes, L., Paul, S., & Williams, H. (2006). Efficiency of specialist rehabilitation in reducing dependency and costs of continuing care for adults with complex acquired brain injuries. *Journal of Neurology, Neurosurgery & Psychiatry, 77*(5), 634–9. doi:10.1136/jnnp.2005.073411

Turner-Stokes, L., Sutch, S., & Dredge, R. (2012). Healthcare tariffs for specialist inpatient neurorehabilitation services: rationale and development of a UK casemix and costing methodology. *Clinical Rehabilitation, 26*(3), 264–79. doi:10.1177/0269215511417467

van Heugten, C. M., Geurtsen, G. J., Derksen, R. E., Martina, J. D., Geurts, A. C. H., & Evers, S. M. A. A. (2011). Intervention and societal costs of residential community reintegration for patients with acquired brain injury: a cost-analysis of the Brain Integration Programme. *Journal of Rehabilitation Medicine : Official Journal of the UEMS European Board of Physical and Rehabilitation Medicine, 43*(7), 647–52. doi:10.2340/16501977-0818

van Heugten, C., Wolters Gregorio, G., & Wade, D. (2012). Evidence-based cognitive rehabilitation after acquired brain injury: A systematic review of content of treatment. *Neuropsychological Rehabilitation: An International Journalehabilitation, 22*(5), 653–73. doi:10.1080/09602011.2012.680891

Vanderploeg, R. D., Schwab, K., Walker, W. C., Fraser, J. A., Sigford, B. J., Date, E. S., Scott, S. G., Curtiss, G., Salazar, A. M., & Warden, D. L.; Defense and Veterans Brain Injury Center Study Group. (2008). Rehabilitation of traumatic brain injury in active duty military personnel and veterans: Defense and veterans brain injury center randomized controlled trial of two rehabilitation approaches. *Archives of Physical Medicine and Rehabilitation, 89*(12), 2227–38. doi:10.1016/j.apmr.2008.06.015

Wade, D. (2012). *Implementing the rehabilitation prescription: A discussion document.* Retrieved from http://www.ouh.nhs.uk/oce/research-education/documents/TVRNRehabilitation Prescription-discussion.docx

Whitnall, L. (2006). Disability in young people and adults after head injury: 5–7 year follow up of a prospective cohort study. *Journal of Neurology, Neurosurgery & Psychiatry, 77*(5), 640–5. doi:10.1136/jnnp.2005.078246

Willer, B., Button, J., & Rempel, R. (1999). Residential and home-based postacute rehabilitation of individuals with traumatic brain injury: a case control study. *Archives of Physical Medicine and Rehabilitation, 80*(4), 399–406. Retrieved from http://www.ncbi.nlm.nih.gov/pubmed/10206601

Wood, R. L., & McMillan, T. (Eds.) (2001). *Neurobehavioural Disability and Social Handicap Following Traumatic Brain Injury.* Hove: Psychology Press.

Wood, R. L., McCrea, J. D., Wood, L. M., & Merriman, R. N. (1999). Clinical and cost effectiveness of post-acute neurobehavioural rehabilitation. *Brain Injury, 13*(2), 69–88. doi:10.1080/026990599121746

Worthington, A. D., Matthews, S., Melia, Y., & Oddy, M. (2006). Cost-benefits associated with social outcome from neurobehavioural rehabilitation. *Brain Injury, 20*(9), 947–57. doi:10.1080/02699050600888314

Worthington, A. D., & Oldham, J. B. (2006). Delayed discharge from rehabilitation after brain injury. *Clinical Rehabilitation, 20*(1), 79–82. doi:10.1191/0269215506cr881oa

18

LOOKING FORWARD

Tom M. McMillan, Jennie Ponsford and Breda Cullen

Epidemiology and neurobehavioural disability

The incidence and prevalence of traumatic brain injury (TBI) is known to be high in Western countries (Tagliaferri et al. 2006; Corrigan et al. 2010) and in low and middle economy countries (Hyder 2013). Some have argued that improvements in acute care have led to greater numbers surviving with disability, although there is no clear evidence to support this. For example, overall mortality rates from head injury have changed little in the past two decades (Hamill et al. 2015). There is little specific evidence about the incidence or prevalence of neurobehavioural disability. Two studies have reported the characteristics of adults admitted to inpatient neurobehavioural units in the UK with a combined sample size of 407 (Worthington et al. 2006; Oddy and Ramos 2013). The majority were males (73%) and age at injury ranged between <1 and 76 years. The most common cause of injury was head injury (54%), and other causes included CVA/intracranial haemorrhage (20%), cerebral hypoxia (13%) and encephalitis (6%). Worthington et al. (2006) list neurobehavioural problems, with the three most frequent being dysexecutive (94%), attention control (81%) and self-awareness (77%); with impulsivity (64%), aggression (52%) and disorders of drive (29%) also reported. Whilst these studies are of interest, they only describe those admitted to neurobehavioural rehabilitation units and do not reflect the broader epidemiological picture that would include, for example, those admitted to less specialist units or who are discharged to the community.

Our understanding of the incidence and prevalence of neurobehavioural disability is therefore limited and it is likely that many are not routinely referred for specialist neurorehabilitation. To advance our understanding of incidence and prevalence of neurobehavioural disability, the long awaited demand for services for brain injury to be systematic and co-ordinated from the point of post-acute care to the community needs to be implemented (McMillan and Greenwood 1993).

From research to practice

Developments in understanding of the nature of brain injury and its effects

A key issue for the future is likely to be our understanding of the causes of the heterogeneous nature of outcome after brain injury. This is associated with, but not clearly explained by, simple factors such as age at injury or severity of injury. Complicating this picture are dynamic changes over time, with improvements and deterioration in outcome for a decade or more after injury, that are evident even late after injury; e.g., between five and ten year follow-ups (Whitnall et al. 2006; McMillan et al. 2012; Ponsford et al. 2008; Ponsford et al. 2014). The risk of mortality is also elevated for at least a decade after head injury (Harrison-Felix et al. 2012; McMillan et al. 2013). These outcomes are likely to be affected by lifestyle issues both pre and post injury that are potentially very relevant to the content of neurorehabilitation programmes and to approaches to the provision of community support (McMillan, Weir and Wainman-Lefley 2014). Indeed it has been argued that brain injury should be considered to be a chronic disease process rather than an 'event' (Masel and DeWitt 2010). However, further work is required to explore, define and evidence this concept of head injury as a chronic disease, including in relation to neurorehabilitation practice.

The biological basis of brain injury and recovery has also received greater interest in recent years. This has arisen particularly from a recent focus on long-term effects of repeated concussion in sports and as a result of war casualties in Iraq and Afghanistan. Many of these casualties may survive an explosion as a result of body armour, yet sustain blast injuries that affect cerebral integrity (Daneshvar et al. 2015). Translational research from laboratory and post mortem studies of single cases and case series have aroused concern that neuropathological changes may lead to long term neurodegeneration and chronic traumatic encephalopathy, even following repeated mild concussion. Such injuries have also been associated with behavioural manifestations that include depression, impairments in memory and executive function, and explosive aggression (Stern et al. 2013; Daneshvar et al. 2015). However, this evidence is based on post mortem studies and retrospective case-note reviews, with a combined sample from all studies of less than 200 cases. Therefore, any association made between concussion and chronic neurodegeneration would seem premature (Gardner et al. 2013) and perhaps overstated. Nevertheless, CTE exemplifies a growing interest in identifying biomarkers that may be associated with neuropathology and long-term psychosocial outcome. It is therefore an area that those with interest in neurobehavioural disability will need to consider.

Assessment for rehabilitation of neurobehavioural disability

Neurobehavioural disability is multifaceted and we do not as yet have a comprehensive choice of assessment tools that are sensitive to the full range of difficulties that may arise (see Chapter 7). We need more appropriate methods of assessing social cognition, such as mentalising and empathy in people with brain injury, and ways to measure complex functions in the real world. Neuroimaging can assist in identifying pathology associated with neurobehavioural disability, but as yet, it is not a diagnostic tool (see Chapter 8). Therefore both now and in the near future practitioners will need to rely on psychometric testing and clinical interviews. Such assessments need to be psychometrically robust yet ecologically valid with the ability to reflect the complex social contexts in which neurobehavioural difficulties are most disabling. The limited ecological validity of tests of executive function is an example that is of particular relevance to neurobehavioural disorders, as discussed in Chapter 7. The development of relatively unstructured assessment methods, such as real-world multiple errands tests, has evolved towards computerised paradigms including virtual reality environments (Neguţ, et al. 2016). Real-time capture of physiological and behavioural measures is now also possible via sensor technology that is embedded in the environment or in mobile devices. Although not new, we envisage that such methods will become more common clinically as quality improves, equipment costs continue to decline, and future generations become increasingly accustomed to interactive technology (see Chapter 16).

Assessment approaches will also be influenced by the expansion of 'personalised healthcare', driven by the increased accessibility of genotyping data and the proliferation of genetic association studies of various traits and diseases. The complex genetic architecture of human behaviour means that a given phenotype may be associated with multiple genetic markers that exert small effects, and, conversely, a genetic marker may be associated with multiple and diverse phenotypic characteristics. In this context, it is perhaps unsurprising, then, that Plomin and Crabbe's (2000) prediction that 'within a few years, psychology will be awash with genes associated with behavioural disorders', eventually 'leading to gene-based diagnoses and treatment programs' (p. 806) has not yet come to pass. Nevertheless, research in this area has opened up new perspectives on mechanisms by which genetic variations can influence behaviour, for example through gene-environment interaction (Ottman, 1996). Our understanding of genetics has had little impact on our knowledge of head injury, its effects and developments in neurorehabilitation. The potential role of APOE genotype has received much attention. Whilst early studies failed to show any clear impact on overall outcome there could be an effect over the long term, linked with ageing (Millar et al. 2003; Teasdale et al. 2005). More recent evidence suggests that the ε4 variant increases the risk of poor functional outcome following head injury (Ponsford et al. 2011). The, genetic variation in the serotonin transporter (5-HTT) gene SLC6A4 has been linked with greater vulnerability to depression following stroke, but carriers of the same genotype may also respond better to psychological interventions for post-stroke depression (see Queirazza and Cavanagh 2014). These studies indicate the potential importance of genetics to outcome, and as genotyping moves from research into the clinical domain, practitioners may be able to make use of such information to identify those people most vulnerable to neurobehavioural disability and those most likely to benefit from interventions.

Developing a stronger evidence base for rehabilitation therapies

Clinical guidelines depend on a robust scientific literature, based on well-designed and adequately powered trials. As a precursor this usually demands in-depth feasibility and pilot studies to develop conceptual models and hypotheses, refine treatment packages and outcome measures, and generate preliminary data to inform the design of full-scale trials with a high chance of success (Craig et al. 2008). Such trials typically require substantial funding, time and resources, thus highlighting the importance of multicentre collaborations and research support networks. There is clearly a need for this in neurobehavioural rehabilitation as discussed earlier in this book (e.g., Chapters 11 and 12) and more broadly in neurorehabilitation as evidenced by reviews of the evidence base for psychological interventions (Bayley et al. 2014; Catelani et al. 2010; Cicerone et al. 2011; SIGN 2013). The conclusions in these reviews overlap significantly (although they do not do so entirely with regard to interventions for specific problems), and they agree that the evidence base required for clinical practice guidelines is limited. There has also been discussion and some criticism of holding RCT designs as the standard for clinical practice guidelines for people with brain injury. Whilst more RCT studies are needed consideration also needs to be given to the value of designs that are more practical in a neurorehabilitation setting. McMillan (2013) and Tate et al. (2014) suggest that single case experimental designs should have greater currency and recommend more rigorous research using single case experimental designs and increased recognition of the value of high quality single case design research evidence in systematic reviews and in clinical practice guidelines.

Bridging the gap between evidence and practice in rehabilitation

Allowing for the above-mentioned deficiencies in evidence underpinning interventions for neurobehavioural problems, there has been enormous growth in the body of scientific evidence in the domain of neurorehabilitation over the past decade. Despite this, there remains a significant gap between this evidence base and real world practice by clinicians working with neurobehavioural disability. At a meeting on knowledge-translation in global health held in 2005, the World Health Organisation (WHO 2005) expressed the view that this endeavour was one of the most important challenges for public health in the twenty-first century. Over the last decade we have seen the development of clinical practice guidelines in the domain of cognitive rehabilitation, guided by best available evidence (Cicerone et al. 2011; Bayley et al. 2014) and there is some evidence to suggest that clinical practice guidelines can improve decision-making and ultimately, clinical outcomes. This was demonstrated in a study by Keris, Lavendelis and Macane (2007) that found an association between clinical practice guideline implementation and outcomes following head injury. However, a recent study auditing the use of the INCOG guidelines by clinicians (Bayley et al. 2014) suggested that a significant gap remains between the availability of clinical practice guidelines and their application in clinical practice, even in specialised brain injury rehabilitation centres. An important next step is the development and evaluation of processes for the implementation of guidelines, which will inevitably lead to changes in those guidelines, but will also hopefully improve evidence-based practice and the effectiveness of neurorehabilitation.

Assistive technology for neurobehavioural rehabilitation and independent living

The continuing trends towards greater longevity in the general population brings with it the potential for survival to an older age in people with neurobehavioural disability. This provokes a tension between the costs of healthcare required for good quality of life and economics. This can only partly be addressed by lifetime cost savings arising from the effectiveness of neurorehabilitation (see Chapter 17). Indeed there is a clear need for the continued development of automated systems that reduce the impact of neurobehavioural disability in the community, which are shown to reduce the need for carer input and which can support return to work in some capacity. There has been continuing development of assistive technology to reduce the impact of cognitive (in particular attention and memory) impairments and the potential to extend this to other domains relevant to neurobehavioural disability, such as executive dysfunction (see Chapter 16; O'Neill and Gillespie 2015). Further developments in automated technology may improve self-monitoring of emotional states in order to facilitate the self-regulation of social behaviour and reduce social isolation (see Chapter 16). Advances in robotics and environmental control systems could also reduce carer costs by providing effective prompts in an interactive fashion (e.g., providing an auditory response to service user questions such as 'have I taken my medication') and otherwise by improving independence for tasks of daily living, by providing safety alerts in the home, reducing falls risk and so on. Systems of this kind need to be validated, to have the capacity to be flexible in order to be tailored to individual needs, to be easily reprogrammed and to be widely available.

Service delivery

Implementing model systems for neurobehavioural rehabilitation

For almost a hundred years many authors have drawn attention to the significance of head injury, as a chronic disabling condition that has a high incidence that needs specialist services, models and pathways (Jefferson 1941; McMillan and Greenwood 1993; Boake 2003; Tagliaferri et al. 2006; Collins et al. 2015). However, despite growing evidence for the cost-effectiveness of neurorehabilitation (see Chapter 17), service provision continues to be patchy and for some depends on the ability to pay where they happen to live (Ettinger et al. 2013). In part this may reflect the fact that most who suffer a severe head injury make a good physical recovery and return to the community with a 'hidden disability', largely a consequence of cognitive and emotional impairment, the day to day consequences of which are not attributed to the head injury. A second reason is that the healthcare costs of post-acute neurobehavioural rehabilitation can seem high, and the longer term financial savings are likely to be associated with different budgetary systems (social care and employment) and may not be seen in overview by healthcare planners. Hence despite banner headlines that emphasise head injury as a very significant problem (Thurman et al. 1999), service provision beyond the stage of acute medical care can often be sub-optimal.

The need is for early identification of those who need post-acute neurorehabilitation and for a flexible and easily accessible system that can respond to changing demands in the daily life of those living in the community (e.g. loss of care support or of employment). This should be combined with the routine presence of head injury in clinical practice guidelines, even where the evidence base is sub-optimal, to emphasise the need for neurorehabilitation to service planners (e.g., see The Matrix of Psychological Therapies: Neurological Conditions 2015).

Maximising opportunities for community-based neurorehabilitation

The methods outlined in this book represent the optimum in neurorehabilitation. However, most individuals, whether receiving such neurorehabilitation or not, will return to the community and, for many, the neurobehavioral impact of their brain injuries will be lifelong. Given the scarcity of residential neurobehavioural treatment units it is not uncommon for inpatient neurorehabilitation to be provided some distance from the individual's home, which can result in limited input from family or other members of their support network. This can also be an obstacle to the generalisation of learned routines into the person's home environment, as well as limiting the opportunities for long-term vocational placement. The frequent presence of persisting impairments of memory, executive function and self-awareness limits the capacity of individuals with brain injury to generalise what is learned in neurorehabilitation units and apply it in their everyday life. For this reason it is optimal for interventions to be applied directly in the real world context, and if possible one in which that individual will be operating in the future. Community-based neurorehabilitation uses a broad range of community resources and natural supports to assist those who have sustained head injury to attain self-determined goals and to attain maximal independence and fulfilment in terms of living situation, employment, recreation and driving, in the most cost-effective manner possible whilst also maximising their control and the quality of their lives.

Despite its importance, the evidence base for the effectiveness of community neurorehabilitation remains very modest. Delivering therapy and follow-up support to people from rural areas also poses significant challenges, and as a consequence there is, for example, emerging interest in the development of tele-rehabilitation programmes. An increasing number of online services and interventions are becoming available although evidence for their efficacy is limited (Wade et al.

2009). Development of cost-effective community-based neurorehabilitation services that meet the lifelong needs of clients with brain injury represents a major challenge for the future.

Global perspectives

More than 1 billion people in the world are disabled (from all causes), and the burden of disability is unequal, with the poor and those in low economy countries being at much greater risk (WHO 2011). Road traffic accidents have been reported to be the third greatest contributor to disease burden in young males and the incidence of consequent injury is predicted to rise significantly as a result of increases in bicycle accidents and the rapid expansion of car ownership that is outstripping infrastructure, safety legislation and enforcement in developing countries. Clearly, prevention is a significant issue. Despite concern about the increase in death and injury arising from RTAs, there has been surprisingly little emphasis on brain injury and the development of services for neurorehabilitation. These services need to take account of local cultural factors including the potential for stigma of the disabled and differing perceptions about injury and recovery and embedding of a Western medical model will often be inappropriate, whereas neurobehavioural principles that take account of fundamental relationships between brain, injury and behaviour in a social context can more easily become associated with cultural specificities. Development of effective services will be a challenge in coming decades, and there is an absolute need for partnerships that combine knowledge and experience of the principles and practice of neurobehavioural rehabilitation and cultural beliefs and customs. This will allow the neurobehavioural approach that is extant in Western countries to be modified to have cultural validity for developing countries, and to retain its effectiveness.

In the West, the challenge will concern the changing trends in epidemiology, with an increasing incidence of head injury in older adults which in part will be related to increasing longevity (Roozenbeek et al. 2013); with this comes a challenge of management and care of neurobehavioural disorders in the elderly with brain injury who tend to have been somewhat ignored in general as well as in terms of provision of specialist neurorehabilitation services.

Conclusions

The rapidly growing knowledge base in genetics and neuroscience will undoubtedly underpin the development of rehabilitative treatments, including pharmacological treatments, the nature of which we cannot yet imagine.

There is a need to further develop, and make available, evidence based systems for the management and treatment of neurobehavioural disability that are provided throughout the patient journey from hospital to community. The evidence base itself needs to be improved, not only in relation to holistic programmes of neurobehavioural rehabilitation but in terms of better evidence for elements that lead to significant change in key outcome domains. For some there may need to be emphasis on specific problems that require psychological therapy and here the evidence base is currently weak. Web based methods of delivery may be developed as cost-effective adjuncts to inpatient or community treatment or maintenance. Quality of life may also be improved or maintained by the use of assistive technology which is ever ready, never subject to fatigue and can be modified to suit needs over the lifespan of chronic disability that can be common after severe head injury.

Finally there is a plea for equality of access to neurorehabilitation that is independent of the ability to pay, racial or cultural background and which embraces vulnerable or disadvantaged groups such as refugees, prisoners and the homeless and supports the emergence of services in developing countries.

References

Bayley, M., Bragge, P., Douglas, J., Ponsford, J., Togher, L., Green, R., Turkstra, L., & Kua, A. (2014). INCOG guidelines for cognitive rehabilitation following traumatic brain injury: Methods and overview. *J Head Trauma Rehabil*, 29(4), 290–306. DOI: 10.1097/HTR.0000000000000070

Boake, C. (2003). Stages in the history of neuropsychological rehabilitation. In: B.A. Wilson, *Neuropsychological Rehabilitation: Theory and Practice*. Lisse: Swets and Zeitlinger, pp. 11–21.

Catelani, R., Zettin, M., & Zoccolotti, P. (2010). Rehabilitation treatments for adults with behavioural and psychosocial disorders following acquired brain injury: A systematic review. *Neuropsychological Review*, 20, 52–85.

Cicerone, K.D., Langenbahn, D.M., Braden, C., Malec J.F., Kalmar, K., Fraas, M., Felicetti, T., Laatsch, L., Harley, J.P., Bergquist, T., Azulay, J., Cantor, J., & Ashman, T. (2011). Evidence-based cognitive rehabilitation: Updated review of the literature from 2003 through 2008. *Archives of Physical Medicine and Rehabilitation*, 92(4), 519–530.

Collins, A., Rankin, P., & McMillan, T.M. (2015). History of neuropsychology. In: J. Hall, G. Turpin, D. Pilgrim, *Clinical Psychology in Britain: Historical Perspectives*, British Psychological Society, Leicester, pp. 270–282.

Corrigan, J.D., Selassie, A.W., & Orman, L.A. (2010). The epidemiology of traumatic brain injury. *J Head Trauma Rehabil*, 25, 72–80.

Craig, P., Dieppe, P., Macintyre, S., Michie, S., Nazareth, I., & Petticrew, M. (2008). *Developing and Evaluating Complex Interventions: New Guidance*. London: Medical Research Council, www.mrc.ac.uk/complexinterventionsguidance

Daneshvar, D.H., Goldstein, L.E., Kiernan, P.T., Stein, T.D., & McKee, A.C. (2015). Post-traumatic neurodegeneration and chronic traumatic encephalopathy. *Mol Cell Neurosci*, 66 (Pt B), 81–90.

Ettinger, C., Hawe, E., Karlberg, S., & Baillie, L. (2013). *Is there a Rehabilitation Postcode Lottery? Advances in Clinical Neurosciences and Rehabilitation*; http://www.acnr.co.uk/2013/05/is-there-a-rehabilitation-postcode-lottery/

Gardner, A., Iverson, G.L., & McCrory, P. (2013). Chronic traumatic encephalopathy in sport: a systematic review. *Br J Sports Med* doi:10.1136/bjsports-2013-092646

Hamill V., Barry S.J.E., McConnachie A., McMillan T.M., & Teasdale, G.M. (2015). Mortality from Head Injury over Four Decades in Scotland. *J Neurotrauma*, 32, 689–703.

Harrison-Felix, C., Kreider, S.E., Arango-Lasprilla, J.C,. Brown, A.W., Dijkers, M.P., Hammond, F.M., Kolakowsky-Hayner, S.A., Hirshson, C., Whiteneck, G., & Zasler,

N.D. (2012). Life expectancy following rehabilitation: a NIDRR traumatic brain injury model systems study. *J Head Trauma Rehab*, 27, E69–E80.

Hyder, A.A. (2013). Injuries in low- and middle-income countries: a neglected disease in global public health. *Injury, Int. J Care Injured*, 44, 579–580.

Jefferson, G. (1941). Discussion on rehabilitation after injuries to the central nervous system. *Proceed Roy Soc Med.*, 35, 295–299.

Keris, V., Lavendelis, E., & Macane, I. (2007). Association between implementation of clinical practice guidelines and outcome for traumatic brain injury. *World J Surg.*, Jun 2007, 31(6), 1352–1355.

McMillan, T.M., & Greenwood, R.J. (1993). Models of rehabilitation programmes for the brain injured adult: II Model services and suggestions for change in the UK. *Clinical Rehabilitation*, 7, 346–355.

McMillan, T.M., Teasdale, G.M., Weir, C., & Stewart, E. (2012). Disability in young people and adults after head injury: 12–14 year follow-up of a prospective cohort study. *J Neurol Neurosurgery Psychiatry*, 83, 1086–1091, doi:10.1136/jnnp-2012-302746

McMillan, T.M. (2013). Outcome of rehabilitation for neurobehavioural disorders. *NeuroRehabilitation – an Interdisciplinary Journal*, 32(4), 791–801. http://doi.org/10.3233/NRE-130903

McMillan, T.M., Weir, C., & Wainman-Lefley, J. (2014). Mortality 15 years after hospital admission with mild head injury: a prospective case-controlled population study. *J Neurol Neurosurgery Psychiatry*, 85, 1214–1220, doi:10.1136/jnnp-2013-307279

Masel, B.E., & De Witt, D.S. (2010). Traumatic brain injury: A disease process, not an event. *J Neurotrauma*, 27, 1529–1540.

Millar, K., Nicoll, J., Thornhill, S., Murray, G.D., & Teasdale, G.M. (2003). Long term neuropsychological outcome after head injury; relation to APOE genotype. *J Neurology Neurosurgery Psychiatry*, 74, 1047–1052.

Neguţ, A., Matu, S.-A., Sava, F.A., & David, D. (2016). Virtual reality measures in neuropsychological assessment: a meta-analytic review. *The Clinical Neuropsychologist*, 30, 165–184.

Oddy, M., & Ramos, S. (2013). The clinical and cost-benefits of investing in neurobehavioural rehabilitation: a multi-centre study. *Brain Injury*, 9052, 1–8, doi:10.3109/02699052.2013.830332

O'Neill, B., & Gillespie, A. (2015). *Assistive Technology for Cognition*. New York: Psychology Press.

Ottman, R. (1996). Gene–environment interaction: definitions and study designs. *Preventive Medicine*, 25, 764–770.

Plomin, R., & Crabbe, J. (2000). DNA. *Psychological Bulletin*, 126, 806–828.

Ponsford, J., Draper, K., & Schönberger, M. (2008). Functional outcome 10 years after traumatic brain injury: its relationship with demographic, injury severity, and cognitive and emotional status. *J Int Neuropsychol Soc*, 2008, 14(2), 233–242.

Ponsford, J., McLaren, A., Schönberger, M., Burke, R., Rudzki, D., Olver J., & Ponsford, M. (2011). The association between Apolipoprotein E and traumatic brain injury severity and functional outcome in a rehabilitation sample. *J Neurotrauma*, 28, 1683–1692.

Ponsford, J.L., Downing, M.G., Olver, J., Ponsford, M., Acher, R., Carty, M., & Spitz, G., (2014). Longitudinal follow-up of patients with traumatic brain injury: outcome at two, five, and ten years post-injury. *J Neurotrauma*, 31(1), 64–77.

Queirazza, F., & Cavanagh, J. (2014). Poststroke depression and 5-HTTLPR. *J Neurol Neurosurgery Psychiatry*, 85, 241–243.

Roozenbeek, B., Maas, A.I., & Menon, D.K. (2013). Changing patterns in the epidemiology of traumatic brain injury. *Nat Rev Neurol*, 9, 231–236.

SIGN (2013). *Brain Injury Rehabilitation in Adults.* Healthcare Improvement Scotland.

Stern, R.A., Daneshvar, D.H., Baugh, C.M., Seichepine, D.R., Montenigro, P.H., Riley, D.O., Riley, B.S., Fritts, N.G., Stamm, J.M., Robbins, C.A., McHale, L., Simkin, I., Stein, T.D., Alvarez, V.E., Goldstein, L.E., Budson, A.E., Kowall, N.W., Nowinski, C.J., Cantu, R.C., & McKee, A.D. (2013). Clinical presentation of chronic traumatic encephalopathy. *Neurology*, 81(13), 1122–1129.

Tagliaferri, F., Compagnone, C., Korsic, M., Servadei, F., & Kraus, J. (2006). A systematic review of brain injury epidemiology in Europe. *Acta Neurochir (Wien)*, 148, 255–268.

Tate, R.L., Perdices, M., McDonald, S., Togher, L., & Rosenkoetter, U. (2014). The design, conduct and report of single-case research: Resources to improve the quality of the neurorehabilitation literature. *Neuropsychological Rehabilitation: An International Journal*, 24, 315–331.

Teasdale, G., Murray, G., & Nicoll, J.A.R. (2005). Association between APOE-e4 age and outcome after head injury: a prospective cohort study. *Brain*, 128, 2556–2661.

Thurman, D.J., Alverson, C., Browne, D., Dunn, K.A., Guerrero, J., Johnson, R., Johnson, V., Langlois, J., Pilkey, D., Sniezek, J.E., & Toal, S. (1999). *Traumatic brain injury in the United States: Report to Congress,* Centers for Disease Control and Prevention, US Government.

Wade, S. L., Oberjohn, K., Burkhardt, A., & Greenberg, I. (2009). Feasibility and preliminary efficacy of a web-based parenting skills program for young children with traumatic brain injury. *J Head Trauma Rehab*, 24(4), 239–247.

Whitnall, L., McMillan, T.M., Murray, G., & Teasdale, G. (2006). Disability in young people with head injury: a 5–7 year follow-up of a prospective cohort study. *J Neurol Neurosurgery Psychiatry*, 77, 640–645.

World Health Organisation (2005). Bridging the "know-do" gap. *Report on meeting on Knowledge Translation in Global Health, 10–12 October 2005.* Geneva, Switzerland: World Health Organisation.

World Health Organisation and World Bank (2011). *World Report on Disability.* Geneva: World Health Organisation.

Worthington, A.D., Matthews, S., Melia, Y., & Oddy, M. (2006). Cost-benefits associated with social outcome from neurobehavioural rehabilitation. *Brain Injury*, 20(9), 947–957, doi:10.1080/02699050600888314

INDEX

Note: Page numbers followed by 'f' refer to figures and followed by 't' refer to tables.

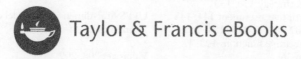